More praise for Mark Torgerson's *Architecture of Immanence*

"*An Architecture of Immanence* is both courageous and challenging. As Mark Torgerson guides us through the difficult terrain of twentieth-century architecture for the church, he is at every turn raising the question *What does our church building say about the Christian life and witness in our time?* With passion and skill he undertakes the daunting task of arranging the diverse manifestations of modern church design into a coherent pattern, and then invites readers to become involved in the process of thinking theologically about their own worship spaces. To step into this book is to understand more deeply the rich interplay between the shape of our churches and the shape of our Christian calling."

— Susan J. White
Brite Divinity School

"As a practicing artist and a trained academic theologian, Mark Torgerson is well qualified to write *An Architecture of Immanence.* . . . I am pleased to recommend this well-written and researched volume enhanced by numerous photographs, useful appendixes, and an annotated bibliography."

— R. Kevin Seasoltz, OSB
editor of *Worship*

"A must-read for any architect designing a church — and very helpful for building committees as well. Torgerson analyzes the interface between modern architecture and the church as servant community with God in its midst. By articulating our words about God and our response as worshiping community, this book will assist in building what we believe."

— Donald J. Bruggink
coauthor of *Christ and Architecture*

The Calvin Institute of Christian Worship Liturgical Studies Series, edited by John D. Witvliet, is designed to promote reflection on the history, theology, and practice of Christian worship and to stimulate worship renewal in Christian congregations. Contributions include writings by pastoral worship leaders from a wide range of communities and scholars from a wide range of disciplines. The ultimate goal of these contributions is to nurture worship practices that are spiritually vital and theologically rooted.

Published

Gather into One:
Praying and Singing Globally
C. Michael Hawn

The Substance of Things Seen:
Art, Faith, and the Christian Community
Robin M. Jensen

Wonderful Words of Life: Hymns in
American Protestant History and Theology
Richard J. Mouw and Mark A Noll,
Editors

Discerning the Spirits: A Guide to
Thinking about Christian Worship Today
Cornelius Plantinga Jr. and Sue A.
Rozeboom

Voicing God's Psalms
Calvin Seerveld

My Only Comfort: Death, Deliverance,
and Discipleship in the Music of Bach
Calvin R. Stapert

A New Song for an Old World:
Musical Thought in the Early Church
Calvin R. Stapert

An Architecture of Immanence: Architecture
for Worship and Ministry Today
Mark A. Torgerson

A More Profound Alleluia: Theology
and Worship in Harmony
Leanne Van Dyk, Editor

Christian Worship in Reformed Churches
Past and Present
Lukas Vischer, Editor

The Biblical Psalms in Christian Worship:
A Brief Introduction and Guide to Resources
John D. Witvliet

MARK A. TORGERSON

AN ARCHITECTURE OF IMMANENCE

ARCHITECTURE FOR WORSHIP AND MINISTRY TODAY

WILLIAM B. EERDMANS PUBLISHING COMPANY
GRAND RAPIDS, MICHIGAN / CAMBRIDGE, U.K.

Published 2007 by
WM. B. EERDMANS PUBLISHING CO.
2140 Oak Industrial Drive, N.E., Grand Rapids, Michigan 49505 /
P.O. Box 163, Cambridge CB3 9PU U.K.
www.eerdmans.com

Printed in the United States of America

11 10 09 08 07   7 6 5 4 3 2 1

Library of Congress Cataloging-in-Publication Data

Torgerson, Mark Allen.
   An architecture of immanence : architecture for worship and ministry today /
Mark A. Torgerson.
     p. cm. — (The Calvin Institute of Christian Worship liturgical studies series)
   Includes bibliographical references and index.
   ISBN 978-0-8028-3209-2 (pbk. : alk. paper)
   1. Church architecture. 2. Symbolism in architecture. 3. Liturgy and architecture —
History — 20th century. 4. Immanence of God.   I. Title.
   NA4800.T67   2007
   726.5 — dc22

                            2006039589

Unless otherwise noted, the Scripture quotations in this publication are from the New
Revised Standard Version of the Bible, copyright © 1989 by the Division of Christian Education
of the National Council of Churches of Christ in the U.S.A., and used by permission.

Portions of Chapters Three and Five have appeared in the essay "Ecumenism, Worship Renewal, and Reforming Spaces for Christian Worship," in *In Spirit and Truth: Essays on Theology, Spirituality, and Embodiment
in Honor of C. John Weborg,* ed. P. Anderson and M. Clifton-Soderstrom (Chicago: Covenant Publications,
2006), pp. 154-79.

In memory of
James Floyd White
(1932-2004)
Scholar, pastor, mentor, and friend

CONTENTS

Preface   ix

1. Worship Spaces: Influenced by God's Nature and Scriptural Models   1

2. God in the Ordinary: Nourishing a Context for Immanence   11

3. Twentieth-Century Worship Renewal: The Elevation of God's People   25

4. Modern Impulses in Church Architecture: Faith Engaging Culture   43

5. The Fruits of Worship Renewal: Emphasizing an Architecture of Immanence   69

6. An Architecture of Immanence: Early Examples in Europe   97

7. An Architecture of Immanence: Selected Examples in America   117

8. An Illustration: The Thought and Work of Edward Anders Sövik   147

9. Where Are We Now? Discernment and Lessons Learned   181

10. Where Can We Go? Directions for the Future   207

Appendix   229

Glossary   267

Bibliography   273

Index   309

PREFACE

"Where is God in the modern world?" Many have wondered about the location of the Holy God in a world that is steeped in scientific reason and economic pragmatism. Historically, the edifice of the church building in a community has functioned as a reference to the presence of God. Christian communities have frequently taken the existing architectural designs of the local community and adapted them to their own use. Over time, unique symbolic elements have been worked into the exterior and interior material expressions of the building. Theological meaning has been developed to explain the symbolism, and the language of church design has been established. Different geographical locales in various time periods have determined what have come to be called "styles" of design. From the vantage point of the twenty-first century, we identify historical styles of church architecture such as Byzantine, Romanesque, Gothic, Renaissance, Baroque, and so on. Each style is interpreted symbolically and theologically as representing particular understandings of God and God's relationship with the world.

Could such a distinct movement and architectural agenda have occurred in the midst of the twentieth century? Have we gained enough distance to identify a "modern" architectural style of church design that will one day gain the respect achieved by other historical ecclesiastical expressions? And what lessons might we have learned from living with the church architecture of the last eighty years or so? These questions and others lie behind the impetus for this book, in which I will explore the development of a particular slice of church design in Europe and the United States in the twentieth century.

An unusual confluence of movements occurred in the twentieth century that changed the face of church architecture across denominational lines in the United

States and Europe. A fusion of ideas emerging from the ecumenical movement, the liturgical movement, and the modern architecture movement produced a distinctive approach to church design that was particularly focused on emphasizing the presence of God in people communally engaged in worship and ministry.

In this book I will not attempt a general survey of church architecture in the twentieth century; instead, I will examine a particular manifestation of Western church design from the 1920s to the 1980s. I have chosen to call this manifestation an "architecture of immanence." I chose this phrase because of the dramatic intentional theological emphasis on God's presence being expressed through the people of God that often underlies the architectural expressions I will explore. Of course, not all churches built during this period reflect the same level of emphasis on the theological notion of God's immanence. Some Christian communities more than others chose to emphasize immanence. For example, monumental church structures tended to minimize references to immanence, while multipurpose churches (those using their worship space for both liturgical and nonliturgical activities) tended to maximize references to immanence. In this volume I will attempt to chart the initiation and development of an architecture of immanence, commenting on its theological grounding, historical development, and visible articulations.

In Chapter One, "Worship Spaces: Influenced by God's Nature and Scriptural Models," I will begin with a discussion of the theological understandings of transcendence and immanence in relation to a proper understanding of God's nature. Next I will discuss ways in which transcendence and immanence can be symbolically represented and interpreted in church design. I will then examine Scripture references addressing the establishment and use of environments for worship. I think it is important to note that Scripture sanctions the building of various environments for worship and to acknowledge that they have an important, if limited, role to play in facilitating religious belief. In this context I will highlight the tabernacle model of Moses and the Temple model of Solomon, along with reflections from Jesus and his early followers on the appropriate use and understanding of places for worship.

In Chapter Two, "God in the Ordinary: Nourishing a Context for Immanence," I will offer a glimpse into the theological context that nurtured an architecture of immanence. Ideas connected to Protestant liberal theology, the writings of Dietrich Bonhoeffer, and reflections of theologians John A. T. Robinson and Harvey Cox will constitute the core of that discussion. Protestant liberal theology downplayed the supernatural intervention of God and optimistically anticipated the translation of

God's presence in and through people acting in accordance with Christian teachings. Bonhoeffer articulated a conception of the faith he called "religionless" Christianity. Bonhoeffer's vision sparked, in part, the launch of a mid-century quest for "secular" expressions of the Christian faith. I will briefly discuss these understandings in an effort to locate a logical theological base for the promotion of an architecture of immanence.

In Chapter Three, "Twentieth-Century Worship Renewal: The Elevation of God's People," I will discuss the development of the ecumenical and liturgical movements in the twentieth century. First I will focus on the establishment of a network for the free flow of ideas across denominational lines through the ecumenical movement. I will note the shared underlying theological concerns for evangelism and service to the world that facilitated this movement. Next I will explore the concern for involving people more actively in corporate worship in reference to the work of the liturgical movement. In this context I will point out common ideas that illustrate a trans-denominational affirmation of choices that allowed for architectural expressions oriented toward emphasizing God's immanence.

In Chapter Four, "Modern Impulses in Church Architecture: Faith Engaging Culture," I will describe modern architecture with the goal of understanding how this movement influenced church design. I will begin by examining the reaction to architectural revival movements of the nineteenth century, and then briefly examine the contributions of Frank Lloyd Wright, Walter Gropius, Ludwig Mies van der Rohe, and Le Corbusier to the genesis of modern architecture. Next I will discuss the emergence of the International Style because of its powerful influence on instilling an ideology of design that rejected the language of traditional architecture. I will correlate priorities found in the promotion of modern architecture to concerns of the liturgical movement, helping to explain the rise and application of a particular aesthetic sense in churches of the early to mid-twentieth century.

In Chapter Five, "The Fruits of Worship Renewal: Emphasizing an Architecture of Immanence," I will trace the evolution of the impulses of the ecumenical and liturgical movements as they were translated into meetings, conferences, and suggestions concerning worship-space articulation. I will review the influential writings of Rudolf Schwarz, Peter Hammond, and John G. Davies, as well as documents such as *Art and Environment in Catholic Worship.* I will also explore materials emerging from denominational sources, illustrating the common themes and the cross-referencing of like materials that over time yielded to greater similarities between Catholic and Protestant church designs.

In the next two chapters, I will explore selected examples of an architecture of immanence. In Chapter Six, "An Architecture of Immanence: Early Examples in Europe," I will discuss early twentieth-century churches by Auguste Perret, Otto Bartning, Dominikus Böhm, and Rudolf Schwarz. I will include descriptions and photographs of a selection of their churches. I have chosen churches by these architects to illustrate the types of models that inspired a more "immanent" form of modern church design in Europe and the United States. In Chapter Seven, "An Architecture of Immanence: Selected Examples in America," I will begin with a discussion of the postwar context that fueled a building boom in the United States. I will then examine a spectrum of churches in the United States, noting the range of ways in which immanence has been referenced in modern design (including examples of the work of architects such as Marcel Breuer, Pietro Belluschi, Philip Johnson, Eliel Saarinen, Eero Saarinen, and Gunnar Birkerts).

In Chapter Eight, "An Illustration: The Thought and Work of Edward Anders Sövik," I will provide an example of how the ecumenical, liturgical, and modern architecture movements came to fruition in the thought and work of a particular architect who designed churches for both Roman Catholic and Protestant communities. Sövik was unusually articulate in his theological approach to church design and prolific in his writing. His visibility earned him an influential role in mid-twentieth-century church design. I will highlight Sövik's reflections from 1960 to 1973, in which he developed a particular approach to design that he called "nonchurch" architecture, intended to enhance the service of the church to the world.

In Chapter Nine, "Where Are We Now? Discernment and Lessons Learned," I will begin with an analysis of the continuing influence of ecumenism and liturgical renewal. I will also note the impact these movements continue to have on church design to illustrate the foundation that remains for a continuing similarity between Catholic and Protestant churches. I will touch on the "death" of modern architecture as well as the rise of postmodern architecture. I will then discuss the strengths and weaknesses of church architecture oriented toward expressing immanence, highlighting recent reservations about an approach to church design that can be interpreted as undermining (even if unintentionally) certain theological realities.

In Chapter Ten, "Where Can We Go? Directions for the Future," I will conclude this study with a series of observations and suggestions that I hope will facilitate a thoughtful process of renovation and new church design in the contemporary church. I will highlight particular resources to establish a broader context for the consideration of church design than is often considered by building committees.

I will also address the benefits of ongoing ecumenical encounters, the consideration of beauty, the significance of sustainable design, and the value of maintaining unique Christian designs.

The birthing and development of a project of this nature is never accomplished in isolation. Appreciation is due to a myriad of individuals who have contributed to the production of this book, only some of whom I can mention here. Thanks to liturgical colleague John Witvliet for the invitation to pursue this project. His vision, ongoing encouragement, and tangible support have enhanced the final text. Thanks to colleagues Todd Johnson, Christopher Miller, Jack Kremers, and John Gallen for their thoughtful comments on various drafts of the book. Their insights have provoked constructive direction and precision (though all errors that may be contained in these pages are due entirely to the author). Thanks to Dale Simmons, Paul Mouw, and the research staff of the Judson College library, who have shared in providing an array of resources necessary to pursue this project. Thanks to the Homer and Margaret Surbeck Summer Research Program, Judson College, which underwrote a portion of the research for this book. Photographs included in the book have been generously shared by many of the faith communities featured in these pages. Special thanks to Keith Bringe, the Reverend David Chandler, John Charles, Mary Jean Del Principe, Thom Karmik, Brother David Klingeman, Father Nock, Denise A. Packer, Tricia Riske, Edward A. Sövik, and Chris Veneklase for their assistance in acquiring images of various churches. Particular documents have been shared through the efforts of Father Gabriel B. Baltes, Joann S. Daily, Father Kevin Seasoltz, and Father Daniel White. I am appreciative of their tangible help with acquiring this information. Thanks to Mary Hietbrink at Eerdmans, who provided insightful editorial direction and support for which I am most grateful. And thanks to my wife, Tracy, for editorial assistance and thoughtful questions, and to children Lukas and Elissa for their willingness to rearrange their lives at times in order that this book might see the light of day.

MARK A. TORGERSON
Elgin, Illinois
August 2006

CHAPTER ONE

WORSHIP SPACES: INFLUENCED BY GOD'S NATURE AND SCRIPTURAL MODELS

The LORD said to Moses: Tell the Israelites to take for me an offering; from all whose hearts prompt them to give you shall receive the offering for me. This is the offering that you shall receive from them: gold, silver, and bronze, blue, purple, and crimson yarns and fine linen, goats' hair, tanned rams' skins, fine leather, acacia wood, oil for the lamps, spices for the anointing oil and for the fragrant incense, onyx stones and gems to be set in the ephod and for the breastpiece. And have them make me a sanctuary, so that I may dwell among them. In accordance with all that I show you concerning the pattern of the tabernacle and of all its furniture, so you shall make it.

EXODUS 25:1-9, NRSV

When Solomon had finished building the house of the LORD and the king's house and all that Solomon desired to build, the LORD appeared to Solomon a second time, as he had appeared to him at Gibeon. The LORD said to him, "I have heard your prayer and your plea, which you made before me; I have consecrated this house that you have built, and put my name there forever; my eyes and my heart will be there for all time."

1 KINGS 9:1-3, NRSV

A FUNDAMENTAL UNDERSTANDING of the nature of God is important in the consideration of building designs for Christian worship and ministry. Churches are public structures associated with the activities of the religious communities that inhabit them. While architectural design cannot, in and of itself, determine the full content of meaning that a person receives when he or she encounters a church, the design can provoke associations based on past and present human patterns of behavior (intuitive and learned). In this first chapter, we will consider some theological reflections concerning the nature of God, highlight certain design factors that can evoke particular meanings, and briefly examine worship environments (and attitudes toward them) in both testaments of the Bible.

The Transcendent and Immanent God

Formulating an understanding of the Holy God is complex. God's people have wrestled with understanding God throughout time. Our sacred writings, as recorded in both testaments of the Bible, speak of God as transcending our existence or dwelling outside of the realm of the earth. The Bible also speaks of God as being in our midst at various times, both through the life of the Spirit of God and through concrete manifestations in material form — especially in the person of Jesus Christ. In theological language, that aspect of the nature of God that is beyond our creation is called the "transcendence" of God. God is present and active beyond our existence. God transcends all time and space. But God is also very close to humanity. God is present in our world through the Holy Spirit, through occasional radical manifestations (for example, miracles), and through the followers of Jesus (the church). That aspect of the nature of God that highlights God's presence among us is sometimes called "immanence."

In the twentieth century, Christians have been particularly fond of remembering that the transcendent, holy God became immanent to us in Christ because of love. Jesus walked this earth as one of us. He lived and died as one of us. He was resurrected from the dead and has returned to his place with God in heaven so that we might achieve restored relationship with God. Christians have always found great joy and comfort in knowing that the Triune God of the cosmos came into our midst in this way. A God who is willing to take the humble form of a servant, to identify intimately with the human condition, is a God who can be trusted, cherished, and adored.

Following the ascension of Jesus, the Holy Spirit was sent to inspire and guide the people of God. Under the influence of the Spirit, the followers of Jesus formed what is now called the Christian church. Saint Paul teaches us that the church is a tangible presence of the body of Jesus Christ in this world. Jesus Christ is central to the life and understanding of the church. Jesus Christ is central to the Christian understanding of God, a reflection of his immanent presence. This focus on the immanence of God in Christ supported a twentieth-century emphasis on evangelism and service to the world in many Roman Catholic and Protestant communities.

FACTORS OF CHURCH DESIGN ASSOCIATED WITH TRANSCENDENCE AND IMMANENCE

Meaning associated with particular church designs can be ascertained intuitively and/or learned through explanation. The physical features of environments for worship can initiate certain feelings in those who occupy the space. For example, one might feel small and humble in a space of great height and volume. Or one might sense "mystery" in a dimly lit space. Such experiences operate on an intuitive level, establishing a sense of meaning in relation to a space. But meanings are also assigned to objects and can be learned over time. People can be taught that particular features of architectural design, objects for worship, and symbols incorporated into a church represent certain theological understandings or interpretations. For example, a long, narrow, intentionally organized space with a primary entrance at one end and a significant focal point at the other end (such as an altar/table) can be said to represent a spiritual "pilgrimage," or "journey," in time and space. An intentional movement from a place of ordinary daily activities to a location of extraordinary religious activities can be established through the specific design and ornamentation of a worship space. One might sense this journey motif on some level, but an intentional explanation of the overall metaphor and accompanying symbolic representations would help those who encounter the space to more fully experience the intended meanings of its design. Impression and catechesis are both important for human engagement with a built environment.

Church buildings are visible witnesses to faith, capable of influencing the belief systems of Christians and non-Christians alike. The transcendent and immanent aspects of God's nature are central to the Christian faith and thus emerge as important themes to reference in church design. However, the radical difference between these two aspects is difficult to navigate in material form. Transcendence refers to the "wholly otherness" of God; immanence refers to "God with us." One could almost think of these two theological notions as polar opposites. If they were to be charted, they would lie on different ends of a straight-line spectrum. For God to be transcendent and immanent at the same time represents a paradox for us. These aspects seem mutually exclusive, but both have been, are, and always will be true of the nature of God for Christians. This paradox is similar (and related) to consideration of the two natures — divine and human — of Christ. For centuries, Christians have struggled to try to define and explain exactly how Jesus could be God and man equally and at the same time. In the end, we have generally agreed that this is a mystery that requires affirmation but defies explanation.

A number of factors in church design can work toward reminding us of the transcendence and immanence of God. Scale (relative size in relation to the human person) and volume, the control of light, the elaboration or simplification of the decor, and the organization of the space have all been used through various designs to help remind the worshiper of the nature of God. But the static nature of material objects does not necessarily lend itself to communicating paradox very effectively. For example, larger scale and volume in a church is often interpreted as emphasizing the significance of God in contrast to humans, reminding us of the transcendent nature of God. A more modest scale and volume in church design is often considered to be inviting and hospitable because people feel more significant in relation to the overall space. The reality of God's immanent nature may more easily be associated with modest scale and volume.

Light can be controlled in an environment through various means. Frequently, diminished light in a worship space is interpreted as more "mysterious" and evocative of wonder, encouraging contemplation of the divine. Often the idea of God's transcendence is coupled with limited light. In contrast, an abundance of light, particularly of bright white light, tends to emphasize the immediate context. The focus of the viewer is on the tangible, visible surroundings. In a corporate worship event, the setting and company of believers could be emphasized by utilizing such light. Focusing on the well-illuminated activities and presence of the people of God (the church as the body of Christ) could be associated with celebrating God's immanence.

Elaboration of the decor of a worship environment can help to focus the person more intentionally on less tangible aspects of God as the object of worship. Contemplation of aspects of God's nature beyond our immediate comprehension can be encouraged through the incorporation of symbolism. Richness and abundance of symbolism and visual articulation can highlight God's transcendence.[1] Symbols can point to more abstract theological understandings (such as God's "otherness," the

---

1. The utilization of symbols in a church can refer to much more as well (including God's immanence), but in this passage I am highlighting a way in which transcendence can be represented more fully through material forms.

Trinitarian nature of God, and God's sovereignty), providing opportunities for pro-longed consideration by the viewer. On the other hand, simplification of the decor of a worship space can tend to focus people more on the immediate activities and occupants of the space as the body of Christ. Highlighting the active participation of God's people at worship through the simplification of the decor could be interpreted as emphasizing God at work in our midst, or the immanence of God.

Elaboration of the worship environment includes an issue related to aesthetic impression as well. For better or worse, people are influenced by the embellishment of spaces. Amplification of the decor of a worship space is frequently associated with the heightening of devotion to a particular deity. The object of worship is considered to be of greater value by virtue of the "offerings" present in the richness of design meant to encourage recognition and adoration. The transcendent qualities of the divine can be emphasized in this way, for we offer unique gifts and expressions through both these design efforts and the sacrifices required to incarnate them. In the Christian tradition there is a long-standing desire to "bring one's best" to God in worship. In the history of the church, the elaboration of decor has sometimes been justified on these grounds. Elaborate churches bore (and still bear) testimony to the holiness of God, his unique place in our world, and the value that ought to be attributed to him. However, not all Christian communities have pursued this material articulation. In the name of stewardship, many Christians have chosen to minimize their worship space decor, setting aside more resources for social ministries. Fear of idolatry has also been given as a reason for creating more spartan environments. Communities that choose to design in this mode must seek other ways to highlight the transcendent nature of God.

Organization of the worship space can also influence focus on the transcendence and immanence of God. Room design and furnishings that tend to minimize the awareness of others in worship can work toward heightening an understanding of God's transcendence. Long, narrow spaces that keep worshipers oriented toward a single focal point can help to emphasize an object of worship outside of themselves. Delineating areas according to a hierarchical understanding of the people of God (clearly differentiated spaces for clergy and laity) can also work toward emphasizing God's transcendence. More centrally planned spaces, where there is an intentional collapse of specific clergy and parishioner domains and where the worshipers are acutely aware of being in community (even to the point of looking into one another's eyes during worship), can help to emphasize the idea that God is in the midst of the company of God's people.

It is important to note that none of the factors mentioned here — scale and volume, use of light, articulation of decor, and organization of space — will adequately communicate either God's transcendence or immanence alone, but they can contribute to an overall emphasis on one or the other to varying degrees. The combining of these factors has a cumulative effect on the perception of the church, especially in conjunction with the ritual activities experienced in the space. The theological disposition of a congregation will also impact perceived meanings in a church. Some Christian traditions naturally lean toward emphasizing either God's transcendence or God's immanence (for example, Eastern Orthodox churches tend to focus on God's holiness, and Southern Baptist churches tend to focus on a personal relationship with Jesus). All traditions affirm both aspects of God's nature, but the general theological focus can vary dramatically and impact the visual impression and interpretation of a church.

All worship environments will exhibit some use of the factors highlighted above. The theological meanings attached to these factors will vary in a given context, according to their articulation and combination, the theological emphases of the Christian tradition using the worship space, the ritual activities embodied in corporate and private worship, and even the past worship experiences of those who occupy the space. For example, larger scale and volume, diminished light, and a singular focus may or may not encourage contemplation of God's transcendence. If these features take the form and shape of the worship practices of a medieval, Roman Catholic, Gothic cathedral, then they probably will emphasize God's transcendence. But if they take the form of a late-twentieth-century Protestant megachurch (think especially of the vast, theatre-type auditorium spaces with ritual engagement bordering on entertainment), God's transcendence may or may not be emphasized by the space. The articulation of church space does not exist without theological context and ritual intention. The architectural design alone will not determine a sense of God's transcendence or immanence. Nevertheless, the features of church design are important for the role they play in helping to provide avenues for glimpsing, pondering, and experiencing different aspects of God's nature.

Scriptural Models for Worship Environments

Two primary models of built environments for worship are mentioned in the Hebrew bible or Old Testament. Both models were initiated by God, and both could be said to highlight the transcendent and immanent aspects of God's character, albeit to different degrees. The model of the tabernacle (see Exodus, chapters 25–40), or tent of meeting, was presented to the people of God when they were sojourning in the wilderness between Egypt and Canaan. Offerings from the people were gathered and fashioned into the requested environment. The tent was mobile, moving with the people as they wandered. It was not considered a "permanent" house for God. It was not thought to "contain" or restrict God in any sense. Rather, it was conceived of as a place in which the presence of God could linger at times in the midst of the people. The scale and volume of the design did not overwhelm worshipers; it appeared to be more inviting by virtue of its more modest expression. By exhibiting these features of design, the tabernacle could be said to have highlighted a fairly strong reference to God's immanence. The tabernacle functioned as a primary symbol of God's presence in the world and among his people, who were "on the move."

A sense of transcendence was also present in the tabernacle model. Elaboration of the tabernacle was achieved through the people's offerings of fine materials and the fashioning of these materials into particular objects by Israel's most excellent artists. In this way, the people publicly proclaimed the holiness of their God and shared in creating a visible sacred place through which to focus their adoration and praise. In addition, the tabernacle space was organized according to a hierarchical plan (certain quadrants were set aside for various people, with entry to some areas restricted) and sometimes limited the amount of light (as in the Holy of Holies, where diminished light could heighten a sense of mystery). So, while a strong emphasis on the immanence of God was active in and through the tabernacle model, references to the transcendent qualities of God were not forgotten.

The building of the Temple by King Solomon (see 1 Kings, chapters 5–8, and 2 Chronicles, chapters 2–7) was sanctioned once a permanent geographical location, Jerusalem, had been secured and a sense of relative peace had been achieved. God shared in guiding the construction and design of an elaborate, permanent place of worship in the capital of the land. The scale and volume of the Temple far exceeded that of the tabernacle. The individual worshiper would have been immediately aware of a sense of the transcendence of the God of Israel by virtue of the diminished significance of the person in relation to the size of the Temple. Delimiting the space in the Temple also accentuated the transcendence of God. The organization of the space was similar to that of the tabernacle: specific locations were assigned to different groups of people, with access to various areas strictly regulated. And the extraordinary elaboration of the space heightened the sense of God's holy otherness and worthiness. The best artists in the nation used expensive materials to create a monument that communicated the glory of God as much to those outside of Israel as to God's people.

Reference to God's immanence was also discernable in the Temple, if less emphasized than in the tabernacle model. The Temple was located within the midst of God's people, in their holy city of Jerusalem. God's presence was promised in the Temple, so a sense of his being among them was maintained. And daily activities in the Temple and its courts would have worked toward building a personal connection with the community of the faithful.

In the Christian scriptures or New Testament, less focus is found on the built environment for worship. The Temple is still present and used by God's people during the days of Christ. Jesus and the disciples are noted for having gathered both at the Temple and at synagogues for worship activities.[2] Neither environment for worship is forbidden, but concern is expressed for having the correct motives for worshiping God (see, e.g., Matt. 21:12-14). Jesus also sees an active walk of faith possible beyond the physical Temple (see Matt. 12:6; John 2:13-22; 4:7-26). While the Temple does remain a "sacred place" in relation to God, Jesus brings a vision that does not in any way limit his presence to the Temple alone. In fact, the presence of God can now be associated with the body of Christ. (For identification of Jesus as "Emmanuel," or "God with us," see Isaiah 7:14 and Matthew 1:23.) In the writings of Saint Paul and Saint Peter, the followers of Jesus become a primary location of God in the world through the activity of the Holy Spirit (see 1 Cor. 3:16; 6:19-20; Eph. 2:19-22; 1 Peter 2:4-10). And in the book of Revelation there is the anticipation that a material location to focus our worship will not always be necessary. The association of the Temple with Jesus will culminate in the New Jerusalem, with his presence alone sufficing for the Temple's existence (see Rev. 21:22-26). The New Testament does not forbid the creation of places of worship, but it is concerned with idolatry and the misuse of such spaces. Worship spaces do serve to facilitate the worship and ministries of the people of God, but they do not limit God's presence or activity in the world. Viewing God's presence as unleashed throughout the entire world points to his transcen-

2. Synagogues are thought to have first been established in the wake of the sixth-century exile of the Israelites by the Babylonians. (However, evidence of a synagogue building exists only from the early third century before Christ.) Journeying to the Temple in Israel for the offering of sacrifices was difficult or impossible for many, so places to gather for prayer, singing, and the reading and preaching of God's Word were established in the Diaspora.

dence. The reality of God's presence located in the midst of God's people, the body of Christ, highlights his immanence.

Overall, it would probably be fair to say that God's immanence was easier to discern in the tabernacle model and that God's transcendence was emphasized more fully in the Temple model. Worship spaces for God's people have been built in a myriad of forms since these biblical times, and the tabernacle and the Temple have remained models of inspiration for Christian communities. Perhaps because of its permanence and visibility to the larger community, the Temple seems to have received more attention than the tabernacle model. It is important to note that political as well as theological motives appear to have been connected to the designs used for Christian worship spaces throughout history also. From the adaptation of the Roman basilican design in the fourth century to the fullness of the Gothic cathedral expression in the late medieval period, the church has sought to publicly declare the presence of the living God and the power of the church. Political and theological concerns can both accentuate transcendence in church design.

CONCLUSIONS

Christian communities wrestle with how best to articulate their faith in material form through the buildings they construct for worship and ministry. Our core religious beliefs impact the articulation of the buildings we construct. Biblical reflections on environments for worship and ministry are important for many Christian communities, although varying interpretations of Scripture sometimes allow us to draw different conclusions. Our perception and understanding of the holy God influences our design choices. Deeply rooted in our faith tradition are oppositional understandings of the nature of God, affirming that God is both transcendent and immanent. When we create church buildings, we often seek to affirm one or both of these aspects of God's nature. It is important to recognize that the intention to emphasize these qualities may or may not be foremost in the minds of those doing the building. But religious buildings, by virtue of their very identification, will still be considered a reflection (to some degree) of the deity in whose name they are built. Design choices related to the scale, volume, light, decor, and organization of the churches we create affect the perception of the God we represent and serve.

Variety in theological emphases among the world's many Christian traditions has yielded a host of expressions for church architecture. Humble beginnings in domestic structures of the first few centuries of the church yielded to Roman assembly halls of the fourth century (the basilica). Over many centuries the basilican design was transformed into the form of elaborate Gothic cathedrals. References to the transcendence and immanence of God can be found in all of these models, but some designs seem to emphasize one or the other more easily and fully. For example, the domestic buildings that were altered to accommodate worship and ministry in the first centuries of the church could be interpreted as more easily reminding early believers that God was in their midst. The particular articulation of the factors mentioned in this chapter tended to underscore the idea of God's immanence in and through the gathered community. In contrast, late medieval cathedrals of Europe, by virtue of the monumental and extravagant articulation they embodied, could be said to more readily remind the worshiper of the transcendent nature of God. Most important to remember is that worthy worship and ministry can be expressed effectively through both house churches and cathedrals.

Because of the paradoxical nature of transcendence and immanence and the static nature of material objects, it may be easier to articulate one end of the transcendence and immanence scale more effectively in built form. Such is the limitation of human existence. In the pages that follow, I will explore an impulse in twentieth-century church architecture that tended to emphasize God's immanence over God's transcendence. A myriad of influences led to this impulse. This historical journey will begin with seeking the presence of God in the ordinary life of our world.

CHAPTER TWO

GOD IN THE ORDINARY: NOURISHING A CONTEXT FOR IMMANENCE

And the Word became flesh and lived among us, and we have seen his glory, the glory as of a father's only son, full of grace and truth.

JOHN 1:14, NRSV

Most people who pass a church's door never enter it. But they do form impressions of the Church from the physical church. There are questions which consciously or unconsciously arise in people's minds: "Is this building and its purposes relevant for me? Or of no particular interest?" People are inclined to wonder if the institution the building represents has anything to say to them really worth hearing. If the church building suggests retreat from the modern world, it is apt to indicate a failure to take the Incarnation of God in man's form seriously.

JAMES F. WHITE, *Protestant Worship and Church Architecture* (1964)

As THE TWENTIETH century progressed, a theological recognition that the holy God was present and active in our ordinary world came to the fore in many Christian circles. A downplaying of supernatural aspects of the faith, a focus on the secularization of European and American cultures, and a desire to serve the community at large all played a part in elevating the theological idea of God's immanence, or "God with us." In this chapter we will examine ideas from Protestant liberal theology, the writings of Dietrich Bonhoeffer, and reflections from theologians John A. T. Robinson and Harvey Cox to better understand how and why many new church buildings in the mid-twentieth century tended to shy away from models of design that appeared "other-worldly."

MODERN THEOLOGY FOR A MODERN WORLD

A Protestant theological movement called "liberal theology" took root in the eighteenth century and flowered in the nineteenth century in Europe. Its influence quickly spread to the United States. Theologians associated with this development expressed concern that the Christian faith remain relevant to the contemporary culture. In an effort to remain appealing to that culture, the movement's leaders were willing to consider modern thought (including philosophical and scientific reflections) as a tool for interpreting the faith. What made these thinkers "liberal" was their willingness to allow modern secular thinking to shape an understanding of the Christian faith.

Liberal theology had its beginnings in the works of German theologians such as Friedrich Schleiermacher (1768-1834) and Albrecht Ritschl (1822-1889). Another German theologian, Adolf von Harnack (1851-1930), helped to disseminate the basic tenets of liberal theology to a broader audience. Three main themes provide a basic understanding of liberal theology: (1) a tremendous focus on the immanence of God (God's immediate presence in and through humanity, even to the point of locating the kingdom of God on this earth); (2) the reduction of the significance of the theological teachings of the Christian faith to ethics; and (3) a belief in the universal salvation of humanity.[1] Liberal theology came to dominate theological reflection in many European and American seminaries in the twentieth century.

Liberal theology developed within a modern cultural mind-set that downplayed or rejected outright any literal understanding of the supernatural in our world. Instead of focusing on a belief system concerned with divine intervention, liberal theology elevated the significance of humanity. There was optimism associated with what Christians could accomplish in the name of God by applying the teachings of Christ to the difficulties of our human culture. Sin and divine punishment receded into the background; the divine goodness inherent in all people came to the fore. In other words, the transcendence of God was on the decline, and the immanence of God *in people* was highlighted. To be fair, liberal theology was not a single, monolithic approach to the faith. Some theologians shaped its interpretation in more radical terms than others — some even eliminated divinity from the nature of Christ. But not all theologians took such extreme positions. What is important to note is

---

1. Roger E. Olson, *The Story of Christian Theology: Twenty Centuries of Tradition and Reform* (Downers Grove, Ill.: InterVarsity Press, 1999), pp. 549-51.

that liberal theology exerted an important influence on the twentieth century and formed a theological climate in which modernist church architecture could focus, intentionally or unintentionally, on the immanence of God.

CHRISTIANITY WITHOUT RELIGION: THOUGHTS FROM DIETRICH BONHOEFFER

Dietrich Bonhoeffer (1906-1945) was a German Lutheran pastor and theologian who was executed by the German Nazi party for his support of a plot to assassinate Adolf Hitler. Bonhoeffer had studied theology in Tübingen and Berlin with theologians such as Adolf von Harnack. He pastored churches in Barcelona (1928-1929) and London (1933-1935), taught theology in Berlin (at intervals from 1931 to 1936), and led a Confessing Church seminary in Finkenwalde, Germany, from 1935 to 1939. As World War II began, Bonhoeffer chose not to flee the turmoil of his country. He ministered, taught, and wrote in the midst of difficult times. Two of his writings, *The Cost of Discipleship* (largely a meditation on the Sermon on the Mount, emphasizing the necessity of faith and obedience in the Christian life) and *Life Together* (reflections based upon his experiences of communal life in the Finkenwalde community), brought him international attention.[2]

Bonhoeffer was unable to wholeheartedly embrace the theological system passed on to him through its liberal interpreters in his seminary training; it was a system of thought that reduced the person of Christ to a good man who embodied the ethical teachings of God better than anyone else. Bonhoeffer found himself drawn to the thinking of a theologian who vigorously challenged liberal theology: Karl Barth (1886-1968). Barth affirmed the unique revelation of the holy Triune God in the person of Jesus Christ as revealed in the Word of God. Whereas liberal theology emphasized a general revelation of God through human religious experiences or in universal history, Barth concentrated on the particularity of the special revelation of Jesus Christ.[3] Bonhoeffer affirmed this unique revelation of God and struggled to articulate this truth in a language and a form that modern humanity could recognize and embrace.

2. Dietrich Bonhoeffer, *The Cost of Discipleship* (New York: Macmillan, 1955), first published as *Nachfolge* (München: Chr. Kaiser Verlag, 1937); and *Life Together* (New York: Harper & Row, 1954), first published as *Gemeinsames Leben* (München: Chr. Kaiser Verlag, 1938).

3. Olson, *The Story of Christian Theology*, pp. 580-81.

Bonhoeffer understood that Jesus Christ was the center of the life of faith and, in fact, the center of life in the world.[4] Jesus was the unique revelation of God in the world. He lived a life of servanthood to humanity, dying and rising, that God's redemptive work might be fulfilled. Jesus laid claim to all of life, not just portions that one might consider "religious" moments of encounter.[5] Jesus established the church so that people might continue to proclaim the presence and activity of God through Christ to the entire world. Bonhoeffer articulated this understanding in *Life Together*:

> A Christian comes to others only through Jesus Christ. Among men there is strife. "He is our peace," says Paul of Jesus Christ (Eph. 2:14). Without Christ there is discord between God and man and between man and man. Christ became the Mediator and made peace with God and among men. Without Christ we should not know God, we could not call upon Him, nor come to Him. But without Christ we also would not know our brother, nor could we come to him. The way is blocked by our own ego. Christ opens up the way to God and to our brother.[6]

The centrality of Christ was essential to Bonhoeffer's understanding of community, both inside and outside of the church. Jesus provided the opportunity for humanity to find reconciliation and peace, with God and with one another. Jesus modeled the way to true human community through his self-sacrificing posture, and we are to emulate that posture with others so that the world might come to find the peace and love that God intends for it.

Toward the end of Bonhoeffer's days, as he was held captive in Tegel Prison in Berlin (where he was incarcerated in 1943), he articulated a vision of "religionless" Christian faith. This was a notion that would capture the imagination of theologians who would come after him. This concept grew out of Bonhoeffer's wrestling with a way to reinterpret his faith to a seemingly unsympathetic modern world. He had a passion for the presence of God in our world, in and through the person of Jesus Christ, and he sought to find language that would effectively introduce the Gospel of Christ to those outside the church. In a letter to a friend dated 30 April 1944, Bonhoeffer reflected,

---

4. Dietrich Bonhoeffer, *Letters and Papers from Prison,* ed. Eberhard Bethge (New York: Macmillan, 1953), p. 191.

5. Bonhoeffer, *Letters and Papers from Prison,* p. 210.

6. Bonhoeffer, *Life Together,* p. 23.

The thing that keeps coming back to me is, what *is* Christianity, and indeed what *is* Christ, for us today? The time when men could be told everything by means of words, whether theological or simply pious, is over, and so is the time of inwardness and conscience, which is to say the time of religion as such. We are proceeding towards a time of no religion at all: men as they are now simply cannot be religious any more.[7]

Bonhoeffer was writing from the midst of a horrific incarceration. He was surrounded by circumstances and questions that defied easy answers. Bonhoeffer believed that Christ was at the center of life in this world, and the church was a primary witness to the presence of Christ. But Bonhoeffer was not sure that unchurched people could — or would — want to perceive the message of the church clearly in the contemporary world. Bonhoeffer began to wonder if "religious Christianity" had become too much of an "insider" phenomenon, using language that was irrelevant and unappealing to secular humanity. He wondered what might happen if instead of using the label *religious* to describe the Christian faith, the label *religionless* were applied to Christianity. Bonhoeffer's underlying concern was for the church to be relevant to the secular culture, as he explained in *Letters and Papers from Prison:*

How do we speak (but perhaps we are no longer capable of speaking of such things as we used to) in secular fashion of God? In what way are we in a religionless and secular sense Christians, in what way are we the *Ekklesia,* "those who are called forth," not conceiving of ourselves religiously as specially favoured, but as wholly belonging to the world? Then Christ is no longer an object of religion, but something quite different, indeed and in truth the Lord of the world. . . .

. . . Man is challenged to participate in the sufferings of God at the hands of a godless world.

He must therefore plunge himself into the life of a godless world, without attempting to gloss over its ungodliness with a veneer of religion or trying to transfigure it. He must live a "worldly" life and so participate in the suffering of God. He may live a worldly life as one emancipated from all false religions and obligations. To be a Christian does not mean to be religious in a particular way, to cultivate some particular form of asceticism (as a sinner, a penitent, or a saint), but to be a man. It is not some religious act which makes a Christian what he is, but participation in the suffering of God in the life of the world.[8]

7. Bonhoeffer, *Letters and Papers from Prison,* p. 162.
8. Bonhoeffer, *Letters and Papers from Prison,* pp. 164, 222-23.

Bonhoeffer wanted all humanity to come to know that the entire world can be experienced as a gift from God. In agreement with liberal theological thinking, Bonhoeffer was not content to imagine that the church could be real and relevant only in a future kingdom to come. He was searching for ways in which to bear witness that God was among us even in the worst of human conditions. The lingering question for Bonhoeffer was, "How can we be 'church' in a meaningful way in the modern world?" I cite Bonhoeffer's fragmentary thoughts on a religionless Christianity here because they would influence modern church architecture, even provoking what Lutheran architect Edward A. Sövik would call "nonchurch" architecture for Christian communities.

The Effort to Relate Faith to the Secular World

Building on the foundation of many years of interpreting the beliefs associated with liberal theology, theologians in the mid-twentieth century launched a new round of writings that demonstrated a real concern for relating their understanding of the Christian faith to modern humanity. These theologians attempted to construct what could be thought of as a "secular" approach to the Christian religion. An underlying assumption of this secular approach to faith was that the average modern person, the product of a post-Enlightenment environment, could no longer embrace supernatural phenomena as convincing or meaningful. Historical, orthodox Christian teachings were thought to be no longer helpful for secular humanity. A renewed effort was made to appeal to universal experiences of humanity for religious connection, seeking to find clues to the presence of God in everyday life. This search focused on what we have been calling the "immanence" of God. In the beginning, this movement affirmed God's existence but sought God outside of traditional religious avenues.[9]

An example of the secular approach to the Christian faith can be found in John A. T. Robinson's book *Honest to God*.[10] Robinson (1919-1983), a bishop at the time in

9. The secular theology movement took different forms with different thinkers. Its most pessimistic conclusion was associated with theologians such as Thomas Altizer and William Hamilton, who concluded that God was no longer relevant or necessary to the spiritual quest of humanity. Their writings are now considered a part of the "death of God" theology.

10. John A. T. Robinson, *Honest to God* (Philadelphia: Westminster Press, 1963). Another theologian writing in a similar vein at this time was Paul van Buren, *The Secular Meaning of the Gospel: Based on an Analysis of Its Language* (New York: Macmillan, 1963). Robinson's work is highlighted here for the unusual popularity it achieved and the influence it exerted in initiating conversation on this interpretive approach.

the Church of England, claimed that he was sincerely seeking an alternative approach to Christian belief. He wrote as someone who believed in the faith but who was seeking to discuss an alternative way of finding God in our world. In his book he noted that he was inspired in his line of thinking in part by Bonhoeffer's reference to a Christianity without religion, although he acknowledged that he was not attempting to reflect Bonhoeffer's larger theological approach.[11] Rather, he highlighted particular passages in Bonhoeffer's work to juxtapose them with certain reflections found in the writings of theologians Paul Tillich (1886-1965) and Rudolf Bultmann (1884-1976). Robinson emphasized Jesus as a man who knew what it was to embody the presence of God through his servanthood. He sought to testify about Jesus, and the God who inspired him, through redemptive, relational experiences in ordinary life. Robinson believed that the Christian faith had the potential to break down the artificial distinctions between "sacred" and "secular."

In Chapter Five of his book, "Worldly Holiness," Robinson discussed Christian worship. He did not view worship as a uniquely religious ritual performed by pious Christians outside of ordinary life. Instead, he saw worship as an opportunity to enliven the ordinary with the revealed truth of God:

> For Christianity . . . the holy is the "depth" of the common, just as the "secular" is not a (godless) section of life but the world (God's world, for which Christ died) cut off and alienated from its true depth. The purpose of worship is not to retire from the secular into the department of the religious, let alone to escape from "this world" into "the other world," but to open oneself to the meeting of the Christ in the common, to that which has the power to penetrate its superficiality and redeem it from its alienation . . . to purify and correct our loves in the light of Christ's love; and in him to find the grace and power to be the reconciled and reconciling community.[12]

Robinson wanted to help people see that the presence of God and the influence of Christ were present in the everyday life of our world, not just in some "religious" realm that was somehow distinct from the secular. He sought an interaction between sacred and secular, religious and nonreligious, that would transform life according to God's intentions. Robinson's understanding of Christ in relation to divinity and the application of his approach to Christian ethics do not conform to

---

11. Robinson, *Honest to God*, pp. 22-23, 36.
12. Robinson, *Honest to God*, pp. 87-88.

traditional, orthodox understandings of the Christian faith, but his writing set the tone for promoting the elimination of the distinction between sacred and secular, a concept that made an impact on modern church design.

In Robinson's wake, a larger conversation concerning secular culture and the church emerged among theologians. The influence of urbanization on American culture and an imagined collapse of traditional religion in America came to the fore in what is sometimes called "The Secular City Debate."[13] In 1965, theologian Harvey Cox published a work entitled *The Secular City* that fueled this debate. Cox (b. 1929) began his book with an examination of biblical material. He concluded that the Bible bore witness to a "desacralization" of three things: (1) nature, by virtue of humanity having received the responsibility to care for the creation; (2) political leadership, in light of the Exodus from the rule of the "divine Pharaoh"; and (3) values, based on the biblical exposure of idols in the Sinai Covenant.[14] Cox's goal was to relativize the understanding of nature, politics, and values in such a way that all three were revealed to be largely influenced by changing human perceptions over time. He pursued this line of thinking to legitimate the "secularization" of the Christian faith in an effort to facilitate conversation about God with secular humanity.

Secularization implied "a historical process, almost certainly irreversible, in which society and culture are delivered from tutelage to religious control and closed metaphysical world-views."[15] Cox felt that modern humanity could not relate to a "religious" Christianity, a religion based largely on the pondering of metaphysical realities (concepts now rejected by secular humanity). Using in part thoughts from Bonhoeffer (particularly the discussion of "religionless Christianity" at the end of *Letters and Papers from Prison*), Cox raised a call to embody an expression of the Christian faith that was primarily concerned about being the people of God in the world through social and political action.[16] Cox sought a theology of social change that would speak to secular humanity, embodying the truth of God through the teachings of Jesus. He felt that the historical theological interpretations of the faith were unable to adapt to modern times. In particular he sought permission to adopt new values and ethics in the name of Christ (allowing for a certain fluidity that was consistent with the au-

13. As an example of the conversation, see *The Secular City Debate*, ed. Daniel Callahan (New York: Macmillan, 1966).

14. Harvey Cox, *The Secular City: Secularization and Urbanization in Theological Perspective* (New York: Macmillan, 1965), pp. 21-37.

15. Cox, *The Secular City*, p. 20.

16. Cox, *The Secular City*, pp. 241-43.

tonomy, freedom, and responsibility that humanity was given by God). Cox's call for a relevant, secular Christian witness exhibited the same focus on God's immanence emphasized by the "liberal theology" movement in the nineteenth century.

I have discussed Bonhoeffer, Robinson, and Cox to establish an important theological current that influenced the development of a modern form of church design. These three thinkers opened up a discussion of the relationship between the church and the world that resonated with insights from existing liturgical, ecumenical, and architectural reform movements of the mid-twentieth century. Pursuing a theology of God in the ordinary world did not, in and of itself, launch or sustain modern church design, but it did facilitate the embracing of ideas that emphasized the presence of God in the midst of real human communities at work in the ordinary world.

ATTENTION TO THE SECULAR IN CHURCH ARCHITECTURE

The collected essays from the First International Congress on Religion, Architecture, and the Visual Arts provide an example of the influence on church design of the theological stream noting God in the ordinary.[17] The Congress was held in New York City and Montreal, Canada, from 26 August to 4 September 1967. More than 800 delegates from twenty countries gathered at this conference to discuss issues related to the contemporary relationship between faith and the arts. Harvey Cox spoke at the conference, calling for a vision to pursue political and social change in urban areas as a response to God's command to serve one another.[18] Cox lifted up the struggles of urbanization in his day, especially the poverty and inequity that he thought the church could help to alleviate.

Other speakers from many fields of study shared their thoughts with the assembly. T. W. Adams, a political scientist associated with the National Aeronautics and Space Administration, expressed a common theme at the conference, the focus on the centrality of the human person:

> If science and resulting technology are unfulfilled without an ultimate application to a human need, so are religious places incomplete without people. Thus, modern times

17. This was published in 1969 as *Revolution, Place, and Symbol,* ed. Rolfe Lanier Hunt (New York: The International Congress on Religion, Architecture, and the Visual Arts, 1969).

18. Harvey G. Cox, "Man's Religious Visions," in Hunt, *Revolution, Place, and Symbol,* pp. 47-51.

compel us to emphasize people over place. I believe God is where man is, wherever he is on earth or in outer space. The place, therefore, may turn out to be less important than the presence of the person.[19]

Adams articulated a desire to focus the concept of place in relation to the presence of humanity, even in religious building (presumably underscoring the holiness of people over the holiness of geographical location). The centrality of the human person in relation to place versus the centrality of God in relation to a specific geographical location was a prevailing theme in the conception of much church architecture of the mid-twentieth century. It could be argued that to try to interpret church architecture as either focused only on God or focused only on people would be to construct a false dichotomy. In truth, churches throughout history have been constructed both to reference the holy God and to facilitate the activities of humanity in relation to God. An overemphasis on either divine presence or human activities can lead to an "overcorrection" of emphasis that yields an imbalance. It is possible that the mid-twentieth-century accent on human activities in church-building was a perceived "correction" to an overemphasis on church buildings concerned primarily with establishing a visible, isolated presence of God in the world. If this is true, then there might be grounds for viewing the mid-twentieth-century theological concern for the needs of people as related to the sixteenth-century theological agenda of the Reformation, in that both spawned church buildings meant to exhibit an accessible God.

John Gordon Davies (1919-1990) was another influential delegate who attended and addressed the Congress. Davies was a professor of theology at the University of Birmingham, England.[20] He had written extensively on the relationship between the Christian faith and church design, including published works such as *The Origin and Development of Early Christian Church Architecture, The Architectural Setting of Baptism,* and *The Early Christian Church: A History of Its First Five Centuries.*[21] Davies was moved by the apparent simplicity, functionality, and hospitality of many early Christian

19. T. W. Adams, "The Space Age and the Meaning of Space," in Hunt, *Revolution, Place, and Symbol,* p. 38.

20. A good introduction to the theological thought and influence of Davies may be found in Daniel W. Hardy, "God in the Ordinary: The Work of J. G. Davies (1919-1990)," *Theology* 99 (November-December 1996): 427-40.

21. *The Origin and Development of Early Christian Church Architecture* (New York: Philosophical Library, 1953); *The Architectural Setting of Baptism* (London: Barrie & Rockliff, 1962); *The Early Christian Church: A History of Its First Five Centuries* (New York: Holt, Rinehart & Winston, 1965).

churches. He sought to apply his understanding of the early church to contemporary congregational life. In his address to the Congress, Davies made these remarks:

> I would sum up the Church's function in one word: service. The Church exists, not for itself, but for others; it should therefore be an agent of reconciliation and liberation; it should concern itself with humanization; it should seek to meet the needs of men in the totality of their physical and spiritual existence. It should therefore plan its buildings in terms of the human needs of that sector of society within which it is serving, irrespective of whether or not those in need call themselves Christian. This is to say that we should plan multi-purpose buildings, the functions of which are determined not primarily by the restricted liturgical needs of a Christian group. The plan I am advocating, and it is capable of infinite variety, is one that embraces both sacred and secular within a single volume; one which neither shuts off the liturgy from the world nor the world from the liturgy. I am able to say this as a Christian, because in Christ sacred and secular are united; for me, therefore, as for the early Christian community, there can be no specially holy places; it is in and through the world of man, the secular, that we encounter the divine. I cannot carve life up into distinct spheres, one sacred, one secular, and I cannot therefore argue for sacred buildings as distinct from secular ones.[22]

Davies sought to place service to secular humanity at the theological center of church design in his day. He sought to break down the distinction between "religious" and "secular" realms of life, focusing on the integration of faith in ordinary activities and ministries. The profound interest he had developed in the relationship between worship and architecture was due in part to the writings of Peter Hammond.[23] In his own later writings, Davies would expand on the themes of faith and secularity, seeking to substantiate his multipurpose approach to church architecture. *The Secular Use of Church Buildings* is an especially good example of how Davies explores the relationship between secular culture and church design.[24] In the preface to this work, he notes the "vital debate" of his day concerning the secular nature of Christianity. In Chapter Seven he mentions Bonhoeffer as he argues for the elimina-

---

22. J. G. Davies, "Architectural Theory and the Appraisal of 'Religious' Buildings," in Hunt, *Revolution, Place, and Symbol*, pp. 169-70.

23. Hardy, "God in the Ordinary," p. 432. I will discuss Hammond in more detail in Chapter Three. Hammond's book entitled *Liturgy and Architecture* (London: Barrie & Rockliff, 1960) was especially engaging for Davies.

24. J. G. Davies, *The Secular Use of Church Buildings* (New York: Seabury Press, 1968).

tion of distinct realms of "sacred" and "secular" in this world, particularly in relation to modern church design. He further explored the subject of God in the ordinary in his book *Everyday God: Encountering the Holy in World and Worship*.[25]

Davies is a wonderful example of a theologian seeking to implement his beliefs through suggestions for changing church architecture in his day. From his perspective, a multipurpose approach to building design (including the design of worship spaces) would best facilitate intended theological reform and renewal. Davies was active in ecumenical dialogue concerning worship and church design, and he was prolific in his writing — and apparently was read quite widely. He had a significant influence on mid-twentieth-century church architects such as Edward A. Sövik; indeed, his writings are mentioned positively in various articles by Sövik.[26] Sövik himself took a "nonchurch" approach to worship space design. He advocated building "houses of the people of God," relating to the secular world, and using a worship space for various activities outside of liturgy:

> The issue is not whether congregations own structures; it is how they conceive their structures, and how they use them. They cannot be conceived as "houses of God," places of ecclesiastical character, in distinction from places of secular character. And they must not be used exclusively for worship. In the first circumstance the implication of architectural style, in the second the implication of special use will inevitably misinform and therefore deform people. They will persist in or come to the sense that God is attached to the place rather than to the Christians.[27]

It could be said that Sövik's approach to contemporary church design focused largely on the immanence of God in our world, primarily through the incarnation of Jesus Christ and the faithful believers as the body of Christ. His architectural practice and his many writings influenced many congregations (both Roman Catholic and Protestant) in the mid-twentieth century. Like Davies, Sövik also made use of reflections from Bonhoeffer, seeking to minister in meaningful visual language to secular humanity. He believed that churches might relate more fully to "secular" people by employing architectural designs that they could understand. The modern architectural styles of that period were thought to "speak" to the people of that day, so church

---

25. J. G. Davies, *Everyday God: Encountering the Holy in World and Worship* (London: SCM Press, 1973).

26. See, for example, E. A. Sövik, "Comment on Multi-Purpose Worship Spaces," *Faith and Form* 2 (April 1969): 20.

27. E. A. Sövik, *Architecture for Worship* (Minneapolis: Augsburg Publishing House, 1973), pp. 42-43.

buildings could — and perhaps should — resemble ordinary urban structures such as schools and office buildings. Theological concerns for relevancy, witness, and service influenced the adoption of modern architectural expressions for church design.

CONCLUSIONS

In the twentieth century, a theological climate emerged in Europe and the United States that emphasized a desire to mobilize the church for meeting the many social needs of the world, particularly those in urban environments. It was assumed that the average non-Christian no longer recognized the supernatural. "Enlightened" humanity was even thought to find religion useless and unnecessary. The church sought to remain meaningful in the face of an uninterested world and was motivated by a desire to bear witness to the truth of Christ and serve others. Accordingly, theological constructs were developed that pushed many faith communities toward adopting architectural expressions for their churches that resembled the contemporary building styles of the day. Some theologians and church leaders chose architectural designs that imitated the nonreligious structures of Western culture, in contrast to those historical architectural styles that sought to refer to the unique, supernatural theological affirmations of the faith (for example, medieval Gothic architecture).

The lingering effects of liberal theology, reflections from Dietrich Bonhoeffer, and popular writings from theologians such as John A. T. Robinson and Harvey Cox produced a climate that promoted the development and building of "servant" churches focused on the humanity whom God loved. The incarnation of God in the person of Jesus Christ became the primary spiritual focus of these communities. The immanence of God's presence in our world, in and through the people of this world, was weighted to an extraordinary degree. The transcendence of God was not denied (at least not by all), but was placed in a subservient position as a theological construct to be pondered later in the face of chaotic political and oppressive economic circumstances of the mid-twentieth century.

Not all churches — and not all believers — pursued the overemphasis on the immanence of God that we have discussed here. Some communities continued to make design choices about their church architecture that maintained references to the transcendence of God (sometimes even to a significant degree, as in those communities that chose designs used for medieval European cathedrals). But many made theological choices for renewing worship and ministry that sought to connect the pious with nonreligious humanity and attempted to help address the physical and spiritual needs of the world. A significant number of the Christian communities that focused on being servants to the world in the 1960s and the 1970s (and even into the 1980s) adopted styles for their churches that intentionally referred to God's immanence.

The theological accent on immanence discussed here is the broad background against which I will now explore two powerful mid-century church phenomena: the ecumenical movement and the liturgical movement. Twentieth-century church design changed rapidly and dramatically across denominational lines, in significant part because of the convergence of these two profound movements.

CHAPTER THREE

TWENTIETH-CENTURY WORSHIP RENEWAL: THE ELEVATION OF GOD'S PEOPLE

Mother Church earnestly desires that all the faithful be led to that full, conscious, and active participation in liturgical celebrations which is demanded by the very nature of the liturgy. . . . In the restoration and promotion of the sacred liturgy, this full and active participation by all the people is the aim to be considered before all else; for it is the primary and indispensable source from which the faithful are to derive the true Christian spirit.

Constitution on the Sacred Liturgy, ARTICLE 14 (1963)

The twentieth century was a unique period of time in which significant, unprecedented cooperation was formally established between various entities of the Christian church. Underlying the impulse for various church bodies to work together was a desire to disseminate the Christian faith throughout the world and a will to minister globally in the wake of urban oppression and world war. As the churches began to coordinate their efforts, similar faith affirmations were recognized. A hunger for unity among Christians grew. The centrality of worship in the life of the church was recognized across traditions, and a desire to renew worship was embraced interdenominationally.

In this chapter I will examine the ecumenical church movement and the liturgical movement. The two movements, ebbing and flowing together, facilitated the establishment of an approach to modern church design that emphasized, for a time, a theological accent on the immanence of God — the immediate presence of God through the worship activities of the people of God.

The Ecumenical Movement

Unity among Christians has been an issue since the days of the early church. Throughout the history of the church, groups of Christians have established formal relationships with one another and cooperated together. Disunity has also accompanied the expansion of the church. In A.D. 1054, after long years of disagreement (theological and political), the church split into two bodies: "Catholic" (following the bishop of Rome) and "Orthodox" (following the bishop of Constantinople). In the sixteenth century, leadership from within the Catholic Church seeking dramatic reform yielded another fracture. "Protestant" churches emerged from the Western church. In each case of separation, most parties made terrible accusations against their opponents. By the beginning of the modern period, the original catholic (or universal) church was organized into three major groups of churches: Roman Catholic, Eastern Orthodox, and Protestant. Each major group had multiple smaller alliances of churches within its organization. Over time, a desire to heal historical conflicts and present a more unified witness of Christ to the world was established and nourished.

Here we will be looking at ecumenical activity primarily in relation to the twentieth century. The word "ecumenical" (derived from the Greek word οἰκουμένη, meaning "the whole inhabited world") has achieved various definitions depending on the point in time to which one is referring and the ecclesial body one is considering. Here we will define "ecumenical" in a broad sense, meaning simply "applying to the whole world" or "universal." In the modern movement we are considering, the primary goal of ecumenism has been to establish a visible unity in Christ among all Christians. Evangelization, social concerns, and ethical questions have been primary points of initiation for ecumenical conversation and cooperation. The modern ecumenical movement has been neither parochial and one-dimensional nor universally accepted, but the reality of its presence has resulted in an unprecedented sharing of theological affirmations and ideas. Because this movement has affected ritual practices and church architectural expressions, we will briefly trace its evolution to better understand the proliferation of similar church buildings across denominational lines in the mid-twentieth century.

A significant missionary effort was undertaken by multiple denominations, especially Protestant sects, in the nineteenth century in Europe and the United States. Improvements in communication and transportation aided the expansion of mission-minded Christian organizations. Through these efforts a global consciousness emerged in churches. As early as 1804, the British and Foreign Bible Society brought together Protestants, Roman Catholics, and Orthodox believers in a common work.[1] Working together was found to increase the amount of effective work that could be accomplished (especially in countries of a vast size) and was less confusing to the newly planted churches as they struggled to understand this new religion of Christianity. Successful cooperation among missionaries sparked additional work together, especially in addressing urban issues. The nineteenth century saw the establishment of the Young Men's Christian Association (1844), the Evangelical Alliance (1846), the Young Women's Christian Association (1854), and the World Student Christian Federation (1895). Thus a significant foundation for ecumenical activity in the twentieth century was laid in the nineteenth century.

Two interchurch events in the early twentieth century provided significant impetus for a modern ecumenical movement: the establishment of the Federal Council of Churches of Christ in the United States and the establishment of the World Missionary Conference in Edinburgh.[2] Thirty-three Protestant American denominations joined together in 1908 to form the Federal Council of Churches of Christ. Approximately 18,000,000 people were represented by the cooperative, interdenominational effort. The Federal Council of Churches sought to encourage fellowship and unity among its many members and to join together in applying the teachings of Christ to the social concerns of the contemporary world. European churches were also engaged in interdenominational efforts. In the first half of the twentieth century, national interdenominational organizations formed in France (1905), Switzerland (1920), and Britain (1942).[3] After years of interdenominational cooperation and conversations with other interdenominational agencies, the Federal Council of Churches joined with other Christian bodies in 1950 to create the National Council of Churches of Christ in the United States.

The World Missionary Conference, held in Edinburgh in 1910, is the second major force that fostered ecumenical activity on a large scale. John R. Mott (1865-1955) and Joseph H. Oldham (1892-1990), both active in the student Christian movement, played significant roles in orchestrating this gathering. Protestant denominations

---

1. William G. Rusch, "Ecumenism, Ecumenical Movement," in *The Encyclopedia of Christianity,* vol. 2, ed. Erwin Fahlbusch et al. (Grand Rapids: Wm. B. Eerdmans, 2001), p. 51.

2. Mark A. Noll, *A History of Christianity in the United States and Canada* (Grand Rapids: Wm. B. Eerdmans, 1992), pp. 307-8.

3. Williston Walker, *A History of the Christian Church,* 3rd ed. (New York: Charles Scribner's Sons, 1970), p. 540.

were represented in abundance, with Orthodox and Roman Catholic churches declining to participate. Approximately 1,200 delegates attended the gathering, representing 160 missionary boards and societies. The conference emphasized themes that would carry through into later ecumenical organizations, including global evangelization, world peace and social justice, and unity among all Christian churches.[4] Many who attended this conference would go on to work at fostering increased interdenominational cooperation.

Momentum for interdenominational cooperation from the Edinburgh Conference was preserved and cultivated in efforts relating to missionary work, Christian education, social concerns, and doctrinal issues. In 1921 the International Missionary Council was established. Representatives from national missionary agencies worked together to coordinate their mission work and to encourage the mission churches to organize and develop their own indigenous national leadership. By 1924 a federation of national, interdenominational, Christian education agencies was established, a group that would eventually become the World Council on Christian Education and Sunday School Association.

Social concerns were addressed through a movement called Life and Work, which sought a unified approach to common ethical action in the world. The first Universal Christian Conference on Life and Work was held in Stockholm in 1925, which yielded the Universal Christian Council for Life and Work in 1930. Those in this movement analyzed the social needs of the world. They sought to mobilize the resources of the universal church and to provide tangible channels for alleviating need. And doctrinal differences between the many church bodies were explored by a movement called Faith and Order. The first World Conference on Faith and Order met in Lausanne in 1927. As early as 1920, the patriarch of Constantinople had issued a call for a permanent organization of fellowship and cooperation among the world's churches. Orthodox church representatives shared in the work of the Life and Work and Faith and Order groups. By 1937 multiple voices seeking a world council of churches encouraged these groups to consider the idea. Nearly ten years of preparation yielded a meeting in Amsterdam in 1948 that established such a council. One hundred forty-seven church bodies from forty-four nations approved the organization of the World Council of Churches. Over time, the World Council became the primary organ through which ecumenical, international efforts in missions, Christian education, social ministries, and doctrinal issues would be accomplished.

4. Rusch, "Ecumenism, Ecumenical Movement," p. 52.

The above discussion demonstrates that both the atmosphere and the interest existed in the twentieth century for international, ecumenical dialogue. Continued improvements in communication and transportation systems throughout the world facilitated unprecedented conversations and the sharing of information at a rapid pace. An emphasis was placed on a theological common ground among the world's various churches. Cooperation was found to yield a powerful witness for Christ in the world and establish avenues for powerful service to address human need.

The Church Builder is an example of a document oriented toward designing churches that emerged from the work of those affiliated with the Federal Council of Churches (FCC). Written by Elbert M. Conover, the director of the Interdenominational Bureau of Architecture and a member of the Committee on Worship of the FCC, this book was published in 1948.[5] An editorial committee of the Church Building Committee of the Home Missions Council of the FCC examined Conover's manuscript before publication. This committee was composed of leaders from twenty-five different Protestant denominations who were involved with church building. *The Church Builder,* which addresses all aspects of church building, is fairly conservative in its direction. Resources recommended for understanding quality church design include books such as John Ruskin's *Seven Lamps of Architecture,* Geoffrey Scott's *The Architecture of Humanism: An Episode in Taste,* Francis Bond's *English Church Architecture,* and Ernest Short's *History of Religious Architecture,*[6] all of which emphasize the advantages of architectural design rooted in historical traditions.[7] According to Conover, modern architecture was to be avoided because it was disconnected from tradition and did not create a church that "looks like a church." Contemporary church designs could be pursued in meeting the current needs of the people, he allowed, but they ought to be visibly connected to traditional styles of church architecture.[8] Although Conover did not mandate any particular architec-

---

5. Elbert M. Conover, *The Church Builder* (New York: Interdenominational Bureau of Architecture, 1948). Twenty years earlier, Conover had written *Building the House of God* (New York: Methodist Book Concern, 1928). Conover was affiliated with the Methodist Episcopal Church (North) and in this earlier work promoted Gothic revival designs as appropriate for Methodist churches.

6. Ruskin, *Seven Lamps of Architecture* (London: Elder Smith, 1849); Scott, *The Architecture of Humanism: An Episode in Taste* (London: Constable & Company, 1914); Bond, *English Church Architecture* (London: H. Milford, 1913); and Short, *History of Religious Architecture* (London: Eyre & Spottiswoode, 1925). Subsequent revised editions of this volume were published in 1936 (second edition), 1951 (third edition, titled *The House of God: A History of Religious Architecture*), and 1955 (fourth edition).

7. Recommended books are noted in Conover, *The Church Builder,* pp. 18, 186.

8. Conover, *The Church Builder,* pp. 34-39.

tural styles, many of the photographs and ground plans included in the book reflect Gothic, Romanesque, and colonial styles. This emphasis could also be seen in the additional planning guides for many aspects of church building that were produced and distributed by the Interdenominational Bureau of Architecture.[9] Real ecumenical cooperation in building churches was fostered through the agency and materials mentioned here, establishing a foundation for the rapid dissemination of ideas and designs across denominational lines.

Eastern Orthodox and Protestant churches were the primary bodies engaging in ecumenical dialogue and cooperation. The Roman Catholic Church had chosen not to participate in these activities when they were initiated, but it experienced a reversal of positions in the mid-twentieth century. As late as 1928, in the *Encyclical on Religious Unity, Mortalium Animos,* Pope Pius XI (1857-1939; in office from 1922 to 1939) insisted upon affirmation of the infallibility of the Roman pontiff as a criterion for interchurch cooperation. But this position was changed under the leadership of Pope John XXIII (1881-1963; in office from 1959 to 1963). An exploration of the role of this pope, especially through his initiation of Vatican II (the Twenty-first Ecumenical Council), is essential for understanding the similarities between Protestant and Roman Catholic church designs supporting a theological understanding of God in our midst.

POPE JOHN XXIII AND VATICAN II

John XXIII took the office of world leader of the Roman Catholic Church in 1958. He first announced his intention to call an ecumenical council of the church in 1959. The council was called to renew the life and faith of the church in the modern world, rebuild unity among Christians, and promote social justice and world peace. In 1960 this pope established the Secretariat for Promoting Christian Unity. This office created a tangible channel through which to support ecumenical dialogue between the Roman Catholic Church and other Christian churches. Both Orthodox and Protestant observers were invited to attend the meetings of Vatican II, and they did come to share in this historic gathering.

The council was opened on 11 October 1962 in Rome. More than 2,600 bishops from around the world met at St. Peter's Church for four sessions, generally in the

---

9. Conover mentions examples in *The Church Builder,* pp. 186-87.

fall of each of four consecutive years. Although Pope John XXIII died in June 1963, his successor, Pope Paul VI (1897-1978; in office from 1963 to 1978), provided able leadership for the last three sessions. The council members adopted sixteen texts. These texts addressed the nature of the church in general (e.g., *Dogmatic Constitution on the Church*), the interior life of the church (e.g., *Constitution on the Sacred Liturgy* and the *Decree on Ecumenism*), and the work of the church in the world (e.g., *Pastoral Constitution on the Church in the Modern World*).[10] Vatican II was brought to a close on 8 December 1965. The media's worldwide coverage of the meetings brought a heightened level of attention to the church's activities and rapidly transmitted the content of the adopted materials. The church around the world experienced an infusion of energy and hope from this ecumenical, renewal-oriented series of meetings.

Two documents from the Vatican II sessions have particular bearing on our exploration: the *Decree on Ecumenism (Unitatis Redintegratio)* and the *Constitution on the Sacred Liturgy (Sacrosanctum Concilium)*. With the promulgation of the *Decree on Ecumenism,* the Catholic Church fully committed itself to the ecumenical movement. The decree is noteworthy for its expressed desire to restore Christian unity among the churches rather than seek a return to the unity of the Catholic Church (an earlier desire). The document acknowledged the sharing of sacred Scripture; a similar focus on the life of grace through the work of Christ; the faith, hope, and charity that all Christians possess; and a common bond in baptism. The decree highlighted fundamental elements that churches shared. For the Orthodox churches, the document confirmed that their sacramental theology and ecclesiology were consistent with Catholic understandings. Vatican II thereby opened up the avenue for sharing fully with the Orthodox in worship together. For the Protestant churches, the document acknowledged, in a spirit of reconciliation, that Christ was at work beyond the boundaries of the Catholic Church and that "both sides were to blame" for historical division in the church.[11] To be sure, the church fathers acknowledged the theological differences that remained between Catholic and Protestant churches. And they did not sanction any quick or easy resolution to thorny issues. But they made a real effort to seek opportunities for dialogue on theological matters, to encourage occasional experiences of praying together, and to foster working together in the name of Christ.

10. The complete text of the sixteen documents adopted at Vatican II in English may be found in *The Documents of Vatican II,* ed. Walter Abbott (New York: America Press, 1966).

11. Abbott, *Documents of Vatican II* ("Decree on Ecumenism," Chapter One, article 3), p. 345.

Of particular interest to our exploration is the formal sanctioning of shared theological reflection between Roman Catholics and Protestants. This decree encouraged laity as well as clergy to pursue ecumenical dialogue. In 1965 the Secretariat for Promoting Christian Unity established a working group with the World Council of Churches. Official Catholic representation at the Faith and Order Commission of the World Council emerged. In the United States, the National Council of Churches and the Bishops' Committee for Ecumenical and Inter-religious Affairs initiated a series of dialogues between representatives of the Roman Catholic Church and other Christian denominations (including Baptist, Disciples of Christ, Episcopal, Lutheran, Methodist, Reformed and Presbyterian, and Orthodox bodies).[12] People were encouraged to discuss their common faith in Christ and to share ideas about how they might cooperate in making that faith relevant to the needs of the world. Decrees such as this one fostered the exchange of theological insights into the design of churches and provided an atmosphere in which a similarity in design might emerge between Roman Catholic and Protestant communities.

The *Constitution on the Sacred Liturgy* was a watershed document for those who were seeking a renewal of worship in the Catholic Church. It was the first of the sixteen texts to be approved by the bishops of the council, gaining approval by a vast majority in November 1962. After revisions, it was promulgated by Pope Paul VI in 1963. The significant role of worship in the life of the church was reflected in initiating the textual work of the council with this document. Also reflected was the tremendous pressure that had been building in the church over many years to renew worship in the context of a modern world. To better understand the significance of this document for church architecture design, it is important to consider the liturgical movement as a whole and then identify how the *Constitution on the Sacred Liturgy* sanctioned the production of guidelines for art and worship.

THE MODERN LITURGICAL MOVEMENT

Worship renewal is a phenomenon that has always been part of the life of the church. However, there have been particular moments in time when remarkable movements toward renewing worship have occurred. In this section I will focus on the liturgical movement of the twentieth century in Europe and the United States

12. Walker, *A History of the Christian Church*, p. 551.

to show how a focus on the activities of God's people in worship shaped the conception and design of churches and their worship spaces. The liturgical movement of this period began in Roman Catholic monastic circles, but a pastoral concern for applying its insights opened up opportunities for the involvement of lay people and ecumenical cooperation.

Benedictine monasteries in Belgium and Germany were at the forefront of the modern liturgical movement in Europe. Liturgical scholars at communities such as Mont-César Monastery in Louvain, Belgium, and Maria Laach Abbey in the German Rhineland promoted active lay participation in the worship of the church beginning in 1911 and 1914 respectively.[13] The writings of the patristic church fathers and the liturgies of the churches in the first centuries became sources of deep inspiration for the monastic scholars. They noted the significance of the ways in which the prayer life of the community at worship shaped the faith and life of these early believers. Leaders such as Dom Lambert Beauduin (1873-1960) of Mont-César and Abbot Ildephons Herwegen (1874-1946) and Dom Odo Casel (1886-1948) of Maria Laach wrote, published, and pursued international dialogue on liturgical renewal. Among the practical reforms they suggested for the pursuit of worship renewal was using the vernacular language in the Mass and increasing the frequency and reception of the Eucharist for laity.

Liturgical renewal was promoted in a profound way through the writing, teaching, and work of another German priest, Romano Guardini (1885-1968). Guardini was an excellent teacher and prolific author. He was passionate about the liturgy of the church and promoted creative ways to celebrate worship. Guardini taught in the area of religion and theology at the University of Berlin from 1923 to 1939, at which time he was dismissed by the Nazi party. In 1922 Guardini had his first contact with a German youth movement called Quickborn,[14] which was centered in a medieval castle, Rothenfel, on the river Main. Burg[15] Rothenfel became important as an environment in which Guardini could put his liturgical reform ideas into practice.

As an example of his willingness to engage creative reform, Guardini participated in informal celebrations of the Mass at Burg Rothenfel. In these celebrations he initiated the singing of the hymns in German instead of Latin, pursued a more conver-

---

13. Frank C. Senn, *Christian Liturgy: Catholic and Evangelical* (Minneapolis: Fortress Press, 1997), pp. 612-13.

14. Regina Kuehn, "Romano Guardini: The Teacher of Teachers," in *How Firm a Foundation: Leaders of the Liturgical Movement*, ed. Robert L. Tuzik (Chicago: Liturgy Training Publications, 1990), p. 42. "Quickborn" is translated as "Fountain of Youth."

15. "Burg" means "fortified castle" in German.

sational style of preaching, and had the young people gather around a freestanding altar with the presider facing them.[16] The chapel that was used at Burg Rothenfel was designed by architect Rudolf Schwarz.[17] After graduating from Berlin Academy in 1923, Schwarz spent six months at Burg Rothenfel. In 1927 Guardini gave him the opportunity to redesign the existing chapel and knight's hall at the castle.[18] The renovated chapel space was nearly square in shape, a little longer than wide. The walls were painted white with no ornamentation. The ceiling and floor were both flat, the floor composed of natural stone. Several large windows with clear glazing brought ample natural light into the space. Seating was flexible: small stools could be arranged on three sides of the altar area. The altar itself was located away from the nearest wall on a low, raised platform. With this arrangement the priest and the people could gather and face one another in their celebrations of the Eucharist. All the choices made in the chapel design were meant to encourage and invite full and active participation among those worshiping.

The young people of the German youth movement and the flexibility of the castle provided a fertile ground for liturgical activity that would later be encouraged through the texts of Vatican II. This is how theologian Karl Rahner expressed the connection on the occasion of Guardini's eightieth birthday: "It is a widely known fact that the Rothenfel experience was the immediate model for the liturgical reforms of Vatican II."[19] In the years following the Vatican II Council, accessible, active, creative celebrations of the Mass in spaces that emphasized the presence of the people in community would come to be normative in many quarters of the church.

The modern liturgical movement took root in the United States especially through the work of Dom Virgil Michel (1890-1938) and his community at St. John's Benedictine Abbey in Collegeville, Minnesota. Because Michel had firsthand contact with the worship renewal centers in Europe, he was able to bring to America the insight and energy of European calls for liturgical renewal, encouraging an active exchange of ideas between the two continents. Michel founded the journal *Orate Fratres* in 1926 (renamed *Worship* in 1951). In that same year, the Abbey started a publishing house, Liturgical Press. Both *Orate Fratres* and Liturgical Press distributed

---

16. Robert Krieg, *Romano Guardini: Proclaiming the Sacred in a Modern World* (Chicago: Liturgy Training Publications, 1995), p. 23.

17. Schwarz's reflections on this chapel can be found in Rudolf Schwarz, *Kirchenbau: Welt vor der Schwelle* (Heidelberg: F. H. Kerle Verlag, 1960), pp. 36-46.

18. James F. White, *Roman Catholic Worship: Trent to Today* (New York: Paulist Press, 1995), p. 74.

19. Kuehn, "Romano Guardini: The Teacher of Teachers," pp. 47-48.

abundant materials from both Europe and the United States concerning liturgical scholarship and suggestions for worship renewal. Michel's own concern for social justice sought a connection between liturgy and life, especially work and worship. Michel was joined by other significant liturgical scholars, including Hans Anscar Reinhold (1887-1968),[20] Reynold Hillenbrand (1904-1979), and Godfrey Diekmann (1909-2002). Their work was pivotal in establishing the critical energy necessary to bring worship reform to the fore in the life of the church, as can be seen in the texts of Vatican II. And leaders such as Diekmann were intimately involved in crafting texts such as the *Constitution on the Sacred Liturgy.*

The *Constitution on the Sacred Liturgy* was profound in its encouragement of liturgical renewal. The hard work that the worship reformers had done for nearly fifty years had finally come to fruition. Major emphases in the text that were approved by the bishops at Vatican II included a call for emphasizing the role of the people in worship and permission to begin to explore actual changes in liturgical rites:

> Mother Church earnestly desires that all the faithful be led to that full, conscious, and active participation in liturgical celebrations which is demanded by the very nature of the liturgy. . . . In the restoration and promotion of the sacred liturgy, this full and active participation by all the people is the aim to be considered before all else; for it is the primary and indispensable source from which the faithful are to derive the true Christian spirit. Therefore, through the needed program of instruction, pastors of souls must zealously strive to achieve it in all their pastoral work.

> For the liturgy is made up of unchangeable elements divinely instituted, and elements subject to change. The latter not only may but ought to be changed with the passing of time if features have by chance crept in which are less harmonious with the intimate nature of the liturgy, or if existing elements have grown less functional.[21]

Celebrations of the Mass that during the medieval period had gradually become more and more focused on the role of the priest in accomplishing corporate worship *for* the people had now yielded to an emphasis on corporate worship *by* the

20. Reinhold wrote on the relationship between liturgy and church architecture over many years. Among his published works are "A Revolution in Church Architecture," *Liturgical Arts* 6 (1937-1938): 122-33; "The Architecture of Rudolf Schwarz," *Architectural Forum* 70, no. 1 (January 1939): 22-27; and *Speaking of Liturgical Architecture* (Notre Dame: University of Notre Dame, 1952).

21. Abbott, *The Documents of Vatican II* ("Constitution on the Sacred Liturgy," articles 14, 21), pp. 144, 146.

people. Specific suggestions for achieving more active participation of the people in the celebrations included educating the priests on the centrality of worship (article 15); emphasizing the "paramount importance" of Scripture in the liturgy (article 24); maximizing the role of the laity in worship-leading (article 29); increasing opportunities for congregational participation through corporately sharing in word and song (article 30); using vernacular languages (articles 36 and 54); revising the official liturgical books of worship according to various cultures (article 38); increasing the role and range of Scripture texts (article 51); emphasizing the significance of preaching (article 52); restoring the "prayer of the faithful" — corporate prayer (article 53); revising initiation rites, the anointing of the sick, funerals, and weddings according to local customs (articles 59-82); and encouraging singing and the use of new musical compositions and new instruments in worship (articles 112-121). These suggestions also had important connections with Protestant worship. In the words of liturgical scholar James F. White, "The vernacular, congregational hymnody, an emphasis on preaching the word of God, frequent communion, and a general raising of the priestly role of all the baptized — all these had been priorities for most of the Protestant reformers."[22] The *Constitution on the Sacred Litrugy* initiated a revolution in worship renewal that would bear fruit for both Catholic and Protestant churches.

In this document, articles 122 to 130 of Chapter VII, "Sacred Art and Sacred Furnishings," are of particular interest here.[23] In anticipation of a modern idiom for church design, no particular style of art (and hence architectural design as an artistic expression) was presented as mandatory:

> The Church has not adopted any particular style of art as her very own; she has admitted fashions from every period according to the natural talents and circumstances of peoples, and the needs of the various rites. . . . The art of our own days, coming from every race and region, shall also be given free scope in the Church, provided that it adorns the sacred buildings and holy rites with due honor and reverence.

> When churches are to be built, let great care be taken that they be suitable for the celebration of liturgical services and for the active participation of the faithful.[24]

---

22. White, *Roman Catholic Worship*, p. 95.

23. The text of Chapter VII from *Constitution on the Sacred Liturgy* may be found in the Appendix.

24. Abbott, *Documents of Vatican II* ("Sacred Art and Sacred Furnishings," articles 123, 124), p. 175.

This opened the door to freely utilize modern architectural designs in church construction and to use art influenced by contemporary expressions. However, it is interesting to note that, under the influence of the liturgical movement prior to Vatican II, Catholic communities had already begun using modern architectural techniques and materials in church construction. Early examples of this phenomenon in Europe include the architectural work of Rudolf Schwarz, Dominikus Böhm, and Auguste Perret. (Specific churches by Schwarz, Böhm, and Perret will be discussed in more detail in Chapter Six.) An example of this phenomenon in the United States is St. Mark's Roman Catholic Church in Burlington, Vermont. Father William Tennien, the priest of the parish at the time, wanted a worship space that would encourage an organic unity between clergy and laity in worship.[25] He also sought to build a church in the spirit of modern architecture. The architectural firm of Freeman, French, & Freeman was engaged to design the church under Father Tennien's direction. A centralized plan was used, with the altar brought out from the wall and surrounded by congregational seating on three sides. Modern architectural design is evident in the expression and construction of the church, which was consecrated in 1942. As this example shows, the influence of the liturgical movement on church architecture was taking tangible form even twenty years before the Vatican II Council meetings.[26]

Following Vatican II, permission was given to officially sanction contemporary architectural designs. Particularly important was utilizing designs that would encourage the active participation of the faithful in worship activities. It could no longer be said that Gothic or other historical church expressions were more inherently ecclesiastical than contemporary designs. It was acknowledged that a wide range of church designs could potentially facilitate the appropriate worship and ministries of God's people.

It should not be forgotten that the *Constitution on the Sacred Liturgy* required careful revision and proper authorization of new materials for Catholic worship. Major revisions of the primary liturgical books for the Catholic Church began to emerge

25. Details concerning the origin of this church are drawn from Joseph T. Popecki, *The Parish of St. Mark in Burlington, Vermont, 1941-1991* (Burlington, Vt.: The Parish of St. Mark, 1991), pp. 15-16.

26. Father Daniel E. White, priest of the parish in 2004, expressed some reservations about the design of the building for his congregation. In electronic correspondence with me, Father White conveyed the difficulties of trying to accommodate later reforms to the liturgy in their worship space. Issues such as establishing a proper location for the presider's chair and tabernacle, the absence of a central aisle for processions, and the lack of a central entrance/exit for greeting parishioners after the Mass proved to be challenging. Father White's observations help to illustrate the point that designs which are innovative in one time period may not always yield ideal arrangements for future worship celebrations. Letter to author, 16 November 2004.

within four years of the closing of Vatican II. (A revised text for the *Roman Missal* appeared in 1969.) For a time there was some confusion in the life of the local church, particularly for those people who were unaccustomed to hearing the liturgy in their own language and who were invited to take a more active role in worship. Years of experimentation in worship followed the release of the *Constitution on the Sacred Liturgy.* Ways of worshiping together, both helpful and unhelpful, were discovered. But a new energy and focus entered the worship life of the church through this work of Vatican II. And Protestant churches initiated their own major revisions of worship materials based, in part, on this bold move of the Catholic Church.

The sponsoring of national worship conferences was one way in which the monastic communities in the United States could mobilize increased lay understanding and involvement in worship renewal. In 1940 the American Benedictines established a board of directors named the Liturgical Conference to direct their national, annual gathering for worship study and renewal called the Liturgical Week. The first Liturgical Week in the United States was held in Chicago. More than 1,200 people attended the multiday event, and both clergy and laity were involved in its leadership. A goal of the annual celebration was to highlight the ongoing need for worship reform; accordingly, education for renewal and models for liturgical practice were pursued. The Liturgical Week gatherings continued into the 1960s, with peak attendance reaching 20,000 in St. Louis.[27] The Liturgical Week meetings helped to actively disseminate the need for liturgical reform and guide its evolution. The Liturgical Conference became ecumenical in 1979, when it merged with the Lutheran Society for Worship, Music, and the Arts. The Liturgical Conference continues to operate today. Its board of directors contains representatives from multiple denominations. It shares its work primarily through its publications *Liturgy* and *Homily Service,* which seek to foster continued worship renewal in ways that support the unity of the whole church.

The concerns for worship renewal raised by the Roman Catholic Church were also recognized by many Protestant churches. Individuals such as Arthur Gabriel Herbert and Gregory Dix influenced Anglican liturgical renewal. Herbert (1886-1963) helped to mediate liturgical insights from the Roman Catholic Church through books such as *Liturgy and Society* and *The Parish Communion* (essays from a worship symposium that were edited by Herbert in 1937).[28] Anglican scholar Gregory Dix

27. Senn, *Christian Liturgy,* p. 621.

28. Herbert, *Liturgy and Society: The Function of the Church in the Modern World* (London: Faber & Faber, 1935); and *The Parish Communion: A Book of Essays by W. S. Baker, D. R. Blackman, J. F. Briscoe, and Others,* ed. A. G. Herbert (London: SPCK, 1937).

(1901-1952) began working in the area of liturgical studies in the 1930s. In 1937 he published a critical edition of an ancient liturgical document, *The Apostolic Tradition,*[29] and in 1945 he published an influential analysis of the evolution of Christian worship entitled *The Shape of the Liturgy.*[30] Although Dix's work has fallen under critical scrutiny today, his suggestions for liturgical renewal were taken up in England and popularized at the parish level through the book *Liturgy Coming to Life* by Bishop John A. T. Robinson.[31] Dix emphasized a particular four-action shape (taking, blessing, breaking, and giving) that he traced throughout the historical development of Eucharistic celebrations. He made suggestions for ways in which current Anglican celebrations could more emphatically mark this fourfold shape. Underlying the reforms was a desire to engage the people more fully in their Eucharistic celebrations and to recognize the implications that our worship activities have for living in the world around us. In 1955 the Church of England initiated a liturgical commission to begin considering the revision of their official liturgies.

In 1946 the American Episcopal Church founded the Associated Parishes for Liturgy and Mission. Its goal was to encourage greater participation in worship, educate the laity concerning the fullness of worship, and seek to link liturgy to everyday life. Worship renewal in the Methodist Church was pursued through the Order of St. Luke, begun in 1948, and the United Methodist Society for Worship, founded in 1975. The Presbyterian Church sought worship renewal through their Church Service Society, and the Lutheran Church established commissions to consider significant liturgical revisions to their service books in the mid-twentieth century. By the 1970s, many mainline denominations were well on their way to revising their worship materials. Layers of conversation between denominations were facilitated through organizations of liturgical scholars such as *Societas Liturgica* (an international forum for liturgical study begun in 1967) and the North American Academy of Liturgy (begun in 1975).

Inspired by the research and insights of Roman Catholic scholars and leaders, enriched through denominational liturgical studies, and fueled by ecumenical

---

29. *The Treatise on the Apostolic Tradition of St. Hippolytus of Rome, Bishop and Martyr,* ed. Gregory Dix (New York: Macmillan, 1937). A second edition with corrections by Henry Chadwick was published in 1968 by SPCK.

30. Dix, *The Shape of the Liturgy* (London: Dacre Press, 1945). A second edition was released shortly after the first. A new edition with contemporary notes on Dix's text was released in 2005 by Continuum International Publishing Group.

31. Robinson, *Liturgy Coming to Life* (London: A. R. Mowbray; Philadelphia: Westminster Press, 1960).

conversations, a series of revised services for Christian worship emerged from the late 1960s into the 1990s. Examples include the *Roman Missal* (the Roman Catholic Church, 1969),[32] the *Lutheran Book of Worship* (the Lutheran Church in America, the American Lutheran Church, the Evangelical Lutheran Church in Canada, and the Lutheran Church–Missouri Synod, 1978),[33] the *Book of Common Prayer* (the Episcopal Church, 1979),[34] *The United Methodist Book of Worship* (1992),[35] and the *Book of Common Worship* (the Presbyterian Church, U.S.A., and the Cumberland Presbyterian Church, 1993).[36] Striking similarities exist between the services for Word and sacrament in these revised documents, the products of extensive sharing of liturgical understandings and dialogues. The similar insights and understandings that are exhibited in these works allowed for similar church designs to serve various denominational liturgical celebrations. Similar emphases in worship practice and common worship services resulted in a common approach to articulating spaces for worship.

With this understanding of the ecumenical and liturgical movements at work in the Christian church in the twentieth century, it is now time to consider the consequences that emerged for modern church design.

CONCLUSIONS

It would be difficult to underestimate the profound effect that the ecumenical and liturgical movements had on mid-twentieth-century church architecture. Pressure to achieve global evangelization and a drive to address the tremendous social problems of urban centers in the twentieth century resulted in an unprecedented "coming together" of the church. First through cooperative mission societies and then through young people's organizations, the church grew in its knowledge of the broader fellowship of Jesus. With increased contact, alliances of churches were formed, yielding national councils in Europe and the United States. National work together was accompanied by global initiatives. A side benefit of the flurry of ecumenical activity in the twentieth century was the drawing together of denominational bodies.

---

32. The *Roman Missal* can be found in *The Sacramentary* (New York: Catholic Book Publishing Company, 1973, 1985).

33. *Lutheran Book of Worship* (Minneapolis: Augsburg Publishing House, 1978).

34. *The Book of Common Prayer* (New York: Seabury Press, 1979).

35. *The United Methodist Book of Worship* (Nashville: The United Methodist Publishing House, 1992).

36. *The Book of Common Worship* (Louisville: Westminster/John Knox Press, 1993).

Lutheran, Methodist, and Reformed churches achieved various levels of "reuniting" among some of their splintered memberships.[37] A significant effort was made to emphasize the common elements embraced by Christians around the world rather than focusing primarily on what distinguished various church bodies from one another. The ecumenical movement created conduits through which conversations about church design could occur on both national and international levels.

The liturgical movement changed the face of Christian worship in Europe and the United States. Frustration with the relatively inactive engagement and limited understanding of worship in many quarters of the Roman Catholic Church initiated renewal rooted in biblical studies and the patristic fathers. Intense scholarship and academic exchanges led to pastoral applications at the parish level. Modest experimentation in a handful of settings fired the imaginations of both clergy and laity. Over many years pressure mounted to initiate the reform of the liturgy at an institutional level. By the grace of God, through the intervention of the Holy Spirit, Roman Catholic leaders boldly embarked on a journey of change that continues to challenge us today.

The ecumenical atmosphere into which the liturgical movement flowered yielded worship reform on a wide scale. Most mainline Protestant denominations began to organize for and investigate their own liturgical history and practice by mid-century. The patristic fathers proved to be a common source for inspiration, as well as the earliest centuries of the Christian church. Committees for worship renewal led to conferences, national and international. Societies of worship scholars emerged. Even university programs in liturgical studies were initiated. Worship was found to be the center of the life of the church. Creativity and imagination found their way into liturgical celebrations, and joy and hope were reintroduced into the rites. And the arts of all sorts were invited to flourish in liturgical events once again. Church design itself was found to be a way to facilitate reform.

---

37. Here are some examples: the merging of the Lutheran Church in America (formed of merging traditions in 1962) and the American Lutheran Church (formed of merging traditions in 1930, 1960, and 1963) with the Association of Evangelical Lutheran Churches to form the Evangelical Lutheran Church in America in 1988; the merging of the Methodist Church (formed of merging traditions in 1939) and the Evangelical United Brethren Church (formed of merging traditions in 1946) to form the United Methodist Church in 1968; and the merging of the Evangelical and Reformed Church (formed of merging traditions in 1934) with the Congregational Christian Churches (formed of merging traditions in 1931) to form the United Church of Christ in 1957.

CHAPTER FOUR

MODERN IMPULSES IN CHURCH ARCHITECTURE: FAITH ENGAGING CULTURE

But we are now being reminded that the church people go to has an immensely powerful psychological effect on their vision of the Church they are meant to be. The church building is a prime aid, or a prime hindrance, to the building up of the Body of Christ. And what the building says so often shouts something entirely contrary to all that we are seeking to express through the liturgy. And the building will always win — unless and until we can make it say something else.

BISHOP JOHN A. T. ROBINSON, *Making the Building Serve the Liturgy* (1962)

ARCHITECTURE DOES NOT develop in a vacuum. Like all of the arts, architectural designs emerge from a combination of historical precedents, cultural influences, and the individual choices of architects and their clients. No architect begins with nothing. All architects are shaped by the existing buildings around them, by the values and ideas of their culture, and by their own interpretations of life experiences. Professional education will add a whole new level of understanding to their intuitive/experiential resources. The same can be said of those who receive architectural designs. They too have been shaped by the buildings around them, by their culture, and by their own impressions. Additional education can also help viewers to learn to appreciate the implicit and explicit qualities of architectural designs. I mention these fundamental understandings to help locate the emergence of a tremendous variety of church expressions in the twentieth century. Occasionally, both architects and those who have reflected upon architecture have been tempted to claim a certain autonomous objectivity. As I examine modern architecture in this chapter, I want simply to reiterate the point that human community and relationships have played an intrinsic role in both the conceptions of architects and the reception of their designs. Our shared human past has always influenced our shared present reality. With this thought in mind, let us now consider modern approaches to church design.[1]

Nineteenth-Century Context

At the beginning of the twentieth century, church architecture exhibited a strong impulse to imitate earlier historical expressions. To be sure, church architects have frequently drawn upon historical styles of design. (For example, the Roman basilican design — with its longitudinal spaces, rounded arches, vaults, and columns — has been used periodically in churches throughout history.) But in the nineteenth century an unusually strong desire to adhere to the details of earlier styles was evident in both Protestant and Roman Catholic circles. One of the most powerful trends of this kind was the movement toward replicating churches in the Gothic style of the European Middle Ages. "Gothic revival," as it is often called, was an architectural movement that lasted for approximately 200 years, from about 1730 to 1930. An influential architectural voice advocating this approach in the mid-nineteenth century in England was Augustus Welby Northmore Pugin.[2] Indeed, Pugin was so moved by Gothic design that he declared it to be the ideal "Christian" architecture.[3] He even attached a sense of morality to Gothic architecture, claiming that it was the design that most effectively conveyed "truth" (via its "honesty" in expression). In the 1840s, the Cambridge Camden Society of England (by 1845 called "The Ecclesiological Society") promoted the adoption of Gothic architectural expressions for Anglican churches, proclaiming Gothic the "best" possible design choice.[4] By the mid-1850s,

---

1. There are some scholars today who would like to substitute the word "modernist" for "modern" in relation to mid-twentieth-century Western architectural design. One reason for desiring this change in label is to recognize that what is commonly called "modern architecture" is a distinct style from other historical expressions. "Modern" is a word that can refer to any contemporary design. To employ the word "modernist" would add a dimension of precision to a style of design that is now being recognized more widely. I acknowledge this reality, but in light of the general use of the label "modern" in reference to mid-twentieth-century architectural design in literature today, I will continue to use the word "modern" throughout this book.

2. Pugin was the son of Augustus Charles Pugin, who wrote a series of detailed studies, *Specimens of Gothic Architecture,* from 1821 to 1823.

3. See A. W. Pugin, *The True Principles of Pointed or Christian Architecture* (London: John Weale, 1841).

4. A well-documented history of this movement can be found in James F. White, *The Cambridge Movement: The Ecclesiologists and the Gothic Revival* (Cambridge: Cambridge University Press, 1962; reissued, 1979).

Gothic revival was the established architectural design for churches in England. Although Pugin and the Cambridge movement did not coordinate their efforts, their combined influence had a profound effect upon church architecture in England.

This influence also found its way to the United States. By the late 1840s, the influence of the Gothic revival movement was visible among American churches.[5] Protestant and Roman Catholic communities began imitating Gothic church design in significant numbers, even up to the middle of the twentieth century. The difficulty with this approach liturgically was that the medieval Gothic layout of a worship space was originally developed for active use by monastic communities that needed to provide an ideal worship area for their own community as well as the parishioners in the surrounding town. Their solution was to create a distinct central hall or nave for local parishioners and a chancel for clergy, such that the chancel could be quite significant in length (at times, up to one-third the length of the nave). The primary altar for the church was elevated and pushed toward or against the east wall inside the chancel, with choir stalls on both sides of the chancel area to accommodate the monastic antiphonal singers of the liturgy. A distinct hierarchy of clergy over laity was visible in the church, with the chancel often "fenced off" from the nave by the rood screen (more or less solid, depending on the design choices). The medieval period also saw a proliferation of altars in the worship space to accommodate multiple celebrations of the mass (public and private). The proliferation of altars impaired the sense of a unified community gathering around a common table of Christ. In addition, a gradual increase in the role of the clergy and a reduction of lay participation in the liturgy had been under way in many church communities throughout the Middle Ages. The Gothic arrangement helped to subtly reinforce parishioner observation over participation. As a consequence, the people gradually came to allow the clergy to perform the worship of the church *for* them rather than share equally in its offering and celebration.

While the Gothic revival movement in England sought to elevate the importance of worship, a worthy pursuit, the chosen "ideal" space in which to celebrate worship emphasized a significant distinction between clergy and laity, de-emphasized a sense of gathering as the unified community around the table of Christ, and divided church choirs. Many who imitated Gothic revival designs were from traditions rooted in the Protestant Reformation. Much Reformation church architecture originally sought to

5. For a thorough examination of the effect of the Cambridge movement on nineteenth-century American church architecture, see Phoebe B. Stanton, *The Gothic Revival and American Church Architecture: An Episode in Taste, 1840-1856* (Baltimore: Johns Hopkins Press, 1968).

reduce the division between clergy and laity, promoted greater proximity between the altar/table and the people, and refrained from setting the Eucharist apart from or above the Word of God. Utilizing Gothic revival spaces tended to emphasize qualities of worship that had been previously downplayed. But many communities seemed to adopt the design without critically reflecting upon such visual emphases.

Ralph Adams Cram (1863-1942) was a noteworthy architect who promoted Gothic revival design in the United States into the twentieth century. Cram believed that Gothic design could promote spiritual values that would counter the negative influences of technological development.[6] He sought to construct churches as explicit "temples to God," finding Gothic architecture — with its scale, organization of space, and limited light — to be helpful in promoting such a model. In 1889 he established an architectural firm in Boston with Charles Francis Wentworth (1861-1897). Bertram G. Goodhue (1869-1924) joined the firm in 1891. When Wentworth passed away suddenly from pneumonia, Frank W. Ferguson (1861-1926) joined Cram and Goodhue (in 1897).[7] Cram's firm completed a number of church projects exhibiting Gothic revival design, including the chapel at the United States Military Academy, West Point, New York (1903-1914);[8] St. Thomas's Church, New York City (1906-1914);[9] Euclid Avenue Presbyterian Church (Church of the Covenant), Cleveland, Ohio (1907-1941);[10] First Baptist Church, Pittsburgh, Pennsylvania (completed in 1912);[11] the chapel at Princeton University, Princeton, New Jersey (1911-1929);[12] Fourth Presbyterian Church, Chicago (1911-1937); and the redesign of St. John the Divine, New York City (1915-1941).[13] How did Cram's ideas achieve such wide circulation and

6. See, for example, Ralph Adams Cram, *The Gothic Quest* (New York: Baker & Taylor, 1907).

7. Cram's architectural office also influenced the spread of Gothic revival church design through the training of young architects. Charles D. Maginnis (1867-1955) is an example of a young architect who trained with Cram and went on to design many Gothic revival churches for Roman Catholic congregations in the northeast part of the United States.

8. Year designations next to church names indicate the time of construction or end date of construction of the building. This will hold true for year designations found in subsequent chapters also.

9. St. Thomas's Church is featured in James McFarlan Baker, *American Churches*, vol. 2 (New York: American Architect, 1915), plates 7-21 and 74.

10. Euclid Avenue Presbyterian Church is featured in Ralph Adams Cram et al., *American Churches*, vol. 1 (New York: American Architect, 1915), plates 146-49.

11. First Baptist Church is featured in Baker, *American Churches*, vol. 2, plates 21-25.

12. The university chapel is featured in *American Church Building of Today*, ed. Ralph Adams Cram (New York: Architectural Book Publishing Company, 1929), pp. 109-14.

13. St. John the Divine is featured in Cram et al., *American Churches*, vol. 1, plates 161-63, and in *American Church Building of Today*, ed. Cram, pp. 103-8.

influence? Besides heading his own firm, Cram was a professor of architecture at the Massachusetts Institute of Technology from 1914 to 1921. He also lectured frequently and wrote prolifically.[14] Roman Catholic and Episcopal communities of faith were naturally drawn to Cram's approach, but he was also able to popularize Gothic revival design among Presbyterian, Congregationalist, Methodist, and Unitarian congregations.[15]

Gothic revival or "neo-Gothic" church design is but one example of a historical model that was replicated among contemporary churches. An interesting fact concerning Pugin's revival of Gothic architecture is that this impulse emerged, in part, from his frustration with the prevailing Georgian church architecture of his day. He felt that church architecture had deteriorated over the centuries and that modern culture was in decline generally. After analyzing historical models for the church, he selected Gothic as the ideal expression, believing that the Middle Ages had captured the best way of ordering life and expressing it. Such frustration with prevailing design choices was not peculiar to Pugin and the nineteenth century. Similar frustrations emerged in or carried over into the twentieth century and resulted in the replication of architectural styles from the past (e.g., Greek, Roman, Romanesque, and Baroque). Nevertheless, at least some architects and theologians felt that the twentieth century, with all its technological advances, warranted a new architectural style for churches. And modern architecture helped to provide a new avenue of possibilities for design.

A Window into Modern Architecture

A thorough exploration of modern architecture is beyond the confines of this book. What I hope to offer are some insights that will help to explain the rationale behind the modern impulse that has shaped many of our present-day church designs.

History provides us with a number of insights. Modernity itself became established and began to develop in so-called Western culture sometime between the sixteenth and eighteenth centuries, especially in northwestern European nations.

14. For example, see Ralph Adams Cram, *Church Building: A Study of the Principles of Architecture in Their Relation to the Church* (Boston: Small, Maynard & Company, 1901), which was released in ever-expanding editions into the 1920s.

15. James F. White, *Protestant Worship and Church Architecture: Theological and Historical Considerations* (New York: Oxford University Press, 1964), p. 138.

During this time period, religious faith became less and less the source of authority for epistemology, or "knowing." Increasingly, human reason became the source for truth and understanding. Coupled with this shift to reason, science developed and flourished. New discoveries were made in many areas of exploration, yielding revelations that seriously challenged and/or overturned previously held notions of how the world worked and had developed over time. Consequently, a "scientific approach" to life developed. Skepticism and autonomy became hallmarks of this approach. "Experts" in various fields gradually emerged, and these individuals became revered for their particular insights (and sometimes went unchallenged in their assertions).

The eighteenth and nineteenth centuries saw industrial revolutions that also changed the face of the West. New methods of production utilizing machines of all kinds, technological inventions (such as the development of new fuel sources), and various materials (such as iron, steel, and reinforced concrete) fostered the establishment of large factories and industrial complexes. Manufacturing launched an explosive expansion of urban areas. Optimism about the ability of humanity to resolve issues such as poverty, illiteracy, disease, and war rose year by year. "Progress" came to be the banner under which humanity labored in the West. Many thought that humanity was evolving quickly and would soon reach an ideal state of existence.

Modern architecture was born into this matrix of rationalism and revolution. New engineering technologies and building materials offered opportunities never before imagined. From the mid-to-late nineteenth century, experiments in iron, steel, and glass construction were being conducted.[16] The fascination with historical models for architectural design, mentioned earlier, was prevalent in both Europe and the United States. But by the late nineteenth century, many were dissatisfied with the replication of historical patterns of design. Some architects called the imitation of historical patterns "romantic," meaning that replicating these expressions was an uncritical approach to design (idealizing a past historical epoch and imagining that imitating its architecture would achieve a reincarnation of that past culture today).[17] The imitative approach was critiqued for ignoring the particular historical and cultural factors that shaped the original conceptions and all that had made them particularly useful for those earlier time periods. In the late nineteenth century, some architectural circles

16. For example, the giant Crystal Palace exhibition hall of Joseph Paxton (London, 1851) is noted for its use of prefabricated steel and glass components, and the Eiffel Tower of Gustave Eiffel (Paris, 1887-1889) for its innovative ironwork (especially the arch and truss work) and extraordinary height (984 feet).

17. Cram's use of neo-Gothic design would be an example of an approach that was considered "romantic" in this sense of the term.

wanted to embrace more rationalistic thinking, seeking designs that might embody the essence of the continuing development of the industrial revolution.

The city of Chicago found a unique opportunity for embracing new buildings of modern design following its devastating fire of 1871. A significant portion of its city center was destroyed, and tremendous rebuilding was necessary. The Chicago school of architecture, to whom architect Louis Sullivan (1856-1924) and the dictum "form follows function" belong, was given the opportunity to contribute to the rebuilding of the city center. The Chicago school focused on the planning of interior spaces, showing concern for the space-per-unit of construction cost and utilizing previously untested materials and technologies (for example, steel-frame construction).[18] Pragmatism and simplicity drove this design approach. The Chicago school paved the way for a leaner style of design by creating structural systems that revealed more of the nature of a building by opening up ground-floor facades and by gradually reducing ornamentation.[19] The form of the building itself was thought of as emerging directly from the particular function of the building. Function was thought to dictate more of the potential design of a building than historical pattern. The Chicago school opened up a way to escape from the revivalist approach to design.

Modern movements in both America and Europe built upon the foundation established by the Chicago school approach. These movements were characterized by an emphasis on structural expressions (seeking "honest" expressions of contemporary materials and building techniques — that is, not trying to disguise the true nature of a material or structural form), a fascination with technology (especially with the speed and the efficiency of machines), a reductionist aesthetic (due in part to the influence of contemporary painting and sculpture), and a functionalist ideology (which elevated structures such as grain elevators and warehouses as paradigms for all types of buildings).[20] Modern architects were also fascinated with pure geometric forms. They often partnered these specifically architectural concerns with the emphases of modernity mentioned earlier, such as optimism about the evolution of

---

18. The twentieth century would achieve a continual flow of new materials and building techniques. Near the beginning of the century, reinforced concrete, steel, and glass found new ways of being utilized in building. As the century progressed, adhesives of many kinds, plastics, and wood products would introduce new opportunities for construction. Economic restrictions also added pressure for exploring the possibilities of these new materials and building techniques (including prefabrication and the use of standardized components).

19. Alan Holgate, *Aesthetics of Built Form* (Oxford: Oxford University Press, 1992), pp. 197-98.

20. Professor Duncan G. Stroik, School of Architecture, University of Notre Dame, letter to author, February 1995.

humanity, a notion of unlimited progress, and an elevation of "experts." Examining the thought and work of several modern architects will help to identify the source of design impulses that bear on modern church design.

FOUR VOICES OF MODERN ARCHITECTURE

In this section I want to focus on four architects who gained international attention and helped to define and establish a widely held approach to modern architecture: Frank Lloyd Wright, Walter Gropius, Ludwig Mies van der Rohe, and Le Corbusier.

Frank Lloyd Wright

Frank Lloyd Wright (1867-1959) was significantly influenced and inspired by the new approach of the Chicago school of architecture, emphasizing function in relation to architectural design. In the early days of his architectural training, Wright studied and worked with Louis Sullivan for six years. Wright took Sullivan's thoughts and applied them with his own particular nuances. He was particularly interested in the idea of continuity, as this quotation from his book *The Natural House* indicates:

> If the dictum "form follows function" had any bearing at all on building, it could take form in architecture only by means of plasticity when seen at work as complete *continuity*. So why not throw away entirely all implications of post and beam construction? Have no posts, no column, no pilasters, cornices or moldings or ornament; no divisions of the sort, nor allow any fixtures whatever to enter as something added to the structure. Any building should be complete, including all within itself. Instead of many things, *one* thing.[21]

With such assertions Wright challenged the traditional architectural thinking of his day. He reduced the traditional "language" of architecture by abandoning fundamental components such as post-and-beam construction, columns, and ornamentation. He worked toward a unified concept of design and space, where form and function merge to express a single reality. For Wright, form and function were one.[22] Form did not follow function in a linear, lockstep fashion; it evolved along

---

21. Frank Lloyd Wright, *The Natural House* (New York: Bramhall House, 1954), p. 20.

22. Frank Lloyd Wright, *An Organic Architecture: The Architecture of Democracy*, 2d ed. (London: Lund Humphries & Co., Inc., 1941), p. 4.

with function in a particular manifestation of space. Both form and function act upon one another to produce an architecture of continuity. An "organic" principle of architecture emerges from this concept of continuity, as Wright explains in *The Natural House:*

> That concept of architecture alive today as *modern* is, first of all, *organic.* "Organic" is the word which we should apply to this new architecture. So here I stand before you preaching *organic* architecture; declaring organic architecture to be the modern ideal and the teaching so much needed if we are to see the whole of life, and to now serve the whole of life, holding no "traditions" essential to the great TRADITION. Nor cherishing any preconceived form fixing upon us either past, present or future, but — instead — exalting the simple laws of common sense . . . determining form by way of the nature of materials, the nature of purpose so well understood. . . . Form follows Function? Yes, but more important now, *Form and Function are One.*[23]

Wright pursued an ideal of allowing the intended function of a building to guide its general design *in concert with* the limitations and potential of modern materials and construction technologies. Neither a preconceived notion of appropriate form nor an over-reliance on function ought to dominate the design process. There was to be no reliance on historical patterns of design, such that the past would dictate or limit visual expressions or utility for the present or future. For Wright, Japanese domestic architecture was an example of an appropriate balance of function, materials, and construction technique guiding design, yielding a truly organic architecture.[24] The respect for the environment, the care taken in the use of materials, and the open planning of the interior space appealed to him. By utilizing his organic approach and employing a flexible design of open planning (not having a predetermined plan for the organization of the interior space),[25] Wright pursued an internal cohesion in building design.[26]

---

23. Wright, *The Natural House*, p. 4.

24. Wright, *The Natural House*, p. 11.

25. It is true that some of Wright's clients complained about a lack of flexibility in his spaces due to his use of built-in furnishings. Wright's spaces may not have been flexible in the sense that they could be rearranged easily into various interior arrangements, but his spaces are noteworthy for the flexible way in which he approached each project and tailored the space to the immediate needs of that community at that time.

26. Sigfried Giedion, *Space, Time, and Architecture: The Growth of a New Tradition,* 5th ed. (Cambridge, Mass.: Harvard University Press, 1967), pp. 405-17.

Above: Exterior of Unity Temple, Oak Park, Illinois (architect: Frank Lloyd Wright, 1904-1906). Wright employed his own "prairie style" design in articulating the first modern church of the twentieth century.

Below: Interior of Unity Temple. The interior space focuses on the people gathered for worship around a modest communion table and a central pulpit.

Wright designed a limited number of buildings for churches.[27] However, his designs opened up new vistas of consideration for how churches might appear in our midst. Unity Temple, Oak Park, was under construction from 1904 to 1906. In this design Wright abandoned the use of tower, steeple, and distinctive nave. His goal was not to build a temple to God but to create a "noble room" in which humanity could reflect upon God. The church was designed in Wright's unique "prairie style" (with its emphasis on the horizontal axis), and it was the first building in the United States to be constructed with poured concrete. The exterior finish of the building, the exposed concrete, was scrubbed to expose the pebble aggregate. Geometric piers with some ornamentation adorn the window areas to integrate them into the large concrete masses of the building. The primary worship area, a rectilinear space with gallery-type seating, is similar in overall design to early New England meeting-houses. It is designed for preaching, with no seating more than 45 feet away from the centrally located, raised pulpit. Skylights and clerestory glass windows (featuring abstract designs by Wright) provide lighting. Hardwood molding and earth-tone colors finish the interior. Unity Temple has been hailed as a unique, genuine expression of American church architecture.

Unity Temple is important to our exploration because of its design, materials, and intention. Wright chose to design a church in a style that had not been used before for church buildings. He felt his design fit the spirit of the modern culture because of its original approach, its simplicity of design, and its reduction of ornamentation. Wright's use of contemporary building materials set a precedent that would be followed freely in other churches built after Unity Temple. And Wright's choice to emphasize the community of people gathered for worship, rather than try to point dramatically to the God who was the focus of worship, is important. Wright did not deny that the building would be used for the function of worship, but he wondered, "Why not, then, build a temple, not to God in that way . . . but build a temple to man, appropriate to his uses as a meeting-place, in which to study man himself for God's sake?"[28] For Wright, the primary focus was the *congregation at* worship rather than the *object of* worship. Clearly, Unity Temple embodies an accent on immanence more than transcendence. Its architecture reinforces one's awareness

27. These include the Annie Pfeiffer Memorial Chapel, Florida Southern College, Lakeland, Florida (Methodist, 1941); the Unitarian Meeting House, Shorewood Hills (Madison), Wisconsin (1947); and the Annunciation Greek Orthodox Church, Wauwatosa, Wisconsin (1956).

28. George A. Lane, *Chicago Churches and Synagogues* (Chicago: Loyola University Press, 1981), p. 116.

and appreciation of the people at worship (God with and among us). This architectural emphasis resonated well with the emphasis on the gathered community at worship prevalent in the liturgical renewal movement and the ecumenical movement of the twentieth century.

Walter Gropius

Walter Gropius (1883-1969) was also an influential architect as well as an educator in Germany and the United States. In 1919 Gropius became the director of a combination of two art schools in Weimar, Germany, that came to be commonly called the Bauhaus. Gropius established a new approach to art education, requiring that all artists and architects study practical crafts to become familiar with materials and processes. Students learned largely by experimenting with new materials and techniques. Historical models and traditions were minimized, with the focus more on new possibilities than previous solutions. In a sense, a historical approach to art education was replaced by a scientific model (similar to the emphasis on experimentation found in the sciences).[29] Gifted painters and sculptors served as faculty at the Bauhaus, including Paul Klee, Wassily Kandinsky, Laszlo Moholy-Nagy, and Josef Albers. From 1920 to 1928, architect Marcel Breuer was both a student and an instructor at the Bauhaus.

In his book entitled *Apollo in the Democracy,* Gropius recalled the effect of Wright's design on his own work, noting especially the opportunity for liberation of the imagination and the straightforward approach Wright insisted upon.[30] Wright's avoidance of historical styles, his appreciation for modern materials and construction techniques, and his pursuit of continuity in design resonated with Gropius's own vision of a modern expression of architecture.

---

29. Dennis P. Doordan, *Twentieth-Century Architecture* (New York: Harry N. Abrams, Inc., Publishers, 2002), pp. 97-98. Gropius's approach can be explored in his own words in his book *The New Architecture and the Bauhaus* (Cambridge, Mass.: MIT Press, 1965).

30. Gropius wrote, "Frank Lloyd Wright was very well known and respected in Europe long before he gained a reputation in the United States. When the Academy of Arts in Berlin arranged an exhibition of Frank Lloyd Wright's work in 1911 . . . I first became attracted to his strong, imaginative approach. I still remember that I was impressed by the Larkin Building in Buffalo and by the Robie House in Chicago, both of which were close to my own thinking and feeling. Their straight-forwardness of unconventional design fascinated me. . . ." See *Apollo in the Democracy: The Cultural Obligation of the Architect* (New York: McGraw-Hill, 1968), p. 167.

By 1922, a rational, objective approach to art production emerged at the Bauhaus, such that many projects produced were meant to be used as prototypes for commercial production. Basic geometric forms, smooth surfaces, regular lines, primary colors, and contemporary materials were emphasized. Architecture was not taught as a separate discipline at the Bauhaus. Rather, the artistic emphases of product designs were applied to building concepts in an effort to achieve a unified expression of contemporary culture. According to architectural historian Sigfried Giedion, Gropius was concerned with the effort to "unite art and industry, art and daily life, using architecture as the intermediary."[31] Gropius believed that the arts could shape culture, and he sought to promote expressions of art and architecture that would capture and inspire the spirit of modern humanity.

In 1925 the Bauhaus was moved to Dessau. Gropius designed the building that housed the academy there. This building, with its "factory" appearance, is considered an enduring example of modern architecture. Its use of simplified geometric form, its emphasis on volume over mass and regularity over symmetry, and its lack of ornamentation are characteristic of what would come to be called the "International Style."

In 1928 Gropius resigned from his position at the Bauhaus. In 1933 the Nazi party closed it down. (Hitler labeled the work of the Bauhaus "un-German.") In 1934 Gropius and his wife escaped to England. Three years later, Gropius emigrated to the United States, where he was appointed a professor of architecture at Harvard University. He was made chair of the department in 1938, and he remained in that position until his retirement in 1952. Gropius's story illustrates the powerful effect of the relocation of prominent modern European architects in the years just before and after World War II. Gropius was able to influence a generation of architects in the United States in his approach to modern architectural design. He did not design any churches himself, but the principles that he taught influenced the churches his students designed in both Europe and the United States.

Ludwig Mies van der Rohe

The third significant modern architect to mention is Ludwig Mies van der Rohe (1886-1969). Mies van der Rohe — or Mies — had worked with Walter Gropius in Germany between the world wars. Mies joined the Bauhaus while the school oc-

---

31. Giedion, *Space, Time, and Architecture*, p. 489.

cupied its complex at Dessau in 1930. Like Gropius, Mies remembered the effect that Wright had on his own work. In recalling the effect Wright had on Europe through his show in 1911, Mies commented,

> The work of this great master presented an architectural world of unexpected force, clarity of language, and disconcerting richness of form. Here, finally, was a master-builder drawing upon the veritable fountainhead of architecture; who with true originality lifted his creations into the light. Here again, at long last, genuine organic architecture flowered. . . . The dynamic impulse emanating from his work invigorated a whole generation. His influence was strongly felt even when it was not actually visible.[32]

In sympathy with Wright, Mies, like Gropius, also sought a reduction in the complexity of the language of architectural design. Unlike those who championed historical styles, he did not advocate the replication or application of any particular style (past or present), and he was concerned with expressing the spirit of contemporary humanity.[33] Mies took over as director of the Bauhaus in 1930, and he remained in this position until its closure in 1933.

Like Gropius, Mies emigrated to the United States. He was appointed the director of architecture for the Armour Institute in 1938 (since 1940 known as the Illinois Institute of Technology or IIT), and he settled into an architectural practice in Chicago. Like others associated with the Bauhaus, Mies equated beauty with utter simplicity in design. Simplicity was linked with clarity and purity, yielding a modern interpretation captured in the phrase "less is more." Having been raised in a Christian environment, Mies allowed the interpretation of his faith to influence his design. In *Apollo in the Democracy*, Gropius wrote about the architectural approach that Mies took:

> A son of a stonemason, he learned his father's craft and simultaneously became influenced by the profound spirit of the great medieval thinkers and writers Thomas Aquinas and St. Augustine, whose words "Beauty is the splendor of truth" struck roots in him. . . . His famous slogan "Less is more," coined when he had already become a

---

32. Philip C. Johnson, *Mies van der Rohe*, 3rd ed. (New York: The Museum of Modern Art, 1978), p. 201.
33. Giedion, *Space, Time, and Architecture*, pp. 480-507.

mature master in this country, expresses in three syllables the long, exhausting effort it must have taken him to penetrate to the essentials of design by resolutely discarding, discarding — everything superfluous. As a lonely seeker of truth, engaging all his spiritual and intellectual qualities with utter disregard for success or failure, he very slowly has acquired authority, but only after what had become a long struggle.

This disciplined process of Mies, the artist, relentlessly distilling the permanent from the transitory and fashionable and "giving the spirit opportunity of existence," attaches an appeal of poetry to his creations. He seeks God in the excellence of proportion, detail, and craftsmanship, but he denies a preconception of form.[34]

In this description one can see Mies following a nearly religious mandate in pursuing a concept of beauty guided by a preference for an aesthetic sense of reduction. Gropius's rather idealized interpretation of Mies's development helps to demonstrate the rationale established for a reductionistic approach to architectural design. Mies truly believed that he had developed an architectural approach to beauty using minimalized forms. In his approach he sought to attach to these minimal forms understandings of "truth" that were rooted in an interpretation of the Christian faith.

Mies designed only one space for worship — a chapel for the IIT campus in 1952.[35] St. Saviour Chapel was built using steel-frame construction, brick, and glass. This chapel is a simple rectangular space. The exterior exhibits a minimalist aesthetic, with its simplicity and lack of ornamentation. The interior is devoid of architectural barriers, suggesting a sense of community among those who used the space. The unified worship area is oriented toward a slightly raised altar/table of travertine marble at one end of the space, with a large metal Latin-style cross located above it. Portable seating for about one hundred can be arranged as desired. Mies was an advocate of great flexibility in the use of space. He did not believe that the future uses of a space could be fully anticipated, or that a space should be inhibited by permanent demarcations, so he planned for change (in this case, providing completely mobile seating).

Mies created a number of buildings for the IIT campus. Sigfried Giedion believes that the buildings Mies designed for IIT demonstrate a careful handling of propor-

---

34. Gropius, *Apollo in the Democracy,* pp. 171-72.

35. This structure was originally affiliated with the Episcopal Church — if with hesitancy, according to a citation found in Albert Christ-Janer and Mary Mix Foley, *Modern Church Architecture* (New York: McGraw-Hill, 1962), p. 187. When I made a recent inquiry of the Episcopal Diocese of Chicago, I was told that the chapel is no longer listed as a parish associated with the Episcopal Church.

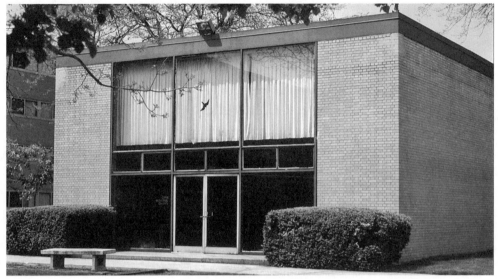

Above: Exterior of St. Saviour Chapel, Illinois Institute of Technology, Chicago (architect: Mies van der Rohe, 1952). St. Saviour Chapel represents an expression of design intended to be consistent with other campus buildings and to exhibit excellence in proportion and material usage.

Below: Interior of St. Saviour Chapel. The organization of this interior and its minimalist aesthetic work to heighten the significance of the people at worship.

tions in concert with a careful handling of materials, transforming common materials into "elements of the highest artistic value."[36] Both Mies's intention and Geidion's assessment reflect a desire to invest profound significance in the least expression of form. St. Saviour Chapel was declared to be "one of the clearest examples of the Episcopal Church's eagerness to be truly contemporary in her church buildings."[37] While Mies's chapel was not widely emulated,[38] it did establish a model focused more on the community of those gathered for worship than on the One being worshiped. The simplicity of Mies's design and the flexibility of his chapel were appreciated by some and added to an impulse in both Roman Catholic and Protestant communities of faith to create worship space focused on God's presence in God's people.

Le Corbusier (Charles-Edouard Jeanneret)

The final modern architect to consider is Charles-Edouard Jeanneret (1886-1965), or, as he referred to himself after 1923, Le Corbusier. Le Corbusier was active both in design and in articulating his thoughts about design in hкis adopted country of France.[39] Beginning primarily with the designing of houses, Le Corbusier conceived of the house as a "machine for living in." He was not really advocating mechanized living, but he admired the clean lines and precision that machines exhibited.[40] He pursued his architectural design with a principle of simplicity, as he once explained:

> Our *search for architecture* has led to the discovery of simplicity. Great art — we must never tire of repeating this — is produced by simple means. History shows that the mind tends toward simplicity. Simplicity, which results from judgments and choices, is a sign of mastery. It gives, through a clearly perceptible play of forms, the means of expressing a

---

36. Giedion, *Space, Time, and Architecture,* p. 603.

37. *Church Buildings and Furnishings: A Survey of Requirements,* ed. Jonathan G. Sherman (Greenwich, Conn.: Seabury Press, 1958), p. 96.

38. However, First Universalist Church in Chicago, designed by Schweikher, Elting, and Bennett, Associated Architects (completed in 1955), is an example of a church based on Mies's chapel.

39. For example, see Le Corbusier, *Towards a New Architecture,* trans. Frederick Etchells (London: The Architectural Press, 1946), originally published as *Vers une Architecture* (Paris: G. Crès et Cie, 1923); and *The City of Tomorrow and Its Planning,* trans. Frederick Etchells (New York: Payson & Clarke Ltd., 1929), originally published as *Urbanisme* (Paris: Éditions Crès, 1924).

40. Le Corbusier, *Towards a New Architecture,* pp. 89-95.

state of mind, of revealing a spiritual system. It is like an *affirmation,* a path leading from confusion to clear geometric statements.[41]

Le Corbusier insisted upon simplicity, a reduced aesthetic approach to modern architectural design.

In keeping with the tenor of modern times, Le Corbusier, like Wright, Gropius, and Mies, also rejected the imitation of historical styles in design:

> The history of Architecture unfolds itself slowly across the centuries as a modification of structure and ornament, but in the last fifty years steel and concrete have brought new conquests, which are the index of a greater capacity for construction, and of an architecture in which the old codes have been overturned. If we challenge the past, we shall learn that "styles" no longer exist for us, that a style belonging to our own period has come about; and there has been a Revolution.[42]

Le Corbusier did not want to turn to past styles of design as a source for primary inspiration for contemporary buildings. The needs and materials of modern humanity provided a more compelling source of insight for him and were elevated in significance in his search for contemporary architectural expressions.

Three components that Le Corbusier mentioned as necessary for modern expressions were an intention to bring order, a concern for materials, and an attention to spirit. In *Towards a New Architecture,* Le Corbusier claimed,

> The business of architecture is to establish emotional relationships by means of raw materials.
>
> Architecture goes beyond utilitarian needs.
>
> Architecture is a plastic thing.
>
> The spirit of order, a unity of intention.
>
> The sense of relationships; architecture deals with quantities.
>
> Passion can create drama out of inert stone.[43]

---

41. Jacques Guiton, *The Ideas of Le Corbusier on Architecture and Urban Planning,* trans. Margaret Guiton (New York: Braziller, 1981), pp. 33-34.

42. Le Corbusier, *Towards a New Architecture,* p. 13.

43. Le Corbusier, *Towards a New Architecture,* pp. 10-11.

Le Corbusier did not believe that function alone was a sufficient starting point for his design work. He recognized the roles that passion and opportunity played in making a unique statement. Perhaps partly because of Wright's influence, he embraced the new materials and construction techniques of his day and developed open, flexible plans according to his own interpretation of space.[44]

Le Corbusier designed four churches during his career.[45] The pilgrimage chapel Notre-Dame-du-Haut near Ronchamp, France, drew the most attention, both appreciative and critical. The chapel was under construction from 1950 to 1955. Le Corbusier's design exhibits a sculptural approach, with flowing lines and sweeping forms. Simplicity in expression, creativity, and dynamism can be found in the Ronchamp structure. It is made of plaster-clad concrete, bereft of ornamentation. The chapel is well-integrated into the hilltop, organized in such a way that pilgrims can naturally find themselves drawn to gatherings either outside (a space meant for large gatherings) or inside (a place intended for small gatherings). Furnishings — such as ambos/pulpits and altars — are provided as focal points for both types of celebrations. The interior space has an asymmetrical arrangement of furnishings and features different-sized windows in a random arrangement, which provides subdued lighting. A minimal aesthetic clearly informs the design of both the interior and the exterior.

The Ronchamp chapel has provided inspiration for the implementation of a contemporary design approach, with its creative articulation of form and its ability to both highlight the gathered community and reference God (the sweeping roof line pointing upward yields a reference to transcendence). Ronchamp was not replicated, but its presence embodies both an authentic expression of modern architecture and a call to a more creative approach to church design in the twentieth century.

The International Congress for Modern Architecture (CIAM) and the International Style

By the late 1920s, articulate European architects were moving toward a common goal of identifying a functionalist approach to modern architecture. In 1928, two

---

44. Le Corbusier, *The Radiant City: Elements of a Doctrine of Urbanism to Be Used as the Basis of Our Machine-Age Civilization*, trans. Pamela Knight et al. (New York: Orion Press, 1967), pp. 20-21.

45. Other projects include his design for La Sainte Baume, 1948, not built; La Tourette monastery, Eveux-sur-Arbresle, completed in 1960; and the church for Firminy, c. 1965, not yet completed.

Vanni/Art Resource, NY

Above: Exterior of Notre-Dame-du-Haut, Ron-champ (architect: Le Corbusier, 1950-1955). Le Corbusier allowed great imagination to guide his singular design for this pilgrimage chapel. The sculptured roofline with three small towers provides a unique focal point.

Right: Interior of Notre-Dame-du-Haut. Seating for a small number of people is provided with fixed pews facing the altar. Three small chapels are located in the bases of the towers, set apart from the nave.

Vanni/Art Resource, NY

dozen architects gathered in Switzerland to discuss the formation of a new organization intended to promote a modern architectural agenda for the twentieth century. The formation of the Congres Internationaux de l'Architecture Moderne (or CIAM) — the International Congress for Modern Architectur — was the result. CIAM sought to promote what they called a functionalist approach to design. Walter Gropius, Ludwig Mies van der Rohe, and Le Corbusier were all foundational members of CIAM. They emphasized a modern ideology of design, rejecting historical models as sources for contemporary emulation. They even considered their own approach "ahistorical." The emphases mentioned earlier in this chapter — a rational approach, a use of geometric forms, a minimalized aesthetic, and the use of new building materials and techniques — were all part of CIAM's architectural agenda. They combined their interpretation of modern architecture with a perhaps naive understanding of urban planning, believing that their buildings could promote a moral approach to life among a city's inhabitants (a belief not unlike that of the "romantic" architects they critiqued).

CIAM was successful in promoting their understanding of modern design. Their influence was prominent in the United States through the teaching and design work of Walter Gropius and Mies van der Rohe. Indeed, work by architects such as Louis Kahn (1901-1974), Richard Neutra (1892-1970), and Philip Johnson (1906-2005) reflected CIAM's approach to design. Although these architects did not always adhere strictly to the tenets of CIAM, they produced work consistent with its values and approach to design. A number of skyscrapers, office and civic buildings, and large-scale housing complexes that were built from the 1930s to the 1970s reflected the design goals of CIAM.

Although the members of CIAM did not advocate any one "style" of design, their approach did achieve a distinctive style that differentiated it from the historical models that had preceded it. This became clear in 1932, when Henry-Russell Hitchcock and Philip Johnson chose to host an art show featuring what they identified as modern architectural design at the Museum of Modern Art in New York City.[46] Work by architects such as Le Corbusier, Gropius, and Mies was featured prominently in the show, which intended to promote their work as well as identify the style of modern architectural design. While the architects themselves made claims of achieving "no style" or being ahistorical, Hitchcock and Johnson identified their work as the International Style. They recognized what the work had in common: an

---

46. The original published articulation of their theory can be found in Henry-Russell Hitchcock Jr. and Philip Johnson, *The International Style: Architecture Since 1922* (New York: W. W. Norton, 1932).

emphasis on volume over mass, a lack of concern for classical symmetry and axiality, and an avoidance of ornamentation.[47]

Hitchcock and Johnson believed that the International Style was the pre-eminent modern expression of architecture from the early to the mid-twentieth century.[48] While not all architectural historians have necessarily agreed with this conclusion, there is no doubt that the International Style affected the design choices of both European and American architects from the 1930s to the 1960s. The work of influential architects such as Alvar Aalto (1898-1976), Pietro Belluschi (1899-1994), Marcel Breuer (1902-1981), Eero Saarinen (1910-1961), Eliel Saarinen (1873-1950), and the firm of Skidmore, Owings, and Merrill (founded in 1937) reflected the adoption of principles associated with the International Style. Many of these architects designed churches that were recognized as significant examples of modern design, and their work inspired the ecclesiastical design work of others.

But CIAM did not survive as long as its influence did. By the mid-1950s, some of the younger members of CIAM began to criticize the rather narrow approach to the interpretation of "modern" espoused by the older members. In 1959 the organization decided to disband. Criticism of CIAM's design agenda grew more significant in the 1960s. Some of the frustration was directed at CIAM's minimalist aesthetic approach and rigid rejection of any references to historical design. Still, the influence of CIAM and the International Style was undeniable.

CONCLUSIONS

The modern approach to building design, especially as embodied in CIAM and the International Style, resonated with some of the emphases of those seeking liturgical renewal and was spread widely through ecumenical activity. These two twentieth-century currents had four main points of connection: the focus on function, the elevation of simplicity, the pursuit of integrity, and the concern for a contemporary expression (a connection to the people using the buildings).

The focus on function in liturgical circles was part of seeking to bring increased congregational participation to corporate worship. The liturgical renewal movement

47. Doordan, *Twentieth-Century Architecture*, p. 36.

48. See thoughts on the movement added to their original reflections in Hitchcock and Johnson's later edition, *The International Style: Art since 1922* (New York: W. W. Norton and Company, 1995).

sought to focus on the essential activities of worship, stripping away those accretions of ritual that undermined the essential purpose and function of communal activities important for various celebrations. Many worship space designs translated these ideas into architectural forms, selecting a scale that would elevate the significance of the gathered faithful, creating unified, centralized spaces for worship (e.g., locating the altar, the clergy, and the people in close proximity to one another), and creating worship spaces with increased opportunity for movement and flexibility. The function of the liturgy in relation to the people sharing in the ritual took on a central role, the goal being to allow the design of a church to flow from this identified communal purpose.[49]

The elevation of simplicity worked hand in hand with the focus on liturgical function. A combination of the proliferation of worship expressions oriented toward private devotions and the frustration with elaborate but inferior decoration in worship environments (both in terms of artistic expression and manufactured quality) predisposed many church leaders to pursue a more minimal aesthetic in space design. Many churches chose to reduce the amount of ornamentation on the exterior of their buildings. Many opted to mimimize the art objects in their worship space, leaving large areas of wall space without adornment. The pursuit of simplicity was also expressed in the reduction of the number of altars in many churches, the clearing of extraneous objects from altars (those not necessary for Eucharistic celebrations), the relocation of the tabernacle to a reservation chapel, and the dismantling or reducing of the elaboration of the screens behind the altar. The overall intention of pursuing simplicity was to concentrate on the essential acts of worship (such as

---

49. In an introductory essay to a discussion of modern church architecture, the Reverend Edward J. Sutfin and Maurice Lavanoux even used some of the jargon of the modern architecture movement when they stated, "It surely follows that many of our building problems can be solved by a return to first principles based upon the liturgy — that is, art in its relation to, and in the service of, the living liturgical community. In this sense we can claim that the formula 'form follows function' takes on a reasonable meaning." See Reverend Edward J. Sutfin and Maurice Lavanoux, "Contemporary Catholic Architecture," in Albert Christ-Janer and Mary Mix Foley, *Modern Church Architecture* (New York: McGraw-Hill, 1962), p. 2. And theologian Peter Hammond articulates the functional priority of modern architecture in this way in considering church design: "Church architecture is subject to the same basic laws as govern every other type of building. If the principles of the modern movement are valid for the construction of a school or a factory, they are equally valid for the making of churches. We cannot have a double standard. . . . The task of the modern architect is not to design a building that *looks like a church*. It is to create a building that *works* as a place for liturgy. The first and essential requirement is radical functional analysis." See Peter Hammond, *Liturgy and Architecture* (London: Barrie & Rockliff, 1960), pp. 8-9.

Eucharist, baptism, and preaching), especially the corporate engagement of God's people in these rituals.

The issue of integrity is perennial in both theological and architectural circles. Professionals in both disciplines seek to pursue their work with the highest quality of performance. Modern architects often spoke of integrity in design, meaning authentic and relevant designs for modern people. Buildings were meant to facilitate the purpose for which they were created. Faith communities began to adopt a similar mind-set as they conceived of church designs in conjunction with modern architects. Functions were established in relation to the wide range of ministries that a community conducted, and then design solutions that would facilitate the articulated needs of the people were suggested. Congruence between need and design was one expression of integrity.

Modern architects also spoke of honesty in construction materials and techniques. Concern for materials meant a respect for the nature of the physical materials being used. Modern architects were not interested in "imitation" or pretending that some materials were something else (e.g., treating wood to make it look like stone or simply covering up reinforced concrete because it was not as "attractive" as stone or brick). Those seeking liturgical renewal were likewise drawn to a desire for integrity. Accordingly, they accepted materials like concrete as alternative building materials for churches. Reinforced concrete was attractive for several reasons: it was generally available and less expensive than many other materials, it was flexible and strong, and it had a surface that could be treated in ways that did not try to disguise its nature. Like stone or wood, concrete could attain its own proper place as a church building material, accepted on its own terms and exploited for its own innate qualities. Integrity meant allowing structural realities to be visible too, so that it was not necessary to hide structural supports or joints that would previously have been disguised. In fact, these exposed structural elements were often considered a part of the overall "beauty" of the design. The church embraced these new materials and construction techniques because of the possibilities they could offer in service to ministry and as evidence that faith communities were willing to share in the architectural expressions of contemporary life.

Many congregations began to consider models of church design based on sources other than traditional historic styles, seeking buildings that would reflect the current culture and relate positively to modern people. As a result, historical revival designs fell out of fashion. Architects trained in modern architecture introduced a host of new expressions to the church, often inspired by the possibilities of new building materials and technologies and even secular building models (such as warehouses, office buildings, schools, and offices). New church buildings often had simple, flat roofs — no steeples. The hope was that the new designs, frequently influenced by the International Style to some degree, would encourage the general public to perceive the church as more accessible. The secular-city debate probably added to the promotion of such designs, in its effort to "connect" the church to contemporary urban life on all levels. To be sure, not all churches fully emulated the CIAM principles. But the aggressive promotion of their ideals into the 1950s (and even beyond among many architects and some architectural critics) and the models of church design provided by some of their outstanding architects did significantly alter church design, both Roman Catholic and Protestant, in the twentieth century.

CHAPTER FIVE

THE FRUITS OF WORSHIP RENEWAL: EMPHASIZING AN ARCHITECTURE OF IMMANENCE

For the churches today are in the midst of a "radical analysis" of their own function in the modern world, an examination so sweeping that it is being called the Twentieth Century reformation. And contained within it are the seeds of an equally sweeping reformation in religious architecture.

DONALD CANTY, "Strength or Banality?
A New Reformation Challenges Church Design" (1963)

The church edifice is constructed to serve men of our age. Its architectural language should not be foreign or archaic, but contemporary and genuine in expression. True Christian tradition accepts the true, good, and beautiful in each age and culture.

"Diocesan Building Directives,"
Diocesan Liturgical Commission, Superior, Wisconsin (1957)

THROUGHOUT THE NINETEENTH and into the early part of the twentieth century, a resurgence of interest in medieval forms of Christian worship took hold in both Protestant and Roman Catholic churches. The "neo-Gothic" churches that were created pointed primarily to the transcendence of God. Frequently, details of medieval church design were duplicated without any real understanding of their purpose — for example, the rood screen, originally meant to enhance a significant crucifix in the space, and divided chancels, originally used to enhance antiphonal singing in churches used by monastic communities. The altar for the Eucharist was placed at the far end of the chancel against the wall, behind the rood screen, where the presider stood with his back to the people. The suggestion, even if unintentional, was that the people were spectators at liturgical celebrations, separated from both the clergy and the altar. The modern liturgical movement sought to promote worship spaces that countered this suggestion of laity as spectators, recognizing that new conceptions of spaces for worship and the ministries of the church would be necessary if real reform was to take root.

By the mid-twentieth century, ideas and materials flowed freely between Christian denominations because of the investment of time and energy in ecumenical dialogue and worship renewal. A common desire to redirect church design away from historical revival patterns flourished. Collaborative conferences brought church architecture to the forefront of discussion in most Christian traditions. And new options for the architecture of the church emerged from multiple denominational sources. Articulate theologians and architects such as Rudolf Schwarz, Peter Hammond, and John G. Davies promoted alternative church designs.

THREE SEMINAL INFLUENCES

Rudolf Schwarz

As early as the 1930s, architect Rudolf Schwarz (1897-1961) was arguing against reproducing designs from the medieval period. Schwarz was conditioned both by his exposure to and work with Romano Guardini and by his training in the architectural theory of his own day. In *Vom Bau der Kirche* (originally published in 1938 and translated into English in 1958 as *The Church Incarnate*), Schwarz stated, "We cannot return to the Middle Ages. The great realities of the cathedral are no longer real to us."[1] Schwarz did not deny the power of the medieval cathedral to move us, but he did not find it to be a genuine expression of the Christian faith in materials and design expressive of our own unique period in history. In *The Church Incarnate* he traced the development of seven general models of liturgical space, seeking to provoke the reconceiving of worship space for modern humanity.

His first model, "Sacred Inwardness: The Ring," provides an example of his approach:

1. Rudolf Schwarz, *The Church Incarnate: The Sacred Function of Church Architecture*, trans. Cynthia Harris (Chicago: Henry Regnery Company, 1958), p. 9.

For the celebration of the Lord's Supper a moderately large, well-proportioned room is needed, in its center a table and on the table a bowl of bread and a cup of wine. The table may be decorated with candles and surrounded by seats for the congregation. That is all. Table, space, and walls make up the simplest church.

　　We cannot continue on from where the last cathedrals left off. Instead we must enter into the simple things at the source of the Christian life. We must begin anew, and our new beginning must be genuine. The small congregation is given us today, the "coming together of two or three," the communion of the table, and certainly for us the Lord is in the midst of men.[2]

Here Schwarz appears to have been moved by the fruits of liturgical studies that had focused on the early development of the Christian church. In this model he hearkens back to the most basic elements necessary to celebrate the Eucharist. He suggests the design of spaces that would highlight the central theme of community around the altar, affirming the immanence of God through Christ in our midst. Schwarz's experiences at Burg Rothenfel seem to be influential in his articulation of this model. In 1968 the Belgian Benedictine priest Frédéric Debuyst, editor of the journal *L'art d'église* ("Church Art"), declared the Guardini/Schwarz chapel to be "a place of celebration which remains probably the most satisfactory ever given us — an astonishing anticipation of our advances of today. . . . In fact, the liturgical arrangement of Schloss ['Castle'] Rothenfels was probably 'optimal,' the best possible solution for an active participation of the faithful in word and sacrament."[3]

　　Schwarz experienced, described, and designed worship spaces that could facilitate focus on the immanence of God. He went on to design several churches that proved influential as models in helping to establish an architecture of immanence. His work gained positive recognition in ecumenical circles and was used as a source of inspiration for new churches in both Europe and the United States.[4]

Peter Hammond

England was far less progressive than continental Europe in embracing any modern expression of church design. Historical revival forms of design (especially neo-Goth-

---

　　2. Schwarz, *The Church Incarnate,* pp. 35-36.

　　3. Frédéric Debuyst, *Modern Architecture and Christian Celebration* (Richmond, Va.: John Knox Press, 1968), pp. 60-61.

　　4. In Chapter Six I will say more about particular churches that Schwarz designed.

ic) continued to flourish among Anglican communities well into the mid-twentieth century. A challenge to the uncritical replication of historical styles of church design emerged in the person of Peter Hammond (1921-1999).[5] Hammond was an Anglican priest and lecturer in the history of art at the Regional College of Art, Hull. In 1957 he founded the New Church Research Group, an ecumenical (primarily Anglican and Roman Catholic) organization that was dedicated to the serious study of church design for contemporary humanity in light of liturgical renewal. In 1960 Hammond published a volume entitled *Liturgy and Architecture,* the purpose of which was not to provide a "handbook" for church design, but to challenge — in light of both the liturgical movement and modern architecture — the historical replication of medieval church plans popular in England.[6] In reference to the liturgical needs of his day, he commented,

> The church building is the house of the Church, in the biblical sense of that word; the house of the people who are themselves the temple of the living God, the habitation of the Spirit; a spiritual house built of living stones. It has no meaning apart from the community which it serves. It is first and foremost a building in which the people of God meet to *do* certain things: to perform the various communal activities known collectively as liturgy, or public service. This is what a church is for. It is a building for corporate worship; above all, a room for the eucharistic assembly. Reduced to its bare essentials, it is a building to house a congregation gathered round an altar.[7]

Hammond was echoing the emphasis that the current liturgical movement placed on the role of the people in the liturgy. Full and active participation was to be promoted, and the building was to be designed with that particular goal in mind. Hammond's list of priorities for designing an appropriate contemporary church included emphasizing the centrality of the Eucharistic celebration, recog-

---

5. For decades Hammond's writings were widely recommended in books concerning church architecture. References to his writings appeared in bibliographies across denominational lines. His work is still recommended in England by the Royal Institute for British Architects (RIBA) for those considering church design. His edited volume, *Towards a Church Architecture* (London: Architectural Press, 1962), is the only book listed for church design in the "RIBA List of Recommended Books 2004-2005." See www.architecture.com/go/Architecture/Reference/Library_825.html (click on "Recommended Books: Design"; then locate under "3.2 Design for building types and structures, Churches").

6. Peter Hammond, *Liturgy and Architecture* (London: Barrie & Rockliff, 1960), p. 31.

7. Hammond, *Liturgy and Architecture,* p. 28.

nizing the significance of the proclamation of the Word of God, and creating a unified space for clergy and laity.[8] A single, freestanding altar was to be the focal point of the worship space, with adequate area for the community to gather and share in the corporate meal. A canopy might be used to set off the significance of the altar. The place of the Word was to be a single pulpit (instead of a lectern for reading and a pulpit for preaching) to emphasize the unity of reading and proclamation. The pulpit should be located in prominent relationship to the altar to indicate that balance between Word and sacrament was essential. Finally, the distinct roles of the clergy and the laity were to be noted, but they were to be recognized in a way that emphasized the corporate celebration of the liturgy, in a space that possessed an "organic unity," avoiding visual or architectural separation. Hammond believed that elevation of the area from which the clergy presided was appropriate, but the distinction must not obscure the unity of Christ's body as expressed in the whole community.

In 1962 a collection of essays by theologians and architects who were members of Hammond's New Church Research Group was published. The book was edited by Hammond and published under the title *Towards a Church Architecture*. These essays championed the priorities of the liturgical movement and the virtues of modern design. The reflections were written by Roman Catholic and Protestant authors and intended for use across denominational lines. Photographs of many churches designed by Rudolf Schwarz were included, along with new church designs by Robert Maguire and Keith Murray (both of whom have essays in the book), Emil Steffann, Rainer Senn, and Ludwig Mies van der Rohe. (More will be said about the significance of some of these architects in Chapters Six and Seven.) The appendix includes two important documents: "Guiding Principles for the Design of Churches According to the Spirit of the Roman Liturgy, German Liturgical Commission (1947)" and "Diocesan Church Building Directives, Superior, Wisconsin (1957)."[9] These were influential pre–Vatican II documents that helped to shape new ways of conceiving of Catholic worship space in light of liturgical renewal. Protestant leaders also found them helpful for clarifying the relationship between worship and architecture in a contemporary setting.

Hammond and his group produced materials that integrated liturgical renewal with modern church design, all in an ecumenical atmosphere. Their work was

8. Hammond, *Liturgy and Architecture*, pp. 35-42.

9. *Towards a Church Architecture*, ed. Peter Hammond (London: Architectural Press, 1962), pp. 245-62.

widely distributed and read in Europe and the United States, helping to set the stage for far-reaching reforms that would emerge from Vatican II.[10]

John G. Davies

Theologian John G. Davies was particularly influenced by Hammond's book *Liturgy and Architecture*.[11] Davies wanted to find ways to help promote the type of liturgical renewal and modern architectural design that Hammond proposed among the churches of England. In 1962 Davies established the Institute for the Study of Worship and Religious Architecture at the University of Birmingham. He was a primary spokesperson for the Institute and their director for many years. The Institute had a cooperative relationship with Hammond's New Church Research Group (it may even have served as a model for Davies, especially with its ecumenical composition and focus). The Institute was influential in guiding church architectural design in Europe and the United States through its research, consultations, and periodic publications.

Examples of their publications include annual research bulletins (from 1965 on, edited by Davies) highlighting particular themes and current church building projects, and the distribution of collected papers in documents such as *Looking to the Future: Papers Read at an International Symposium on Prospects for Worship, Religious Architecture, and Socio-Religious Studies, 1976*.[12] Davies, along with Gilbert Cope, who

10. An additional example of suggestions for church design from the New Church Research Group (NCRG) can be found in a series of articles published in successive issues of the British architecture periodical *The Architects' Journal* (from 9 August to 18 October 1967). Members of the NCRG prepared documents concerning the particular worship and ministry needs of the Church of England, the Roman Catholic Church, the Presbyterian Church of Scotland, the Methodist Church, the Society of Friends, and the Salvation Army. The guidelines provided reflect the theological and liturgical priorities of renewal explored in this chapter. Also present is the influence of the priorities of modern architectural design. The bibliographies provided recommend books discussing the importance of liturgical renewal and its implications for church architecture as well as books illustrating European and American churches of modern design from the early to mid-twentieth century. For wider distribution and accessibility, the articles were published together in the document entitled *Church Buildings*, ed. The Architects' Journal (London: Architectural Press, 1970).

11. Daniel W. Hardy, "God in the Ordinary: The Work of J. G. Davies (1919-1990)," *Theology* 99 (November-December 1996): 432.

12. *Looking to the Future: Papers Read at an International Symposium on Prospects for Worship, Religious Architecture, and Socio-Religious Studies, 1976*, ed. J. G. Davies (Birmingham: Institute for the Study of Worship and Religious Architecture, 1976).

was the deputy director of the Institute, also published occasional collections of essays with others. Two examples are the collection edited by Cope entitled *Making the Building Serve the Liturgy: Studies in the Re-ordering of Churches* (the preface of which is written by Bishop John A. T. Robinson), and the collection edited by William Lockett entitled *The Modern Architectural Setting of the Liturgy: Papers Read at a Conference Held at Liverpool, September 1962.*[13] Lockett and Cope contributed half of the ten essays of an additional title edited by Cope, *Christianity and the Visual Arts,*[14] in which they encouraged an active embrace of liturgical renewal and modern art and architecture in the life of the church.

Priorities of the liturgical movement and modern architectural design are evident in the writings of the Institute and its leadership. Designs for churches of Roman Catholic and Protestant traditions are addressed in their research too. Evidence of the depth of their ecumenical commitment can be seen in a statement from a document jointly published by the Institute and the Diocese of Chichester, with whom they were consulting on new church designs:

> It is very desirable that there should be as much consultation between the different denominations as possible at every stage. The Diocesan Planning Officer himself might well be responsible at every stage, not only to the diocesan authorities, but also to a joint churches planning committee. In some places (notably the deanery of Woolwich) a scheme is being considered whereby joint use can be made of a single group of buildings, and whereby ministers of different denominations might be members of the same group ministry. If this can be managed, it means not only greater economy, but also a valuable demonstration of a common unity of purpose which should do much to commend the Christian Gospel.[15]

Such a statement is a profound example of the influence of ecumenicity on church building in the mid-twentieth century.[16]

---

13. *Making the Building Serve the Liturgy: Studies in the Re-ordering of Churches,* ed. Gilbert Cope (London: A. R. Mowbray & Company, 1962); *The Modern Architectural Setting of the Liturgy: Papers Read at a Conference Held at Liverpool, September 1962,* ed. William Lockett (London: SPCK, 1964).

14. *Christianity and the Visual Arts,* ed. Gilbert Cope (London: Faith Press, 1964).

15. *Buildings and Breakthrough: Report of the Diocese of Chichester Buildings Study Group,* published in association with the Institute for the Study of Worship and Religious Architecture, University of Birmingham. No date is given, but internal evidence suggests a date close to 1967.

16. Evidently the idea of Christian congregations across denominational lines using the same church

The publications mentioned here remain cited in bibliographies of books addressing church architecture in the United States at least into the late 1980s, a testimony to the value of the insight the Institute provided for the larger church in the world.

Ecumenical Collaboration across Continents

A building boom in church construction followed in the wake of World War II, especially from 1945 to 1959, both in Europe and in the United States.[17] A strong trend of building continued into the 1960s. The National Council of Churches and the World Council of Churches established conduits to facilitate dialogue about theological and architectural issues related to church building in light of these trends. The National Council of Churches launched a department of church planning and architecture and a department of worship and the arts and sponsored national church architecture conferences.[18] The World Council of Churches held periodic meetings discussing church architecture.

An example of some conclusions reached concerning modern church architecture in these international, ecumenical gatherings can be found in the notes of a gathering of theologians and architects at the World Council of Churches' Ecumenical Institute meeting in Bossey, Switzerland, from 6 to 13 May 1959. The conference name for this

---

building became a reality in some European locations. In 1988 Randall Lindstrom noted two communities in Europe (one in Ettwig, West Germany, and the other in Steinhausen, Switzerland) where Roman Catholic and Protestant communities were sharing new joint church facilities. See Lindstrom, *Creativity and Contradiction: European Churches since 1970* (Washington, D.C.: The American Institute of Architects Press, 1988), p. 15.

17. Henry C. F. Arnold, "Religious Buildings: Stability after the Boom," *Architectural Record* 134 (July 1963): 18.

18. Members at the first meeting (in 1954) of the National Council of Churches Commission on Architecture of the Department of Worship and the Arts initiated the drafting of a bibliography on church architecture that could be circulated among its constituencies. Herbert W. Johe, a faculty member of the Department of Architecture at the University of Michigan, agreed to undertake this task. His nineteen-page bibliography of recent book and periodical resources was released in January 1959. The bibliography, which referred to both books and periodicals, included materials both Roman Catholic and Protestant, some of which were written by leaders associated with promoting the liturgical movement (such as Louis Bouyer, Yngve Brilioth, Gregory Dix, Theodor Filthaut, Peter Hammond, Anton Henze, H. A. Reinhold, and Rudolf Schwarz). Johe also included a list of articles related to contemporary Protestant churches in the United

particular gathering was "Church Building as an Expression of the Presence of the Church in the World." The report from the conference concluded with a series of statements that were "unanimously accepted" by those in attendance:

1. Our twentieth-century material and scientific progress and discovery, our new ways of thought and living do not invalidate the ageless message of Christianity. The considerations of life today are calling the Church into the common life of man, away from the enclosed sanctuary, to witness in daily work. This may create new forms of Christian community life which will also lead to expression in buildings which represent, like other buildings of our time, the thinking of modern man. New buildings are often needed to consolidate this evangelistic work and to draw men together in Christian fellowship.

2. In earlier times the church building was one of the finest expressions of the age. This does not solve our problem. We have to face our task in our time to find a new expression of Christian life today through the buildings we make.

3. The serving and not the dominating role of the Church should be kept in mind. This can be expressed not only in the building, but also in the way in which it is related to the town plan. The church building should not be a venture in personal expression, an architectural tour de force, or merely a sensuously satisfying achievement.

4. The Church must take account of the needs of modern society. . . .[19]

At this conference, service was deemed the focal point of the church. The building was to be a genuine expression of the architecture of the day, serve the people who built the space, and facilitate ministry to the world. Human relationship was to be

---

States, as well as a list of articles related to Roman Catholic and Protestant churches in many European countries (including new churches by architects such as Auguste Perret, Le Corbusier, Otto Bartning, Dominikus Böhm, Rudolf Schwarz, and the French chapels at Assy, Audincourt, and Vence developed under the leadership of Father M.-A. Couturier). See Johe, *Architecture and the Church,* vol. 1: *A Bibliography on Architecture for the Church* (New York: Department of Worship and the Arts, National Council of Churches of Christ in the USA, 1959). Additional reports that the NCC Commission on Architecture produced and distributed in the 1950s include "The Church, the Arts, and Contemporary Culture," "Round Table Report . . . Theology and Architecture," "Architecture and the Church" (addresses by Joseph Sittler Jr. and Leonard J. Trinterud), "The Shape of the Church's Response in Worship" (address by Joseph Sittler Jr.), "The Blight of Hillbillyism in Religion" (by A. W. Tozer), "The Church and Contemporary Culture" (by Paul Tillich), and "The Spiritual Function of the Church Building."

19. "Church Building as an Expression of the Presence of the Church in the World," *Report of the Conference for Architects and Theologians, May 6th-13th, 1959* (Bossey, Switzerland: The Ecumenical Institute, 1959), p. 6.

the primary way in which the presence of God would be mediated through the new churches. In this model God's immanence through the presence and activities of the human "body of Christ" became paramount.

The Liturgical Conference was an effective organization through which ideas of worship renewal were exchanged among theologians, church leaders (especially members of liturgical and building commissions), artists, and architects. In 1965 the annual meeting of the conference pursued the theme of church architecture. A three-day gathering was held from 23 to 25 February in Cleveland, Ohio. Approximately 500 people attended the proceedings. Individuals who were actively involved in liturgical renewal shared papers. Architect Edward A. Sövik and theologians such as Bernard Cooke, Gerard Sloyan, Godfrey Diekmann, Aelred Tegels, and Kevin Seasoltz made presentations. Momentum from the elevation of the people at worship from the new *Constitution on the Sacred Liturgy* oriented the focus toward re-imagining designs that would declare a "house of the Church." Although the gathering was specifically addressing Catholic concerns, it had an ecumenical spirit. In the introduction to the published essays from the conference, the ecumenical hope is explicit:

> Directed specifically at the requirements of Catholic liturgy, these chapters should nevertheless be helpful to architects and others responsible for building the "house of the Church" in other confessional traditions. Our basic problems are much the same. And emphases which at one time were pressed so strongly as to seem contradictory have begun to integrate in the perspective of a vision at once catholic and evangelical.[20]

Discussions included seeing the Eucharist as a communal meal, seeking to encourage active engagement of the whole congregation in worship, heightening the significance of the Word in the Eucharistic celebration, accenting the significance of initiation (baptism), contemplating the pursuit of "noble simplicity" in the liturgy, discovering an appropriate place for private devotional practices, and enlisting the aid of professionals in designing churches. Design suggestions included making the freestanding altar a more modest size, removing the tabernacle from the altar to encourage a single focus on the action of the shared Eucharist in the Mass, empha-

---

20. *Church Architecture: The Shape of Reform,* Proceedings of a Meeting on Church Architecture Conducted by the Liturgical Conference in Cleveland, Ohio, February 23-25, 1965 (Washington, D.C.: The Liturgical Conference, 1965), p. 1.

sizing the significance of the ambo (the place of the Word of God), highlighting the space for initiation in the corporate space, and making a place for devotional objects in an alternative area (other than the primary worship area).

In the late 1960s and early 1970s, a series of three international congresses on religion, architecture, and the visual arts were jointly sponsored by institutes of architects, councils of churches, and research centers for church architecture from around the world.[21] (The first international congress in 1967 was mentioned in Chapter Two.) Liturgical renewal, concern for the social needs of urban humanity, and contemporary church design were discussed at length at these conferences. The congresses were fertile contexts for bringing together architects, artists, theologians, church leaders, and other academics to exchange ideas. Four of the published essays from these congresses were even reprinted in a French collection of essays entitled *Espace sacré et architecture moderne.*[22] Writings by authors such as J. Lercaro, Edward A. Sövik, John G. Davies, and Frédéric Debuyst were included in this collection, increasing the influence of these agents of liturgical reform.

Concern for a church design focused on immanence can be discerned in comments from various essays from the first conference. In his address "The Meaning of Religious Places," Frédéric Debuyst quoted the late Dutch bishop Monsignor Bekkers, who conceived of the church as a "kind of great living room, a place where the faithful come together to meet the Lord and one another in the Lord."[23] Debuyst was advocating a domestic model for church design in opposition to what he called "monumental" designs, those that seemed to overwhelm the people who occupied them. For Debuyst, hospitality was a key quality of church design. In fact, Debuyst's own book, *Modern Architecture and Christian Celebration,* published the following year, would focus on the domestic house as a primary model to consider when designing churches.[24] Debuyst had the urban concerns of Harvey Cox in mind when he noted

21. The first international congress was held in New York City and Montreal in 1967, the second in Brussels in 1970, and the third in Jerusalem in 1973. Papers from the first conference were published in *Revolution, Place, and Symbol: Journal of the First International Congress on Religion, Architecture, and the Visual Arts, New York City and Montreal, August 26 through September 4, 1967,* ed. Rolfe Lanier Hunt (New York: International Congress on Religion, Architecture, and the Visual Arts, 1969). Papers from the third conference were published in *Sacred Space: Meaning and Form,* ed. David James Randolph (New York: International Congress on Religion, Architecture, and the Arts, 1976).

22. *Espace sacré et architecture moderne* (Paris: Les Éditions du Cerf, 1971).

23. Frédéric Debuyst, "Meaning of Places," in *Revolution, Place, and Symbol,* p. 155.

24. Frédéric Debuyst, *Modern Architecture and Christian Celebration,* pp. 30-41.

the need for pursuing humility and tangible responses to real human needs in and through modern church design.[25] In effect, Debuyst appears to have been calling for the church to be considered more of a "house of the people of God" than a "house for God" per se.

ROMAN CATHOLIC RECOMMENDATIONS FOR RENEWAL THROUGH CHURCH DESIGN

Various published works to guide contemporary Roman Catholic church design that appreciated the priorities of the liturgical movement and modern architecture were released in the decades leading up to the Vatican II Council meetings. Three examples from American publishers — one each from the 1930s, the 1940s, and the 1950s — will help to illustrate the powerful influence of the liturgical movement in conjunction with modern architecture.

Church Architecture: Building for a Living Faith by Frank Brannach, a member of the Federation of Catholic Art and Liturgical Arts Society, was published in 1932.[26] Brannach's book was a historical survey of church design that culminated in a word of appreciation for many qualities of modern architectural design.[27] Brannach mentioned the influence of Frank Lloyd Wright, discussed the emerging International Style, and featured European and American churches that seemed to emulate the concerns of modern design.[28] He could not sanction wholesale imitation of secular architecture, but he encouraged creative new designs for churches in the spirit of modern sensibilities.[29]

Churches: Their Plan and Furnishing by Peter F. Anson (revised and edited by Thomas F. Croft-Fraser and H. A. Reinhold to "Americanize" the original English edition) was released in 1948. In his foreword to the book, Anson remarked,

25. Debuyst, "Meaning of Places," pp. 158-59.

26. Frank Brannach, *Church Architecture: Building for a Living Faith* (Milwaukee: Bruce Publishing Company, 1932).

27. Brannach, *Church Architecture*, pp. 164-234.

28. One can get a sense of Brannach's approach in this brief passage from the book's foreword: "Great churches have been built in the past in many various styles, but we must make our contribution and interpret the Church to the present age. Borrowing Gothic forms from the past, or Romanesque or Renaissance modes of expression, means nothing to the living present. Old forms are not even interesting." Brannach, *Church Architecture*, p. xv.

29. Brannach, *Church Architecture*, p. 224.

The trouble with so many churches erected during the past century is that architects have been far more concerned with the superficial "beauty" than with the nature of the building. Their object, so it seems, was to create a building that *looked* what most people believed a church *ought* to look like rather than a building that fulfilled the practical functions of a place of worship. . . . The aim of a church architect should be, first and foremost, to create a "house" in which the public worship of the Church can be carried out according to canonical requirements. "The aim is not a 'style,' whether past or present, but the meaning of the *Mysteria* and the true purpose for which this House is to be built."[30]

In this quotation one can discern the objectives and language of the liturgical movement in relation to church architecture: traditional architectural designs were not to be reproduced without regard for contemporary function. Anson was concerned with giving proper emphasis to the activities of the liturgy and creating an environment that would facilitate active engagement in worship. He emphasized that all the people (clergy and laity) in worship are themselves a locus of the mystery of God in Christ. The last statement of the excerpt here is a quotation from Reinhold, an indication of the closeness in thought between Anson and this significant leader in the liturgical movement. Anson occasionally mentioned renewal concerns (often via comments by artist Eric Gill), such as moving the central altar toward the people and accentuating the organic unity between clergy and laity.[31] But many of his specific suggestions tended to be conservative, a consequence of his trying to navigate renewal in the face of contemporary church legislation.

Church Building and Furnishing: The Church's Way by J. B. O'Connell was published in 1955.[32] O'Connell examined liturgical law in the Roman Catholic Church with the intent of discerning specific guidance for the design, decoration, and furnishing of Catholic churches. O'Connell used the pre–Vatican II liturgical materials available to him, including European documents such as "The Directives of the Bishops of

30. Peter F. Anson, *Churches: Their Plan and Furnishing* (Milwaukee: Bruce Publishing Company, 1948), pp. x-xi.

31. Anson, *Churches: Their Plan and Furnishing*, pp. 33-35. Even models of churches exhibiting a central altar with congregational seating on several sides are occasionally represented.

32. J. B. O'Connell, *Church Building and Furnishing: The Church's Way* (Notre Dame: University of Notre Dame Press, 1955). This book was an early text in a liturgical studies series under the direction of the Liturgical Committee of the University of Notre Dame. Other authors in the series included liturgical scholars such as Louis Bouyer, Balthasar Fischer, Josef Jungmann, and Jean Danielou.

Germany on Church Building" (1947) and "The Directives of the Bishops of France regarding Sacred Art" (1952).[33] The influence of the liturgical movement can be discerned in a number of his recommendations, such as embracing (within reason) expressions of modern art, reducing the ornamentation in the church to maintain proper focus on the main altar, inviting people to actively participate in worship through particular architectural design choices, and allowing the presider to face the people during the Mass celebration.[34]

Reflections from the three books by Brannach, Anson, and O'Connell help to provide a window of understanding into the development that led to the directives ultimately found in the document *Environment and Art in Catholic Worship*.

Prior to the Vatican II Council meetings, dioceses in Europe and the United States articulated suggestions for church design based on a desire to support worship renewal in conjunction with modern art and architecture. In 1947 the German Liturgical Commission published a document entitled *Richtlinien für die Gestaltung des Gotteshauses aus dem Geiste der romischen Liturgie,* or "Guiding Principles for the Design of Churches according to the Spirit of the Roman Liturgy."[35] The guidelines were fairly conservative overall but did add some intriguing insights reflective of the priorities of the liturgical renewal movement. Concern for the people and needs of the present day were addressed, as guideline six shows:

> 6. A church is meant for a congregation of our time. It must therefore be so constructed that men and women of today may feel at home in it. Their noblest aspirations must find fulfillment there: the urge towards community and fellowship, the search for the true and genuine, the desire to get away from what is peripheral to what is central and essential, the striving after clarity, the longing for peace, for warmth and shelter.[36]

---

33. I will say more about the content of the German guidelines later in this chapter.

34. O'Connell, *Church Building and Furnishing: The Church's Way,* pp. 36-41, 48-52, 160-61.

35. *Towards a Church Architecture,* ed. Hammond, pp. 248-54. According to Hammond, these principles were primarily the work of Theodor Klauser in collaboration with a commission appointed by the hierarchy of the German church in 1940. The principles appeared in English in the journal *Orate Fratres* 24 (December 1949): 9-18, and were reprinted in *Documents for Sacred Architecture* (Collegeville, Minn.: Liturgical Press, 1957), pp. 15-23. In the appendix of his book (pp. 248-54) Hammond reproduced the principles from a translated edition of a revised text, c. 1955, by Hildegart Nicholas. The entire text of the principles has also been reproduced in the appendix of *An Architecture of Immanence*.

36. *Towards a Church Architecture,* ed. Hammond, p. 249.

There is a clear emphasis here on creating an appropriate environment for authentic, communal expressions of worship. The people are central to this statement. The church building needs to be designed to help focus the people on what is essential for worship and ministry: providing hospitality and care. The guidelines go on to mention that the altar is to remain central to the worship space, with care taken to relate it organically to the congregation. The altar is to be freestanding, significant in and of itself (not hidden as a repository for other artifacts), and allow for the presiding clergy to face the congregation at Mass. The choir is to be located so that they are perceived as part of the community at worship. And the font is to have a significant presence and be located near the entrance of the space to remind the faithful of their initiation.[37]

In 1957 the bishop of the diocese of Superior, Wisconsin, released a brief document of directives intended to guide church design in support of liturgical renewal. The "Diocesan Church Building Directives" emerged from the work of a panel that included artists, architects, liturgists, a pastor, a canonist, and an artist.[38] The directives were intended to be a working document subject to future revision.[39] Like the German guidelines, the American directives were largely conservative. Concern for contemporary expression in architectural design was present, as directive seven indicates:

> 7. The church edifice is constructed to serve men of our age. Its architectural language should not be archaic or foreign but contemporary and genuine in expression. True Christian tradition accepts the true, good, and beautiful in each age and culture.[40]

This directive expresses appreciation for the artistic expressions of the modern world. Though no particular architectural style of design is endorsed here, the search for contemporary and authentic expressions of beauty is supported. The directives go on to state that the art used in service to the church is to be neither too

---

37. *Towards a Church Architecture*, ed. Hammond, pp. 250-53.

38. *Towards a Church Architecture*, ed. Hammond, p. 245.

39. The directives were reproduced in two parts: *Liturgical Arts* 26, no. 1 (November 1957): 7-9; and *Liturgical Arts* 26, no. 2 (February 1958): 43-44. A revised text (c. 1962) was published in the appendix of Hammond's book, *Towards a Church Architecture*, pp. 255-62, although it is largely the text from the original document of 1957. The text of the directives is also reproduced in full in the appendix of *An Architecture of Immanence*.

40. *Towards a Church Architecture*, ed. Hammond, p. 256.

naturalistic nor too abstract, and the decoration of the church "should be simple, organic, and unpretentious." Humility and integrity are a priority here. Permission to remove inferior expressions of art is implied. A unified, organic arrangement of the worship space is endorsed in this directive: "Although distinct in treatment, the sanctuary which contains the altar and the nave which houses the community of the baptized ought to be visually and psychologically one." The baptistery is to be located near the entrance of the church, allowing for a substantial emphasis on initiation. The altar is to be the primary focal point of the space, away from any wall, illuminated by natural light as possible, and not diminished by auxiliary appointments (such as the tabernacle, altar cross, and candleholders).[41]

Prior to the Vatican II Council meetings, many in the liturgical renewal movement had expressed concern that environments for worship frequently tended to overemphasize individually focused, personal devotional activities through an abundance of artifacts (for example, many statues and multiple altars). Often the artistic work was thought to be of an inferior quality, with many churches using mass-produced, inexpensive objects. It is true that churches function as places to collect devotional artifacts over time, most of which are notoriously difficult to remove at a later date. Both of the sets of guidelines discussed here intend to counter such impulses, emphasizing the whole gathered community at worship, recommending the simplification of the worship environment with a single altar as the primary focal point, and allowing for high-quality contemporary art and architecture. Both sets of instructions were reproduced in multiple journals and books, both Catholic and Protestant. These statements served as sources for conceiving of church design in new ways, with the intention of enhancing more active communal engagement among the faithful at worship.

The *Constitution on the Sacred Liturgy* initiated a fresh approach to consideration of the environment for Catholic worship. Article 128, located in Chapter VII, "Sacred Art and Sacred Furnishings," seemed especially fruitful for promoting renewal through the material environment. The article states in part,

> There is to be an early revision of the canons and ecclesiastical statutes which govern the provision of material things involved in sacred worship. These laws refer especially to the worthy and well-planned construction of sacred buildings, the shape and construction of altars, the nobility, placing, and safety of the eucharistic tabernacle, the

41. *Towards a Church Architecture*, ed. Hammond, pp. 257, 258, 260-61.

dignity and suitability of the baptistery, the proper ordering of images, embellishments, and vestments. . . . According to the norm of art. 22 of this constitution, the territorial bodies of bishops are empowered to adapt such things to the needs and customs of their different regions; this applies especially to the materials and form of sacred furnishings and vestments.[42]

This statement granted permission to reconsider church architecture and the worship environment. Of particular significance is the fact that the bishops of various geographical locales were empowered to adapt to the "needs and customs" of the people they served. Some of the renewal ideas that had been circulating for years in liturgical renewal circles (and that had sometimes been applied to individual churches) could now be applied more broadly and precisely for the benefit of the whole church.

In an effort to provide a little more precision to article 128, the preparatory commission on the liturgy generated an appendix.[43] The appendix was only a handful of pages long, with fourteen points, but nonetheless significant. Important emphases that sought to promote the communal nature of worship included accenting the organic unity of clergy and laity in worship (no. 1); using a freestanding primary altar, with "noble simplicity of design," located midway between the clergy and the laity (no. 3); recommending that side altars be located in special chapels rather than in the main body of the church (no. 4); granting permission to move the tabernacle from the primary altar and locate it in a chapel for the Blessed Sacrament (no. 6); properly elevating the ambo/lectern for reading and proclamation of God's Word (no. 7); and honoring the baptistery through strategic placement (no. 8). A clear priority of the appendix was encouraging a fullness of corporate worship around a primary altar. (Many of the points mentioned in this appendix will be reiterated in later reflections on article 128 of the constitution.)

Additional directives were issued in subsequent years. On 26 September 1964, "The First Instruction for the Proper Implementation of the Constitution on the Sacred Liturgy" *(Inter Oecumenici)* was released. In Chapter Five of this instruction (numbers 90-99), entitled "The Proper Construction of Churches and Altars to Facilitate Active Participation of the Faithful," altars (major and minor), the

42. *Church Architecture: The Shape of Reform*, pp. 97-98.
43. *Church Architecture: The Shape of Reform*, p. 87.

presider's chair, the lectern (ambo), and the location of the faithful and the baptistery were mentioned in more detail.[44] Of interest here is number 91, which contained the directive to remove the altar from the wall so that the presider could face the people in celebrating the Eucharist. It also mentioned that the altar needed to have a "truly central" place in the building. This instruction required the moving of altars in most Catholic churches and a significant emphasis on establishing a more intimate connection between the priest, the altar, and the people. The people were to be able to see and hear the clergy clearly in worship. And in number 99, the baptistery was required to express the dignity of the sacrament and to be "well suited" for communal celebrations. In each case, the place of the gathered people at worship was elevated, and the space was to be altered to accentuate this intention.

The release in 1969 of the revised *Roman Missal* for celebrating the Mass initiated a set of guidelines for its implementation, "General Instruction of the Roman Missal."[45] Chapter Five of the instruction is entitled "Arrangement and Furnishing of Churches for the Eucharistic Celebration" (numbers 253-280). Additional detail was given in these instructions also, but there was much latitude for expression requiring excellence in design and implementation. The arts and artists were welcome to serve the church, allowing for new expressions from all peoples and parts of the world (no. 254). The altar needed to be set apart in distinction (at least slightly elevated), freestanding, ordinarily fixed (although mobility was allowed), and central as a focal point of the space (nos. 258, 260, 262, and 264). The celebrant's chair was to be significant (but humble) and face the congregation (no. 271). The lectern or ambo should be a natural focal point and suitable location for proclamation of the Word of God (no. 272). A chapel suitable for private adoration and prayer was suggested for the location of the tabernacle (no. 276). Images for veneration were to be limited and located in areas that would not distract the faithful from communal celebrations (no. 278). Overall, the suggestion was that the decorative style of a church was to be "a means to achieve noble simplicity, not ostentation" (no. 279). The spirit of reform was evident in these directives, allowing for new forms of art, a simplified environment for Word and table, and a focus on the active participation of the whole community gathered for worship.

---

44. The entire text of Chapter Five is reproduced in the appendix of *An Architecture of Immanence*.

45. This emerged in a fourth edition issued by the Sacred Congregation for Divine Worship on 27 March 1975.

A lengthier set of guidelines entitled *Environment and Art in Catholic Worship* (EACW) was formally released in 1978.[46] The Bishops' Committee on the Liturgy, a committee of the American National Conference of Catholic Bishops, produced EACW. EACW was meant to function as a more complete guide for appropriating the rather broad directives concerning worship art and space present in texts such as the *Constitution on the Sacred Liturgy.* EACW appeared fourteen years after the constitution, an official response to the invitation and hope expressed for bishops in article 128. EACW was not a long document — approximately fifty pages of text in the original booklet, with relatively few footnotes that were quite brief — but it was significant nonetheless. In contrast to an approach to church design that seemed rooted in particular historical forms, EACW encouraged an openness to contemporary designs and priorities:

> The norm for designing liturgical space is the assembly and its liturgies. The building or cover enclosing the architectural space is a shelter or "skin" for a liturgical action. It does not have to "look like" anything else, past or present. Its integrity, simplicity, and beauty, its physical location and landscaping should take into account the neighborhood, city, and area in which it is built.[47]

This statement acknowledged modern architectural design as appropriate for churches. A church no longer had to imitate a recognized historical style of architecture in order to "look like" a church. Modern design was concerned with issues such as integrity, simplicity, and beauty, priorities for religious communities as well. The statement specifically mentioned geographical location and context, concerns relevant to the "secular city" debate and the immediate presence of the church in the world. And the assembly or congregation gathered for worship and its liturgies were central for guiding church design. The church building was not to be thought of as an autonomous structure but as a servant that facilitated the worship and ministries of God's people.

In the years between 1964 and 1978, the year EACW was published, many conversations had occurred on national and international levels between priests, laity,

---

46. Bishops' Committee on the Liturgy, *Environment and Art in Catholic Worship* (Washington, D.C.: National Conference of Catholic Bishops, 1978). Select articles from EACW have been reproduced in the appendix.

47. *Environment and Art in Catholic Worship,* article 42.

architects, and theologians of many Christian traditions. Robert Hovda, a Roman Catholic priest and member of the Liturgical Conference, is recognized as a primary author of EACW.[48] Convergence in Catholic and Protestant thought and mutual appreciation had occurred during the years following Vatican II. Themes from ecumenical gatherings concerning worship renewal and modern church design can be discerned from titles of subsections of the document: "A Climate of Hospitality" (article 11), "Quality and Appropriateness" (articles 19-23), "The Serving Environment" (article 24), "The Action of the Assembly" (articles 29-32), and "A House for the Church's Liturgical Celebrations" (the title over several subsections encompassing articles 39-54, including "Primary Demand: The Assembly," articles 40-43, and "Unity of Space," articles 53-54). Even the possible need for a multifunctional worship space was considered in article 65, in which case "a certain flexibility or movability should be considered even for the essential furnishings." Human interaction and active participation in worship were mentioned frequently in EACW. Its guidelines encouraged creating a space that facilitated a simple, noble beauty, relevancy, hospitality, and a "human scale." Specific suggestions that illustrate the emphasis on communal action, hospitality, and simplicity include the allowance for mobility of liturgical appointments if needed; seating that emphasized community; a single altar scaled to the celebration by a single priest in the primary liturgical environment (holding only the bread, wine, Eucharistic vessels, and ritual book); removal of the tabernacle from the central altar to an appropriate location for accommodation of private devotions; a room or rooms for reconciliation; and a reduction in the proliferation of symbols (such as crosses or candles) to heighten the effect of their presence.[49]

EACW is, in part, an example of how ecumenical work over many years could shape concrete suggestions for church design encouraging worship renewal that would resonate across denominational lines. It could be said that the emphasis on God's presence in and among those at worship heightened the acknowledgment of God's immanence in the document (and potentially in the churches that followed its guidelines). However, an acknowledgment of mystery was not absent from EACW. Articles twelve and thirteen explicitly discuss "the experience of mystery" in the liturgical environment:

---

48. James F. White, *Roman Catholic Worship: Trent to Today* (New York: Paulist Press, 1995), p. 119.
49. *Environment and Art in Catholic Worship,* articles 65, 68, 71-72, 80, 81, 86.

12. The experience of mystery . . . involves a certain beneficial tension with the demands of hospitality. . . . A simple and attractive beauty in everything that is used or done in liturgy is the most effective invitation to this kind of experience. . . .

13. Incarnation, the paschal mystery, and the Holy Spirit in us are faith's access to the transcendence, holiness, otherness of God. . . .[50]

Beauty was highlighted as a primary vehicle through which mystery could be experienced in the worship environment.[51] Those seeking to encounter transcendence could contemplate beauty, both in objects and in the liturgy itself; this provided an alternative to the sense of mystery suggested by overwhelming scale or dim illumination (common qualities of many Gothic revival worship spaces). If hospitality was to be prioritized in the liturgical environment, then compatible ways of acknowledging transcendence were also necessary. Accordingly, the guidelines also mentioned other ways that transcendence might be encountered in a setting emphasizing God's immanence: by contemplating the mystery of the incarnation of God in Christ; by contemplating the mystery of the passion, death, and resurrection of Christ; and by contemplating the mystery of God's Spirit in us.[52]

Many churches applied these guidelines, to varying degrees, in the renovation of older spaces and in plans for new churches. Critical voices noted an overemphasis on God's immanence at the seeming expense of transcendence, the application of a more spartan modern aesthetic, and the de-emphasis on private, devotional practices. (In Chapter Nine I will say more about the critique of modern church design focused on God's immanence.)

---

50. *Environment and Art in Catholic Worship,* articles 12 and 13.

51. Architect Edward A. Sövik, who was active in ecumenical dialogue, was drawing a connection between expressions of beauty and the mystery of holiness as early as 1967. See Sövik, "What Is Religious Architecture?" *Faith and Form* 1 (Special issue, 1967): 24.

52. Consideration of these fundamental mysteries of the Christian faith is built on another important strand of the liturgical movement that we have not explored: the mystery theology of the Benedictine monk from Maria Laach, Odo Casel (1886-1948). Especially important was his emphasis on the activity of Christ in the whole liturgical celebration, evident in the entire gathered community rather than isolated in particular acts performed by the clergy. Casel's theological reflections are fundamental for locating a sense of God's transcendence/mystery in the congregation and their worship activities. For a brief introduction to Casel, see Patrick Malloy, "Odo Casel: Theologian of the Mystery," in *How Firm a Foundation: Leaders of the Liturgical Movement,* ed. Robert L. Tuzik (Chicago: Liturgy Training Publications, 1990), pp. 50-57. English translations of Casel's writings on mystery and worship can be found in Odo Casel, *The Mystery of Christian Worship and Other Writings,* trans. Burkhard Neunheuser (Westminster, Md.: Newman Press, 1962).

PROTESTANT RECOMMENDATIONS FOR
RENEWAL THROUGH CHURCH DESIGN

Protestant scholars and documents also played an influential role in establishing mid-century church design. A range of representative materials will be considered here.[53]

In the 1950s the Joint Commission on Architecture and the Allied Arts of the Protestant Episcopal Church in the U.S.A. released two documents for its congregations to use for guidance in building new churches. The first was *Architecture for the Church,* edited by Darby Wood Betts, published in 1952.[54] This fifty-five-page booklet addressed basic issues such as considering purpose, considering style of design, hiring an architect, and using contemporary arts in service to the church. It made allowance for appropriate contemporary expressions of architecture, but gave little evidence of the priorities of the ecumenical and liturgical movements. The book's bibliography was primarily resources published in the 1920s and 1930s, including *Church Building* by Ralph Adams Cram (1906 edition).[55]

The second book (130 pages long) was *Church Buildings and Furnishings: A Survey of Requirements,* edited by Jonathan G. Sherman and published in 1958.[56] This second volume was a sequel to the first and contained contributions by many architects and theologians. It examined particular issues in more detail (such as site planning, the ground plan, Christian education needs, and architectural style). It also contained a new bibliography that removed Cram's title but retained the core of resources from the first book and added titles from the 1940s and 1950s (including *Betonkirchen* by Ferdinand Pfammatter and *Religious Buildings for Today,* edited by John Knox Shear).[57] As in the first book, there was little evidence here of the influence of the ecumenical and liturgical movements, but the shift to modern architectural design was acknowledged. Near the end of the book, this comment appeared:

> But whereas the Gothic architect-builder had only wood and stone at his disposal and
> thus his structures were heavy and extremely expensive, the architect and engineer of

53. The materials examined here are not exhaustive. The bibliography contains many additional materials, including those generated by members of denominations not represented here.

54. *Architecture for the Church,* ed. Darby Wood Betts (Greenwich, Conn.: Seabury Press, 1952).

55. *Architecture and the Church,* ed. Betts, p. 55.

56. *Church Buildings and Furnishings: A Survey of Requirements,* ed. Jonathan G. Sherman (Greenwich, Conn.: Seabury Press, 1958).

57. Ferdinand Pfammatter, *Betonkirchen* (Zurich: Benziger Verlag Einsieldeln, 1948); *Religious Buildings for Today,* ed. John Knox Shear (New York: FW Dodge Corporation, 1957).

the twentieth century has steel, laminated wood plastic, and reinforced concrete as well as new forms of glass. His buildings are thus light and airy in construction, they are flexible, they can be erected quickly, they are expendable. . . . Quite naturally the Church is following suit as she always has. Man is now meeting God through the Prayer Book in a "meeting house" that is as much like the representative buildings of this age as the churches have been like the representative buildings of any age. To say that there is some relation between the appearance of a church, a factory, a theatre, or an exhibit hall is to proclaim its contemporaneousness and in no sense to condemn it.[58]

By the late 1950s, at least some in the Episcopal Church were willing to embrace modern architecture and its impulse to imitate secular designs in service to the church. St. Saviour Chapel (completed in 1952), the chapel that Ludwig Mies van der Rohe created for the campus of the Illinois Institute of Technology, Chicago, was even mentioned as "one of the clearest examples of the Episcopal Church's eagerness to be truly contemporary in her church buildings."[59] With comments such as these, the ground was being prepared for additional ideas about renewal that would enter into materials for guiding Episcopal Church design in the latter decades of the century.

As was mentioned earlier, the 1960s saw Anglican theologians such as Peter Hammond and J. G. Davies publishing materials promoting liturgical renewal, ecumenical dialogue, and the use of modern architecture in church design. By the late 1980s and 1990s, American authors were publishing materials intended for the Episcopal Church (and other traditions) reflecting similar insights. Titles representing this shift in thought include Arthur Pierce Middleton's *New Wine in Old Skins: Liturgical Change and the Setting of Worship,*[60] Charles Fulton and Patrick Holtkamp's *The Church for Common Prayer: A Statement on Worship Space for the Episcopal Church, April 1, 1994,*[61] Richard Giles's *Re-Pitching the Tent: Re-Ordering the Church Building for Worship*

---

58. *Church Buildings and Furnishings,* ed. Sherman, p. 95.

59. *Church Buildings and Furnishings,* ed. Sherman, p. 96.

60. Arthur Pierce Middleton, *New Wine in Old Skins: Liturgical Change and the Setting of Worship* (Wilton, Conn.: Morehouse-Barlow, 1988).

61. Charles N. Fulton and Patrick J. Holtkamp, *The Church for Common Prayer: A Statement on Worship Space for the Episcopal Church, April 1, 1994* (New York: Episcopal Church Building Fund, 1994). In this statement a centralized approach to worship space is represented, similar to the designs proposed by many others active in the liturgical movement. The bibliography contains materials by authors from a variety of traditions, including Protestant and Roman Catholic. Also released was a companion videotape, "Churches for Common Prayer," which illustrated the approach to worship space design presented in the statement.

and Mission,[62] and William Seth Adams' *Moving the Furniture: Liturgical Theory, Practice, and Environment.*[63] Although a little behind other denominations, the Episcopal Church did eventually reflect the ecumenical, liturgical, and modern architectural priorities evident in other traditions.

In Lutheran circles, the Department of Church Architecture of the United Lutheran Church in America published a manual entitled *Organizing and Operating the Building Program* in 1954. In 1958 a revised edition of this booklet was released as *Manual for Organizing and Managing the Building Program.*[64] The revised, sixty-six-page booklet outlined details for establishing the various committees deemed necessary for pursuing a new or renovated church building project. Evidence of the influence of the ecumenical and liturgical movements could be seen in the inclusion of references to materials, both Roman Catholic and Protestant (including many National Council of Churches materials), intended to enhance the congregation's understanding of worship and architecture. Modern architectural designs for churches were featured in some of the recommended resources, but not always in a positive way. An example is this statement listed under the heading "Principles for the Use of the New Church" (drawn from a "dedication booklet" of the Evangelical Lutheran Church of the Redeemer, Atlanta, Georgia): "The new church proper shall be used exclusively for prayer, meditation, and worship. All business, social, and educational meetings shall be held in other parts of the church plant."[65] Twenty years later, not all Lutheran materials would promote this principle. Theological concerns for stewardship and ministry would cause some Lutheran congregations to seek to develop multipurpose worship spaces, and permission to do so was incorporated into materials supported by the denomination (see below).

In 1965 the Missouri Synod Lutheran Church released *Architecture and the Church.*[66] A commission composed of professional architects and theologians

---

62. Richard Giles, *Re-Pitching the Tent: Re-Ordering the Church Building for Worship and Mission* (Norwich: Canterbury Press, 1996; revised and expanded edition, 1999). The book was also published by the Liturgical Press (Collegeville, Minn.: Liturgical Press, 1999).

63. William Seth Adams, *Moving the Furniture: Liturgical Theory, Practice, and Environment* (New York: Church Publishing Incorporated, 1999).

64. *Organizing and Operating the Building Program* (New York: Department of Church Architecture, The United Lutheran Church in America, 1954); *Manual for Organizing and Managing the Building Program* (New York: Department of Church Architecture, The United Lutheran Church in America, 1958).

65. *Manual for Organizing and Managing the Building Program,* p. 46.

66. The Commission on Church Architecture of the Lutheran Church–Missouri Synod, *Architecture and the Church* (St. Louis: Concordia Publishing House, 1965).

produced this approximately 100-page document addressing the entire process of church design and execution. It mentioned everything from establishing the building committee to master planning to using modern building techniques and materials. Photographs included at the end of the book feature outstanding Missouri Synod churches designed by architects of international renown such as Pietro Belluschi and Eero Saarinen, as well as churches of Episcopal, Congregational, and Methodist traditions.

In 1975 the Lutheran Church in America released *Space for Worship: Some Thoughts on Liturgy, Architecture, Art* by Ralph R. Van Loon. Van Loon was a theologian who focused on creating a worship environment that would accommodate the whole range of liturgical celebrations of the community *and* would accommodate a variety of nonliturgical activities.[67] Although he did not quote him directly, Van Loon appears to be building on the work of the Lutheran architect Edward A. Sövik in his booklet. In 1973 Sövik published *Architecture for Worship,* a book delineating his own theological reflections on church design and recommendations for contemporary church architecture.[68] Many of the ideas in *Space for Worship* paralleled Sövik's suggestions for church architecture (and Sövik's book was noted in the bibliography). Van Loon mentioned paying attention to the engagement of the congregation in worship, along with considering flexibility in the worship space (for example, moveable chairs and furnishings). He spoke of the architecture of the space as the servant of the liturgy, designed to enhance the work of the people of God. In his bibliography Van Loon directed his readers to several ecumenical resources, all of which highlighted similar concerns for worship space design.[69]

In 1987 the Lutheran Church in America released *Where We Worship* by Walter C. Huffman and S. Anita Stauffer and *Where We Worship: Leader's Guide and Process Guide* by Walter C. Huffman and Ralph R. Van Loon (edited by S. Anita Stauffer).[70]

---

67. Ralph R. Van Loon, *Space for Worship: Some Thoughts on Liturgy, Architecture, Art* (Philadelphia: Lutheran Church in America, 1975; revised edition, 1982), p. 7.

68. Edward A. Sövik, *Architecture for Worship* (Minneapolis: Augsburg Publishing House, 1973).

69. In the second edition the bibliography included titles such as *When Faith Takes Form* by D. Bruggink and C. Droppers; *Making the Building Serve the Liturgy,* edited by Gilbert Cope; *Modern Architecture and Christian Celebration* by Frédéric Debuyst; *Environment and Art in Catholic Worship;* and *Liturgy and Architecture* by Peter Hammond.

70. Walter C. Huffman and S. Anita Stauffer, *Where We Worship* (Minneapolis: Augsburg Publishing House, 1987); Walter C. Huffman and Ralph R. Van Loon, *Where We Worship: Leader's Guide and Process Guide* (Minneapolis: Augsburg Publishing House, 1987).

These books emerged from a joint committee on worship, with representatives from the Association of Evangelical Lutheran Churches, the American Lutheran Church, the Evangelical Lutheran Church in Canada, the Lutheran Church in America, and the Lutheran Church–Missouri Synod. Unlike Van Loon's earlier book, the guide he co-authored with Huffman mentioned Sövik explicitly in the preface: "Edward Sövik has profoundly influenced church architecture through his designs, writings, and lectures, and the spirit of his work has greatly shaped our approach to worship space."[71] As testimony, the guide features photographs of several of Sövik's churches. The guide also emphasizes the role of the people in worship, the importance of Word and sacrament (especially as shared meal), and qualities of the "serving" liturgical environment such as hospitality, flexibility, and unity (to encourage the connection in the priesthood of all believers). And accents on simplicity and beauty in the space, with an orientation toward God in the ordinary (via the incarnation of Christ), are familiar themes drawn from ecumenical, liturgical renewal dialogues of the mid-twentieth century.[72]

The Presbyterian and Reformed traditions had figures such as Donald J. Bruggink, a theologian, and Carl H. Droppers, an architect, to provide guidance for church architectural design in the mid-twentieth century. In 1965 Bruggink and Droppers released their substantial work (just over 700 pages), *Christ and Architecture: Building Presbyterian/Reformed Churches*.[73] The first section of the book (almost 500 pages) was written by Bruggink, who taught historical theology at Western Theological Seminary, Holland, Michigan. He explored a Reformed understanding of the Christian faith and its implications for contemporary church design. He was passionate in his analysis, seeking to restore an earlier Reformed central focus on Word *and* sacrament in worship. Bruggink made use of ecumenical reflections, quoting from current thought in Roman Catholic and Protestant circles concerned with liturgical renewal, and illustrated his preferences through many images of contemporary churches from the Netherlands (primarily), Switzerland, and Germany. He clearly emphasized the community in worship, gathered around the Word and sacrament. He discussed the power of the symbol at length, and encouraged simplicity and

---

71. Huffman and Stauffer, *Where We Worship*, p. 5.

72. Ultimately Sövik's approach would be promoted in videotape form as "Architecture for Worship" (2002), produced and distributed by Luther Productions from Luther Seminary, St. Paul, Minnesota.

73. Donald J. Bruggink and Carl H. Droppers, *Christ and Architecture: Building Presbyterian/Reformed Churches* (Grand Rapids: Wm. B. Eerdmans, 1965).

"honesty" in aesthetic expression. Droppers, an architect grounded in modern architectural design and on the faculty at Western Reserve University, wrote the second section of the book. He outlined a process by which to pursue church building, making many design suggestions consonant with Bruggink's theological reflections.

In 1971 Bruggink and Droppers published *When Faith Takes Form: Contemporary Churches of Architectural Integrity in America*.[74] This volume promoted the combination of liturgical renewal and modern church design across denominational lines, featuring twelve new churches for Baptist, Presbyterian, Roman Catholic, United Methodist, Reformed, and Lutheran congregations. Over half of the churches utilize a centralized plan for the worship space, gathering the congregation around a slightly elevated altar/table and ambo/pulpit area.

Both books by Bruggink and Droppers were recommended in the bibliographies of church-building guides intended for multiple traditions at least into the late 1980s, a testimony to the value others found in their work and suggestions.

CONCLUSIONS

The renewal of the liturgy would not have been sustainable if the environments for worship had not changed. Orienting churches toward placing more emphasis on communal worship activities and seeking to encourage full and active participation required altering worship spaces. The deep desire to relate to the secular communities in which the church found itself, and to minister to the deep needs of the hurting world, were combined with the elevation of the people at worship. The servant church was challenged to engage both the faithful and the unfaithful in life and in ministry. Service to the faithful and to the world came to be viewed as critical. Hospitality, flexibility, simplicity, and beauty were emphasized as appropriate pursuits in consideration of designs for spaces for worship and other ministries.

Contemporary expressions, styles, and forms of architectural design that bore the mark of modern authenticity found a place in the aesthetic repertoire of the mid-twentieth-century church. Sources of inspiration for the art and architecture of the church were not restricted to past ecclesial traditions, but could be located in the ordinary (or vernacular) expressions of this world. Twentieth-century architects,

---

74. Donald J. Bruggink and Carl H. Droppers, *When Faith Takes Form: Contemporary Churches of Architectural Integrity in America* (Grand Rapids: Wm. B. Eerdmans, 1971).

often suspicious of historical styles of design, shaped churches according to an expression we now identify as uniquely "modern." In the wake of ecumenism, similar approaches to design were established across denominational lines. Theologically, one could sense the immanence of God to a significant degree in many modern churches because of the implementation of directives emerging from both the liturgical renewal movement and the modern architecture movement.

It is now time to see this phenomenon as it took embodied forms in Europe and the United States. In Chapter Six I will feature early examples from Europe, and in Chapter Seven I will explore churches from the United States that exhibit a sense of immanence.

AN ARCHITECTURE OF IMMANENCE: EARLY EXAMPLES IN EUROPE

The church edifice today is intended for the people of our times. Hence it must be fashioned in such way that the people of our times may recognize and feel that it is addressed to them. The most significant and the most worthy needs of modern mankind must here find their fulfillment; the urge toward community life, the desire for what is true and genuine, the wish to advance from what is peripheral to central and essential, the demand for clarity, lucidity, intelligibility, the longing for quiet and peace, for a sense of warmth and security.

THE REVEREND THEODOR KLAUSER and the CATHOLIC BISHOPS OF GERMANY,
"Directives for the Building of a Church" (1947)

A HOST OF CHURCHES in Europe and the United States that were built in the twentieth century reflect the integration of influences from the ecumenical movement, the liturgical movement, and modern architecture. In this chapter I will feature a variety of church buildings from Europe to help illustrate the resulting range of design expressions. I will briefly explore certain Roman Catholic and Protestant churches to help illustrate some early models (from the 1920s and 1930s) that functioned as prototypes for a more "immanent" church architecture. In particular I will feature the work of architects Auguste Perret, Otto Bartning, Dominikus Böhm, and Rudolf Schwarz.

Church of Notre Dame, Auguste Perret

If Unity Temple (1906-1909), designed by Frank Lloyd Wright, could be called the first modern church in the United States, then Auguste Perret's Church of Notre Dame, Le Raincy, France, completed in 1923, is a good candidate for the first modern church in Europe.[1] Perret (1874-1954), a French architect, used reinforced concrete as a primary building material for his church. Although reinforced concrete had been invented early in the nineteenth century, it had been used primarily for civil engineering projects. It was considered too crude, at least when left exposed, for churches.

Notre Dame du Raincy is longitudinal, resembling a basilican design, but it has walls composed of thin reinforced concrete pierced with pieces of colored glass that function largely as screens. The weight of the roof is borne by slender columns slightly tapered from top to bottom. The roof is also reinforced concrete, molded in the shape of a barrel vault down the center with shallow vaults along both side aisles. A rectangular bell tower is located at one end of the church, with the same design of glass piercing concrete used in the walls of the church. The interior, designed to seat up to 2,000 people, exhibits a unified space of nave and chancel, with the altar elevated at the front. Chairs are provided for seating. Light is ample in the space via the large curtain walls of glass. The color of this glass intensifies in hue as one approaches the altar area.

In seeking to capture a modern architectural spirit of design, Perret used contemporary building materials without hiding them, made tremendous use of light, and articulated the space in such a way that the interior areas are revealed in accordance with the exterior massing of volumes. In other words, a structural simplicity was evident in his design, with correspondence between the form of the building and its intended function. (The materials Perret chose to use also kept the cost of the church modest for its time.)[2] The unified worship space removed the choir area of neo-Gothic design that separated the congregation from the altar. Perret presented a space that sought to draw the congregation closer to the clergy at the altar and to foster increased unity and participation in the celebration of the Eucharist.

---

1. It is true, as Nikolaus Pevsner recalls, that Anatole de Baudot used concrete in 1894 as a primary construction material for St. Jean de Montmartre (completed in 1902), even choosing not to conceal the material. But de Baudot continued to employ a Gothic model in his design of the church, remaining attached to the principles of his training under Labrouste and Viollet-le-Duc. See Nikolaus Pevsner, *The Sources of Modern Architecture and Design* (New York: Oxford University Press, 1968), p. 150.

2. The construction cost was 600,000 francs, approximately $120,000. See Albert Christ-Janer and Mary Mix Foley, *Modern Church Architecture* (New York: McGraw-Hill, 1962), p. 11.

Foto Marburg/ Art Resource, NY

Exterior of the Church of Notre Dame, Le Raincy (architect: Auguste Perret, 1923). Perret took a traditional basilican plan for a church and applied a modern architectural aesthetic to its articulation.

Interior of Church of Notre Dame, Le Raincy. Especially striking are the thin, exposed columns bearing the support of the structure, the pierced concrete and stained-glass walls in gradually changing hues, and the drawing together of the traditional nave and chancel areas.

Perret's unified approach to worship space, which sparked some of the goals of the liturgical movement, became commonplace in church building after World War II. Notre Dame du Raincy was Perret's first church commission. He garnered several other church commissions, but he is primarily remembered for his first modern church design.[3]

CHURCHES DESIGNED BY OTTO BARTNING

While France gave us Perret, who initiated an approach to modern church architecture, Germany proved to be an even more significant source for prophetic voices. Otto Bartning (1883-1959) was an influential, early architectural voice. He designed a number of churches displaying concerns for both modern aesthetic sensibilities and congregational participation, including *Die Sternkirche,* or the Star Church, 1922 (not built); *Auferstehungskirche,* or Resurrection Church, Essen, 1930; and *Die Stahlkirche,* or the Steel Church, 1928.

A hypothetical ground plan for "The Star Church" (Die Sternkirche; architect: Otto Bartning, 1922). The pulpit is in the center of the space, with the altar in close proximity. The choir and organ are located in two sections behind the pulpit, with congregational seating gathered around the pulpit in the remaining five sections.

3. Other churches include Church of St. Thérèse, Montmagny (completed in 1925), and Church of St. Joseph, Le Havre (completed in 1959). The latter is interesting for its square plan and its location of the altar in the center of the congregational seating.

The design for the Star Church showed a series of overlapping, external shells formed around a circular, heptagonal shape. Modern materials were projected for use in this plan. The unified interior space was designed to facilitate worship. It featured raked (inclined) flooring on the interior for congregational seating around three-quarters of the worship space, and pulpit and altar areas that were pushed toward the center of the space (a central pulpit with the altar elevated behind it). In this design Bartning sought to emphasize a strong sense of the community gathered around Word and sacrament.

Although the Star Church was never built, Bartning used many of the same ideas in his execution of his Resurrection Church in Essen. However, instead of using an overlapping shell form for the exterior, Bartning stacked several circular levels, in decreasing size, one on top of another. The exterior is constructed of brick, concrete, glass, and metal. The interior is circular, with a baptismal font located in the absolute center of the space. Near the font is a slightly elevated altar, with the pulpit located above and to the side of it. Spaces for the choir and the organ are located behind and above the altar area. Seating for the congregation is placed on a raked surface in a semicircle, oriented toward the pulpit and altar areas. Levels of clerestory glass provide ample light in the worship area.

Bartning also achieved a contemporary design using modern materials in his Resurrection Church. His centralized plan seeks to remind the people that they are the community gathered around both Word and sacrament. The congregational seating, spread out in a semicircle, helped to keep the environment from being too static. This was an influential design: worship spaces with centralized seating arrangements (especially semicircular or fan-shaped) would come to be reproduced with various exteriors in many countries throughout the twentieth century.

Bartning's Steel Church was a massive structure of copper, steel, and glass, built to house the Evangelical Exhibition at the International Press Exhibition in Cologne in 1928.[4] Following the exhibition, the church was taken down and rebuilt in Essen in 1929. Sadly, in 1944, the church was bombed and destroyed.

In conceiving his design, Bartning was particularly concerned about architectural expressions for a modern age:

If this gathering of the community be not only a passing historical pageant, but a living force in modern life, the church structure itself must be more than a passing histori-

4. D. Otto Bartning, *Die Stahl Kirche* (New York: Copper & Brass Research Association, 1930), p. i.

Foto Marburg/Art Resource, NY

Foto Marburg/Art Resource, NY

Top: Exterior view of Resurrection Church, Essen (sometimes called the "Round Church"; architect: Otto Bartning, 1930). Bartning used contemporary building materials to create a centralized worship space. He used height to complement the strong horizontal accent on the gathered community.

Left: Interior view of Resurrection Church. The font was originally the central point of the space, with the altar and pulpit in close proximity. The large bank of gleaming organ pipes may diminish the significance of the cross as a focal point.

cal display. It must reveal the essential eternity of the Christian ideal in purely modern terms. It must be built in a modern manner with modern materials of construction, using the best and newest methods.[5]

Bartning used a steel frame structure and longitudinal design; vast areas of wall in stained glass encompassed his worship space. The few wood wall panels that were used, located near the floor level beneath the glass, were specially fitted between supports and covered entirely on the outside with sheet copper. The entire steel frame of the structure was exposed, with all glass and wood simply attached to the frame. The roof was copper. A bell tower was located near the structure's primary entrance. With this church, Bartning had achieved a structural expression in steel similar to that executed by Perret in reinforced concrete.

The interior worship space of the Steel Church was rectangular, but rounded at the end that held the altar. A unified nave and chancel design was used, with the altar area only slightly raised from the floor of the nave. Slender steel columns supported the roof. Tremendous light flooded the space. Featuring "three materials which have been melted in fire — glass, steel, and copper," Bartning's modern church was completed in just four months.[6] With this structure Bartning proved that churches of significance could be built faster and more efficiently without dependence on replicating historical models or using traditional materials and construction.

Both Perret's Notre Dame du Raincy and Bartning's Steel Church were heralded as "successful" modern architectural expressions because of their use of new building materials, their exposure of those materials, their ample use of natural light, their dramatic reduction in ornamentation (both inside and outside), and their pursuit of open interior planning. And both helped to further the aims of the liturgical movement by unifying the worship space and focusing the people on their primary corporate celebrations as a single, gathered community.

Churches Designed by Dominikus Böhm

Dominikus Böhm (1880-1955) was another early pioneer of modern church design in Germany. Böhm taught at the School of Architecture and Applied Arts at Offenbach am Main for eighteen years, beginning in 1908. One of his students at Offenbach,

5. Bartning, *Die Stahl Kirche,* p. 1.
6. Bartning, *Die Stahl Kirche,* p. 2.

Martin Weber (an oblate at the Abbey of Maria Laach), introduced Böhm to the concerns of the liturgical movement. Böhm became aware of the deep desire to stimulate more active and conscious participation in Christian worship. In 1926 Böhm was invited to head the division of church art at the Cologne Werkschule.

Böhm's early churches are not noted for remarkable changes, but in 1927 he collaborated on a design for Our Lady of Peace Church (or *Frauenfriedenskirche*) in Frankfurt with Rudolf Schwarz (who had joined the faculty of the Offenbach in 1925).[7] Böhm and Schwarz won the design competition for the church. Although the design was never implemented, it was striking:

> [The interior was] an unadorned rectangular room, with the congregation ordered in
> a double column toward the sanctuary. The latter was undifferentiated from the nave
> except by its dramatic elevation and large windows, the only breaks in the side walls, to
> illuminate the single table altar.[8]

The Böhm/Schwarz design embodied priorities of the liturgical movement and the simplicity of modern architecture. The focus of the space remained on the altar, but the use of a unified space predisposed clergy and laity to have a more direct relationship with one another during worship. The design also featured minimal adornment and ample use of natural light, which would become favorite characteristics of many modern church designs.

Böhm had submitted an additional design to the Our Lady of Peace competition, a circular plan that eventually was translated into his design for St. Engelbert Church in Cologne-Riehl (1930-1932). St. Engelbert is a structure consisting of a series of radiating parabolic vaults in a circular shape, built of brick and concrete and sheathed in copper. The altar is located in one of the parabolic vaults, amply lighted by windows to retain a strong focal point in the interior. Böhm achieved a contemporary expression for this church, drawing the congregation together for their celebrations, although he maintained a certain distinction between the nave and chancel areas.

In 1935–1936, in the parish church of Ringenberg, Germany, Böhm achieved one of Europe's earliest modern expressions of a Roman Catholic worship space.[9] Here

---

7. Schwarz's reflections on Frauenfriedenskirche can be found in his book entitled *Kirchenbau: Welt vor der Schwelle* (Heidelberg: F. H. Kerle Verlag, 1960), pp. 12-14.

8. *Macmillan Encyclopedia of Architects*, 1st ed., s.v. "Böhm, Dominikus," p. 236.

9. Hugo Schnell, *Twentieth Century Church Architecture in Germany: Documentation, Presentation, Interpretation*, trans. by Paul J. Dine (Munich: Verlag Schnell & Steiner, 1974), p. 43.

Foto Marburg/Art Resource, NY

Foto Marburg/Art Resource, NY

Exterior view of St. Engelbert Church, Cologne-Riehl (architect: Dominikus Böhm, 1930-1932). A series of radiating parabolic vaults arranged in a circular pattern articulates the exterior structure of this building, made of brick and concrete.

Interior view of St. Engelbert Church. An elevated altar, located against the wall in one of the arches designed as a functional apse, serves as the focal point of the interior space. Both the exterior and the interior of the church exhibit minimal ornamentation.

Foto Marburg/Art Resource, NY

Foto Marburg/Art Resource, NY

Exterior view of Mary the Queen Church, Cologne-Marienburg (architect: Dominikus Böhm, 1953-1954). For this church Böhm used a design based on a square, thus reducing the distance between clergy and laity in the space. He also made the church of modest height and used minimal exterior and interior ornamentation.

Interior view of Mary the Queen Church. A shallow apse holds the altar, which is slightly elevated above the area for congregational seating. A pulpit is located to one side of the altar area. The minimal aesthetic applied to the interior focuses the faithful on the altar and the activities of the people at worship.

the altar is pushed out from the wall and surrounded by seating on three sides. A later church, Mary the Queen, Cologne-Marienburg (1953-1954), is another example of Böhm's ability to address the concerns of the liturgical movement and modern architecture. Here he created a nearly square room with a low platform extending forward from a shallow apse to locate the altar in a more intimate relationship to the congregation. The south wall, to the side of the congregation, is made entirely of stained glass in a gray-green leaf pattern.

Böhm's work received international attention and sparked interest in contemporary church design.

CHURCHES DESIGNED BY RUDOLF SCHWARZ

Rudolf Schwarz is an architect I have already referred to in earlier chapters. Several of Schwarz's churches deserve to be mentioned here for the tremendous influence they had in igniting new possibilities for church expressions.[10]

The Church of Corpus Christi (or Fronleichnamskirche), built in Aachen, West Germany (1928-1930), was an especially thought-provoking church from Schwarz (designed with the help of Hans Schwippert).[11] Corpus Christi has a simple rectangular shape and volume, white on both the interior and the exterior surfaces. Small square windows of clear glass provide light for the stark, unadorned interior, along with pendant lights on wires that stretch from the ceiling down to just above the people. The structure has a low-pitched roof, with a plain bell tower located near the worship space. The building exhibits a certain purity of form, having been reduced in detail to a minimal structure that is useful for sheltered corporate worship. Some observers suggested that the church resembled a modern factory building from the outside because of its utilitarian expression of design.[12]

Inside, there are two rows of pews, with a large central aisle and side aisles. One side aisle is wider, with a low ceiling and colonnade next to the bank of pews in the nave. A pulpit of black marble is wrapped around one pillar of this wider side aisle,

10. A recent exploration in English of Schwarz's theory and design in relation to church architecture can be found in Richard Kieckhefer, *Theology in Stone: Church Architecture from Byzantium to Berkeley* (New York: Oxford University Press, 2004), pp. 229-64.

11. Schwarz's reflections on the Church of Corpus Christi can be found in Schwarz, *Kirchenbau: Welt vor der Schwelle*, pp. 16-30.

12. Robert Maguire and Keith Murray, *Modern Churches of the World* (New York: E. P. Dutton, 1965), p. 22.

with the font located in a side chapel. The freestanding altar, also of black marble, is elevated seven steps above the floor at the front of the space. In this design Schwarz focused on simplicity and the function of the space in facilitating communal celebration of the Eucharist. He was particularly cognizant of Romano Guardini's emphasis on the meaningfulness of emptiness.[13]

It is interesting to note that the design of the Church of Corpus Christi coincided with the establishment of CIAM (the International Congress for Modern Architecture mentioned earlier). Although it is important to acknowledge that Corpus Christi preceded the height of influence of the International Style movement and to avoid the claim that Schwarz depended on CIAM, the church's design does appear to reflect many of CIAM's principles. While some found Schwarz's approach too sterile, he did open up new avenues for considering the significance of the gathered community in worship through his application of an aesthetic of reduction. Corpus Christi may even have functioned as a necessary purge for many in the church, a powerful rejection of excessive historical trappings that could be augmented slowly over time once a suitable minimal base had been established. Those championing liturgical renewal in the early twentieth century wanted to make a tangible statement that the people at worship are more important than the building that shelters them, and Corpus Christi is an excellent example of a logical architectural expression of such an emphasis.

Later churches that Schwarz designed are not quite as spartan as Corpus Christi, but they reflect similar impulses of design. The Church of St. Anna, Düren, West Germany (1956), was a pilgrimage site destroyed during World War II.[14] Rubble from the old church was incorporated into the new church building. Steel, reinforced concrete, stone, and glass brick are the primary materials used for the church. Schwarz's design here is similar in shape and style to that of Corpus Christi, but the addition of a shorter nave to the side creates an "L" shape instead of a simple rectangle. The roof is flat. Natural light floods the interior through the ample use of glass brick along the two walls that form the inside of the "L" (the longer of the two walls is set at a slight angle). There is seating capacity for 800 people, with two rows of pews provided in the longer nave (used especially for occasional services) and one row of pews in the shorter nave (used for the regular parish services). Adjoining the two naves is a wide aisle with a lower ceiling that contains the main entrance to the

---

13. Maguire and Murray, *Modern Churches of the World*, p. 24.

14. Schwarz's reflections on the Church of St. Anna can be found in Schwarz, *Kirchenbau: Welt vor der Schwelle*, pp. 223-35.

Exterior view of the Church of Corpus Christi, Aachen (architect: Rudolf Schwarz, 1928-1930). Designing with the assistance of Hans Schwippert, Schwarz gave Corpus Christi a longitudinal orientation but used a radically simplified articulation of design. The general unification of nave and chancel and the focus on a single altar were unusual at this early date.

Interior view of the Church of Corpus Christi. The bare white walls and clear glass brought tremendous light into the space. This approach encouraged focus on the congregation at worship, gathered before a common, freestanding altar.

building. This wide aisle houses the font and a small altar with reliquary and votive lights. A slightly elevated, freestanding altar is located at the joining point of the two naves, with the pulpit nearby to one side. An abstracted "tree" form is made of stone and glass brick in the exterior wall behind the altar, but otherwise there is little additional adornment to the warm tone of the natural stone. The white, "cold" appearance of Corpus Christi is exchanged for earth tones here, but the dramatic reduction of ornamentation remains.[15]

Toward the end of his architectural career, Schwarz experimented with a more centralized plan in churches with smaller seating capacities. At Holy Family Church, Oberhausen, West Germany (1956-1958),[16] he used a square plan for the worship space, placing the freestanding altar on a slightly elevated area in the center of it.[17]

15. Schwarz used the longitudinal plan in other churches, sometimes adding elliptical forms to the ends of the primary form and to additional small arms of extended space (e.g., at the Church of St. Michael, Frankfurt, Germany, 1954, and Mary the Queen, Saarbrücken, Germany, 1959).

16. Schwarz's reflections on this chapel can be found in Schwarz, *Kirchenbau: Welt vor der Schwelle*, pp. 269-76.

17. As early as 1935, architect Hans Herkommer used a centralized plan for Mass to be said facing the people (with a freestanding altar and congregational seating on three sides of it) for a parish church in Ringenberg, Germany. (Hugo Schnell attributed this church design to Dominikus Böhm; Herkommer is

Exterior view of Holy Family Church, Oberhausen (architect: Rudolf Schwarz, 1956-1958). Schwarz used a square plan for the worship space in this church. The lower half of the worship space is brick; the upper half is concrete pierced with rectangular glass panels.

Interior view of Holy Family Church. Schwarz used a central, slightly elevated altar here. Congregational seating is located on three sides of the altar area, with one side left as open space. The font is located just outside the primary worship space in an area used as a day chapel.

There is congregational seating on three sides of the altar area. The baptistery is located in an adjacent side chapel. Four tapered columns stand near the four corners of the altar area. There is little adornment of the space. Steel, reinforced concrete, brick, and glass brick are the primary components of the structure. Natural light is allowed in the worship space through the use of glass brick on the upper half of all four walls.

One of Schwarz's last churches, the Church of St. Christopher, Cologne-Niehl, West Germany (1960), also uses the centralized plan.[18] Here, however, the minimally

known to have been influenced by Böhm's design work which may have led to the confusion.) Drawings of this arrangement are featured in Peter F. Anson, *Churches: Their Plan and Furnishing*, ed. Thomas F. Croft-Fraser and H. A. Reinhold (Milwaukee: The Bruce Publishing Company, 1948), pp. 20, 59. At St. Laurentius Church, Munich, 1955-1956, architects Emil Steffann (1899-1968) and Siegfried Ostreicher also used this centralized plan of locating the people on three sides of a minimally elevated altar area in the execution of a Roman Catholic church in Germany. A number of significant European architects were addressing liturgical reforms through this centralized plan nearly ten years before the closing of the Vatican II Council meetings. Other denominations also utilized a centralized approach to arranging worship space. Two examples from this time period are structures for Anglican congregations — St. Paul Church, Bow Common, London, England, 1956-1960 (Robert Maguire and Keith Murray, architects) and St. Columba Church, Glenrothes, Scotland, 1960 (Wheeler and Sproson, architects).

18. Schwarz's reflections on this chapel can be found in Schwarz, *Kirchenbau: Welt vor der Schwelle*, pp. 296-303.

Exterior view of St. Christopher Church, Cologne-Niehl (architect: Rudolf Schwarz, 1960). St. Christopher's was the last church that Schwarz completed. The church is slightly longer than it is wide, with a minimally pitched roof. Colored glass with geometric shapes is used for clerestory illumination.

Interior view of St. Christopher Church. A simple stone altar, minimally raised, is the focal point of the space. Congregational seating is located on three sides of the altar (much like the arrangement at the chapel of Burg Rothenfel).

elevated altar area is located near one side of the slightly elongated space, with seating on three sides of the freestanding altar. Four columns stand at the corners of the primary seating area for the congregation, with the baptistery centered on a wall to one side of the worship space. Steel, reinforced concrete, and brick are the primary structural components. The roof is very slightly pitched; little exterior ornamentation is used. But there is the addition of colored glass in the industrial metal windows set in all four walls of the worship space, the use of marble and tile in the flat surface of the floor, and the presence of an abstract depiction of the resurrected Christ behind the altar. While Schwarz remains true to his reduced aesthetic, the minimal additions he allowed add a symbolic focus to the otherwise plain space.

Over the span of his architectural career, it appears that Schwarz gradually increased the amount of symbolic content in his churches. While conscious of not wanting to draw attention away from the primary communal celebrations, he did acknowledge the place of various artistic expressions. By the end of his career, he had provided a range of church designs that prompted not precise replication but inspiration for a new generation of architects in service to the whole church.

Four Architects and Their Legacy

Part of the reason that the church designs of Perret, Bartning, Böhm, and Schwarz were so influential was that their ideas were repeatedly reproduced with positive remarks in books featuring ideas for modern church design. From the late 1940s to the mid-1960s, a host of books featuring modern churches in both Europe and the United States were published. Several German titles that are cited in many English-language sources are *Betonkirchen* by Ferdinand Pfammatter, *Neue Kirchen im Erzbistum Köln, 1945-1956* by Willy Weyres, *Kirchen unserer Zeit* by Richard Biedrzynski, and *Kirchen: Handbuch für den Kirchenbau* by Willy Weyres and Otto Bartning.[19] It is important to remember that Bartning was not the only one writing about his approach to church design; Rudolf Schwarz was also publishing works on his ideas (some of which, like *The Church Incarnate,* were translated into English).[20] And with influential architects such as Walter Gropius and Ludwig Mies van der Rohe teaching at outstanding schools of design in the United States, it is not hard to see how European designs came to be important for mid-century modern church design in the industrialized West.[21]

Titles of books in English featuring modern churches by Perret, Bartning, Böhm, and Schwarz during this same chronological period include *Modern Church Architecture* by Edward Maufe, *Churches and Temples* by Paul Thiry, Richard M. Bennett, and Henry L. Kamphoefner, *Modern Church Architecture* by Joseph Pichard, *Liturgy and Architecture* by Peter Hammond, *Modern Church Architecture: A Guide to the Form and Spirit of Twentieth-Century Religious Building* by Albert Christ-Janer and Mary Mix Foley, *The New Churches of Europe* by G. E. Kidder-Smith, and *Modern Churches of the World* by Robert Maguire and Keith Murray.[22] These titles

---

19. Ferdinand Pfammatter, *Betonkirchen* (Zürich: Benziger Verlag Einsiedeln, 1948); Willy Weyres, *Neue Kirchen im Erzbistum Köln, 1945-1956* (Düsseldorf: Verlag L. Schwann, 1957); Richard Biedrzynski, *Kirchen unserer Zeit* (Munich: Hirmer Verlag, 1958); Willy Weyres and Otto Bartning, *Kirchen: Handbuch für den Kirchenbau* (Munich: Verlag Georg D. W. Callwey, 1959).

20. One of these publications is *Kirchenbau: Welt vor der Schwelle,* where Schwarz discusses his many church projects.

21. Church designs by Frank Lloyd Wright, Mies van der Rohe, and Le Corbusier were often reproduced in these sources also.

22. Edward Maufe, *Modern Church Architecture* (London: Incorporated Church Building Society, 1948); Paul Thiry, Richard M. Bennett, and Henry L. Kamphoefner, *Churches and Temples* (New York: Reinhold Publishing Company, 1953); Joseph Pichard, *Modern Church Architecture* (New York: Orion Press, 1960); Peter Hammond, *Liturgy and Architecture* (London: Barrie & Rockliff, 1960); Albert Christ-Janer and Mary Mix

featured the European churches discussed here in a positive light (along with a host of churches from countries around the world).[23] Resources such as these were produced both for architects and for those in churches who sought guidance for contemporary church design.

Roman Catholic and Protestant church projects were featured in all of the above titles, often without distinct sections labeled by denomination. In light of the momentum of the ecumenical movement and the accelerated church-building in the mid-twentieth century, the Roman Catholic and Protestant designs featured in these books were given a wide and appreciative audience. Most readers could appreciate the virtue of emphasizing the altar/table and ambo/pulpit areas of a worship space, as well as the desire to promote active congregational participation in celebrations. It is certainly true that new insights helpful for particular denominations (e.g., a renewed emphasis on the ambo for Roman Catholic communities and a renewed emphasis on the table for many Protestants) were transmitted through these resources. However, as liturgical renewal took root and yielded some level of homogenization in worship practice, similar church designs came to be used across denominational lines. Cross-pollinization between traditions flourished through the ecumenical approach pursued by the publishers of these materials.

Foley, *Modern Church Architecture: A Guide to the Form and Spirit of Twentieth-Century Religious Building* (New York: McGraw-Hill, 1962); G. E. Kidder-Smith, *The New Churches of Europe* (New York: Holt, Rinehart & Winston, 1964); Robert Maguire and Keith Murray, *Modern Churches of the World* (New York: E. P. Dutton, 1965).

23. Not all books discussing modern church design found the early twentieth-century European churches featured here desirable. Dom E. Roulin expressed disappointment with Corpus Christi, Aachen, and the trend in Roman Catholic church architecture toward a reduction of interior ornamentation that he associated with the "Protestant church meetinghouse." See Dom E. Roulin, *Modern Church Architecture* (St. Louis: B. Herder Book Company, 1947), pp. 132-33. William Watkin is rather dismissive of postwar churches in Europe in his guide for designing the modern church. He expresses admiration for the work of Ralph Adams Cram and Charles D. Maginnis, however, and he suggests that extending their exploration of Gothic designs for our contemporary time could bear good fruit. He does acknowledge the value of refocusing on the centrality of the altar and pulpit areas of the worship space, including a simplification of ornamentation, but he continues to suggest elements of Gothic revival, such as placing the choir in front and to both sides of the altar (pushed to the wall) in an extended chancel area. See William Ward Watkin, *Planning and Building the Modern Church* (New York: F. W. Dodge Corporation, 1951), pp. 1-3, 73-75.

Conclusions

In highlighting the work of Perret, Bartning, Böhm, and Schwarz, I do not mean to imply that the work of many other fine architects was inconsequential for modern church design. To name but one example, Switzerland produced a school of architects under the influence of Karl Moser and Fritz Metzger (including two students of Moser, Hermann Baur and Otto Dreyer), who were responsible for articulating a modern church approach exhibiting sensitivity to the concerns of modern architecture and the liturgical movement.[24] Moser himself was particularly moved by Perret's church at Le Raincy, as can be seen in his church, St. Antony (St. Antonius), Basel, Switzerland (1925-1927). In the words of Edwin Heathcote, "The church [St. Antony, Basel] was not only a dramatic leap forward for ecclesiastical architecture in Switzerland but one of the first significant moments in the history of Swiss modernism, representing one of the first truly modern constructions in the century."[25] Many architects in Europe were producing significant work that helped to foster a growing sense of the immanence of God in modern churches. But Perret, Bartning, Böhm, and Schwarz occupy a unique place in providing an inspiring body of work that sparked creative modern church design for a generation of architects.

The European churches mentioned in this chapter illustrate the ushering in of a modern architectural approach to church design in concert with a desire to achieve liturgical reform meant to enhance congregational participation in worship. The approach to modern design included rejecting the significant use of historical architectural styles as models for churches, using new building materials and construction techniques, highlighting the function and utility of the building, incorporating ample natural light, and reducing the ornamentation of exterior and interior surfaces. The influence of early twentieth-century liturgical reform on church design resulted in several characteristic features, some of which overlapped with those just mentioned: using simple geometric forms for the basic layout of many churches;

---

24. In thinking of the church design work of Fritz Metzger, Peter Hammond once commented, "Switzerland was the only country in Western Christendom which, by the late thirties, had created a living tradition of church architecture. There is still no other country where modern churches of real quality take their place so naturally among the best secular buildings of their day. The 'ecclesiastical' architect does not exist. The finest Swiss churches are the work of the same architects who have created some of the most outstanding schools, hospitals, and houses of the last thirty years." See Peter Hammond, *Liturgy and Architecture* (London: Barrie & Rockliff, 1960), p. 62.

25. Edwin Heathcote and Iona Spens, *Church Builders* (New York: Academy Editions, 1997), p. 36.

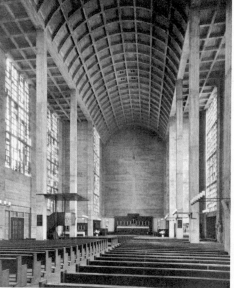

Foto Marburg/Art Resource, NY

Foto Marburg/Art Resource, NY

Exterior view of Church of St. Antonius, Basel (architect: Karl Moser, 1927). Inspired by A. Perret's Church of Notre Dame, Le Raincy (1923), Moser expressed a traditional basilican plan for a church in concrete and steel. St. Antonius was one of the earliest expressions of modern architecture in Switzerland.

Interior of Church of St. Antonius, Basel. Moser used a barrel vaulted ceiling in the space, echoing Le Raincy, though there the ceiling is unadorned, while here it is covered with a pattern of recessed squares. As at Le Raincy, narrow columns support the barrel vault. The chancel area is fairly low and shallow (as at Le Raincy, but less elevated), the goal being to unify clergy and laity in worship.

reducing the height of churches to a more modest scale; using ample light in the interior spaces; and reducing ornamentation on the exterior and interior surfaces. Traditional symbols and liturgical appointments were retained, but they were manifest in simplified ways that sought to provide a more significant focus on communal, ritual celebrations of the faith. And a unity between spaces designated for clergy and laity was pursued, often resulting in a centrally planned arrangement of seating focused on the altar/table and ambo/pulpit. An increasing sense of the immanence of God was communicated through the environments achieved through this combination of architectural and liturgical renewal.

The models of modern church architecture in Europe featured in this chapter came to influence design in other countries as well. Increased contact between Europe and the United States because of the world wars and the educational exchanges of ideas through direct contact, printed resources, and teaching in schools of architecture promoted these modern design priorities and expressions to faith communities on both continents. It is time now to examine some representative churches from the United States to develop a sense in which "God with us" came to be emphasized in worship environments in America.

CHAPTER SEVEN

AN ARCHITECTURE OF IMMANENCE: SELECTED EXAMPLES IN AMERICA

The hiatus between architecture for the church and architecture for other institutions and groups in society exposes the shallowness of our understanding of the Gospel and its relevance to all areas of our common life and all realms of society. The continuing penchant among many churches for Gothic and Renaissance denies their assertion that Christianity has significance for all aspects of man's life. It is an architectural denial of the meaning of the Incarnation and the belief that God continues to speak his Word in the language of each new age.

MARVIN HALVERSON, "On Getting Good Architecture for the Church" (1957)

CONTRASTS ARE OFTEN helpful for teasing out particular distinctive qualities in objects. With that in mind, I will follow the examination of European churches expressing immanence with an exploration of a variety of churches in the United States from the 1940s to the 1980s that emphasize immanence.[1] I will feature a range of churches that could be said to reflect an increasing emphasis on God's immanence. As noted earlier, no church is completely devoid of some references to tran-

---

1. The limitations of this study will only allow for the examination of modern churches reflecting immanence to varying degrees in the United States. Such a choice will illustrate the gradual emergence of and emphasis on immanence (and related emphases discussed in Chapters One to Five) among certain American churches. A similar spectrum could be illustrated among select European churches as well. *Contemporary Church Architecture* by Reinhard Gieselmann (London: Thames & Hudson, 1972) surveys primarily European churches from the 1950s and 1960s. The pattern in modern church building pointing increasingly to God's immanence could be located within its pages. *New Trends in Church Architecture* by Justus Dahinden (New York: Universe Books, 1967) also features churches that reflect a pattern of "immanent" design. More recent

scendence as well, since the very designation of "church" indicates both a reference to the Divine who is beyond our world and a reference to the building itself, which is made for use by people in this world. But as the 1960s and 1970s progressed, many churches resonating with the liturgical renewal concern for locating God's presence in the assembly and engaging the social and material needs of local communities tended to adopt architectural forms that pointed increasingly to God's immanence.

AMERICAN RELIGION, CULTURE, AND THE GROWTH OF THE CHURCH

The early European church buildings examined thus far were built between and just after the world wars. The activity of the wars created circumstances that fueled the dissemination of similar ideas in Europe and the United States in relation to liturgical renewal, ecumenical activity, and modern expressions of architecture. Common concerns for political, social, and economic stability increased the amount of contact between these various nations. The consequences of the wars encouraged many intellectuals to flee across Europe, with many emigrating to the United States, including architects of renown. Several of these prominent architects took up teaching positions in schools of architecture in the United States. Continued joint efforts to combat common political threats fostered strong ties between European nations and the United States. And the wars themselves gave Americans (including future architects) increased exposure to modern European architecture and created opportunities for rebuilding numerous churches throughout Europe.

Economic prosperity and optimism after the wars helped to foster an atmosphere conducive to a major movement toward church building. In the United States, people began to earn better incomes and have children in greater numbers. As a consequence, they wanted homes for their families outside of traditional urban areas, and

---

books in English that significantly feature modern European church architecture of the type I am examining in the second half of the twentieth century include Hugo Schnell, *Twentieth-Century Church Architecture in Germany: Documentation, Presentation, Interpretation*, trans. Paul J. Dine (Munich: Verlag Schnell & Steiner, 1974); Randall S. Lindstrom, *Creativity and Contradiction: European Churches since 1970* (Washington, D.C.: American Institute of Architects, 1988); Edwin Heathcote and Iona Spens, *Church Builders* (New York: Academy Editions, 1997); Wolfgang Jean Stock, *European Church Architecture, 1950-2000* (Munich: Prestel Publishing House, 2002); and Wolfgang Jean Stock, *Architectural Guide: Christian Sacred Buildings in Europe since 1950* (Munich: Prestel Publishing House, 2004).

thus developments in domestic architecture grew rapidly in areas that became known as suburbs. The thinking was that the suburbs required a support infrastructure — including churches — outside of the city. In reflecting on the state of religion in the United States following World War II, sociologist Robert Wuthnow commented,

> To some extent, the prevailing mood was indeed optimistic. Even before the war had ended, religious leaders were looking to the future to determine what role their organizations should play. Some emphasized new fields in which missionary work could take place as a result of peace, trade, and new regimes. Others, recognizing the serious devastation wrought by the war, encouraged congregations to shoulder the responsibility of providing relief. Preaching, church schools, fighting communism, guarding against totalitarianism, offering inner security in the coming atomic age were all discussed as priorities for ministry. . . . Wartime prosperity had generated what one editorial described as "immense funds for postwar building needs." As soon as restrictions on building materials were lifted, these funds were expended to bring long-anticipated plans for renovation and expansion to fruition.[2]

The euphoria of winning a war that engaged much of the world, optimism about confronting the challenges of modern life together, economic prosperity, and a baby boom all helped to foster rapid growth among churches in the United States in the years immediately after World War II. Church building was pursued with great vigor to keep pace with increasing membership, as Wuthnow explains:

> Between 1946 and 1949, the Southern Baptist Convention alone established 500 new churches at a cost of $97 million. In the same years, Methodists were spending almost as much on new buildings and improvements as their entire operating budget. And more was to come: by late 1949, it was reported that a billion dollars of new construction was underway in Protestant denominations. Nor was the building limited to Protestants; Catholics also embarked on major programs: 125 new hospitals were under construction, over 1,000 new elementary schools were being opened, and 3,000 new parishes were being added.[3]

2. Robert Wuthnow, *The Restructuring of American Religion: Society and Faith since World War II* (Princeton: Princeton University Press, 1988), pp. 35-36.

3. Wuthnow, *The Restructuring of American Religion*, p. 36.

Church building was pursued at unprecedented rates in the 1950s and into the 1960s. In an article published in 1955 by the F. W. Dodge Corporation, George Cline Smith shared these words with architects who were considering designing buildings for faith communities in the United States:

> The economic aspect of the situation boils down simply to this: it is reasonable to expect that in the coming ten years, some 70,000 churches and synagogues will be constructed or substantially altered at a total cost of nearly six billion dollars. . . . This is considered to be a conservative estimate, in the light of past and present trends. . . . It is entirely possible, therefore, that the estimate may be on the low side, in view of our rapid population growth and movement, current prosperity, and the increasing emphasis on church-going. . . . Current activity in church construction is running at the highest rate in history. Contract awards for religious building in the 37 eastern states during the first three months of 1955 totaled $128 million. That's an increase of 60 per cent above the previous first-quarter record set in 1951, and 61 per cent above the first quarter of 1954.[4]

Optimism, prosperity, mobility, and increasing church growth forged extraordinary interest in building new churches. An increasing number of architects were becoming interested in helping to address the visible needs of these faith communities. The influences of the liturgical movement, the ecumenical movement, and modern architecture all came together to shape this flood of new churches. Because of the many new modern materials and building techniques that had become available, modern churches took on a host of new shapes and expressions. In response to the liturgical movement and Vatican II, a newly discovered emphasis on the people at worship and in ministry to the world was pursued. And much sharing of ideas concerning all areas of church life, including the design of churches, took place between traditions because of the concern for ecumenical exchanges.

In what follows I will examine select examples of mid- to late-twentieth-century modern churches. Each of the churches examined expresses a modern architectural design using contemporary building materials and construction techniques. In the tremendous array of new churches built in the United States following World War II, references to both the transcendent and the immanent characteristics of God's nature can be identified in nearly all of them. I will highlight those aspects of

4. George Cline Smith, "Seventy Thousand Churches in Ten Years," in *Religious Buildings for Today* (New York: F. W. Dodge Corporation, 1957), p. 33.

design, both interior and exterior, that emphasize an understanding of God's presence in, with, and through the people of God. In the process I will note the interesting range of emphasis on qualities accenting immanence in both monumental edifices and humble structures.

MODERN CHURCH BUILDINGS REFERRING TO GOD'S IMMANENCE TO A LESSER DEGREE

Benedictine Abbey Church of St. John the Baptist, Collegeville, Minnesota

Marcel Breuer (1902-1981) was chosen as the architect for this Benedictine community in Minnesota that had been active in promoting the liturgical movement in the United States. Breuer had been trained at the Bauhaus in Germany. He had studied with both Walter Gropius and Ludwig Mies van der Rohe. Breuer too had emigrated to the United States by 1930. In 1937 he joined Walter Gropius at Harvard University as a professor of architecture. Breuer chose to work with the plasticity of reinforced concrete for the Benedictine community church, seeking a more monumental presence in design.[5] The church was built from 1958 to 1961.

For the structure Breuer designed a great bell tower or, as it is sometimes called, a bell "banner." The tower consists of a large rectangular slab of reinforced concrete mounted on four legs that stretch down across the church entrance, forming a sort of gate to the worship space. The slab is 100 feet wide, and the tower is 112 feet high. An oak cross is mounted in the slab near the top, and a row of bells is mounted beneath the cross. The exterior wall of the church just behind the bell tower is a honeycomb pattern of reinforced concrete inset with colored glass. The stained-glass pattern, referring to liturgical seasons and the life of the church, was designed by Bronislaw Bak. Light reflects off the large slab of the tower and illuminates the interior through the stained glass.

The church has the general shape of a trapezoid, with the two sides of the church angled toward one another as they meet with the shorter rear wall. The side walls are folded slabs of reinforced concrete that assume an upside-down V-pat-

---

5. Breuer's St. Francis de Sales Church, Muskegon, Michigan (1964-1966), which Breuer designed with his partner, Herbert Beckhard, is another outstanding example of his ability to work with reinforced concrete in a creative and monumental fashion. He uses a geometry of hyperbolic paraboloids to give this award-winning church a unique form and presence in the community.

Exterior view of the Abbey Church of St. John the Baptist, Collegeville, Minnesota (architect: Marcel Breuer, 1958-1961). The trapezoidal shape of this church — with its flat roof, angled exterior walls, and honeycomb facade filled with stained glass — marks this building as an icon of modern church architecture.The unusual shape of the bell tower is a significant departure from historical rectangular designs.

tern as they rise to meet the flat concrete roof. Local granite is used to face exterior surfaces. The interior walls are unfinished concrete, with the patterns of the wooden molds visible in the surface texture.

The baptistery is located in the narthex of the church, with a statue of St. John the Baptist sculpted by artist Doris Caesar. The baptistery is on an axis with the free-standing altar inside the worship space; this arrangement symbolically represents the journey from initiation to celebration of the Eucharist.

The worship space is centrally planned. The freestanding altar sits slightly raised on a granite platform near the center of the church. Four banks of pews face the altar and fill half of the space that serves as the nave. The other half of the space holds choir stalls formed in a semicircle around three sides of the altar area, where the brothers can celebrate the Eucharist and pray the daily office together. The seat-

Interior view of the Abbey Church of St. John the Baptist. The central plan of this space is striking, with the monastic brothers and others who gather for worship brought into relatively close proximity around the slightly elevated, freestanding altar.

ing capacity for the nave and the choir stalls is 1,450. The abbot's chair is located in the middle of the monks' seating, on a granite platform directly behind the altar. A large red silk screen was originally located near the rear wall of the church, behind the abbot's chair. A cantilevered balcony above the nave provides additional seating for 500 people. Clear glass in the lower side walls adds to the natural light coming in through the stained-glass wall.

The unified space that allows clergy and laity to worship together clearly reflects the priorities of the liturgical movement. The tremendous scale of the bell tower and the church itself remind one of the transcendence of God at the same time that the interior organization of the space reminds one of the focus on God with us.[6]

6. Additional information concerning the planning and building of St. John's can be found in Whitney S. Stoddard, *Adventure in Architecture: Building the New St. John's* (New York: Longmans, Green & Company, 1958).

Exterior view of the Cathedral of St. Mary of the Assumption, San Francisco, California (architect: Pietro Belluschi; engineer: Pier Luigi Nervi, 1965-1970). Hyperbolic paraboloids were the inspiration for the warped surfaces exhibited in the design of St. Mary's. The exterior is covered in travertine marble, but exhibits minimal ornamentation.

Interior view of St. Mary's. A slightly elevated altar area is surrounded on three sides by congregational seating in the worship space. The coffered, angled ceiling is pierced by the stained glass of artist Gyorgy Kepes.

The Cathedral of St. Mary of the Assumption, San Francisco, California

Architect Pietro Belluschi (1899-1994) and engineer Pier Luigi Nervi (1892-1979) consulted with the architectural firm of McSweeney, Ryan, and Lee on the design of a new cathedral for San Francisco following a fire that devastated the previous church building in 1962.

In this structure, under construction from 1965 to 1970, Belluschi and Nervi exploited the ability of reinforced concrete to achieve warped surfaces in their design. Reinforced concrete and steel are the primary materials employed to create the unusual form of the cathedral. Belluschi and Nervi used permutations of hyperbolic paraboloids to express both a base for the church and a 190-foot-high cupola in the form of a three-dimensional Greek cross to rest upon this base. The exterior of the cathedral is covered in travertine marble but does not feature elaborate ornamentation.

The church features a centralized plan for the primary worship space. It has seating (for up to 2,500) on three sides of a slightly elevated altar area. A freestanding altar is located in the center of this area, with the cathedra behind the altar. A low rosewood reredos is behind the cathedra, and an ambo is set to one side of the altar. No seat is more than 100 feet from the altar area. The interior space features minimal adornment, but two installations of art are significant. The first is the stained-glass windows designed by Gyorgy Kepes. Six feet wide by 130 feet long, they are featured at the junctures of the hyperbolic paraboloids along the sides of the cupola and overhead. The second is a baldachino of aluminum rods, designed by Richard Lippold, suspended from the cupola by slender gold wires. In the center of the baldachino is a simple gold cross. The underside of the cupola is coffered in triangular forms of exposed concrete.

The arrangement of the congregation at worship and the creation of a unified space for celebrations point to the intention of achieving a sense of "God with us" in this church. At the same time, the extraordinary expressions of form in the building and its art installations suggest a sense of God's presence above and beyond our world.[7]

The Crystal Cathedral (Garden Grove Community Church), Garden Grove, California

Architect Philip Johnson (1906-2005), with the help of partner John Burgee, was chosen to design Robert Schuller's primary worship space for his large church in the Reformed Church in America denomination. Johnson had studied architecture with Walter Gropius at Harvard University in the late 1930s. He had worked with Mies van der Rohe, and with the help of Henry-Russell Hitchcock he had helped to identify the International Style in modern architecture. Although his earlier work reflected the influence of this style, he abandoned this approach by the 1980s, choosing instead to refer to historical design styles in his work.[8]

The vast structure of the Crystal Cathedral, 207 feet by 415 feet, was completed in 1980. Johnson chose a four-pointed star shape for the church. The structure is composed of a white, tubular steel space frame covered by more than 10,000 mir-

7. Additional information concerning the churches of Pietro Belluschi can be found in Meredith L. Clausen, *Spiritual Space: The Religious Architecture of Pietro Belluschi* (Seattle: University of Washington Press, 1992). St. Mary's Cathedral is discussed in particular on pages 126-35.

8. Johnson and Burgee's design for the AT&T Corporate Headquarters building in New York City (1984) is thought to be one of the first major projects to intentionally reflect historical idioms in opposition to the abandonment of such an approach in the International Style movement. Johnson holds an interesting historical position as a "high-profile" architectural leader who was both tremendously in favor of and opposed to the International Style of modern architecture over the span of his career.

Exterior view of the Crystal Cathedral or Garden Grove Community Church (architect: Philip Johnson with John Burgee, 1980). A four-pointed star shape functioned as the guiding inspiration for the church. A white tubular frame supports the church, with mirrored glass panels covering the wall and ceiling surfaces.

rored glass panels. A bell tower was added to the building ten years after the church was built. The tower is composed of highly polished stainless steel prisms and houses a fifty-two-bell carillon.

The interior of the church, which has no columns, reaches a height of 128 feet at points. A 185-foot stage provides room for the choir (and can accommodate over 1,000 singers and instrumentalists), the organ, the cross (17 feet high, gold-leafed), the altar, and the pulpit. The altar and the pulpit are made of granite. Two 90-foot-high doors, which can be opened electronically as desired, are located near the pulpit. The worship space has a seating capacity of 2,890. Seating in the nave is provided through pews fixed in rows on a raked surface, facing the stage. Balconies also face the stage from three sides of the space. Other than the exposure of the frame and glass panels of the structure, there is little adornment of the worship space.

The Crystal Cathedral does facilitate the worship of the congregation as they are gathered around the large stage. While the organ and the choir become the primary focal points of worship by virtue of their size, the altar and the pulpit are also important focal points. The design of the seating — with people sitting side by side

Interior view of the Crystal Cathedral. A significant stage area with a dramatic organ installation faces the seating areas for the congregation. The organ and choir appear to be dominant focal points for the people, although a large cross, altar, and pulpit are also located on the stage.

in the pews and even facing one another in the balconies — also attempts to remind worshipers of the human manifestation of the body of Christ and connect with the idea of "God in our midst." However, the grand scale and unusual appearance of the church itself in relation to the ordinary structures of the surrounding community place a prominent accent on the idea that the church reflects a God who is quite "other" than us.

Summary

Each of the churches mentioned in this section facilitates authentic expressions of Christian worship. Each takes some care to ensure that a sense of "God in our midst" is realized, especially by centrally organizing the congregation in the church interior and by reducing ornamentation that might distract people from focusing on their corporate worship activities. But all of these churches also allow for an understanding of God as the object of worship. The size, volume, and unusual shapes of these churches set them apart from other buildings in their settings. They have intentionally been designed in this way, in part so that people would become aware of the unique role of the church in the world. Each building is capable of reminding those who worship in it that the God of the universe is vast in relation to us, different from us, a transcendent presence. Each building is also non-traditional: the architects used modern building materials and designs differentiated from traditional church expressions. For these reasons we can identify these churches (and others like them) as offering modern and revealing accents on a theological understanding of God's immanence. Perhaps even more dramatically present, however, is the visual emphasis on the transcendent nature of God.

MODERN CHURCH BUILDINGS REFERRING TO GOD'S IMMANENCE TO A MODERATE DEGREE

First Christian Church (originally Tabernacle Church of Christ), Columbus, Indiana

Eliel Saarinen (1873-1950) designed First Christian Church for the Disciples of Christ denomination. The church was completed in 1942. First Christian is a rectangular building containing a longitudinal worship space. The building is largely made of brick, with a supporting frame of steel and reinforced concrete. The exterior of the structure has minimal ornamentation. However, at the short end of the building containing the primary entrance, panels of Indiana limestone (in a pale buff color) have been applied to the entire surface, with a large wooden cross attached to the panels just off-center. Near the church entrance stands a rectangular bell tower of significant height, also made of brick with minimal ornamentation. Additional educational and office spaces are located toward the rear of the primary worship space.

The interior worship space is basically rectangular, but asymmetrical in design. A center aisle is set slightly off-center between two banks of pews facing toward an elevated chancel area. The two side aisles vary in width. One is located under a ceiling dramatically lower than that of the adjoining nave, and it exhibits a colonnade next to the pews. The other aisle is next to a wall with floor-to-ceiling clear glass panels

Author photo

Exterior view of First Christian Church (architect: Eliel Saarinen, 1942). For this church Saarinen used a simple rectangular shape, longitudinal in orientation. A large cross, set just off-center in limestone facing, has been attached to the end of the building featuring the primary entrance.

Interior view of First Christian Church. Asymmetry marks the interior space, with the large chancel cross located off-center on the wall and an off-center central aisle creating aisles of pews of different widths for congregational seating. In recent years a small projection screen has been placed in the chancel.

Author photo

that allow much natural light into the nave. Floor-to-ceiling strips of clear glass set near the immersion baptistery at the rear of the chancel area bring additional striking illumination to the front of the space. An elevated, tub-type pulpit is located to one side of the chancel area. The altar is located behind the pulpit in the center of the chancel, with the baptistery (covered by a wooden screen that opens in the center) placed in the area behind the altar. A large wooden cross is asymmetrically located on the wall above the chancel area. A tapestry has been installed on one side of that area, but the remaining surface areas of the worship space are unadorned, revealing the structural materials of lightly colored brick and wood.

First Christian Church is reminiscent of Schwarz's Corpus Christi Church, Aachen (built from 1928 to 1930). The general basilican design with unified nave and chancel, the use of ample clear glass, the lightly colored surfaces, the varying widths of side aisles with the lower ceiling on one side, and the greatly reduced ornamentation — all are parallel expressions. First Christian clearly achieves simplicity in its design. The focus of the space is on the ritual activities of the community at worship, but the volume and orientation of the space also make reference to the significance of God as the object of worship.[9]

Trinity Lutheran Church, Walnut Creek, California

Trinity Lutheran Church, completed in 1956, was designed for the Missouri Synod Lutheran tradition.[10] It represents a collaborative effort between architect Pietro Belluschi and the firm of Skidmore, Owings, and Merrill. Trinity is basically rectangular in shape, with sides that flare out like a trapezoid above an angular base. The roof is slightly curved. The lower walls are reinforced concrete sided with stone (on both the exterior and the interior). The upper walls and roof are wood supported by angular laminated arches that are exposed on the interior. There is a wall of stained glass at the end of the building used as a primary entrance, and gray-colored cathe-

9. In 1950 Eliel Saarinen produced a very similar design in Christ Church Lutheran for a Missouri Synod Lutheran congregation located in Minneapolis, Minnesota.

10. Other Missouri Synod Lutheran churches acclaimed for their exhibition of modern design include Zion Lutheran Church, Portland, Oregon (1949-1950), designed by Pietro Belluschi, and Kramer Chapel, Concordia Theological Seminary, Fort Wayne, Indiana (1957), designed by Eero Saarinen. Kramer Chapel is important for the "A-frame" model it provided. The A-frame design, often constructed of laminated wood products, was a less expensive way to achieve a sense of height and volume in a church. Following its construction, Kramer Chapel was featured in numerous journals and books. A host of congregations adopted the A-frame design for their churches in the late 1950s and 1960s.

Exterior view of Trinity Lutheran Church (architect: Pietro Belluschi and Skidmore, Owings, & Merrill, 1956). This rectangular, longitudinal space has walls that angle inward toward a slightly rounded roof. At one end of the building a wall of stained glass rises from the entry to the roof.

Interior view of Trinity Lutheran Church. A rich wooden roof forms an arch over the stone walls of the space. Two rows of pews face the slightly raised chancel area holding the marble altar and pulpit.

dral glass flanks the floor-to-ceiling wood reredos. Glass admitting natural light is used at the chancel end of the space on both sides of the reredos and at the juncture between the lower stone walls and the upper wooden walls. Here, where the upper walls overhang the lower walls, are horizontal glass panels that run the entire length of the nave on both sides. Nave and chancel areas are unified in the space, with two rows of pews (providing seating for 300) facing the slightly raised altar area. On one side of the altar is a pulpit, and on the other side is a font. Both the exterior and the interior of the church are minimally adorned. However, on the reredos is a large cross composed of colored glass strips that contrast with the warm tones of the wood and stone.

Trinity Lutheran exhibits characteristics of the earlier European prototype churches examined earlier: it uses modern materials with minimal ornamentation and houses a unified space for worship. Trinity Lutheran perhaps has a warmer feel than some of the European prototypes because of the extensive use of wood in the design, but the same goals were pursued and achieved in this church. The longitudinal orientation of the space suggests basilican design, but its length is limited in an effort to create a greater sense of intimacy in corporate celebrations of worship.

North Christian Church, Columbus, Indiana

North Christian Church was designed by Eero Saarinen (1910-1961), son of Eliel Saarinen, and completed in 1964. North Christian was a daughter congregation of First Christian Church in Columbus, born of theological conflict within the community. Saarinen used a hexagonal shape and centralized plan for the worship space of North Christian. From a distance, the viewer notes the presence and rise of the roof, culminating in a needlelike spire (192 feet high) sheathed in copper steel plates. A small cross has been placed at the tip of the spire, but it is difficult to distinguish from afar. From the spire six prominent steel spines covered in copper run down the sides of the roof, attaching to steel arches that are grounded in a reinforced concrete foundation. Offices and meeting rooms surround the hexagonal worship space placed at the center of the structure.

North Christian Church. Used with permission.

Exterior view of North Christian Church (architect: Eero Saarinen, 1964). Saarinen chose a hexagonal design for this centrally planned church. The building is nestled in the ground and topped by a needlelike spire rising from a roof of copper plates.

Author photo

Interior view of North Christian Church. The articulation of the interior space creates an intimate chamber for gathering. A slightly elevated central altar is surrounded on five of six sides by raked congregational seating. The sixth side of the space features the pulpit, organ, and choir.

One ascends slightly as one enters the worship space, which has minimal ornamentation. Seating consists of pews placed in five sections on a significantly inclined floor. The pews provide seating for 455 people; an upper perimeter bench extending around the space provides room for 150 more. The pulpit, the seating for clergy, the organ, and the choir space are located on the sixth side of the hexagon. In the center of the space, set on a three-step elevated hexagonal platform, is the altar (composed of twelve tables representing the twelve apostles and a taller table representing Christ). Natural light in the space is subdued, coming in through an oculus immediately above the altar and indirectly through glass panels located behind the seating areas. An immersion pool is located in a chapel (seating fifty), approachable via the hallway that circles around outside the primary worship area.

A real sense of intimacy is achieved through the centralized design of North Christian. The interior creates a strong sense of the community at worship, while the symbolism of the exterior creates a sort of axis mundi, indicating the close relationship between heaven and earth.

Summary

Each of the churches in this section exhibits a significant amount of concern for the people gathered to worship in community. All of them are much smaller than the churches mentioned in the previous section. The buildings themselves are more modest in size and volume, have less seating capacity, and generally do not exhibit the unusual shapes utilized in the examples from the last section. North Christian Church does have a less traditional shape, but its low profile and extraordinary emphasis on focusing the community on corporate ritual in the interior of the space heighten its focus on "God with us." Other hallmarks of modern design that characterize each church are minimal ornamentation and the use of contemporary materials and building techniques. The exterior facades of these churches (and others like them) in some ways adopt patterns similar to secular building designs, evidence perhaps of congregations seeking to "connect" to the communities in which they reside. This emphasis is consistent with the fact that some theologians and architects believed that relating the ordinary world to God could be done more effectively through the use of nonreligious architectural expressions than traditional ecclesiastical designs (e.g., those used in Byzantine, Gothic, and Puritan meetinghouse churches). But the buildings represented here do not eliminate transcendence. They do utilize primary Christian symbols and possess a scale and/or volume that point the occupants to qualities of God that transcend this world. Still, they have an increased focus on the presence of God in our midst, largely due to the interior planning emphasizing communal activities and the external appearance exhibiting a move toward more common, vernacular designs.

MODERN CHURCH BUILDINGS REFERRING TO GOD'S IMMANENCE TO A HIGH DEGREE

Church of the Blessed Sacrament, East Hartford, Connecticut

Russell Gibson von Dohlen designed a completely flexible worship space for a Roman Catholic community that was built in 1973. Church of the Blessed Sacrament is based on a simple square shape, built primarily of reinforced concrete and steel. An exposed frame is used for the church, with nine columns placed throughout the

David F. Chandler. Used with permission.

Above: Exterior view of Church of the Blessed Sacrament (architect: Russell Gibson von Dohlen, 1973). A simple square is used in this design, with minimal ornamentation exhibited. A parish hall was later added next to the worship space.

Below: Interior view of Church of the Blessed Sacrament. An open plan was used for the interior arrangement of the church. A low platform centrally located near one side of the space now holds the altar and ambo, with seating (chairs and pews) on three sides.

David F. Chandler. Used with permission.

space. The exterior is quite plain, clad in cedar boards painted white. In the lower part of the walls are small, rectangular windows that run in a band all around the building, providing some natural illumination. The primary entrance is also of clear glass, providing additional light for the interior. The church is about a single story in height, very much in scale with nearby community buildings.

The interior of the church exhibits an open plan, with only a small circular chapel and an oblong area (containing the sacristy, storage room, kitchen, and restrooms) fixed in the space. The altar, font, ambo, and clergy seating are moveable, and flexible seating for 500 people can be arranged around them in a variety of patterns. The interior walls are white; installations of liturgical art are periodically included in various celebrations and can easily be changed with the season or feast. This extraordinarily flexible interior arrangement accommodates all kinds of activity in the life of the church.

Church of the Blessed Sacrament is the logically extreme expression of a worship space desiring to focus on "God in our midst." The people are a significant focal point during communal celebrations, and they can encounter one another around the altar/font/ambo in many configurations. The tabernacle is located in a permanent circular chapel, providing a fixed location for private devotional activities. (Regular services are also held in this prayer chapel.)[11] A continuing sense of God's presence (through the consecrated elements located in the tabernacle) is retained alongside the larger, flexible worship area.

Willow Creek Community Church, South Barrington, Illinois

The first primary building constructed for worship by Willow Creek Community Church was designed by the architectural firm of O'Donnell, Wicklund, and Pig-

---

11. More elaborate yet still simple expressions of this flexible design have also been built. An example would be Church of Our Divine Saviour, Chico, California (completed c. 1973), designed by Patrick J. Quinn and Francis Oda. Quinn and Oda developed a more complex but minimally ornamented exterior for their church. The interior is also based on a square centralized plan (able to seat up to 300 people), with moveable seating and liturgical furnishings. The sacristy, tabernacle, prayer chapel, and ancillary rooms are located on the perimeter of the larger open worship space (which can be divided into two sections if desired). Additional information on flexible-space church buildings of the 1970s can be found in Elizabeth Kendall Thompson, "Building Types Study 450: Flexible Space in Religious Buildings," *Architectural Record* 145, no. 1 (July 1973): 117-32.

Above: Exterior view of Willow Creek Community Church (architect: O'Donnell, Wicklund, and Pigozzi, 1981). The worship space is roughly hexagonal in shape and resembles a contemporary auditorium. An intentional choice to eliminate all Christian symbols from the exterior was pursued in an effort to be hospitable to those unfamiliar with the Christian faith.

Below: Interior view of Willow Creek Community Church. A raked main floor of theatre seats, with two main-floor risers and three balconies, provides congregational seating. The seats are oriented toward a thrust stage with multiple projection screens.

ozzi and was completed in 1981.[12] The church was constructed primarily of steel, reinforced concrete, glass, and brick. From the outside, the building resembles those used for community theaters, schools, and shopping centers. No Christian symbols adorn the exterior of the church, and there is little ornamentation of any kind. The general shape of the main auditorium used for worship is roughly hexagonal on the main floor, with a thrust stage equipped for theatrical performances serving as the focal point of the space. The auditorium is composed of a main floor, two main-floor risers, and three balconies (west, center, and east) on a single upper level, with a seating capacity of 4,500 people.[13] Theater seating on a sloped floor is wrapped around the stage in a semicircular pattern. A large projection screen is centered at the back of the stage, with two smaller projection screens on either side (and one against the back wall for those onstage). These screens are used during the services to project song lyrics, live video feed of the worship leaders, and various other images.

Large areas of clear glass flank both sides of the platform (beginning at the edge of the side screens), providing for much natural light during the daylight hours and a view of a five-acre lake in which immersion baptisms are often celebrated. The space is devoid of any symbols usually associated with a church. No cross, pulpit, altar, or baptismal facilities are permanently installed in the space. Permanent installations of visual art, paraments, and candles are not present either. Traditional symbols are occasionally included in various worship events, but they are viewed more as "props" to heighten emotional engagement in worship.[14]

---

12. Architect Douglas Pasma (of the firm Goss/Pasma) designed a larger auditorium (with a seating capacity of 7,200) for Willow Creek that was completed in 2004. The same basic design approach was used for both the exterior and the interior of the new auditorium. It has a "familiar," contemporary facade and an interior with balconies and theater seating on a raked floor. The seating focuses on a thrust theater-type stage featuring audiovisual enhancements and the latest technological advancements in lighting. Both the exterior and the interior remain devoid of traditional religious symbols. Now that the new auditorium is ready, the original auditorium will be renovated to accommodate smaller gatherings of people for worship and other events.

13. Originally the seating capacity for the auditorium was 1,600. Subsequent expansions have increased that capacity dramatically.

14. See Stewart M. Hoover, "The Cross at Willow Creek: Seeker Religion and the Contemporary Marketplace," in *Religion and Popular Culture in America*, ed. Bruce David Forbes and Jeffrey H. Mahan (Berkeley and Los Angeles: University of California Press, 2000), pp. 145-59.

Church of the Servant, Grand Rapids, Michigan

Gunnar Birkerts was the architect chosen to design Church of the Servant, which was completed in 1993. The Christian Reformed congregation that built this church was organized in the late 1960s, but it was reluctant to build a permanent structure for its worship and ministries. A strong theological argument was made in the community for renting facilities from others and using the majority of resources for ministry outside the church. The congregation rented space from various local groups for approximately twenty years before enough impetus was generated to construct a building of their own. In the end, the time and energy needed for weekly set-up and tear-down in temporary spaces and the lack of flexibility in determining how and when their rented spaces could be used drove the decision to construct a permanent building. The congregation wanted a multipurpose church that would allow for maximal service to the outside community, as well as accommodate Christian worship using the many artistic, material offerings of their members (including liturgical appointments, paraments, banners, and many forms of visual art).

Birkerts sought to design a structure that would embody the concept of "a village clustered around a town square — the traditional place of community."[15] The worship space is the "square" around which an arcade for fellowship and adjoining classrooms, offices, kitchen, and art and music rooms are gathered into "houses" (the organization of which is visible from the exterior). From the outside, the church appears to be a collection of small buildings, sheathed in textured plywood siding and painted an array of colors, including forest green, golden brown, periwinkle blue, ash gray, and mulberry purple. Building materials include steel, concrete block, plywood, and standard residential windows. The roofs on the small buildings are flat, but over one section of the worship area there is a spire and a translucent skylight (thirty-two feet in diameter). A cross has been placed on top of the spire, the overall height of which is sixty feet. The skylight and additional translucent material installed as clerestory allow for ample natural light in the central interior of the church.

The interior of the worship area is centrally planned, in the shape of a rectangle, with the front area set in the middle of one long side. Generally the interior is white or off-white in color, with moveable chairs for congregational seating (for 500) ar-

---

15. This quotation is from a self-published church brochure by James Vander Molen, "A Self-Guided Tour" (Grand Rapids: Church of the Servant, n.d.), p. 1. Many details concerning the church mentioned here are drawn from Vander Molen's two-page document.

Above: Exterior view of Church of the Servant (architect: Gunnar Birkerts, 1990). The square worship space features adjoining areas that from the exterior resemble a collection of multicolored smaller buildings. The worship area, in the center of the clustered buildings, is topped with a translucent skylight and spire.

Below: Interior view of Church of the Servant. The primary worship area is rectangular. All liturgical appointments — altar, font, and lectern — and all congregational seating are moveable. Seasonal art installations add color and variety to the interior environment.

ranged in a semicircle around a lectern, font, and communion table. The lectern and table (and other interior furnishings) are made of clear birch. The font is a small ceramic bowl set in a birch stand on one corner of the long communion table, and both are raised on a single-step platform. (There is also a mobile processional cross and stand in the front area.) The three primary liturgical appointments are located beneath a large structural steel support shaped to represent a tree. The tree supports the skylight and allows those gathered for Eucharist to share the bread and wine in a circle of believers beneath its "branches." Set to one side of the worship space is a small, birch-lined chapel for private devotions and meditation.

Summary

Each church featured in this section is primarily concerned with emphasizing the presence of God in the midst of God's people. The Church of the Blessed Sacrament and Church of the Servant are buildings that are modest in visual expression and articulated in forms that reflect the secular architectural design of the day. Centralized organization of the worship space encourages a sense of unity in Christ among both leadership and congregation during ritual activities. These churches also feature minimal ornamentation and modern materials and building techniques.

The 1970s in particular saw a tremendous emphasis, in both Roman Catholic and Protestant circles, on developing and using multipurpose spaces for worship. Economics may have been a factor in this development. Church building in the United States continued at a rate of 3,500 to 4,000 new buildings a year into the 1970s even as the costs associated with such buildings continued to increase.[16] Theological issues related to economics (being good stewards of material resources), relevancy (being useful for the community beyond the activities of the faithful), and accessibility (expressing an inviting and familiar appearance) were mentioned earlier as important issues for churches to consider as they sought to build new structures for worship and ministry. The churches featured here reflect such theological priorities in the buildings they created. The application of a minimalist aesthetic allows each congregation to maximize the visual impact of daily, weekly, or seasonal installations of art. (Church of the Servant is a congregation especially blessed with many artists whose work appears regularly in long-term and short-term installations.) The buildings themselves tend to reflect God's immanence more than God's transcen-

16. Thompson, "Building Types Study 450: Flexible Space in Religious Buildings," p. 117.

dence through the use of secular architectural expressions and flexible, open interior plans. These churches have not completely eliminated transcendence, of course, because worship activities are still primary, and the spaces retain some symbols (e.g., the cross, the crucifix, the altar, and the tabernacle) that point to God's transcendent qualities. But, theologically speaking, the accent points more significantly to the immanence of God in and through the people of God. And the buildings play an important role in emphasizing this orientation.

Willow Creek Community Church is set apart from Church of the Blessed Sacrament and Church of the Servant in that it represents a nondenominational permutation of immanent church architecture. According to research conducted by the Hartford Institute for Religion Research, Hartford Seminary Foundation, approximately ten million people in the United States identify themselves as non-denominational.[17] According to this research, about 70 percent of these churches have organized since 1950. Individual churches will sometimes spawn whole networks of affiliated churches, such as the Willow Creek Association, the Association of Calvary Chapels, the Association of Vineyard Churches, and Purpose Driven Churches.[18]

In relation to church architecture, nondenominational communities sometimes employ church complexes that mirror shopping malls or community colleges. Their spaces of worship often resemble fine-arts auditoriums for dramatic productions or concerts, including the occasional use of "black box" type theatre spaces. Frequently they have a prominent stage with the type of seating found in contemporary theatres (often on an inclined surface). In spaces of this kind, since the stage and the seating are fixed, flexibility often refers to being able to use the worship auditorium for non-worship events rather than being able to alter the interior environment for worship. Facilities resembling health clubs, bookstores, restaurants, and coffeehouses are often included in the overall master plan of their campuses. Willow Creek ad-

17. See the "Faith Communities Today" project, coordinated by Carl Dudley and David Roozen, 2001, Hartford Institute for Religion Research, Hartford Seminary Foundation; and the "Organizing Religious Work" project, coordinated by N. Ammerman, A. Lummis, D. Roozen, and S. Thumma, 1997-1998, Hartford Institute for Religion Research, Hartford Seminary Foundation. Data from both projects is available at www.hirr.hartsem.edu/org/faith_congregations_nondnmcong/html. A helpful overview considering nondenominational church identity can be found in Scott Thumma, "What God Makes Free Is Free Indeed: Nondenominational Church Identity and Its Networks of Support," at www.hirr.hartsem.edu/bookshelf/thumma_article5.html.

18. In effect, many of these associations seem to be in the early stages of forming their own distinct denominations.

opted such a design approach, and because of its enormous influence, it is modeling this approach to a wide audience. Such a development may represent an application of the earlier-discussed priority among churches to relate to ordinary community life; it is another permutation of a multipurpose church.

Willow Creek has intentionally chosen to reflect architectural design familiar to the uninitiated in order to facilitate transition into their community. This choice is reminiscent of the use of vernacular architecture among denominational bodies wanting to relate to secular culture. However, whereas denominational churches still use historical symbols in their buildings, Willow Creek removes this last vestige of connection and all evidence of permanent Christian symbol. Those who have developed Willow Creek believe that some people are anxious in environments that exhibit symbols unique to the church. They have employed an architectural design highlighting the immanence of God for much the same reason as denominational churches (seeking to enhance connection with people through familiarity and hospitality in order to serve them in Jesus' name), but their independent status has probably made them less influenced by the thought and work of liberal theology, the liturgical movement, and the historical church.[19]

Conclusions

In the mid-twentieth century, various factors — including global war, economic prosperity, population growth, mobile populations, and interest in joining churches — fostered unusual opportunities for building new churches. The modern architecture movement avoided using historical styles of design and encouraged much experimentation in designing buildings, including churches. The liturgical movement sought to mobilize the activity of the laity in worship and noted that church designs based on historical styles (such as Gothic revival) often hindered this goal. In a sense,

---

19. Nondenominational churches are often fairly conservative theologically and evangelical. Such churches have often been suspicious of Roman Catholic and mainline denominations. This suspicion has frequently kept them more removed from the effects of the ecumenical and liturgical movements. In recent years, however, especially through the efforts of evangelical scholars like Robert E. Webber (a prolific author and currently a professor of worship at Northern Baptist Theological Seminary), some leaders of nondenominational churches are showing interest in the work and worship of other Christian traditions. It will be interesting to see if a relationship of mutual interest and respect develops between denominational and nondenominational churches in years to come.

the ideal of a "house for God" alone shifted to include the ideal of a "house for the people of God" too.

In architectural and theological circles the impulse to depend on historical styles of design was quashed, which ensured that no one model from the past would be established as absolute for achieving adequate Roman Catholic or Protestant church design. Although no particular style was mandated, the tendency of human nature is to adopt the cultural style of the times, and that is what prevailed. For all of the seeking among modern architects to create a "non-style," the ideals and priorities of design as reflected in the International Style became dominant for many decades. The strong geometric forms and simplified, machine aesthetic of this modern design gradually filtered into church architecture. Given the convergence of strands of the ecumenical movement, the liturgical movement, and modern architecture, the logical extreme of an architecture of immanence — the so-called multipurpose church (with spaces created to facilitate both religious and nonreligious needs) — came to be possible across denominational lines. In the multipurpose church, the focus on the immanence of God in human community can yield very flexible rooms where the majority (if not all) of the religious furnishings are mobile. Primary Christian symbols are frequently minimal (in some cases, completely absent) and often as mobile as the furniture for worship. The primary room for worship is intentionally designed to facilitate a host of other communal activities, including dinners, various sorts of entertainment, meetings of all kinds, and even sports activities.

In light of the strong influence of ecumenism and liturgical renewal in Europe and the United States, it makes sense that churches in the twentieth century increasingly focused on the presence of God in the midst of God's people. Not all Christian communities pursued this emphasis to the same degree, but a host of churches that embraced modern design began to look less and less distinct in the urban landscape. Theological meaning was attached to these design choices. More familiar, contemporary architectural designs were chosen by churches interested in evangelism and service, in relating to non-Christian constituencies. Because no single architectural path was mandated or sanctioned as ideal by any ecclesial authorities, a variety of experiments in design emerged. The logical end of an architecture of immanence can be found in the multipurpose churches of the late 1960s and 1970s. While a trend toward increasingly spartan expressions continued into the 1970s, some architects never went to a reductionistic extreme, and others augmented their designs with increasing symbolism and ornamentation.

It is hard to imagine a different course of progression in the development of church design in the last century. It was perhaps helpful that a significant break was made with an approach that interpreted the mere replication of historical architectural styles as ideal.[20] The nature of our infinitely creative God could be discovered and represented anew through fresh, contemporary building designs. In the end, permission to pursue modern designs may even have promoted a rediscovery of the richness of historical designs of the past. In the mid-twentieth century, the minimalism of modern design was already evoking some discontent in both architectural and religious circles. Over time, this discontent would grow. I will say more about this response later; here it is sufficient to recognize that positive growth and change resulted from the ecumenical exploration of modern church design emphasizing God's immanence.

20. Choosing to not simply reproduce historical styles of design was not an idea unique to modern architecture. In the history of Western architecture there have been voices that have suggested using historical styles as sources for contemporary design without pursuing thoughtless imitation. But architects do not always agree upon the line between outright imitation and careful adaptation. It appears that many advocates of modern architecture felt that abandonment of historical models was the only viable way to purge a dependence on past styles and force a truly innovative approach that would accurately reflect the dramatic distinctions of the modern day from all previous time periods.

CHAPTER EIGHT

AN ILLUSTRATION:
THE THOUGHT AND WORK
OF EDWARD ANDERS SÖVIK

This, then, is the challenge to us, that comes out of an incomplete reformation, from a heritage of ersatz medievalism, from a growing resource of studies in the field of worship, and from an example being set by our Roman Catholic brothers: can we in the Lutheran churches open ourselves to a renewal of forms which will affect every congregation, and every liturgy, and every church building?

EDWARD ANDERS SÖVIK, "Reformation Is Still Needed" (1966)

And if we are to carry the logic of the "servant church" to its undeniable end, we must proceed even further. Jesus was the "Man for others"; Christians are called to be the "men for others." Their structures should not be built unless they are directed to the service of the community of people around them and become a means for the Christian community to provide as effectively as possible not only for its own needs, but for the needs of the community.

What this ultimately means is that there can be no more church building in the sense that is meant when we talk about "houses of God," shrines, temples, naves, chancels, or sacred edifices. We need to return to the non-church.

EDWARD ANDERS SÖVIK, *Architecture for Worship* (1973)

EXPLORING A SPECIFIC example of a phenomenon is often helpful for illustrating a discussion. For that reason, I want to use this chapter to examine the work of Edward Anders Sövik, which illuminates the ways in which the ecumenical movement, the liturgical movement, and modern architecture have affected the design of twentieth-century churches. I mentioned Sövik briefly in earlier chapters, but here I will explore his thought and work more fully, seeking to discern how his approach to church architecture illustrates the convergence of ecumenism, worship renewal, and modernity.

Edward Anders Sövik (b. 1918) is an architect of Christian faith, a member of the Evangelical Lutheran Church in America, who primarily has designed church-es throughout the latter half of the twentieth century in North America.[1] Sövik, a Fellow in the American Institute of Architects since 1967, has designed approxi-mately 400 church-related projects for Protestant and Roman Catholic communi-ties. He has received numerous awards for excellence in architectural design: in 1981 he was the first recipient of the Edward S. Frey Memorial Award for "great talent and long-term commitment in the field of religious architecture" from the Interfaith Forum on Religion, Art, and Architecture (IFRAA, formerly the Church Architectural Guild of America/Guild for Religious Architecture); in 1982 he received the Gold Medal of the Minnesota Society, American Institute of Archi-tects (MSAIA); and throughout his career he has received numerous competitive awards from IFRAA and the MSAIA for specific projects.[2] In addition to receiving awards for excellence in architectural design, Sövik has also been recognized for his sensitivity to liturgical concerns through architecture. In 1993 he was awarded the Twentieth Anniversary Bene Award for "most influential liturgical architect of the last 20 years" by *Modern Liturgy*, an award given to honor his design work,

1. A detailed examination of the theological reflections and church architecture design work of Sövik may be found in Torgerson, "Edward Anders Sövik and His Return to the 'Non-church'" (Ph.D. diss., Uni-versity of Notre Dame, 1995).

2. Significant awards include the following: honor award from the Church Architectural Guild of Amer-ica for Our Savior's Lutheran Church, Austin, Minnesota (1962); for Westwood Lutheran Church, St. Louis Park, Minnesota (1964); and for Lutheran Church of the Good Shepherd, Moorhead, Minnesota (1968); mer-it award from the Guild for Religious Architecture for Trinity United Methodist Church, Charles City, Iowa (1973); honor award from Interfaith Forum on Religion, Art, and Architecture for Knutson Center (Centrum and Commons), Concordia College, Moorhead, Minnesota (1977); and for Our Savior's Lutheran Church, Jackson, Minnesota (1982); merit award from Interfaith Forum on Religion, Art, and Architecture for Trinity Lutheran Church, Princeton, Minnesota (1978); for Summit United Methodist Church, Columbus, Ohio (1983); for Saints Peter and Paul Cathedral, Indianapolis, Indiana (1987); and for Worship/Drama/Communi-cations Center, Augsburg College, Minneapolis, Minnesota (1989); merit award from the Minnesota Society, American Institute of Architects, for Westwood Lutheran Church, St. Louis Park, Minnesota (1964); and for Lutheran Church of the Good Shepherd, Moorhead, Minnesota (1968); honorable mention (works in prog-ress) from the Liturgical Conference for Saint Leo's Catholic Church, Pipestone, Minnesota (1968).

teaching, writing, and participation in interfaith organizations.[3] And in 2003 Sövik was the first recipient of the Godfrey Diekmann award from the North American Academy of Liturgy for having made a significant contribution to liturgical life in North America.[4] As these awards indicate, Sövik is an extraordinary architect who can help us understand how ecumenism, liturgical renewal, and modern architecture could all converge to yield a particular church design highlighting the reality of God's immanence.

Sövik has pursued the architectural design of Christian churches using an approach he has called the "nonchurch." Sövik's worship spaces are particularly interesting to examine under this rubric, because they are the opposite of traditional "church" designs, which produce inflexible, single-purpose (liturgical) spaces dependent upon particular historical design styles associated with Christianity. By contrast, a Sövik worship space is flexible (meaning most furnishings are portable and can be moved with relative ease) and multifunctional (capable of hosting both liturgical and nonliturgical activities), exhibiting a "modern" architectural design idiom (especially in contrast to revival expressions of the nineteenth century). His work does not emphasize the structure but rather underscores the importance of the people who gather in these spaces, the body of Christ as church and their mission of service to the world as modeled by the incarnation of God in Christ. Sövik named the flexible, humble, missional worship space the "centrum."[5] This new name was meant to help people understand the concept of the unified worship space, to move beyond the ordinary designations of "nave" and "chancel."

Sövik developed, articulated, and implemented his nonchurch design in response to certain theological and architectural currents he encountered. First I will examine some theological influences, remembering the ecumenical and renewal-oriented atmosphere in which Sövik operated. Then I will reflect on Sövik's architectural training and locate him in the wave of postwar church-building that swept across Europe and the United States. Finally, I will examine two examples of Sövik's church design, one Roman Catholic and one Protestant, to illustrate his expression of an architecture of immanence.

---

3. *Modern Liturgy* 20, no. 9 (November 1993): 46.

4. Gilbert Ostdiek, "Introduction, Godfrey Diekmann, O.S.B., Award," in *Proceedings of the North American Academy of Liturgy Annual Meeting* (2003): 29-31.

5. Sövik used the word "centrum" for approximately fifteen to twenty years. He then abandoned it in favor of the word "assembly." From Edward A. Sövik, letter to the author, 24 May 1993.

KEY THEOLOGICAL CONCEPTS:
INCARNATION, SERVANTHOOD, AND HUMILITY

During the 1920s and 1930s, Sövik grew up and was educated in mainland China on a foreign mission field of the Norwegian Lutheran Church of America. His Lutheran heritage emphasized the theological centrality of the Word of God, a personal commitment to Jesus Christ, and a living out of his faith in service to both God and neighbor. Studies at St. Olaf College, Northfield, Minnesota (where he received a BA in 1939), and Luther Theological Seminary, St. Paul, Minnesota (where he took various courses from 1940 to 1942), grounded Sövik in Lutheran theological interpretations and allowed him to be conversant with other theological understandings present in Christianity. In his mainline theological training, Sövik was exposed to the emphasis on "God in the ordinary" that I described in Chapter Two. Emphasizing the humble, servant posture of Christ in the world became central to his theological approach.

Sövik articulated aspects of his understanding of the incarnation of Christ in at least twelve published articles and his book entitled *Architecture for Worship*.[6] He emphasized three aspects of incarnation he saw as important: (1) incarnation as being God's initiative; (2) incarnation as indicating God's unrestricted presence in the world; (3) incarnation as indicating God's appreciation for the "ordinary" of this earth. God entered our world in human form by his own choosing and according to his own timing, an orthodox theological interpretation of incarnation. God was present in Christ, Christ was directly involved in the world, and Christ continues to be present and active in the entire world through the church. Sövik saw all places on earth

---

6. See specifically E. A. Sövik, "The Faith Our Forms Express," *Dialog* 4 (Autumn 1965): 296; E. A. Sövik, "A Theology of Architecture," *Study Encounter* 2, no. 4 (1966): 174; Edward A. Sövik, "The Architecture of Kerygma," *Worship* 40, no. 4 (April 1966): 202-3; E. A. Sövik, "What Is Religious Architecture?" *Discourse* 9 (Winter 1966): 79; Edward A. Sövik, "Images of the Church," *Worship* 41, no. 3 (March 1967): 132-33; E. A. Sövik, "The Valley of Decision," *Dodge Construction News (Chicago edition)*, 25 August 1967, section 2, column 4, p. 18; a brief reference — "I have wondered whether there is a better symbol of incarnation and redemption than this — that one cherishes the earthy and natural things enough to invest to the limit in them and thus to transform them into something superlative, without ever changing them into something synthetic or exotic" — in Edward Anders Sövik, "Tea and Sincerity," *Liturgical Arts* 37, no. 1 (November 1968): 5; E. A. Sövik, "House of God to House of God's People," *The Priest* 25, no. 4 (April 1969): 214-15; E. A. Sövik, "The Return to the Non-Church," *Faith and Form* 5 (Fall 1972): 13-14; E. A. Sövik, "The Place of Worship: Environment for Action," in *Worship: Good News in Action*, ed. Mandus A. Egge, 94-110 (Minneapolis: Augsburg Publishing House, 1973), pp. 96-99; Sövik, *Architecture for Worship* (Minneapolis: Augsburg Publishing House, 1973), pp. 35-37, 57; Edward A. Sövik, "Elements of the Christian Tradition in Building," *Reformed Liturgy and Music* 16, no. 2 (Spring 1982): 82; Edward Sövik, "The Mirror of the Church," *Faith and Form* 22 (Fall 1988): 17.

become potentially sacred via the work of God's Holy Spirit (versus identifying God's presence with only a limited number of geographical locales). And God's choosing to become incarnate in and through the ordinary material of our world (having humble beginnings and a ministry focused on ordinary people and located largely in ordinary places) indicates that God operates outside of a limited, sacred realm.

Sövik found God's activity in the ordinary paradigmatic for the design of his worship spaces. He sought to create ordinary environments that could host the extraordinary but that did not pretend to *be* extraordinary (e.g., did not try to imitate what may lie in the heavenly realm). Sövik's concern was that the church remain intimately connected to this world and not drift off in pursuit of another realm, abandoning its responsibility for service to others as the people of Christ. Such an interpretation of the incarnation of Christ allowed for a weighting of the immanence of God.

Although Sövik focused on God's immanence, he did not ignore God's transcendence. From at least 1965 onward, he spoke about the mystery of God being accessible architecturally through beauty rather than exotic expressions (such as an overwhelming scale or the dramatic reduction of natural light, both of which were used in neo-Gothic church designs).[7] He highlighted ordinary beauty, experienced in all expressions of "good" art, as capable of suggesting the mystical or the holy to the viewer.[8] The object of beauty (whatever it may be — perhaps even an entire building) does not become "holy" in and of itself, but functions as a means by which to contemplate the holiness of God. Sövik's discussion of beauty makes more sense in the context of his larger theological view that God's activity is not limited to particular sacred locations. All creation is God's domain. Beauty becomes a means by which we are reminded that the ordinary is capable of conveying the extraordinary. With this understanding of encountering God's transcendence, Sövik cultivated design choices that accentuated his own predisposition toward humility and service to others.

Sövik periodically mentioned theologian J. G. Davies in his writings.[9] Sövik was especially appreciative of his book *The Secular Use of Church Buildings*. Davies sought

---

7. Edward A. Sövik, "Role of the Architect in Liturgical Renewal," in *Church Architecture: The Shape of Reform: Proceedings of a Meeting on Church Architecture Conducted by the Liturgical Conference, February 23-25, 1965, in Cleveland, Ohio* (Washington, D.C.: The Liturgical Conference, 1965), pp. 21-23.

8. Edward A. Sövik, "What Is Religious Architecture?" *Faith and Form* 1 (Special issue, 1967): 24. See also, Sövik, *Architecture for Worship*, pp. 60-62.

9. For example: E. A. Sövik, "Comment on Multi-Purpose Worship Spaces," *Faith and Form* 2 (April 1969): 20; Edward A. Sövik, "The Second International Congress: The Architecture of Religion," *Faith and Form* 4 (April 1971): 20; Sövik, "The Return to the Non-Church," p. 13; Sövik, *Architecture for Worship*, p. 8.

to blur the distinction between imagined "sacred" and "secular" realms in our world (as did Dietrich Bonhoeffer) in many of his published reflections, finding the two united in the incarnation of Christ. In *The Secular Use of Church Buildings*, Davies noted that Jesus did not endorse the construction of buildings for worship and that New Testament writers emphasized the idea that the "living stones" of the Temple of God are the *people*, not the building. Davies continued,

> The early Christians then did not put their church buildings to secular use, simply because they had no church buildings as such, but the physical location of their particular acts of worship witnessed to their understanding of the unity of sacred and secular in and through Christ — they assembled in private houses.[10]

Sövik appreciated this theological interpretation of the actions of early Christians. His own writings would reflect a similar understanding of a more domestic environment for worship. Davies perhaps emphasized a choice on the part of early Christians that did set them apart from other organized religions. Davies lifted up this theological emphasis and ultimately defined the function of the church in terms of service to the world.[11] Davies did acknowledge that tangible issues, such as fairly small gatherings, minimal resources, and occasional persecutions, may also have factored into the selection of anonymous domestic environments for early gatherings.[12] But he did not want those issues to be seen as the exclusive rationale for use of nonreligious architecture for worship.

Sövik was drawn to a theological interpretation of early Christianity that broke down the distinction between sacred and secular. As an architect, he appreciated a perspective that emphasized the elevation of nonreligious architecture by the church in service to the world. Sövik would eventually be so bold as to make this statement:

> It is conventionally supposed that the reasons that Christians of the first three centuries built almost no houses of worship were that they were too few, or too poor, or too much persecuted. None of these is true. The real reason they didn't build was that they didn't

---

10. Davies, *The Secular Use of Church Buildings* (New York: Seabury Press, 1968), pp. 2-4, 5.

11. J. G. Davies, "Architectural Theory and the Appraisal of 'Religious' Buildings," in *Revolution, Place, and Symbol* (New York: The International Congress on Religion, Architecture, and the Visual Arts, 1969), pp. 169-70.

12. Davies, *The Secular Use of Church Buildings*, pp. 1-2.

believe in ecclesiastical buildings. For Christians, as the church fathers (echoing New Testament writers) said repeatedly — Christians are the temples of God. His presence is where they are, and the Christian religion finds its fundamental expression in a life of love and human concern, the reflection of God's love and his concern. Christians were known as the community who loved each other.[13]

In this statement Sövik was making use of Davies' thought, but adding a stronger accent than Davies himself did. Sövik used Davies' writings to substantiate his emphasis on the incarnation of Christ and to ground his nonchurch (flexible and multipurpose) design historically and theologically.

In considering the servanthood of Christ, Sövik drew on the writings of St. Paul in the New Testament and of Lutheran theologian Dietrich Bonhoeffer. In his letter to the churches at Philippi, St. Paul stated, "Let the same mind be in you that was in Christ Jesus, who, though he was in the form of God, did not regard equality with God as something to be exploited, but emptied himself, taking the form of a slave, being born in human likeness."[14] At times Sövik would quote this passage and highlight it as a crucial understanding of Jesus to be emulated in the world.[15] Sövik joined this reflection from St. Paul with Bonhoeffer's focus on the servanthood of Christ in *Life Together.*[16] In this book Bonhoeffer spoke of the centrality of Christ's self-giving, the effect that his action had on humanity, and the importance of Christians emulating the model he gave us in serving God and others. Sövik's explicit references to Bonhoeffer come in these two published statements: "Bonhoeffer described Jesus as being *the man for others,* and said that it was only proper that his followers should also be men for others";[17] and "If Jesus was the *Man for Others* (to use Bonhoeffer's phrase), then Christians must be *men for others,* a servant community."[18] Sövik chose to pursue a similar central focus on the self-giving of Christ in his own nonchurch

---

13. Sövik, "The Place of Worship: Environment for Action," p. 98. See similar statements in Sövik, "The Return to the Non-Church," p. 13; and Sövik, *Architecture for Worship,* p. 14.

14. Philippians 2:5-7a, New Revised Standard Version.

15. Sövik, "The Faith Our Forms Express," p. 296.

16. Edward A. Sövik, interview with the author, 3 August 1993.

17. Edward A. Sövik, "Church Architecture — A Public Language," *Cutting Edge* 7, no. 4 (July-August 1978): 2; Edward A. Sövik, "Church Architecture — A Public Language," *Liturgy* 4, no. 4 (Spring 1985): 84.

18. Sövik, "Elements of the Christian Tradition in Building," p. 82. Use of the phrase "the man for others" can also be found in "House of God to House of God's People," p. 214; "The Place of Worship: Environment for Action," p. 103; *Architecture for Worship,* p. 39; and Edward A. Sövik, "Sitting Proper: Notes on Seating for the Assembly," *Environment and Art* 3, no. 12 (February 1991): 92.

approach, promoting a worship space that could act as "servant" to the world, litur-gically and nonliturgically.

Sövik was also drawn to Bonhoeffer's speaking of Christianity as a secular re-ligion. In his book *Architecture for Worship*, he noted that the New Testament por-trayed Jesus as doing ministry predominantly in secular places.[19] Jesus was born and grew up in ordinary places, and he did not restrict his ministry to places of special re-ligious significance but spent much of his time wandering through the countryside, bringing honor to God and caring for people. Sövik appreciated Jesus' preoccupation with earthly places (e.g., the stable at Bethlehem, the hillsides of Galilee, roadsides, homes, and the upper room in Jerusalem), linked this observation with Jesus' focus on serving others in those places, and from them drew conclusions about designing worship spaces. In an unpublished address Sövik made these remarks:

> Consider, for example, Bonhoeffer's catalytic reflections, that Christianity is not a religion like other religions but a "secular" religion, not a category of life but all of life, not an escape from the world but *in* the world, not esoteric but earthy. God incarnated; Christ the Real Man; God present in the life of Christians and in the world. If one be-lieves this, how can one build a temple, a House of God, a shrine, a fane, implying that God's presence is attached to a building? People used to say (some still do) that "a church should look like a church." But it is better to say that a church should look like a part of the world, not something different; because it is in the world that God meets his chil-dren, not in some heavenly enclave. The world is God's house; the church building is the *domus ekklesia* [house of the church].[20]

Sövik interpreted Bonhoeffer's pursuit of secular religion, a religion that is rel-evant to the ordinary of this world and everyday life, as a mandate for the construc-tion of his nonchurch. Bonhoeffer probably did not envision such an interpretation with respect to church buildings, but Sövik does seem to share the same essential passion with him: to make what Christians bring to the world relevant for more than those who belong to the church. Since Sövik was responsible for creating worship spaces, he sought (in keeping with Bonhoeffer's servant emphasis) the opportunity to design spaces that would be of maximum use to their communities. Sövik high-lighted particular aspects of Bonhoeffer's thought — the image of servant and the

19. Sövik, *Architecture for Worship*, p. 36.
20. Quoted in Torgerson, "Edward Anders Sövik and His Return to the 'Non-church,'" p. 55.

call to service — and used these to promote servanthood and service in the life of the church through his architecture.

As a church architect, Sövik was concerned with how this servant model affected the construction of worship spaces. He expressed this concern initially by having each church client evaluate the needs of the larger community around it in determining what potential spaces would be needed for ministry.[21] Sövik recognized that believers must have gathering places in which to conduct their liturgical activities and in which they can care for one another, but ministry was not restricted to liturgical activities. Ministry entailed a broad range of activities in one's life, both liturgical and nonliturgical, both inside and outside the walls of the worship environment created for the body of Christ. The church structures that Christians erected and inhabited needed to allow for the exercising of ministry in this larger sense of service to God and humanity. This nonliturgical emphasis was foundational for Sövik's promotion of a multipurpose worship space.

In considering the implications of a servant posture for church architecture, Sövik emphasized the quality of humility. Church architecture that focused on testifying to the transcendence of God often used designs that confronted the viewer, often making him or her feel rather small in relation to an overwhelming scale. Such designs, sometimes categorized as "monumental," went against Sövik's theological agenda of "servant to the world." In critiquing the creation of monumental structures for worshiping communities, Sövik once said,

> In many large buildings and even some which are not so large, the combinations of site, of shapes and surfaces are designed so as to be imposing or even imperious. The building says, in effect, to the people who use it, "I am the ruler; when you approach me, you must be impressed by me, and I wish you to behave in certain ways and assume an attitude of awe and subservience in my presence. My geometry and my space are independent of you. They exist autonomously and represent an ideal order by which I intend to dominate you." . . . This is what we often call "monumentality," and churches are often classified as monumental buildings. Such buildings often seem to be independent of the service they are meant to perform. They confront people rather than meet them. They aim at greatness rather than goodness. . . . But the mind of Christ and the form of the servant are not recognizable in them.[22]

21. Sövik, "The Place of Worship: Environment for Action," p. 103.
22. Sövik, "The Faith Our Forms Express," p. 296.

Sövik was expressing his concern that the structure of the church be a visible sign reflecting the nature of the church. He believed that monumentality in architecture diminished the possibility of perceiving the church structure as a servant to the world. Sövik was focusing on the humanity of Christ in emphasizing servanthood and found monumentality less than adequate in communicating humility and servanthood.

Sövik was not alone in viewing monumentality in this way. In 1959 he attended a conference at the Ecumenical Institute, Bossey, Switzerland, which had this title: "Church Building as an Expression of the Presence of the Church in the World." The report of the conference reflected a preference for congregations occupying nonmonumental structures:

> In the discussions, the participants seemed to be agreed on the fact that a church building can only grow out of the deep-rooted faith of a congregation who have understood something of the nature and mission of the Church and are not interested in creating an attractive monument as the highly individual expression of a group or even a single architect.[23]

The nature and mission of the church, which for Sövik translated into the nature and mission of Christ, were to be the foundation for the structure of the church. Given his theological conviction, Sövik was attracted to "vernacular" or ordinary expressions of buildings (domestic or commercial).

In the early part of the twentieth century, vernacular architecture was elevated as a rich source for design inspiration. In reflecting on this kind of architecture, Sövik once commented,

> It is usually industrial architecture, barns, warehouses, factories — and most often the designer's name is unknown. Its virtues are various: it is absolutely ingenuous, authentic, real. The structural materials are not disguised or cosmetized; there is no intent to impress or to manipulate people, only to serve.[24]

In the development of modern architecture, vernacular designs were briefly celebrated for their simplicity, authenticity, and utility. Sövik was trained during this

---

23. "Church Building as an Expression of the Presence of the Church in the World," *Report of the Conference for Architects and Theologians, May 6th-13th, 1959* (Bossey, Switzerland: Ecumenical Institute, 1959), p. 2.

24. E. A. Sövik, "Triumphalism, Sacred and Secular — A Christian Architect's Reflections," *Living Worship* 6, no. 1 (January 1970): 3.

period and found vernacular designs to resonate well with a theological posture of humility and servanthood. He was intentional in seeking to develop a design approach for worship spaces from his particular theological understanding of incarnation, servanthood, and humility in relation to Jesus Christ.

KEY THEOLOGICAL INFLUENCES: ECUMENISM, VATICAN II, AND LITURGICAL RENEWAL

The Lutheran denomination of which Sövik was a part was active in the ecumenical movement of the twentieth century. Ecumenical cooperation was a part of Sövik's experience from his earliest days, since his tradition often worked with other Christian traditions on the mission field to address common needs (such as the education of missionary children). Sövik's early exposure to interdenominational cooperation and his tradition's interest in ecumenical dialogue predisposed him to be open to the activities of the liturgical movement that were at work in both Europe and North America. Sövik once remarked, "I suppose that growing up with very close associations with so many non-Lutherans whose piety, if not theology, was shared, made me a bit skeptical about taking denominationalism too seriously and putting too much stock in Luther himself."[25] Sövik read scholars such as Josef Jungmann, Gregory Dix, and Rudolf Schwarz, combined their insights for promoting corporate worship with the new modern church expressions of Europe and America, and focused on those theological insights and architectural expressions that tended to conceive of the church building as a "house of the people of God" as opposed to a "house of God."

Sövik also recognized Vatican II as a major force in renewing Christian worship and allowing for new expressions of worship. He resonated with Vatican II's emphasis on the importance of the laity in worship and the pursuit of opportunities for their full participation in worship. In fact, in 1966 he used the momentum of Vatican II to challenge his own Lutheran tradition to renew their understanding of worship in relation to the worship environment. Sövik was particularly interested in reforming worship space design so that it might reflect more accurately the theological concerns of twentieth-century humanity as he understood them. He followed his challenge with remarks concerning several things he believed were important for

25. Edward A. Sövik, letter to the author, 25 June 1994.

Lutheran churches: an emphasis on the community in worship (participation in worship by *all* assembled), the elimination of the distinction between nave and chancel areas (seeking a church that was all "chancel"), the abolition of the communion rail, the practice of a basilican posture by clergy when presiding at the altar/table, and the celebration of the Eucharist in an atmosphere of joy.[26] Sövik's predisposition to emphasize the importance of all the faithful in worship was encouraged by Vatican II's pursuit of worship renewal, and he continued toward a nonchurch concept that sought explicitly to elevate the presence of the people, draw them fully into all liturgical celebrations, and provide opportunities for serving the larger community by using the space for nonliturgical activities.

An example of Sövik's ecumenical interest in liturgical renewal would be his active participation in the Liturgical Conference. In 1965 the Liturgical Conference gathered in Cleveland, Ohio, to focus on church architecture as its theme. At this meeting Sövik presented a paper that specifically addressed the role of the architect in liturgical renewal.[27] The following year the Liturgical Conference met in Houston, Texas. A strong theme running through this gathering was concern over the role of the church in a secular culture. After the meeting, the Liturgical Conference published a collection of essays, *Worship in the City of Man,* that dealt with concerns for service to the world and the implications that such a pursuit had for the reform of Christian worship. One essay addressed the subject of sacred space in this way:

> Sacred space is humanizing space; it is there that the Church happens. For this purpose the storefront may or may not be a better place than a Gothic cathedral. The test is whether the space is for men and whether it is a place where a thoroughly secularized world can be itself. Beauty and style, elegance and simplicity are never to be disregarded in the humanizing of God's world. Beautiful buildings are not a luxury; they are a desperate necessity. On the other hand, pouring enormous amounts of money into enormous rock piles that look like what churches are supposed to look like is hardly the great need of our day.[28]

Emphases important to Sövik can be discerned in this brief excerpt: concern for the people gathered in the sacred space (the "humanizing" potential of the space);

26. Sövik, "Reformation Is Still Needed," pp. 12-13.

27. Sövik, "Role of the Architect in Liturgical Renewal," pp. 12-25.

28. Brother Gabriel Moran, "The Theology of Secularity: What Happens to Worship?" chapter in *Worship in the City of Man* (Washington, D.C.: The Liturgical Conference, 1966), pp. 88-89.

concern for relationship to the secular (or ordinary) world all around; and concerns for beauty, simplicity, and stewardship. Openness to new forms of worship spaces is evident, and Sövik responded positively to this desire for change. Although Sövik has never claimed any dependence on Harvey Cox or the "secular city" debate, he was exposed to the social concerns that emerged from this debate and has admitted to being influenced (to some degree) by Cox's concerns for a Christian faith that had connection to and relevancy for everyday life.[29]

While Sövik did not attend the 1966 gathering of the Liturgical Conference, he did serve as a member of their board of directors from 1965 to 1971 and as their secretary from 1969 to 1971. One of the publications the Liturgical Conference produced while Sövik was secretary is *There's No Place Like People: Liturgical Celebrations in Home and Small-Group Situations* by Robert Hovda and Gabe Huck. The introduction to this book began by mentioning that the "church is both worshipping community and mission." The first chapter began with this line: "Biblical faith drew the Jewish and then the Christian people toward a more pure awareness that the 'place' of worship, of holy action, was the community of God's children, God's people, rather than any sacred place, building, or temple."[30]

At this time, when Sövik's association with the Liturgical Conference was the strongest, a significant focal point of worship reform was the gathered community in service to the world, addressing both liturgical and nonliturgical needs. Clearly his association with the Liturgical Conference was one of the things that influenced him to design worship spaces that were multifunctional.

In the mid-1960s Sövik was on the steering committee for the First International Congress on Religion, Architecture, and the Visual Arts. He attended this conference in New York City in 1967. In an article published two years later, Sövik reflected on the fact that there was a major focus on urbanization at the conference:

Sociologists, politicians, and planners made emphatic the urgency of examining the role of the institutional church in relation to the new kinds of human communities and their frightening problems. Nowhere have I heard more clearly made the position which asserts that if humanity is to be served the church may need to abandon its traditional institutional patterns, focus on the "humanitarian" programs, and allow the cultic life to

---

29. Edward A. Sövik, interview by the author, 1 July 1995, Northfield, Minnesota.

30. Robert Hovda and Gabe Huck, *There's No Place Like People: Liturgical Celebrations in Home and Small-Group Situations* (Washington, D.C.: The Liturgical Conference, 1969), pp. viii-ix, 3.

emerge in whatever new patterns grow organically from the situation.[31]

Sövik was concerned about the immediate needs of those in urban areas and identified with the emphasis on "humanitarian" service. After this conference he continued to work toward developing a nonchurch that could accommodate this goal of humanitarian assistance and remain open to the changes that liturgical life would undergo in the years to come.

At the First International Congress, Sövik encountered the thought of theologians such as Father Frédéric Debuyst. In his address to the conference, Debuyst defined the church building in terms of function and domesticity:

> A good definition of the church has been given by a Dutch bishop, the late Monsignor Bekkers. The church for him is essentially a "kind of great living room, a place where the faithful come together to meet the Lord and one another in the Lord." Such a room in itself has no specific architectural character, except on a functional side — functional in a fully human sense, to offer the community a space for active living and loving celebration. . . .
>
> This definition points towards domestic rather than monumental architecture . . . and hospitality over monumentality.[32]

Sövik commented enthusiastically on Father Debuyst's comments in his reflections on the congress meetings.[33] That Sövik was not alone in seeking a "house of the people of God" for Christian worship was underscored by theologians such as Debuyst, who were highlighting the actions of the community in worship gatherings and promoting expressions of architecture that related directly to the significance of their active worship celebrations and mission.

A final example of Sövik's ecumenical sensitivity and striving for liturgical renewal is his applying his approach to church design to a whole range of Christian communities. Throughout his career, Sövik maintained a consistent application of his nonchurch design to communities both Roman Catholic and Protestant (including Lutheran, United Methodist, Presbyterian, Episcopal, United Church of Christ,

---

31. Edward A. Sövik, "Revolution, Place, and Symbol: Reflections Two Years Later," *Worship* 43, no. 8 (October 1969): 497.

32. Dom Frédéric Debuyst, "Meaning of Religious Places," in *Revolution, Place, and Symbol*, p. 155.

33. Sövik, "Revolution, Place, and Symbol: Reflections Two Years Later," p. 498.

and Mennonite communities). He was careful to study the various theological interpretations of each tradition and design according to particular ministry (liturgical and nonliturgical) needs. He also studied denominational documents that articulated the construction of appropriate places for worship. An example of this effort is his endorsement of the North American bishops' document *Environment and Art in Catholic Worship* in the journal *Liturgy*.[34] Sövik was especially appreciative of the way in which this document articulated its design principles without resorting to a prescribed formula for each community. Sövik encouraged both Protestants and Catholics to use these reflections in a common effort to emulate Christ in the world through the built environment.

MODERN ARCHITECTURE AND SÖVIK'S CONCEPT OF THE NONCHURCH

Sövik completed his degree in architecture at Yale University in 1949. There he was exposed to the primary currents in architecture discussed earlier. Great emphasis was placed on using modern building materials and techniques with integrity. The influence of the International Style was evident in architectural schools at that time, particularly through the teaching and work of figures such as Walter Gropius and Ludwig Mies van der Rohe (Mies). A resistance to the adoption of historical styles of design, an appreciation of simplicity in expression, and an aversion to ornamentation yielded the reduced aesthetic discussed previously.

In his writings Sövik mentioned three modern architects who had a significant influence on his church design work: Frank Lloyd Wright, Mies, and Le Corbusier.[35]

---

34. Edward A. Sövik, "Ecumenics and High Art," *Liturgy* 23, no. 5 (September 1978): 19-20.

35. References to these architects and particular churches they designed can be found in the following: Le Corbusier (Ronchamp, 1950-1955) in Edward A. Sövik, "Church Design and the Communication of Religious Faith," *Architectural Record* 128 (December 1960): 138; Wright, Mies, and Le Corbusier (general observations) in Edward A. Sövik, "Fundamentals for Church Builders," *Your Church* 7, no. 3 (July/August/September 1961): 35; Wright, Mies, and Le Corbusier (general observations) in Edward A. Sövik, "New Visions for Church Builders," *Church Management* 38 (October 1961): 26; Mies (IIT chapel, 1952, and general observations) in Sövik, "The Faith Our Forms Express," pp. 297-98; Mies (IIT chapel, 1952) in Sövik, "What Is Religious Architecture?" *Discourse*, p. 80; Mies (IIT chapel, 1952) in Sövik, "The Architecture of Kerygma," pp. 203-4; Le Corbusier (Ronchamp, 1950-1955) in Sövik, "A Theology of Architecture," p. 182; Wright (general observation) in Sövik, "What Is Religious Architecture?" *Faith and Form*, p. 8; Wright and Le Corbusier (general observation) in Sövik, "Triumphalism, Sacred and Secular — A Christian Architect's Reflections,"

Sövik had read a number of works by Wright and Le Corbusier, even publishing reviews of *The Radiant City* by Le Corbusier and *An Organic Architecture* by Wright.[36] In reflecting generally upon the work of these three men, Sövik found the integrity and passion with which they pursued architectural design to be compatible with his understanding of Christian values (focus on a single higher cause or good for humanity).[37]

Sövik was impressed by Wright's concern for an organic principle in architecture. He noted how Wright applied this organic principle to both the physical environment and the human community. Just as Wright instituted and used an organic principle, creating physical spaces in harmony with the materials at hand and in concert with the environment that surrounded them, so Sövik used designs and materials that were in concert with pre-existing structures in the communities in which the worship spaces were to be built. Sövik took Wright's organic principle further by striving to make these worship spaces a part of the whole life of the community, spaces capable of hosting both liturgical and nonliturgical activities.

Mies reflected a beauty and truth in simplicity that Sövik adopted in his own design. Mies developed an architectural approach seeking to express beauty in minimalized forms. Rather than trying to design only according to function, Mies sought to design structures with pure, simple volumes and spaces. He realized that the needs of any community can change so rapidly that it is impossible to anticipate planning for them very far in advance; better to generate spaces that can be adapted for future needs with a minimum of effort.[38] Consistent with the IIT chapel that Mies designed, Sövik's worship structures are generally simple, centrally planned spaces. The interiors are usually devoid of physical barriers and allow for changes in liturgical activities as well as multiple uses for nonliturgical activities. A careful

---

p. 4; Mies (IIT chapel, 1952) in Sövik, "The Return to the Non-Church," p. 12; Le Corbusier (general observation), Wright (Unity Temple, Oak Park, 1908) and Mies (IIT chapel, 1952) in Sövik, *Architecture for Worship*, pp. 26-27, 49, 52-54; Mies (general observation) in E. A. Sövik, "Notes on Sacred Space," *The Christian Century* 99 (31 March 1982): 365; Le Corbusier (general observation) in Ed Sövik, "The Environment for Sight, Sound, and Action," *Dialog* 25, no. 4 (Fall 1986): 276.

36. Edward A. Sövik, review of *The Radiant City* by Le Corbusier, *Liturgical Arts* 36, no. 4 (August 1968): 120; Edward Anders Sövik, review of *An Organic Architecture: The Architecture of Democracy* by Frank Lloyd Wright, *Liturgical Arts* 39, no. 2 (February 1971): 53-54.

37. Sövik, "Fundamentals for Church Builders," p. 35.

38. Alan Holgate, *Aesthetics of Built Form* (Oxford: Oxford University Press, 1992), p. 217.

handling of proportion, a clarity of expression, and an attention to beauty are also evident, albeit with a developed theological interpretation.

Le Corbusier provided Sövik with a model of creativity, passion, and concern for contemporary expressions that he appreciated. In reflecting on Le Corbusier's architectural design, Sövik once wrote,

> One can discover in this [Le Corbusier's] architecture, I think, a most intense commitment to a series of ideas which can hardly be thought of except in terms of religion. There is, for instance, the Modular, which is Corbu's system of measure and proportion — a reflection of his faith that the created world hangs together, that visual order and mathematical order are related elements in a total order. There is the insistence that the architect's problem is to put the world in orderly form — encompassing the whole range from furniture to city — and that this order must serve the fulfillment of people. There is the unflinching and persistent enthusiasm for the real in preference to illusion, artificiality, or affectation. There is the implied assertion that the forms of the material may be invested with the spiritual. Is not this incarnationism? And there is a reflection in all the surprising and beautiful things that this man was in touch with wonder and mystery which are beyond reason.[39]

Le Corbusier affirmed order, people, the real, and sought a sense of the spiritual in architecture. Sövik confirmed these as important emphases in his own design work by creating worship spaces that exhibited order, by focusing on the people, by paying attention to truth or honesty in materials and expression, and by recognizing the power of architectural beauty to spark connection to the holy.

When Sövik began his architectural practice, some of the most progressive Christian worship spaces were being built in Europe. Liturgical renewal movements at work in Belgium, Germany, and Austria in the wake of World War I brought renewed emphasis on the notion of corporate worship and a "rediscovery of the scriptures" that influenced a reappraisal of the function of Christian art and architecture.[40] Christian architects like Rudolf Schwarz were raising concerns about the honesty of structural expression, the use of materials, and the expression of function with respect to contemporary church design.[41] And there was concern about

---

39. Sövik, review of *The Radiant City* by Le Corbusier, p. 120.
40. Peter Hammond, *Liturgy and Architecture* (London: Barrie & Rockliff, 1960), pp. 50-51.
41. Hammond, *Liturgy and Architecture*, p. 57.

the relationship between the *ecclesia* (the gathered people) and liturgy, about seeking a "house" for divine worship related directly to the community.[42]

Sövik had begun his exploration of European church design while at Yale. The devastation of World War II had provided the opportunity for a tremendous rebuilding of places of worship throughout Europe. In Sövik's day, there was a free flow between Europe and the United States of texts and images of modern church designs, materials that were especially interesting to young architects.[43] Sövik recalled those days:

> In the late forties, I gleaned the pages of European and American books and periodicals to study examples of "modern" church architecture and made a list of about 180, going back perhaps 60 years. Such things were thought of then as daring. . . . Many of them would not be thought modern now, but at least they ventured at change.[44]

After his studies at Yale, Sövik continued to read many architectural works in both French and German that featured contemporary European church designs.[45] (He also traveled to visit churches in France, Germany, and Switzerland from the year 1959 onward, finding European church designs more progressive and possessing more integrity than many church designs that he encountered in the United States.)[46] One German book that Sövik found particularly helpful was *Betonkirchen* by Ferdinand Pfammatter.[47] This volume contained text about and photographs of Roman Catholic and Protestant churches, primarily in Europe, especially those in France, Germany, and Switzerland. Outstanding architects to whom Sövik was

---

42. Hammond, *Liturgy and Architecture*, p. 57. H. A. Reinhold once commented, "I think Rudolf Schwarz has made the church anew *a house for* divine worship, not an autonomous, architectural expression of religious feeling. . . . That is a step forward." See H. A. Reinhold, "The Architecture of Rudolf Schwarz," *Architectural Forum* (January 1939): 26. See also Frédéric Debuyst, *Modern Architecture and Christian Celebration* (Richmond, Va.: John Knox Press, 1968), for an extended discussion of church design in relation to the "modern house."

43. References to many of these volumes can be found in Chapter Five, pp. 101-2.

44. Quoted by Torgerson, "Edward Anders Sövik and His Return to the 'Non-church,'" p. 96 n. 144.

45. Edward A. Sövik, interview by the author, 3 August 1993, Northfield, Minnesota. Sövik even published reviews of some of the works he read: E. A. Sövik, review of *Europaische Kirkenkunst der Gegenwart* by Erich Widder, and *L'architecture religieuse contemporaine en France* by Georges Mercier, *Faith and Form* 2 (April 1969): 4.

46. Edward A. Sövik, interview by the author, 3 August 1993.

47. Ferdinand Pfammatter, *Betonkirchen* (Zurich: Benzinger Verlag Einsieldeln, 1948); mentioned by Edward A. Sövik, interview by the author, 3 August 1993.

particularly drawn included key figures mentioned previously, such as Auguste Perret, Dominikus Böhm, Otto Bartning, and Rudolf Schwarz.[48] The churches that Sövik was especially interested in featured characteristics of modern church architecture, including an intentional rejection of historical architectural styles, the use of contemporary construction materials and techniques, exterior walls with little, if any, ornamentation, ample glass enclosing unobstructed interior spaces, flat roofs, and spartan interiors. A number of the spaces also used flexible seating (open space or chairs as opposed to long, fixed pews).[49] Sövik went on to incorporate many of these characteristics in his own architectural design work for worship spaces.

The first model of built environments that had a profound effect on Sövik's conception of worship space as nonchurch was the domestic living and dining room. With the liturgical movement's tremendous emphasis on the corporate nature of worship and full participation in its incarnation, conceiving of the church as "family" came up from time to time in both Protestant and Roman Catholic circles. Sövik was especially drawn to this image of church and used this metaphor to rail against the common distinct spaces of "nave" and "chancel" in historical models of worship space design. In seeking an alternative arrangement based on the family metaphor, Sövik began to reflect on the environments that families occupy, especially living and dining rooms, seeking to identify qualities of those spaces that might be transferable into spaces for Christian gatherings.

As mentioned earlier, Sövik had encountered Frédéric Debuyst at the First International Congress on Religion, Architecture, and the Visual Arts. Debuyst's likening of a worship space to a "great living room" captured Sövik's imagination.

48. Sövik refers to specific churches of these architects in the following: Böhm (St. Maria-Königin, Cologne-Marienburg) in Sövik, "Church Design and the Communication of Religious Faith," p. 138; Schwarz (*Fronleichnamskirche,* Aachen, 1928-1930, and *The Church Incarnate*) in Sövik, "The Faith Our Forms Express," pp. 292-93; Schwarz (general observation) in Sövik, "The Architecture of Kerygma," p. 198; Schwarz (*Fronleichnamskirche,* Aachen, 1928-1930) in E. A. Sövik, "Images of the Church," *Worship* 41, no. 3 (1967): 134; Schwarz (*Saint Christoforus,* Cologne, 1957-1960) in E. A. Sövik, "Tea and Sincerity," *Liturgical Arts* 37, no. 1 (November 1968): 7; Böhm (general observation) and Schwarz (*The Church Incarnate*) in Edward A. Sövik, "House of God to House of God's People," p. 215; Auguste Perret (*Notre-Dame du Raincy,* Paris, 1922-1923), Bartning (*Stahlkirche,* Cologne, 1928, and *Sternkirche,* 1922), and Böhm (St. Engelbert, Cologne, 1930-1933) in Sövik, "The Return to the Non-Church," pp. 12-14; Auguste Perret (*Notre-Dame du Raincy,* Paris, 1922-1923), Bartning (*Stahlkirche,* Cologne, 1928, and *Sternkirche,* 1922), and Böhm (St. Engelbert, Cologne, 1930-1933) in Sövik, *Architecture for Worship,* pp. 26-27, 29-31.

49. Pfammatter, *Betonkirchen,* pp. 38-41, 53, 62, 80, 84. In an interview with the author on 3 August 1993, Sövik spoke of another architectural book of religious spaces that he appreciated: Paul Thiry, Richard M. Bennett, and Henry L. Kamphoefner, *Churches and Temples* (New York: Reinhold Publishing Corporation, 1953).

In 1968 Sövik was delighted to find Debuyst's approach articulated more fully in his book *Modern Architecture and Christian Celebration*. Debuyst had compiled six lectures in a short volume that discussed the importance of celebration in Christian worship and focused on the modern house as a potential model for Christian churches:

> A church is not an architectural monument built to symbolize God's glory, but a "Paschal meeting-room," a functional space created for the celebrating of Christian assembly. It is a real interior, and it has to express a very fundamental kind of hospitality.
>
> . . . the churches of tomorrow, if they are to be really good churches, will have to look much more like simple houses than like the churches of today or yesterday. In fact, they will have to combine the freedom of the modern house with the basic qualities of the early Christian churches.[50]

Sövik resonated with Debuyst's focus on the activities of the gathered community, worship as a celebratory activity, and spaces of simplicity, flexibility, and hospitality in which to accommodate new and existing forms of worship. In his book Debuyst also expressed a desire to promote church designs that he felt were more in tune with the spirit and needs of modern humanity, both contemporary in design and humane in expression.[51] Debuyst even featured churches in his book by architects whom Sövik admired, including the Church of Corpus Christi, Aachen, the Church of St. Christopher, Cologne-Niehl, and the chapel at Schloss Rothenfels, all by Rudolf Schwarz; St. Saviour's Chapel, Illinois Institute of Technology, Chicago, by Mies van der Rohe; and Notre Dame du Haut, Ronchamp, by Le Corbusier. Sövik mentioned Debuyst and *Modern Architecture and Christian Celebration* in published articles from 1969 to 1982.[52] Sövik favorably reviewed *Modern Architecture and Christian Celebration* in the journal *Faith and Form,* and he wrote a foreword to a second edition of Debuyst's book (which was never released).[53]

In considering domestic living and dining room models, Sövik identified the centralized, undivided space and the flexibility of these rooms as important qualities

50. Debuyst, *Modern Architecture and Christian Celebration,* p. 30.

51. Debuyst, *Modern Architecture and Christian Celebration,* pp. 40-41.

52. Sövik, "House of God to House of God's People," p. 219; Sövik, "The Place of Worship: Environment for Action," pp. 100-101; Sövik, "Notes on Sacred Space," p. 365.

53. E. A. Sövik, review of *Modern Architecture and Christian Celebration* by Frédéric Debuyst, *Faith and Form* 2 (January 1969): 30.

to incorporate into his nonchurch worship spaces. The centralized, undivided space would help to ensure that no one person would be any great distance from another and would underscore that the environment implied no distinction between clergy and laity. Flexibility encouraged the ability to incorporate changes (changes in worship or changes between liturgical and nonliturgical activities) and allowed for the focus of the activities embodied to shift, all working ultimately toward the goals of meeting various needs and extending inclusiveness (both inside and outside of the Christian community).

Sövik was drawn primarily to those churches that not only exhibited use of modern architectural principles, materials, and techniques, but also combined this modern approach and liturgical sensitivity to produce a centralized worship space of intimacy, humility, flexibility, and light. The Church of St. Christopher (Cologne-Niehl, 1960) by Rudolf Schwarz is a good example of a space using a reduced aesthetic that Sövik thought worthy of considering a model worship environment. The central plan based on the square, the seating on three sides of the altar, the minimal wall, roof, and floor treatments, and the asymmetrical arrangement of liturgical focal points all appealed to Sövik.[54] Indeed, these qualities would find their way into Sövik's expressions of the nonchurch.

The second model of built environments that profoundly affected Sövik's conception of worship space as nonchurch was the Japanese teahouse. Sövik's use of the teahouse as a source of insight for designing Christian worship spaces was noted in the *New York Times* in 1968.[55] His interest in this model grew from an earlier experience of encountering teahouse designs in July of 1965. The Board of World Missions of the Lutheran Church in America sent Sövik to Tokyo to discuss plans for a new Lutheran theological seminary that was to be built in the city. While in Japan, Sövik spent time examining historical and modern Japanese sites and structures, especially in Kyoto and Tokyo. He contrasted the secular architecture of Kyoto Palace and Katsura Villa with the sacred architecture of the Nikko temples and shrines, opting for the former as a more genuine expression of "truth" (or expression of the "religious").[56] Given his predisposition toward seeking God in the ordinary and his ap-

54. Edward A. Sövik, letter to the author, 4 November 1994.

55. "Edward Anders Sövik, a theologically sophisticated architect in Northfield, Minn., has suggested that, except for size, the best analogy for church designing is now the Japanese tea room." From "New Church Designs Reflect Changes in Liturgy," *New York Times*, 6 July 1968, col. 2, p. 23.

56. Sövik, "A Theology of Architecture," p. 172.

preciation of domestic design, it is not surprising that Sövik suggested the Japanese teahouse as a model for Christian worship spaces.[57]

Sövik was moved by the environment that sheltered the ritual of the Japanese tea ceremony. He appreciated the choice of readily available materials used in constructing the teahouse and the great skill and care taken in composing these materials into expressions of utility and beauty:

> The materials are ordinary, the structure simple and forthright. Bamboo, thatch, unfinished timbers and boards, mud and straw plaster, paper, stone for the footings and hearth, woven grass floor mats — these are the typical materials. . . . One has a sense that the environment is one of absolute ingenuousness.
>
> . . . the humble material is invested with the most thoughtful and skillful artistry of design, and the finest possible craftsmanship. I have wondered whether there is a better symbol of incarnation and redemption than this — that one cherishes the earthy and natural things enough to invest to the limit in them and thus to transform them into something superlative, without ever changing them into something synthetic or exotic.[58]

His architectural training at Yale had predisposed Sövik to favor respecting the nature of materials in building, using the strengths of the materials chosen, and allowing them to be what they were in presentation (no masking or pretending the material was something that it was not) — themes present in the development of modern architectural design. Sövik recognized these same concerns for honesty and integrity in the structure of the teahouse and applauded them. He then took the example of care taken in the construction of the teahouse, raising the value of simple, humble materials by investing them with great craftsmanship, and compared this to the incarnation of Jesus Christ, imagining God to be the craftsperson who takes the humble, earthy material of this world and infuses that substance with worth far beyond measure. Sövik's concern to emphasize the truth that God uses the ordinary of this world to convey the extraordinary was again evident. Christian worship

---

57. Sövik, "A Theology of Architecture," p. 178. Additional references to the Japanese teahouse can be found in Sövik, "What Is Religious Architecture?" *Faith and Form*, p. 22; Sövik, "Images of the Church," pp. 139-41; Edward A. Sövik, "The Building and the Music," *The Diapason* 58, no. 4 (March 1967): 44; Edward Anders Sövik, "What Is a Church? A Place for Holding Family Reunions," *World Encounter* 5, no. 4 (April 1968): 10, 13; Edward Anders Sövik, "What Is an Altar? What Is a Pulpit? What Is a Baptismal Font? Why?" *World Encounter* 5, no. 4 (April 1968): 18-19; Sövik, "Tea and Sincerity," pp. 4-7; Sövik, *Architecture for Worship*, pp. 76-77.

58. Sövik, "Tea and Sincerity," p. 5.

spaces could convey beauty and nobility through simplicity and honesty, just as the Japanese teahouse did.

Sövik was also drawn to the asymmetrical arrangement of the Japanese teahouse space. In thinking about the significance of its asymmetry, Sövik commented,

> This quality is an expression of the awareness of imperfections, the sense of incompleteness and tension, the consciousness that life is movement rather than stability. . . . This asymmetric composition has nothing of chaos; it is simply a different kind of order from the stable classic and geometric. And since the most profound truth is in paradox, there is nothing contradictory in the fact that the tea room exhibits at once the qualities of tension and of utmost serenity.[59]

Sövik believed that asymmetrical arrangements of space could provoke an awareness of finitude, tension, and movement in those who occupied the spaces. He was cognizant of the paradoxes of the Christian faith: that God is transcendent yet immanent; that God would need to die that we could live; that humanity is initiated into faith through "dying and rising" with Christ; that our mysteries of faith will never find complete resolution in this life. He also knew that in the course of worship celebrations, the focal point of the space might need to shift from location to location (between pulpit, altar, font, choir, congregation, etc.). Sövik hoped that asymmetrical arrangements of the interior space might help worshippers to embrace the natural shifts in focus that would occur and to contemplate paradox in their experiences of worship.

SÖVIK'S NONCHURCH:
DESIGN GUIDELINES AND TWO EXAMPLES

Sövik's guidelines for nonchurch design took roughly twenty years to crystallize. Particular preferences with regard to exterior and interior design of the nonchurch worship space can be discerned in his work.

The exterior of Sövik's nonchurches generally reflect architectural expressions similar to those in the community (e.g., schools, office buildings, and factories). In an attempt to relate the worship structure more directly to the community, Sövik

---

59. Sövik, "Tea and Sincerity," pp. 5, 7.

intentionally emulated secular designs in his nonchurches. He sought to relate his churches to the mundane of this world (thinking of how God chose to incarnate Godself in the ordinary of this world):

> To be consistent with the idea of the incarnation, the architect, it seems to me, must deal unabashedly with the finite, the ordinary, the secular, the everyday, the contemporary, the particular. And he ought to avoid the strange, the curious, the stylistic, the exotic, and all those temptations to make of a church something different, special, or "religious."
>
> . . . religious architecture is not limited to church building any more than the religious life is limited to church going. A church building has to serve a particular sort of function, but the materials, the structural techniques, the design details, and the attitude of the designer are not necessarily or ideally different from those which ought to be present to other architectural problems.[60]

Sövik is not denying that the building for the church is different or special with respect to function; rather, his concern is that the intent of the architect and the materials and techniques employed need to be oriented toward the best manifestations of contemporary architectural design. Buildings for worship need to be understood as important for their relationship to *this* world, not interpreted as structures that are relegated to the world that is to come.

Focus on the incarnation of Christ affects the interior design of the nonchurch in a number of ways. To be consistent with the model of the servant Jesus reflected in his earthly ministry, Sövik seeks to create interiors that are humble and accessible. He seeks to incarnate hospitable worship spaces by generally limiting the height of his structures to roughly two stories (paying particular attention to scale so that people do not feel diminished) and using a simple rectangular shape for the interior of the space, slightly longer than it is wide, so that no one is too far away from the center of activity. Common materials such as brick, steel, concrete, hardwoods, and glass are left exposed (not altered to imitate other materials) and combined with colorful textiles to produce a rich and inviting environment.

Sövik's nonchurch interiors have level floors (to provide easily accessible and flexible spaces for liturgical and nonliturgical activities) and are generally devoid of

---

60. Sövik, "The Architecture of Kerygma," p. 203.

balconies or galleries (which might split the community, reducing a sense of unity). The interior has minimal ornamentation, allowing liturgical furnishings to become the primary symbolic foci of the worship space.[61] Sövik usually locates a platform of rectangular wooden units along one long side of the space (out about ten feet from the wall) with seating (usually upholstered wooden chairs, sometimes simple pews) set on three sides of the low platform. Three unequal sections of chairs are often arranged around the platform and are frequently located at right angles to one another, thus increasing the individual's awareness of being in the midst of community. A wooden altar/table, often nearly square in shape, is placed on the two-step-high platform area along with a wooden pulpit, chairs for those presiding, and stands for candles and plants. A processional cross is provided for the worship space, usually a Greek-style cross (sometimes with a corpus and sometimes without) set on a pole, which is to reside in the midst of the people during the worship event (indicative of Christ being present "in our midst"). Usually the seating and liturgical furnishings are designed to be portable; this allows for various arrangements for worship and makes it easy to remove these objects to accommodate nonliturgical events in the space.

A stone font for baptism is located near the entrance of the worship space. The fonts are usually substantial in size (often between three and four feet in diameter and just over two feet high) and frequently square or octagonal in shape. Fresh water is fed into these fonts, with drainage systems provided. The font reminds Christians entering the space of their baptism, and appeals to the uninitiated as an attractive fountain or water pool. Its location minimally inhibits the multiple uses of the space. Other liturgical furnishings such as tabernacles, ambries, and communion rails are included as required.

Facilities for music are provided by locating an organ (if requested) near one corner or one short side of the space (to minimize problems with flexibility). A piano is sometimes included in the same general vicinity. The choir is frequently placed in a section of chairs located on one side of the platform area near the organ and/or piano. Placing the choir here (facing the altar/pulpit area) preserves a sense of their unity with the larger community and allows them to be visible when they present performance pieces.

---

61. Minimal ornamentation also meant that the space could more easily be used for nonliturgical functions. With the primary liturgical appointments and symbols being removable, it would be easier for people to transition to nonliturgical activities in a space they identified with worship.

Sövik pursues an asymmetrical arrangement of furnishings in his worship spaces to encourage a focus that can shift easily depending on which liturgical center requires attention at any given time.[62] There is no attempt to emphasize one liturgical center over another; this conveys an equality of significance, such that God can be perceived as equally present in the Eucharist, baptism, and preaching.[63] An asymmetrical approach also maintains a certain tension in the space, avoiding a static environment, and even allows attention to move toward the worshippers when they are the focus of the celebration (e.g., during the singing of songs).

Completed in 1969, St. Leo's Roman Catholic Church, Pipestone, Minnesota, is a good example of Sövik's nonchurch approach.[64] The exterior is composed of concrete bands with brick in-fill. These bands, visible from both the exterior and the interior, emphasize the horizontal dimension of the space. The building resembles a contemporary commercial structure, and at the time of its completion it did not have a cross fixed to any exterior surface of the building.[65] The primary entrance to the space is marked by a pair of clear glass doors, leading into a substantial gathering area with an angular concrete overhang.

The overall shape of the worship space is a rectangle, a little wider than it is long, with a level floor. The materials used to construct this space are steel, concrete, brick, wood, and glass. Internal piers of concrete mark two open aisles the length of each of the longer sides of the space. Most of the window panels are composed of angular, irregularly sized pieces of leaded glass — some clear, the rest in a variety of colors (light hues of lavender, orange, yellow, green, blue, rose, brown, and gray). These windows are nonrepresentational and contain no explicit Christian symbols. They are features of all four walls of the space — clerestory along the two longer walls and asymmetrically placed panes on the two shorter walls. Open brickwork is placed at irregular intervals in the walls to create variety in wall treatment and to shield acoustic panels. The floor is also made of brick. Fixed pews of red oak are arranged in an asymmetrical pattern on three sides of an altar/table island.

---

62. Sövik, *Architecture for Worship*, p. 76.

63. E. A. Sövik, "Westwood Lutheran Church, St. Louis Park, Minnesota," *Northwest Architect* 28, no. 3 (May/June 1961): 63.

64. Reflections on the genesis of this church can be found in Father Paul Evers and William Stolte, *An Incarnational Church: Saint Leo Catholic Church* (Pipestone, Minn.: Nicollet Press, 1969).

65. Later, the parish added the name of the church and a Latin-style cross to the exterior of the building near the primary entrance.

Above: Exterior view of St. Leo's Roman Catholic Church (architect: Edward Sövik, 1969). St. Leo's is a rectangular building resembling the commercial buildings of its day. Although the exterior features minimal ornamentation, the church is identified by its name and a cross.

Below: Interior view of St. Leo's Roman Catholic Church. The rectangular worship space is centered on a focal point along one long side of the building. Fixed pews arranged in an asymmetrical pattern around three sides of the raised platform provide congregational seating.

Near the entrance of the space is a significant font (four feet square by two feet high) of gray granite with running water.[66] Along one of the long interior walls is a fixed, minimally raised area made of brick that holds the altar, ambo, credence, and chairs for clergy seating. (All furniture is made of red oak.) The altar is rectangular and can be moved if necessary. The choir area is located on one end of the altar/table area near the organ, which has been placed along one of the short sides of the space.

The only easily visible cross is a Greek-style cross with corpus on a standard that is carried into the space during each liturgical celebration. Stations of the Cross are located in an aisle behind the raised platform area, but in keeping with the uncomplicated design approach, they are simple Greek crosses of wood embedded in the brick floor of the space. The stations lead one to the tabernacle. The bronze tabernacle, designed by Frank Kacmarcik, is set on a stand of red oak and located to the right of and just behind the altar/table area. Red oak kneeling benches and padded red oak chairs are set to the right of the tabernacle and create a space used as a "reservation chapel" within the main worship space.

In most respects, St. Leo's represents Sövik's understanding of a nonchurch. St. Leo's reflects concerns present in the wake of post–Vatican II developments: a concern for breaking down the perceived gulf between clergy and laity in liturgical celebrations (by placing the clergy in the midst of the laity), an emphasis on baptism and preaching in the worship service (by avoiding an altar-dominant space), and an emphasis on the *people* as the body of Christ on earth (through seating arrangements that made the people aware, perhaps uncomfortably, of their communal gathering). A modest scale, ample light, beautiful furnishings, and space for easy movement create a hospitable environment for many activities.

A Protestant space that epitomizes the Sövik nonchurch is Trinity United Methodist Church, Charles City, Iowa, completed in 1972.[67] The exterior is composed of concrete bands with brick in-fill. A pair of clear glass doors serve as the primary en-

66. According to Michael E. DeSanctis, St. Leo's may exhibit one of the first instances of locating the font near the entrance of the worship space in a post–Vatican II Catholic church in the United States. See Michael E. DeSanctis, "Renewing the City of God: The Reform of Catholic Architecture in the United States," *Meeting House Essays*, No. 5 (Chicago: Liturgy Training Publications, 1993), p. 55 n. 16. Many other churches, Catholic and Protestant, have located their font/pool near the entrance (instead of in a more secluded area) in the last thirty years in an effort to elevate the significance of initiation in relation to the community (reminding people of their own baptism as they enter and allowing for ample room and visibility for celebrations of the rite of initiation).

67. Trinity United Methodist Church is featured prominently in Sövik's book *Architecture for Worship.*

Author photo.

Author photo.

Above: A small, fixed, elevated platform area holds the altar, the ambo, and the seating area for clergy. A tabernacle is located just behind and to the right of the altar area. St. Leo's Roman Catholic Church, Pipestone, Minnesota.

Left: The granite baptismal font is located near the entrance of the worship space. St. Leo's Roman Catholic Church, Pipestone, Minnesota.

Above: Exterior view of Trinity United Methodist Church (architect: Edward Sövik, 1972). Sovik designed a generally rectangular building featuring a steel frame and exterior walls of concrete bands with brick in-fill. Concrete columns holding four bells and a small Greek-style cross are located on one end of the worship space.

Below: Interior view of Trinity United Methodist Church. The rectangular interior of this church features a low platform along one long side of the space as a focal point. The altar, pulpit, and clergy seating are located on this platform. The seating — padded wooden chairs — is flexible.

trance to the gathering space of the facility, with another entrance just off a parking lot on the opposite side of the building. Concrete columns resembling a simple scaffold hold four bells and a small Greek cross at a minimal height above the worship space on the side opposite the primary entrance (invisible from there). From the outside, Trinity looks like a school or other auditorium facility, a feature that allows it to discreetly integrate itself into its more residential community setting.

The worship space is generally rectangular in shape, a little wider than it is long, with a platform area located along one longer side. The interior of the worship space has a flat floor of paving brick. Open and closed brickwork cover the lower walls, with wood panels covering much of the upper walls. Stained glass is placed in three of the four walls: there are two large sections on the lower part of one wall, two on the upper part of the opposite wall, and clerestory panels along a third wall (opposite the platform area). The stained glass, designed and crafted by Rambusch, Inc., New York City, is abstract, angular geometric shapes in various hues. (Blue and gray are the dominant colors in the large section on one side; red and yellow are dominant in the panels opposite; and yellow, gray, and brown are dominant in the clerestory panels along the third wall.) A primary gathering area containing tables and chairs is located immediately outside the main worship space.

A granite baptismal font with flowing water is located near the primary entrance to the worship space. Trinity United Methodist Church.

Author photo

The baptismal font is placed near the entrance to the space, against the wall. The font is made of gray flamed granite, three feet square by thirty-two inches high. Immediately above the font is a fourteen-inch pipe by which water flow can be controlled. (There is also a drain in the bottom of the font's basin.) The font can hold enough water to allow an infant to be baptized by immersion.

A platform of multiple oak panels is placed along one longer wall of the space (with an open aisle behind it marked by concrete piers, as in St. Leo's). Because the platform is made of oak, it stands in contrast to the floor of brick pavers. The platform area provides a slight elevation for the altar/table, pulpit, and chairs for those presiding at liturgical celebrations. The modular panels that compose the platform are substantial in weight, but mobile. Congregational seating consists of chairs that Sövik himself designed. Originally the seating was placed on three sides of the platform area, with the two side banks of chairs facing at right angles to the bank set in front of the platform. The choir was originally located to the left side of the platform area, near the pipe organ. Sövik designed two Greek-style processional crosses for the church, but it had no permanent installation of a cross. The congregation used and appreciated the processional crosses, but they eventually installed a Latin-style cross, front and center, above the platform area.

The congregants at Trinity have found their nonchurch space hospitable and flexible. They have used their worship space for all kinds of congregational events, including various meetings, conferences, performances, and dinners. The space is also available to the community, and over the years they have had many community groups use their space for all kinds of meetings and events. The service that Sövik envisioned has truly been achieved in and through Trinity's nonchurch space.

Conclusions

Sövik is a thoughtful, articulate Christian architect whose church design work exhibited a convergence of the ecumenical movement, the liturgical movement, and the modern architecture movement. His ability to converse with theologians and his interest in sharing in ecumenical dialogue exposed him to the prevailing impulses of liturgical renewal. His prolific speaking and publishing disseminated his ideas in Protestant and Roman Catholic communities throughout North America and beyond.

Sövik's nonchurch approach grew from his background and life experiences, which included his roots in missionary work in China, his theological training in an atmosphere emphasizing Christian service to the world, his participation in liturgical renewal exhibiting a focus on the activities of the people of God, and his architectural preparation in the midst of particular priorities of modern architectural design. Important emphases that emerge from Sövik's approach to twentieth-century church design include a blurring of boundaries between sacred and secular geography; a potential sacralization of the ordinary materials of our world; a focus on the people who will use the buildings provided for ministry (liturgical and nonliturgical); a strong sense of stewardship (both of financial resources and of utility in relation to the buildings that are erected); an elevation of beauty as an avenue for encountering God's "otherness"; and a concern for public presence or witness. Humility, simplicity, and excellence are hallmarks of Sövik's churches. Theologically, it would be fair to say that his churches exhibit a pronounced accent on "God in our midst."

As an architect, Sövik responded to the theological emphases of his day with a nonchurch design that could address the perceived needs of the church. He made a decision to highlight the human dimension of the incarnation of Christ because of his concern for service and perhaps to counter the tendency of some churches to emphasize primarily liturgical activities. He did not deny the need for liturgy, but through his passion for mission he could conceive of a worship environment that was capable of embracing both liturgical and nonliturgical activities. In a sense, Sövik's nonchurches stand as a quintessential form of an architecture of immanence.

CHAPTER NINE

WHERE ARE WE NOW? DISCERNMENT AND LESSONS LEARNED

One can say that every new church in a new style is an experiment. Without the risk of experiments that fail, there is no creation. Perhaps people in the future will point to many failed experiments; but they will also point to the wondrous success: the triumph over the dishonest, the unquestioned, the anxiously conservative. New church building is a victory of spirit, of the creative human spirit of God that breaks into our weakness.

PAUL TILLICH, "On the Theology of Fine Art and Architecture" (1961)

THE TWENTIETH CENTURY was a period of unprecedented discovery, change, and consequences good and bad. Developments in the areas of science and technology have changed the way in which we understand our world, our universe, and one another. Our living patterns have changed as we have applied the fruits of our discoveries. Both positive and negative consequences have often emerged in the wake of our enthusiastic pursuit of "progress." For example, we have created many ways of manufacturing products that require less human labor. On the positive side, this can often reduce the initial cost of certain products and increase the rate of production. On the negative side, jobs are eliminated, human craftsmanship may be compromised, and an ethos of "disposability" may emerge (which creates more waste in landfills). In the field of medicine, we have uncovered numerous ways to enhance human life. On the positive side, effective treatments for many illnesses are alleviating much suffering, and life expectancy is increasing in some parts of the world. On the negative side, our technological abilities exact increasing costs for medical care (often negatively affecting availability) and are providing opportunities for research and development that may compromise the ethical beliefs of many communities.

I could mention numerous other examples in the areas of agriculture, economics, transportation, energy development, and urban planning, but the point is that the applications of many discoveries in the twentieth century have often been found, in the end, to yield destructive consequences — even if unintended. The rather simple, naive view of progress that people had at the beginning of the twentieth century was over time replaced by a recognition of the complexity of the application of insights, with advancement and retreat occurring simultaneously depending on the particularity of human constituencies.

So I begin these final reflections on church architecture in the twentieth century with the recognition that progress for some is not progress for all. While certain goals for the dramatic changes in church design were helpful in some ways, unintended consequences also emerged. The solutions that were intended to express a theological affirmation of the people of God did achieve their effect in the built environment, but sometimes this was achieved at the cost of affirming the significance of God's holiness (at least from the perspective of some believers). I will conclude this exploration of an architecture of immanence by commenting on the continuing efforts of ecumenism and liturgical renewal, the demise of modern architecture, and the lessons learned thus far from an extraordinary period of experimentation in church design.

Modulation in Ecumenism

Ecumenism has continued to bear fruit in the final decades of the twentieth century. The World Council of Churches (WCC) continues to work through its offices in Geneva, Switzerland. The WCC claims a current membership of more than 340 churches, denominations, and church fellowships in over one hundred countries (representing some 400 million Christians who are Orthodox or Protestant, with the Roman Catholic Church maintaining a working relationship with the WCC).[1] Its original membership of European and North American entities has expanded to include constituencies in Africa, Asia, the Caribbean, Latin America, the Middle East, and the Pacific. World assemblies of members have continued to hold meetings regularly through the end of the twentieth century, including meetings in Evanston, Illinois (1954), New Delhi (1961), Uppsala (1968), Nairobi (1975), Vancouver (1983), Canberra (1991), and Harare (1998). The National Council of Churches (NCC), the

1. See www.wcc-coe.org/wcc/who/index-e.html.

largest cooperative body for ecumenical work in the United States, continues its work from its offices in Washington, D.C. The NCC claims 36 Orthodox and Protestant member denominations, representing about 50 million people in more than 100,000 local congregations.[2] Five primary program commissions guide most of the work of the NCC. The commissions have representatives from 54 denominations (including the Roman Catholic Church), seeking to foster constructive theological dialogue and cooperative ministry in the United States and around the world. While the presence and work of the WCC and the NCC continue, the initial impetus of the ecumenical movement, with its heavy investment of financial resources and high-profile presence, has been transmuted into an effort involving fewer financial resources and a lower visible profile depending increasingly on grassroots efforts.[3]

Theological conversations and official statements by entities such as the World Council of Churches have clarified the understandings of various traditions, highlighting points of both agreement and disagreement. An extraordinary example of cooperative, ecumenical theological reflection related to worship was the release of *Baptism, Eucharist, and Ministry* (BEM) by the Faith and Order Commission of the WCC after its meeting in Lima, Peru, in January 1982.[4] The Faith and Order Commission had been working on issues related to the theology and practice of baptism, the Eucharist, and ministry since its 1927 meeting in Lausanne. Thus BEM represented the results of a fifty-year process of exploration. BEM was unanimously recommended for transmission to the world's churches by more than a hundred Orthodox, Protestant, and Roman Catholic theologians gathered at Lima.[5] The primary text

2. See www.ncccusa.org/members/index.html.

3. In mentioning the continuing work of the WCC and NCC, I do not mean to ignore the significant activities of other ecumenical bodies in the United States and Europe, such as the following: the Conference of European Churches (founded in 1959, a fellowship of 126 Orthodox, Protestant, and Old Catholic churches of Europe and 43 associated organizations; see www.cec-kek.org); the World Evangelical Alliance (founded in 1951, representing approximately 200 million evangelicals in 123 countries; see www.worldevangelical.org); the National Association of Evangelicals (founded in 1943, representing 54 denominational bodies and additional organizations; see www.nae.net); and the European Evangelical Alliance (founded in the 1950s, representing 15 million European evangelicals in 35 countries of the European Union; see www.europeanea.org). All of these ecumenical organizations remain committed to facilitating ministry in the name of Jesus Christ across sectarian boundaries.

4. Faith and Order Commission, *Baptism, Eucharist, and Ministry,* Faith and Order Paper No. 111 (Geneva: World Council of Churches, 1982).

5. This includes Eastern Orthodox, Oriental Orthodox, Roman Catholic, Old Catholic, Lutheran, Anglican, Reformed, Methodist, United, Disciples, Baptist, Adventist, and Pentecostal traditions. Source: Faith and Order Commission, *Baptism, Eucharist, and Ministry,* back cover.

represents points of theological agreement on baptism, the Eucharist, and ministry, with commentary highlighting areas of disagreement. The document was offered to facilitate conversation among the world's Christians on these essential aspects of the faith. Its presence was an unusual example of mutual recognition and appreciation, seeking the development of additional common ground for tangible expressions of the Christian faith.

The creation of human institutions is not without its difficulties, especially large organizations such as the WCC and the NCC. In the years that followed their creation, reports began to surface of occasional fiscal mismanagement and the pursuit, now and then, of particular political agendas. Increasing efforts at accountability have often followed these allegations. Such realities do take a toll on enthusiasm, however, and the idealistic thoughts of establishing an easy uniformity of Christian presence faded. A general decline in the growth of many mainline denominations in the United States in the latter half of the twentieth century also contributed to the consolidation of the efforts of the WCC and the NCC. The popular practice of the Christian faith in both Europe and the United States from the 1960s forward has also been less vigorous in many quarters of the church. All of these factors hampered, to some extent, the maintenance of a high level of energy for ecumenical activity. Ecumenism has not died over the years, but it has matured somewhat and now pursues a slightly different path at a slower but still steady pace.

The ecumenical movement's early goal of achieving an increase in uniformity in faith and practice across denominational lines has gradually shifted to an emphasis on affirming unity around a common theological center expressed in a diversity of patterns and expressions.[6] To this end, significant achievements in the last few decades would include the Leuenberg Agreement (1973),[7] the Roman Catholic Church and Lutheran World Federation Joint Declaration on the Doctrine of Justification

---

6. For example, unity in diversity with respect to worship can be discerned in *Worship Today: Understanding, Practice, Ecumenical Influences,* Faith and Order Paper No. 194, ed. Thomas F. Best and Dagmar Heller (Geneva: WCC Publications, 2004).

7. The Leuenberg Agreement was signed by ninety-nine European Protestant churches (five were churches located in South America derived from European immigrant communities), allowing for "pulpit and altar fellowship" between Lutheran, Reformed, United, and Hussite churches. This agreement was a significant early movement to demonstrate visible unity among Protestant churches, especially those divided by historical Lutheran and Reformed differences. In the wake of the agreement a Leuenberg Fellowship was organized, with a general assembly meeting at least every six years, to nurture continuing cooperation and theological development.

(1999),[8] the relationship of "full communion" achieved between the Evangelical Lutheran Church in America and the Episcopal Church (2001),[9] the continuing cooperation exhibited in the three emerging statements from an American movement entitled "Evangelicals and Catholics Together,"[10] and the *Charta Oecumenica* statement entered into by the Conference of European Churches and the Council of European Bishops' Conferences (2001).[11] Fifty years of talking and working together is yielding new respect, understanding, and appreciation among the majority of Christian churches today. An enduring achievement of the ecumenical movement has been the cooperation of churches from a broad spectrum of Christian traditions in various local worship celebrations and social ministries. Ecumenical cooperation has taken root in numerous towns and cities throughout Europe and the United States, with congregations celebrating the one shared faith in Jesus Christ through many ways of praying and cooperative ministries extending mercy to others.[12]

An odd sort of phenomenon that could be attributed in part to the continuing effectiveness of the ecumenical movement is the growth of the so-called nondenomi-

8. This document is the culmination of many decades of intentional conversation. The mutual condemnations of the sixteenth century were put into historical context and no longer found to be helpful in light of recent theological conversations, and an affirmation of justification by faith in the saving action of God in Christ was affirmed by both traditions.

9. As stated in the document "Called to Common Mission," this was the culmination of a thirty-year dialogue between the two traditions. This document does not represent a merger of the two denominations, but it does provide for clergy and laity to move freely between the two churches.

10. The conversation partners of "Evangelicals and Catholics Together" began their exchanges in 1985. They have produced three formal statements: (1) "Evangelicals and Catholics Together: The Christian Mission in the Third Millennium," in *First Things* 43 (May 1994): 15-22; (2) "The Gift of Salvation," in *First Things* 79 (January 1998): 20-23; and (3) "Your Word Is Truth," in *First Things* 125 (August/September 2002): 38-42.

11. This agreement is an expression of a common commitment to continue to dialogue and work together cooperatively in ministry among the majority of Roman Catholic, Orthodox, and Protestant churches in Europe.

12. My own theological education and academic vocation might be my personal testimony to the effect and influence of the ecumenical movement in the last forty years. I was raised in the Evangelical Covenant Church, a small, conservative, evangelical Protestant tradition (such denominations are often identified as "free-church" for their insistence on local congregational autonomy and resistance to prescribed patterns of worship). Following preparation for ministry at North Park Theological Seminary, the only denominational seminary for the Covenant Church, I spent six and a half years at the University of Notre Dame pursuing theological graduate studies and teaching undergraduates. The majority of my teaching experience following my graduate work has been at Protestant mainline schools, including my present position at Judson College, a school affiliated with the American Baptist Church. Such a free-flowing movement in academic circles between free-church, Roman Catholic, and mainline Protestant traditions would have been rare, if not impossible, in the early part of the twentieth century.

national or community churches.¹³ I mention these churches in relation to ecumenism because the people affiliated with this growing movement do not appear to exhibit a denominational loyalty, but prefer to give allegiance to a local church.¹⁴ Ecumenism may have played a role in eroding the necessity of denominational affiliation by emphasizing the central importance of unity in Christ over a particular denominational label.

In the wake of tremendous intentional ecumenical activity throughout the twentieth century, Roman Catholic and Protestant churches have come to resemble one another in exterior appearance and in interior arrangement. The breaking down of barriers between Christian traditions has allowed for the sharing of church design ideas across sectarian boundaries. Christian architects frequently serve parishes across denominational lines. Members of congregations today often feel more comfortable with visiting a host of Christian churches as they dream about new ways of designing their own worship and ministry environments. They talk with each other to discern the strengths and weaknesses of a particular church design. Exchanges in theological understandings have also worked toward respecting distinctive furnishings (such as ambries, tabernacles, and reconciliation rooms) among various churches. Communities can now more freely exchange questions that allow for renewed understandings of how we can more effectively bear testimony to and adore the holy God through built environments.

CONTINUING LITURGICAL RENEWAL

Liturgical renewal has continued throughout the twentieth century among Christian traditions, both in academic scholarship and in application to congregational celebrations. John Fenwick and Bryan Spinks have identified a number of important emphases of the liturgical movement in their analysis of its influence over the past hundred years: developing community in worship and in the surrounding society (versus focusing

---

13. Not all community churches are nondenominational. It seems that even some denominational churches today are adopting the label of "community" in their name to downplay denominational identification. This shying away from denominational affiliation may be another manifestation of the deep influence of the ecumenical movement.

14. It is also true that many Christian churches are finding that some of their members both drift in from and drift out to other denominations rather freely. The emphasis on mutual respect and appreciation of various Christian bodies through ecumenical activity may have precipitated ease of movement between denominations.

on the individual); decentralizing the performance of worship in seeking to mobilize greater congregational involvement; seeking principles of worship from early Christian models; emphasizing a broader range of Scripture use in worship; recovering the significance of the Eucharist; using vernacular forms of expression (e.g., in language and music); engaging in intentional ecumenical cooperation and sharing of theological resources; and viewing worship as sharing in the renewal of society (seeking justice).[15]

Evidence of these emphases can be discerned from the books of worship mentioned earlier: the *Roman Missal* (Roman Catholic, 1969), the *Lutheran Book of Worship* (Lutheran Church in America, the American Lutheran Church, the Evangelical Lutheran Church in Canada, and the Lutheran Church–Missouri Synod, 1978), the *Book of Common Prayer* (the Episcopal Church, 1979), *The United Methodist Book of Worship* (1992), and the *Book of Common Worship* (Presbyterian Church U.S.A. and the Cumberland Presbyterian Church, 1993).[16] These books of worship have made use of insights from liturgical scholarship examining the worship practices of the first five centuries of the early church, they reflect a wide range of Scripture through their inclusion of similar lectionaries, they highlight both Word and sacrament, they encourage active engagement of clergy and laity, and they make use of vernacular, contemporary materials. The similarities among these resources illustrate active ecumenical exchanges and priorities.[17] The revision process of books of worship has not ended, either. The *Common Worship* project in the Church of England and the *Renewing Worship* project in the Evangelical Lutheran Church in America are two examples of this ongoing work in relation to books of worship.[18]

15. John Fenwick and Bryan Spinks, *Worship in Transition: The Liturgical Movement in the Twentieth Century* (New York: Continuum Publishing Company, 1995), pp. 5-11.

16. *Roman Missal,* as found in *The Sacramentary* (New York: Catholic Book Publishing Company, 1973, 1985); *Lutheran Book of Worship* (Minneapolis: Augsburg Publishing House, 1978); *Book of Common Prayer* (New York: Seabury Press, 1979); *The United Methodist Book of Worship* (Nashville: United Methodist Publishing House, 1992); *Book of Common Worship* (Louisville: Westminster/John Knox Press, 1993).

17. Liturgical scholar Frank C. Senn has done a helpful comparative analysis of the "common shape" of liturgies found in these books of worship in *Christian Liturgy: Catholic and Evangelical* (Minneapolis: Augsburg Fortress Press, 1997), pp. 645-51. While the orders for Word and sacrament are not completely identical, the shared characteristics are remarkable.

18. For *Common Worship,* see the revised service book, *Common Worship: Services and Prayers for the Church of England* (London: Church House Publishing, 2000), and *Common Worship Today: An Illustrated Guide to Common Worship,* ed. Mark Earney and Gilly Myers (London: HarperCollins Publishers, 2001). For an example of a document related to the Renewing Worship project (only one of many preliminary documents being circulated for examination by churches throughout the denomination), see Evangelical Lutheran Church in America, *Principles for Worship* (Minneapolis: Augsburg Fortress Press, 2002).

The liturgical movement inspired the establishment of doctoral programs in liturgical studies for people of all Christian traditions at major American universities, such as the University of Notre Dame and Catholic University of America. Eventually, through ecumenical contact and increasing interest among Protestants for renewing worship, Drew University also established such a program. Scores of scholars have been trained specifically in worship and are contributing to the continuing liturgical renewal process as teachers in colleges and universities, seminary appointees, and parish clergy.

An interesting insight emerging from liturgical scholarship that has developed in the latter part of the twentieth century is liturgical historian Paul Bradshaw's challenge to an imagined uniformity of worship practice among the earliest centuries of Christians. Throughout the eighteenth to twentieth centuries, many liturgical scholars worked from the presupposition that a core of material must exist that would demonstrate a certain uniform practice of rituals such as baptism and the Eucharist in the earliest centuries of the Christian church. Belief in such a notion has been especially attractive among those Christians seeking to "purify" contemporary worship practices by celebrating the faith in the same way as the earliest followers of Christ. By 1987, Bradshaw was beginning to publicly question this assumption of uniformity in practice and the quest to discover a hidden common text guiding early Christians.[19] Through his own examinations of early Christian materials and the studies produced by numerous other scholars, Bradshaw found evidence of multiple ways for celebrating baptism and the Eucharist from the earliest of days. Instead of seeking an early common practice, Bradshaw says, we might be better served by affirming a variety of practices from the very beginning of the faith.

Bradshaw's insights can be useful for us today, when we have a plethora of ways in which to celebrate our faith. The mystique of early Christian practice has sometimes been applied to church building design too. We saw evidence of this kind of privileging in relation to the "house church" model of Frédéric Debuyst and Edward Sövik. Both Debuyst and Sövik appreciated the imagined domestic and humble qualities of these early worship spaces. In an effort to reproduce these qualities in worship environments for contemporary communities, they sought to promote

19. See Paul Bradshaw, "The Search for the Origins of Christian Liturgy: Some Methodological Reflections," *Studia Liturgica* 17 (1987): 26-34. Further refinement and elaboration of his thesis can be discovered in the two editions of Paul Bradshaw, *The Search for the Origins of Christian Worship: Sources and Methods for the Study of Early Liturgy* (Oxford: Oxford University Press, 1992, 2002).

church designs that would reflect more common (or vernacular) domestic building designs. Use of vernacular, domestic spaces by the early church became a part of the justification of such designs in our day.

Toward the end of the twentieth century, some liturgical scholars began to openly question elevating the liturgical life of one historical model of the church above another when seeking to reform contemporary worship patterns. Fenwick and Spinks raised such a concern when they asked, "Why has the Liturgical Movement 'stopped the clock' at the third and fourth centuries?"[20] They were following the lead of Paul Bradshaw, who, in a 1982 essay, asked if the liturgical movement might not be guilty of "patristic fundamentalism."[21] Fenwick, Spinks, and Bradshaw were reflecting on the widespread replication of forms of Eucharistic prayers in revised books of worship based upon particular third- and fourth-century liturgical materials. They did not deny the power of these early Christian models but wondered whether such broad dependence was wise for the diversity of our contemporary church communities. Might liturgical scholars have inadvertently hindered the use of other creative materials by selecting a narrower band of authoritative source materials? Similar questions have been asked about the application of modern architecture to church design in the twentieth century. Might the use of a narrow range of models for church architecture have yielded unintended consequences? I will return to this question later.

Musical compositions and their role in worship have dramatically affected liturgical renewal in the last fifty years. Congregational participation in music in worship became an increasing priority among Roman Catholics following Vatican II, as can be discerned in documents such as "The Place of Music in Eucharistic Celebrations" (1967), *Music in Catholic Worship* (1972, 1982), and *Liturgical Music Today* (1982).[22] These documents granted permission to produce appropriate music for worship events in light of the needs of people in contemporary cultures. Consequently, there was much musical experimentation in celebrations of the Mass, some helpful and some less than adequate. Over the years, a substantial body of music has emerged from Roman Catholic composers and is now present in hymnals of both Catholic and

---

20. Fenwick and Spinks, *Worship in Transition*, p. 172.

21. Paul Bradshaw, "The Liturgical Use and Abuse of Patristics," in *Liturgy Reshaped*, ed. Kenneth Stevenson (London: SPCK, 1982), pp. 134-45.

22. All of these documents were prepared by the Bishops' Committee on the Liturgy, National Conference of Catholic Bishops (Washington, D.C.).

Protestant traditions. Protestant composers have also remained active, producing a vast array of new music and alternative settings for classic hymns for choirs and congregational song. In addition, ecumenical communities in Europe established in the mid-twentieth century, concerned with the priorities of the liturgical movement, introduced unique musical compositions for worship that have entered hymnals and songbooks around the world.[23] And as an increasing awareness and availability of musical compositions for ethnic communities from around the world have emerged, Western hymnals and songbook supplements have added an international range of songs to their repertoires.[24]

Mid-century pop music has also played a role in worship renewal. A part of the energy behind this development has been the charismatic movement, which gradually emerged from the modern Pentecostal movement.[25] The charismatic movement represents a sort of neo-Pentecostal phenomenon, highlighting the significance of the activity of the Holy Spirit in believers which can ignite faith and ministry in the life of the church. By mid-century, the charismatic movement was infusing new energy into the Roman Catholic Church and most major Protestant churches in the United States, especially through young people. In the 1960s, young Christian musicians began to experiment with contemporary rock-and-roll instrumentation and compositional patterns for devotional music. Use of this music in small group gatherings and concert venues led to a gradual incorporation of their offerings in corporate worship events.[26]

Finally, new electronic technologies, hardware, and software that have been developed in the last thirty years have affected liturgical renewal. The generation, edit-

23. Examples are the Iona Community in Scotland, founded by the Reverend George MacLeod in 1938, and the Taizé community in France, founded by Brother Roger in 1940.

24. For a discussion of this topic, see C. Michael Hawn, *Gather into One: Praying and Singing Globally* (Grand Rapids: Wm. B. Eerdmans, 2003).

25. The modern Pentecostal movement is generally recognized as having been initiated through the ministry of the Reverend William J. Seymour in the work of his Apostolic Faith Gospel Mission (founded in 1906) on Azusa Street in Los Angeles, California. A new emphasis on the work of the Holy Spirit was present in his ministry. Ultimately, denominations using the designation Church of God (beginning as early as 1907) and the Assemblies of God (established in 1914) would emerge from this work.

26. Calvary Chapel, Costa Mesa, California (founded in 1965), is an early example of a nondenominational church that incorporated so-called contemporary Christian music into its worship events. Their ministry, under the direction of the Reverend Chuck Smith, founded and promoted "Maranatha! Music" resources. Today, Calvary Chapel represents a network of over 500 affiliate churches around the world, claiming a membership of over 35,000. See www.calvarychapelcostamesa.org.

ing, final production, and distribution of liturgical materials have been facilitated and accelerated via these new technologies. Resources from worship books and hymnals have grown increasingly available in electronic formats. Revisions of existing materials and new materials can be distributed at an accelerated rate. Scripture, prayers, creeds, service components of all kinds, and songs of all types can now be downloaded easily into printed documents for worship or projected via screens (through various means) in worship gatherings. And use of the Internet and other electronic forms of transmitting information are allowing for an unprecedented sharing of worship resources. The electronic forms of worship resources can be shared easily and instantly around the globe. A new chorus in a congregation one week can easily be shared in congregations in multiple other countries within days. Older worship resources are even finding new life as they are "discovered" and shared electronically by enthusiastic believers.

The work of the liturgical movement has continued to affect the shape of church design throughout the twentieth century. Centrally planned worship spaces have become much more common for both Roman Catholic and Protestant traditions through the continued emphasis on active congregational engagement in liturgical celebrations.[27] Usually fan-shaped or semicircular arrangements of seating are oriented around a slightly elevated common focal point consisting of the primary liturgical appointments of altar/table and ambo/pulpit.[28] When longitudinal spaces are used (especially helpful for those communities that incorporate processions

27. In his essay examining Catholic church architecture since Vatican II, "Renewing the City of God," Michael E. DeSanctis mentions the movement toward a more unified worship space with a focus on the faithful who are gathered together under the headings of "hall church," "fan-shaped church," and "modified long church." See Micheal E. DeSanctis, "Renewing the City of God: The Reform of Catholic Architecture in the United States," *Meeting House Essays,* No. 5 (Chicago: Liturgy Training Publications, 1993), p. 15. Richard Kieckhefer, in an analysis of church design through the centuries, labels this twentieth-century pattern of centralized space for worship "modern communal." See Richard Kieckhefer, *Theology in Stone: Church Architecture from Byzantium to Berkeley* (New York: Oxford University Press, 2004), pp. 11-15.

28. The proliferation of fan-shaped seating arrangements was anticipated by the liturgical movement leader and priest Hans A. Reinhold in a 1938 article discussing contemporary German design. Reinhold commented, "The church which eventually may crystallize out of the considerations of these architects [Rudolf Schwarz, Dominikus Böhm, and others] may have the shape of an open fan, thus giving reality to the favorite word of all liturgists of true understanding: that through the *character indelebilis* we are all partakers of Christ's sacerdotal character and, therefore, should be *circumstantes* at the altar." See H. A. Reinhold, "A Revolution in Church Architecture," *Liturgical Arts* 6 (1937-38): 126. Full circular arrangements for congregational seating have also been tried now and then, but have been found to be problematic because the leadership always have their back to some portion of the community at any given moment.

into their celebrations), they are often wider and shorter today than they were at the beginning of the twentieth century; these changes have been made in an effort to bring the congregation closer to the altar/table and ambo/pulpit. Flexibility in the worship space (often limited to a portion of the space, although some churches are continuing to make all furnishings mobile) has also become important to many church designs. Christian communities that wish to celebrate with a variety of artistic expressions are increasingly choosing to use facilities that can accommodate some change in seating orientation and location of altar/table, font, and ambo/pulpit. Changes in musical instrumentation or personnel, inclusion of paintings or sculptures, theatre or dance (especially congregational) might require reconfiguring worship spaces from time to time. And the inclusion of high-tech materials in worship is requiring the addition of projectors, screens, and other equipment.[29] Use of this increasing range of worship resources will probably continue to fuel the necessity of incorporating flexibility into church designs.[30]

In Roman Catholic circles, there is a general tendency to design churches giving attention to a full range of ministries instead of providing a more singular focus on worship alone. Whereas many early twentieth-century Catholic churches had facilities that were underdeveloped for nonliturgical activities, by the end of the century the inclusion of ample spaces for meeting, eating, and serving others is quite common. Because the homily and congregational singing have become more liturgically prominent, the worship space emphasizes the location of the ambo/pulpit, the choir, and the instrumentalists. Often a larger area near the front of the worship space is used to emphasize these components of the worship event. Locating the choir in the rear balcony has generally been abandoned in order to help the choir become more a part of the visible community and actively lead congregational song. Generally a single altar in close proximity to the congregation continues to be used (since Vatican II) as a focal point to emphasize the significance and communal nature of the Eucharist.

In Protestant circles, concern over space for both liturgical and nonliturgical activities remains. The creativity and imagination of many Roman Catholic church

29. The list includes computers, CD and DVD equipment, cameras, and elaborate controls for sound and lighting.

30. Many churches today are using a master plan for new construction that also guides the entire building project incrementally over time. Flexibility of space is often an important component of church design here because it allows various buildings to be used for different purposes up until the full project is completed.

designs from the middle to the latter half of the century have inspired many Protestant churches to consider a renewed role for the arts in relation to church design.[31] To acknowledge this connection is not to diminish the role of theologians such as Paul Tillich, Francis Schaeffer, and Hans Rookmaaker in preparing Protestants for a wider appreciation of modern art in relation to the church. Rather, it is to affirm the significance of ecumenical contact in relation to liturgical renewal. A heightened sense of God's holiness is also becoming apparent in and through Protestant church design at times — for example, through the creation and setting aside of some space or material objects solely for liturgical use (including private devotions). Lutherans and Episcopalians have been conscious of this important activity all along, but an increased interest in "spirituality" in the larger culture is causing more Protestants to reconsider the value of highlighting God's transcendent nature in this way. Emphasis on celebrating the Eucharist (even with joy!) has led to a renewed prominence of the altar/table among some Protestant communities. New respect for the significance of the altar/table (not viewing it as a "coffee table" to collect miscellaneous items) has led to its becoming a focal point equal to the ambo/pulpit in some traditions (sometimes even accompanied by more frequent celebrations of communion).

And both Roman Catholic and Protestant traditions have seen a new emphasis on Christian initiation in the last fifty years. Catholic and Protestant churches have produced many new materials for preparing candidates and sponsors for baptism.[32] Increasingly, the small baptismal fonts for baptism inherited from the past have been replaced or supplemented by pools allowing for full immersion.[33] Ample use of

31. A good example is the efforts of Fathers Marie-Alain Couturier and Pie-Raymond Régamey, Dominican priests who wrote about and worked toward the inclusion of modern design in church art and architecture. Couturier even commissioned artists such as Georges Rouault, Jean Lurçat, Fernand Léger, Jacques Lipchitz, Marc Chagall, Pierre Bonnard, and Henri Matisse to create visual art and objects for chapels at Assy, Audincourt, and Vence, France. See William S. Rubin, *Modern Sacred Art and the Church at Assy* (New York: Columbia University Press, 1961), and Henri Matisse, M.-A. Couturier, and L.-B. Rayssiguier, *The Vence Chapel: The Archive of a Creation,* trans. Michael Taylor (Milan: Menil Foundation/Skira Editore, 1999).

32. A primary source of inspiration for renewing initiation has come from the 1972 release of the *Rite of Christian Initiation of Adults* (RCIA) by the Roman Catholic Church (adapted for the United States in 1988). The RCIA represents a model for adult catechesis. The rite of baptism was also revised in the wake of Vatican II. The production of these materials and their application has inspired some Protestant churches to renew their own initiation materials and rites.

33. For examples of the theology and history behind vessels for baptism and how they could be reclaimed for churches today, see S. Anita Stauffer, "A Place for Burial, Birth, and Bath," *Liturgy* 5, no. 4 (1986): 51-57; S. Anita Stauffer, *Re-examining Baptismal Fonts: Baptismal Space for the Contemporary Church* (videotape

water and oils has brought a renewed sense of the significance of initiation into the church and the public celebration of this reality.

The Death of Modern Architecture

Modern architecture, especially as embodied in the principles of the International Congress for Modern Architecture (CIAM), was particularly influential from about 1925 to 1965. Primary proponents of this functionalist approach were given the opportunity to design buildings not only throughout Europe and the United States but also in South America, Africa, and Asia. While it is generally acknowledged today that the International Style never really achieved universal application (because not all architects accepted the core beliefs of this approach), elements reflective of this style continued to be evident in building designs even into the 1980s (e.g., an overt emphasis on functionality, volume over mass, an open interior plan, and aesthetic minimalism).

Architecture critic Charles A. Jencks (b. 1939) has been reflecting on the demise of modern architecture and the rise of postmodern architecture for nearly thirty years.[34] He has often used a certain sarcastic tone in his commentary. In discussing the grip that modern design had on the formation of students at schools of architecture in the United States in the mid-twentieth century, Jencks stated,

> Modern seminaries were formed at the major universities such as Cambridge and Harvard and from there the Purist doctrines of John Calvin Corbusier, Martin Luther Gropius, and John Knox van der Rohe were dispersed. Their white cathedrals, the black and white boxes of the International Style, were soon built in every land, and for a while (until 1960) the people and professors kept the faith. Ornament, polychromy, metaphor, humour, symbolism, place, cultural identity, urban context, and convention were put on the Index, and all forms of decoration and historical reference were declared taboo.[35]

---

produced by the Liturgical Press, Collegeville, Minn., 1991); and Regina Kuehn, *A Place for Baptism* (Chicago: Liturgy Training Publications, 1992). A moving celebration of initiation using a pool for baptism at an Easter vigil can be seen on the videotape *This Is the Night: A Parish Welcomes New Catholics* (Chicago: Liturgy Training Publications, 1992).

34. His first edition of *The Language of Post-Modern Architecture* was published in 1977 (New York: Rizzoli). This title went through numerous editions into the late 1980s.

35. Charles Jencks, *What Is Post-Modernism?* 4th ed. (London: Academy Books, 1996), p. 22.

Jencks may not have been far off the mark in comparing the vigor of modern architectural educational formation with the pursuit of particular theological agendas of sixteenth-century Protestant Reformers. If one thinks about the concern that the early Reformers had for simplifying and purifying the Christian faith, the parallel becomes even more striking. Proponents of modern design felt that they were trimming away centuries of bondage to past expressions, releasing a fresh approach and purity of design for the modern world. The adamant certainty of universal truth and philosophical idealism of architects like Le Corbusier, Walter Gropius, and Ludwig Mies van der Rohe has drawn criticism in the wake of living with and in their buildings for decades. Flat roofs have proven problematic in the face of weather. Vast glazed surfaces entail maintenance and modesty concerns. Not everyone has found the simple, geometric designs with minimal ornamentation (or the absence of it) either beautiful or inspiring. Some people have missed the distinctiveness of designs based on a shared public language (e.g., churches that have a unique appearance) or culture (the distinctive influence of various ethnic expressions of visual art). And ideal human behaviors did not necessarily emerge from living in buildings of ideal architectural design.

Jencks located the death of modern architecture (perhaps a little tongue-in-cheek) in the destruction of a large portion of the award-winning Pruitt-Igoe public housing project in St. Louis, Missouri, on 15 July 1972, at precisely 3:32 P.M.[36] The fourteen-story structure, designed by Minoru Yamasaki, incorporated many of the ideals of CIAM and had received an award from the American Institute of Architects in 1951.[37] The housing project, constructed from 1952 to 1955, was intended to inspire a sense of goodness and constructive communal relationship in its inhabitants through its rational expression and purist forms and its use of a minimal aesthetic. But that did not seem to happen. Despite the investment of millions of dollars in ongoing maintenance over nearly two decades, vandalism and crime were higher in this complex than in other public housing units, so the decision was finally made to destroy it.[38] It is safe to say that the idealistic goals of those who supported the International Style were never fully achieved through design choices alone.

36. Charles Jencks, *The New Paradigm in Architecture: The Language of Post-Modernism* (New Haven: Yale University Press, 2002), p. 9.

37. Yamasaki would go on to design the World Trade Center, New York City, in the early 1970s.

38. Jencks, *The New Paradigm in Architecture*, pp. 8-9.

In the 1960s the rational theories of modern architecture fell under heavy criticism from some professional quarters. In 1966 architect Robert Venturi (b. 1925) published a critique of the International Style entitled *Complexity and Contradiction in Architecture*.[39] He challenged many of the presuppositions of modern architecture, such as the elevation of explicit function in design, the reduction of symbolism, and the disconnection of design from historical precedents. Venturi was concerned about the complexity of the language of architecture. He sought the incorporation of insights from popular cultural artifacts as well as the inspiration of a professionally trained architectural elite. Following Venturi's challenge, scholars and other architects began more actively questioning the basic tenets of modern architecture.

"Plurality" is the word that best describes the myriad of approaches to architectural design in Europe and the United States since 1960. The increasing use of computer hardware and software in generating designs has accelerated and facilitated the variety of conceivable designs (whether for good or ill is currently open to debate). Jencks has developed an elaborate "family tree" in an attempt to describe the design landscape from 1960 to 2000. He begins with six main classifiers to group primary movements he sees emerging from modernism, and then notes twenty-one trends, 500 influential buildings, and nine major architects as well as a host of other significant ones.[40] His chart is a wonderful visual illustration of the vast array of designs that have been implemented in the recent past. Important insights that might be gleaned from the tremendous exploration of design alternatives in a postmodern period include the following: (1) the importance of historical architectural symbolism and its role in society; (2) the importance of the specific context of a building; (3) the importance of paying attention to treasured regional architectural expressions; (4) the importance of collaborative approaches to design; and (5) the importance of acknowledging the very real limitations of design in promoting ideal human behavior. At its best, architectural design today can be more flexible, particular, and complex than the proponents of the International Style had allowed. To be sure, not all modern architectural principles and priorities have been abandoned. But their application has been modulated since the early days of their implementation, creating a richer variety of environments.

The demise of the predominance of modern design in church architecture did not have an immediate effect, but the consequences have been important over time. Schools

---

39. Robert Venturi, *Complexity and Contradiction in Architecture* (New York: Museum of Modern Art, 1966).

40. Jencks, *The New Paradigm in Architecture*, pp. 50-51.

of architecture began to explore the significance of historical models of design with renewed vigor, influencing architects who would be employed by churches. Buildings exhibiting a broader range of design expressions appeared in professional and popular books, journals, and magazines. Interest in historic church designs was re-established, but this time both the strengths and the weaknesses of historical models were more actively discussed by professional architects and theologians. And an accompanying critique of liturgical practice emerged in the midst of the re-evaluation of modern church architecture (not as a contingent phenomenon, but as a parallel phenomenon), fostering important insights for the renovation and building of new churches.

THE STRENGTHS AND WEAKNESSES OF ARCHITECTURE EMPHASIZING GOD'S IMMANENCE

Time frequently works to the advantage of the one doing critical evaluation. Identifying the weaknesses in church architectural design that emphasizes the theological understanding of "God in our midst" is easier to do in the current context, when examples are more abundant. In the early twentieth century, when modern architecture was in an early stage of development in Europe and the United States, much church architecture, both Roman Catholic and Protestant, was dominated by revivalistic designs that seemed more imitative than thoughtfully interpreted and applied. The proliferation of neo-Gothic designs tended to emphasize the holiness, the "otherness," or the transcendent nature of God. As I said earlier in this book, such an emphasis is absolutely proper in a place intended for Christian worship and ministry. But the church has also affirmed a fundamental oppositional truth: that the holy Triune God chose to make himself intimately accessible to humanity. The latter truth became the focal point of much theological discussion in the twentieth century and ultimately affected church design.

Modern architectural design, especially as manifest in the International Style, may simply have unintentionally ushered in the latest opportunity for Christians to manifest a church architecture accentuating God's immanence instead of God's transcendence.[41] That modern architectural design became prominent in the mid-twen-

41. Other historical periods of the church have exhibited similar impulses, such as the twelfth-century churches designed by the Cistercian order and the seventeenth- and eighteenth-century meetinghouses used by early American Congregationalists.

tieth century, when the effects of the ecumenical and liturgical movements were also increasingly prominent, is a case of extraordinary timing. Both Roman Catholic and Protestant communities were looking for tangible ways to focus on how God is present in our world, active in and through the deeds of clergy and laity alike, and yearning to relate to and care for the needs of all people, and modern architecture appeared to speak to these concerns.[42] Political and economic circumstances were such that an unusual number of opportunities occurred to build and renovate churches in both Europe and the United States (especially in the 1950s and 1960s). As a result of the confluence of these factors, Christian communities began to use modern architectural design in an effort to promote worship renewal and ministry to a hurting world in the name of Christ. These efforts produced both positive and negative consequences.

On the positive side, the construction and renovation of churches according to the principles of modern architectural design allowed for relatively quick completion times. The use of modern materials and building techniques, along with simplified exterior and interior designs, helped to facilitate more rapid construction. New materials and techniques helped to usher in additional design alternatives, improved sight-lines for visibility in worship (especially in larger spaces), creative acoustic solutions, and lower construction costs. The flexibility of reinforced concrete and steel construction, along with a host of breakthroughs in the use of glass, plastics, and adhesives, helped to achieve many of these positive results.

Exterior facades often adopted features of modern vernacular architecture (especially features common to commercial buildings), a strategy that many supporters of modern design continue to believe is effective in helping those less familiar with the Christian faith connect to the church (e.g., Willow Creek Community Church).[43] Evidence to support this belief is largely anecdotal, but the lack of significant alterations to many modern facades and their continuing presence in new construction today does tend to support such a conclusion. A theological overlay that sometimes accompanies the justification of this approach is that God has laid claim to every-

---

42. It is interesting to note that Orthodox communities chose not to adopt the conventional architectural designs of the twentieth century in spite of their desire to embrace fellow Christians and minister to the larger world. Neither did they feel compelled to revise their liturgical rituals in the same way that Roman Catholic and Protestant churches did. They appear to remain committed to sharing in active contemporary Christian ministry in the companionship of centuries-old building designs and liturgical texts.

43. Economic factors may play a role in choosing to adopt vernacular designs too, in that costs for building construction may be lower when using materials that are more readily available and easy to use.

thing in our world, so even ordinary building designs can be used as a vehicle for God's grace. And some believe that if a familiar building design for the church helps people integrate their place of worship into the larger fabric of their community, it is worth pursuing.

With respect to the interior design of modern churches oriented toward immanence, several benefits continue to be espoused. Spaces that are more open and flexible facilitate a wider variety of liturgical possibilities (e.g., in terms of seating arrangements, the location of liturgical appointments, the incorporation of special artistic expressions, and congregational movement for seasonal or occasional gatherings). Open planning can also facilitate a wider range of use for ministry, especially in churches where either geographical area or financial resources are limited. It is true that it takes additional time and energy to effectively use space not dedicated to particular functions, but for some parishes with real limitations this is a valuable advantage.

Many churches appreciate the physical drawing together of chancel and nave (ordinarily with some elevation of the chancel area), both for its symbolic and its tangible benefits. The symbolic significance of both clergy and laity sharing in a mutual offering of thanksgiving and praise in worship, each with distinctive ministerial roles, is powerful. In most Christian traditions, both groups are important to liturgical celebrations, and that mutual necessity is conveyed in this modern organization of the worship space. The physical proximity of clergy and laity enhances the symbolic meaning, but it also allows for increased access to the altar/table in the communal celebration. This proximity increases not only the visibility of the central activities but also the communal sense of solidarity simply by bringing the laity closer to this important liturgical appointment. A theological sense of being gathered at the "table of the Lord" (in reference to the imagery of the communal meal of the feast) is also much enhanced through the physical closeness of the chancel and nave areas.

The application of a reduced aesthetic also continues to be seen as helpful for some communities. Parishes concerned about the misuse of visual artifacts in relation to worship can have deeply rooted theological understandings that support these concerns. For congregations that are concerned about losing focus on the significance of particular visual elements, a less elaborate aesthetic approach can help properly highlight important artifacts or features of the church design. A simplified aesthetic can always be adapted over time, depending on the desired level of expression. On the other hand, elaborate designs are more difficult to regulate, since they are usually more difficult and more expensive to simplify (on physical, financial, and/or emotional levels).

Although the use of modern design has many positive consequences, it also has negative consequences, even if some are unintended. Robert Venturi's earlier cited critique of modern architecture — that a reduction in symbolism and an ahistorical approach to design were not necessarily ideal — has also been leveled against modern church design. Indeed, warnings about abandoning traditional (historical) church design were issued even as modern design was gathering momentum. Here is an example of such a warning, articulated by Ernest Short, in the late 1940s:

> There exists in the present day a certain tendency in favor of avoiding ecclesiastical conventions in church building. To some of these undoubtedly sincere reformers it seems that a distinctively ecclesiastical church building is a hindrance and not a help to his work.
>
> Although one cannot help admiring the enthusiasm and originality of those who search for new methods of contending against indifference, which is nowadays a more serious danger than hostility, it should be remembered that in the "ages of faith" ecclesiastical buildings have always been distinguishable, as far as possible, from secular ones. . . . Sometimes the studious avoidance of ecclesiastical trappings may have unexpected results.[44]

While some communities revel in the ways in which their church "blends into" the fabric of the community through a common design strategy, others lament the loss of the distinctiveness of church design.[45] Historically the church has often had a unique form of architecture that has set it apart from other public institutions. This uniqueness depended on the specific symbolic elements of church design, which were applauded for their ability to bear witness to the presence of a Christian community in the midst of secular entities. The classic scale and detail of a Gothic cathedral or the facade and steeple of a traditional New England meetinghouse are examples of this symbolic architectural language. While it is true that some churches have cast off all symbols that would identify them with the historical church, others still merge traditional Christian symbols with contemporary architectural design. The virtue of retaining at least a basic historical, communal, and symbolic

---

44. Ernest Short, *Post-War Church Building* (London: Hollis & Carter, 1947), p. 65.

45. For example, see Elizabeth M. Farrelly, "How Great Thou Aren't," *Faith and Form* 38, no. 2 (2005): 20-21.

vocabulary for both the exterior and the interior design of the church building is to acknowledge that the Christian faith offers an alternative way of existence to the ways of the world, is rooted in a movement that transcends time, and retains a connection to believers across cultural boundaries.

Several voices in Roman Catholic architectural circles have echoed Short's call to remember the riches of historical church design. Steven J. Schloeder, Duncan G. Stroik, and Michael S. Rose have all expressed disappointment with the reduced symbolism and the disconnection of modern church design from the language of traditional church architecture. In his book *Architecture in Communion: Implementing the Second Vatican Council through Liturgy and Architecture,* Schloeder voices his frustration with the "white-washed barns" of modernity. He seeks to recapture a connection with the historical patterns of church design, producing designs that "look like a church."[46] Schloeder also seeks to emphasize procession in worship, create a more pronounced visual hierarchical distinction between clergy and laity, reintroduce more traditional iconography, and elevate the significance of the tabernacle in the worship space.[47]

Stroik teaches architecture at the University of Notre Dame, South Bend, Indiana.[48] In 1998 Stroik initiated the journal *Sacred Architecture* to support a "restoration" of Catholic church architecture in concert with historical models of design.[49] Among other things, Stroik was critical of the post–Vatican II document *Environment and Art in Catholic Worship* (EACW). EACW was a product of its time, a first attempt at broad, official ecclesial guidance for religious art and architecture intended to facilitate the implementation of the liturgical reforms of Vatican II in Catholic churches throughout the United States. Stroik's difficulties with the document are evident in this excerpt from his published critique of it:

46. Steven J. Schloeder, *Architecture in Communion: Implementing the Second Vatican Council through Liturgy and Architecture* (San Francisco: Ignatius Press, 1998), pp. 233, 225.

47. Schloeder, *Architecture in Communion,* pp. 50-60, 225-43.

48. I was privileged to have Stroik as an articulate and thoughtful reader for my doctoral dissertation on Sövik at the University of Notre Dame from 1993 to 1995.

49. His recent critiques of modern church design include "The Roots of Modernist Church Architecture," *Catholic Dossier* (May-June 1997), "Ten Myths of Contemporary Church Architecture," *Sacred Architecture* 1, no. 1 (Fall 1998), and "Environment and Art in Catholic Worship: A Critique," *Sacred Architecture* 2, no. 1 (Summer 1999). In 1999 a collection of new sacred buildings and works of art exhibiting the priorities of Stroik's approach was published: Duncan Stroik, *Reconquering Sacred Space 2000: Rediscovering Tradition in Twentieth-Century Liturgical Architecture,* ed. Cristiano Rosponi and Giampaolo Rossi (Rome: Editrice il Bosco e la Nave, 1999).

Its [EACW's] authority has been invoked to require theater-shaped interiors, removal of tabernacles from sanctuaries, removal of religious imagery, and a puritanical style. The lack of a good alternative to EACW coupled with its heavy promotion by the liturgical establishment has resulted in EACW exerting an undue influence over the face of our sacramental architecture during the past two decades. It has also been supported by a secular architectural profession often willing to strip older churches and design new buildings in a reductionist mode.[50]

Stroik raises a number of criticisms that have been leveled at EACW over the years, including the tremendous freedom to design churches according to contemporary trends in art and architecture and the perceived lack of attention paid to the significance of private devotional practices. These criticisms are understandable in light of the fact that the majority of the thirty-nine photographs that accompanied the text of the document featured the work of a single liturgical design consultant, Frank Kacmarcik, who modeled a unique contemporary design reflective of the International Style.[51] Stroik seeks to re-establish a richer language of church architecture today, applying the vocabulary of historical design to the contemporary needs of congregations.

Michael Rose offers a sharp critique of modern church design in his books *The Renovation Manipulation: The Church Counter-Renovation Handbook* and *Ugly as Sin: Why They Changed Our Churches from Sacred Places to Meeting Spaces — and How We Can Change Them Back Again*.[52] He holds "misinterpretations" of Vatican II documents, architects such as Edward Sövik, and liturgical consultants such as Richard Vosko accountable for the perceived demise of contemporary church architecture.[53] Rose appears to be seeking a return to a unique expression of Catholic church design based on select historical models. Rose's critique is certainly provocative, although he often seems to focus on only the most "immanent" of modern expres-

50. Stroik, "Environment and Art in Catholic Worship: A Critique," p. 8.

51. Bishops' Committee on the Liturgy, *Environment and Art in Catholic Worship* (Washington, D.C.: National Conference of Catholic Bishops, 1978). All photographs and notes for the photographs mentioning Kacmarcik are located at the end of the booklet.

52. Michael Rose, *The Renovation Manipulation: The Church Counter-Renovation Handbook* (Cincinnati: Aquinas Publishing Ltd., 2000); Michael Rose, *Ugly as Sin: Why They Changed Our Churches from Sacred Places to Meeting Spaces — and How We Can Change Them Back Again* (Manchester, N.H.: Sophia Institute Press, 2001).

53. Rose, *Ugly as Sin*, pp. 135-74. Such a position seems to ignore important advances achieved through the liturgical and ecumenical movements and the application of renewal-oriented insights to liturgical architecture.

sions (ignoring contemporary designs that have incorporated more complex symbolism and historical references), and his approach seems to discount the newly established "tradition" of modern church architecture that we have traced in this book.[54]

Schloeder, Stroik, and Rose all offer a postmodern critique of modern design. They may all be correct: Church architecture may indeed have been impoverished on some level because many modern designs avoided using familiar historical church designs. It is important to note, however, that modern church buildings can often be fairly easily altered in various ways because of their original neutral color palettes and minimal ornamentation. When decisions are made in this regard, Christian communities need to remain very conscious of the messages their church buildings communicate, especially in a time as visually literate and savvy as our own.

The extraordinary emphasis on functionalism evident in much modern architecture has only limited usefulness in relation to building churches. While the practices of Christian worship and the variety of ministries to be accomplished in and through a built environment are important to consider, it is difficult to support the idea that these functions alone will dictate the overall design of a church building. The very history of buildings for Christian communities demonstrates that a wide variety of designs can be employed to accomplish orthodox worship and ministry.

A radical accent on function can even undermine the fullness of the witness of the church. Focusing on utility alone or mere pragmatism (such as cost per square foot or ultimate seating capacity) can yield structures that neither inspire the imagination nor reflect the creative side of the holy God.[55] Mere functional containers may unintentionally communicate the vision of a God who is oblivious to beauty. A theological parallel with respect to life in the church would be the false choice between emphasizing either evangelism of the unbeliever or discipleship of the faithful. Both are essential components of authentic Christian living. To address only one or the other creates a distorted vision of the faith. Similarly, to emphasize either function or beauty in design is a misrepresentation of our faith. Both beauty and

---

54. Bartlett Hayes noted this phenomenon of innovation becoming tradition over time in his book *Tradition Becomes Innovation: Modern Religious Architecture in America* (New York: Pilgrim Press, 1983).

55. The presence and proliferation of manufacturers ready to supply Christian communities with prefabricated materials can be a real risk with respect to creating churches of substantial and lasting beauty. While prefabricated materials can find an appropriate place in church building today, there are companies eager to erect sheds or warehouses for Christians to occupy that visually communicate an impoverished understanding of God. Economics alone is not an adequate base upon which to design or build a church. Frugality can be a virtue, but only if kept in creative tension with a variety of other priorities connected to an adequate communication and embodiment of the Christian faith.

function must remain in creative conversation as churches seek to create a material, visible presence.

In the last fifty years, concerns have also been raised over the application of a modern understanding of open and flexible interior planning. An extreme example of this approach would be the multipurpose worship space. Multipurpose worship spaces are not a new development in the history of the church. The establishment and use of Puritan meetinghouses give evidence of that. And in the late 1960s, J. G. Davies's book entitled *The Secular Use of Church Buildings* reminded Christians of all traditions of the long-standing use of church buildings for many purposes. Other books and journals featuring new church architecture from the mid-twentieth century also included multipurpose designs, albeit some with reservations.[56] But not all Christian communities have chosen to endorse this manifestation of worship space. Those who oppose a multipurpose space express a concern about retaining a sense of the holy in a space used for secular activities.[57] They are also concerned about maintaining a readily accessible location for personal prayer and reflection, a "sanctuary" for the individual, if you will. While it is true that an alternative setting for personal devotions can be established with appropriate artifacts or liturgical appointments, there is significance in having the space typically used for communal worship used for devotional faith encounters as well. Private devotional activities can actually be enhanced when they take place in a communal worship space that is rich with past experiences and memories. Clearly, the particular theological convictions of each faith community will need to inform the limits of use associated with their place of worship.

56. For example, see *Sixty Post-War Churches: Churches, Church Centres, Dual-Purpose Churches* (London: Incorporated Church Building Society, 1956). Articles entitled "A Dual-Purpose Architecture?" and "Planning for the Dual-Purpose Church" are included in this book. Although acknowledgment is made of economic realities that might necessitate a dual-purpose church, the following statement is also made in "A Dual-Purpose Architecture?": "The term 'dual purpose' is begging the question. A building can either be a church or a hall, either religious or secular, but it cannot architecturally be both, and the term 'architecturally' is here used as meaning fit for its particular purpose" (p. 6). Ambivalence toward the concept was sometimes present even when it was being featured.

57. Memory is a powerful force with which to reckon. A space that has been used for the celebration of powerful ritual events such as religious conversion, baptisms, weddings, funerals, rites of reconciliation, and other moments of transformation is not always easily stripped of that experiential imprint. There appears to be something in human nature that finds it important to have special geographical locations in this world that can facilitate encounters with the divine. To affirm such a reality is not to diminish the omnipresence of the holy God, but to recognize the limitations and vulnerabilities of being human.

CONCLUSIONS

The theological idea that God is immanent has been a fundamental affirmation of Christian communities down through the ages. Reminders of this truth have been discerned in church architecture, to varying degrees in different periods, through design elements and / or specific artifacts. Aspects of early Christian, Cistercian, Reformation, and Puritan architecture have been said to convey significant reminders of God's immanence. Church architecture has never emerged in a vacuum: architecture of the surrounding culture has frequently influenced the shaping of church design. The use of principles associated with the International Style of modern architecture is simply another chapter illustrating the interplay between the architecture of the world and the architecture of the church. A renewed sense of "God in our midst" was accomplished, in part, by using aspects of modern architecture in church design.

Modern church architecture of the twentieth century may one day be remembered for the significant role it played in facilitating a renewed sense of the holy God dwelling actively in the midst of people engaged in worship and ministry. In his book entitled *Jesus through the Centuries,* Jaroslav Pelikan recalls the ways in which the divine aspects and the human aspects of Christ have alternately become the focus of believers through the years.[58] Different generations of believers have come to celebrate different facets of his being based on many theological and cultural issues. Perhaps the twentieth century will be another time period remembered for celebrating the Jesus who is like us and as close as our neighbor. Modern church design as we have explored it in relation to expressions such as the International Style has functioned as a catalyst in revealing this truth. But Jesus is more than human too. He remains the heavenly king who rules in eternity, creator of everything and final judge of all.

The slice of modern church architecture that we have examined may ultimately be judged to have been less capable of sustaining references to these theological realities. Nevertheless, the modern church design we have explored has had a unique role to play in twentieth-century faith and has effectively pointed to select and important understandings. Its inadequacies — and perhaps the inadequacies that can be found in all expressions of church architecture — may play the positive role of

---

58. Jaroslav Pelikan, *Jesus through the Centuries: His Place in the History of Culture* (New Haven: Yale University Press, 1985).

provoking us to anticipate the day when all such static material forms are no longer necessary (see Rev. 21:22-26). In the meantime, a variety of church designs will be employed to help focus our congregations on the infinite God and bear witness to his reality to the world.

CHAPTER TEN

WHERE CAN WE GO?
DIRECTIONS FOR THE FUTURE

§16. Just as the term *Church* refers to the *living temple,* God's People, the term *church* also has been used to describe "the building in which the Christian community gathers to hear the word of God, to pray together, to receive the sacraments, and to celebrate the eucharist." That building is both the house of God on earth *(domus Dei)* and a house fit for the prayers of the saints *(domus ecclesiae).* Such a house of prayer must be expressive of the presence of God and suited for the celebration of the sacrifice of Christ, as well as reflective of the community that celebrates there.

NATIONAL CONFERENCE OF CATHOLIC BISHOPS, *Built of Living Stones* (2000)

THE ASSUMPTION OF Protestant liberal theology that modern people were no longer interested in the supernatural aspect of God has been proven false. In the latter half of the twentieth century, a large volume of material has been produced and distributed that explores a continuing quest for a God who is not only with us but beyond us. In Christian circles, both Roman Catholic and Protestant, spiritual disciplines are being reinvigorated to help people explore this side of God's existence. With this resurgence of interest in the transcendence of God's nature, a search for church architecture that acknowledges this reality has been launched. The concerns of Steven Schloeder, Duncan Stroik, and Michael Rose, mentioned in Chapter Nine, represent this movement of people within the church who are missing, among other things, a more explicit reference to the mystery of God in church design. It should not be forgotten that the clericalization of the faith, with its more objective ritual practices, was a primary barrier that the liturgical movement tried to overcome by emphasizing the role of the people in worship. In fact, much of the energy of the liturgical movement in the twentieth century centered on elevating the significance of the laity. It is possible that this focus on the people has sometimes been interpreted as an overemphasis, an accent that has inadvertently downplayed the awe and wonder of our celebrations. In other words, the significance of God's immanence could have been so emphasized that the mystery of God's transcendence was downplayed. But perhaps corrections of this kind need to occur in the history of the faith in order to re-establish a more appropriate balance in our finite human understanding of transcendence and immanence in relation to worship.

Maintaining a proper balance between these two oppositional truths is an ongoing challenge, given the limits of static material forms and objects. In the twenty-first century, we must continue to seek visual expressions that support both aspects of God's nature appropriately. I will now explore the potential that church design holds today, highlighting some ideas that could bear constructive and fruitful witness to central Christian teachings.

THE BENEFITS OF WORKING IN A POSTMODERN ARCHITECTURAL WORLD

While a postmodern world seems to make some Christians anxious, it is important to recognize that the world of architectural design is exploding with exciting possibilities for church design. The rich language of historical designs has once again been sanctioned as an appropriate source for architectural inspiration, a windfall for church architects. Some professors of architecture in schools around the world are now encouraging their students to reclaim the traditional language of architecture as they design new buildings for a wide range of purposes, including churches. An ever-increasing variety of contemporary building materials and construction techniques is still employed, but there is no longer the same drive to articulate expressions that are disconnected from the historical roots of architectural design or from regional styles of design. In truth, even modern architecture was never *completely* disconnected from its historical roots. All expressions of art are built on *some* foundation, whether or not that foundation is recognized. All architects study historical building designs in their vocational preparation, and they cannot help but be influenced by and incorporate aspects of these designs.

Our new century will continue to see reflections of modern architecture in churches, but the dogmatic, monotone expression of movements like the International Style is not likely to be replicated widely again. What modern architects most feared — mere imitation of past expressions of architectural styles in church design — is not something that today's most thoughtful architects will pursue. What we can anticipate is the creative incorporation of traditional designs with the contemporary needs of congregations for worship and ministry. For example, we can anticipate features of Gothic or Renaissance architecture (which were never completely eliminated in the twentieth century) in new church designs. It also seems likely that features associated with reference to the transcendence of God will find new life. Congregations both Protestant and Roman Catholic are now discovering "new" (in actuality, often simply "new" to them) worship resources in the texts, music, visual arts, and spiritual practices of past generations of Christians from around the world. Some are calling this an "ancient/future" movement, in which the resources of the past are being celebrated again with new energy.[1] Church architecture is likely to benefit from this impulse. Those more familiar with resources that point to God's immanence will probably be attracted to resources reminding us of God's "otherness." A desire to reinvest our churches with symbols pointing to the mystery of God has been prevalent for the last decade or so and will likely bear much fruit in years to come. The spartan designs of modern church design can be augmented as necessary to reflect transcendence in rich ways.

Some aspects of modern design have now moved from being "innovative" to "traditional." Many of the materials and building techniques of the early twentieth century that were new then have become the bedrock of design and construction today, with innovations continuing to present new opportunities for creative expressions. Emphasis on the roles of function and simplicity endures in many architectural circles (especially in light of rising building costs), albeit as conversation partners with a wider range of issues. Concern over authentic design for our own day and time persists, but the imagined "ahistorical" approach to architecture has ended. Historical approaches and patterns for building design are being reclaimed, inspiring expressions that no longer fear a connection to the past. The strict ban on ornamentation has been lifted, allowing for a richer iconographic language in building design. The emphasis on the horizontal axis (prevalent in some expressions of early modern design) is being enhanced with more attention to verticality, and the basic geometric forms once idealized are yielding an increasing range of expressive, organic forms

---

1. For instance, see Robert Webber, *Ancient-Future Faith: Rethinking Evangelicalism for a Postmodern World* (Grand Rapids: Baker Book House, 1999).

(including many curvilinear surfaces). The plurality of forms that has been exhibited in modern architecture has carried over into postmodern architecture. Given these factors, churches can expect to benefit from the opportunity to both draw on the riches of past design and imagine a vast array of new designs for their buildings.

Preliminary Suggestions to Prepare for Church Design Today

Understanding the local and regional history of a parish or congregation can be helpful as a community assesses its current church design. Examining the evolution of worship practices and ministries supported by the church can help to illuminate why certain design choices in the building(s) may have been made in the past and whether or not the choices have been found to be effective. Local church historians or archivists may be able to provide important materials to consider (and/or suggest individuals with whom to speak). Evaluation of present theological beliefs and desired patterns for worship expression should be discerned. Built realities can both shape theological understanding and unleash or restrict ritual practice and ministry. Building committees need to determine whether the built environment of their church has helped or hindered the worship expressions and ministries of their community.

Architectural styles in a particular area sometimes reflect various local or regional patterns, both indigenous and introduced. Christian communities generally want to be perceived as "good neighbors" in the world. Being sensitive to particular architectural characteristics of a geographical locale can help a community to show its appreciation of local culture and traditions. Paying attention to the architectural expressions of a neighborhood or a region can also help to explain certain design choices that have been incorporated into the building(s).

Two general resources will be helpful in considering these broader preliminary issues. The first is entitled *Houses of God: Region, Religion, and Architecture in the United States* by Peter W. Williams.[2] Williams provides a narrative of the gradual

2. Peter W. Williams, *Houses of God: Region, Religion, and Architecture in the United States* (Urbana: University of Illinois Press, 1997). Additional details concerning select churches (organized by region and state, including brief historical remarks of an introductory nature) can be gleaned from *America's Religious Architecture: Sacred Places for Every Community* by Marilyn J. Chiat (New York: John Wiley & Sons, Inc., 1997). Discussion of an eclectic collection of thirty-six country churches from different states and a variety of Christian traditions can be found in William Morgan, *American Country Churches* (New York: Harry N.

development of church architecture by region throughout the United States. He mentions important religious beliefs, historical events, circumstances, and people in various considerations of a wide range of Christian traditions. Excellent bibliographies accompany each regional exploration. The second resource worth perusing is *Houses of Worship: An Identification Guide to the History and Styles of American Religious Architecture* by Jeffery Howe.[3] Howe provides a brief overview of the history of religious architecture in the United States, followed by chapters examining a wide variety of church designs according to designated time periods. A multitude of color photographs and pages of drawings help to clarify Howe's descriptions of each period. From these resources, individuals or committees charged with charting a community's renovation or new church design needs could glean much insight into where their present building fits into the larger fabric of American church design and gain exposure to a wide array of architectural possibilities.

Specific Resources for Denominational Guidance

Denominational guidance for church building is still sought by most faith communities and is quite useful for exploring the distinctiveness of our many Christian traditions. For all that Christians have affirmed that we hold theologically in common among denominations, we do continue to recognize that there are some ways in which Catholic and various Protestant theological interpretations and patterns of worship are different.

Abrams, Inc., 2004). In recent years a small wave of titles focusing on specific American states and cities and their historical places of worship has also emerged. Some titles of note include Marc Trieb, *Sanctuaries of Spanish New Mexico* (Berkeley and Los Angeles: University of California Press, 1993); Dell Upton, *Holy Things and Profane: Anglican Parish Churches in Colonial Virginia* (New Haven: Yale University Press, 1997); Frank L. Greenagel, *The New Jersey Churchscape* (New Brunswick: Rutgers University Press, 2001); Robert Berger and Alfred Wills, *Sacred Spaces: Historic Houses of Worship in the City of Angels* (Glendale, Calif.: Balcony Press, 2003); Alan K. Lathrop, *Churches of Minnesota: An Illustrated Guide* (Minneapolis: University of Minnesota Press, 2003); David W. Dunlap, *From Abyssinian to Zion: A Guide to Manhattan's Houses of Worship* (New York: Columbia University Press, 2004); Panos Fiorentinos, *Ecclesia: Greek Orthodox Churches of the Chicago Metropolis* (Chicago: Kantyli, Inc., 2004); Denis R. McNamara, *Heavenly City: The Architectural Tradition of Catholic Chicago* (Chicago: Liturgy Training Publications, 2005); and Roger W. Moss, *Historic Sacred Places of Philadelphia* (Philadelphia: University of Pennsylvania Press, 2005).

3. Jeffery Howe, *Houses of Worship: An Identification Guide to the History and Styles of American Religious Architecture* (San Diego: Thunder Bay Press, 2003).

In considering the particular needs of Roman Catholic communities, the 2003 English edition of the General Instruction of the Roman Missal (GIRM) devotes Chapter Five to the subject: "The Arrangement and Furnishing of Churches for the Celebration of the Eucharist" (numbers 288-318).[4] Much of the material here closely parallels the instructions from the earlier edition of GIRM, although some passages are presented in a different order. Emphases remaining consistent include allowing for artistic expressions of all peoples and regions (no. 289), creating an overall design reflecting noble simplicity (no. 292), making appropriate choices to meet contemporary needs (no. 293), conveying an overall sense of unity in ordered community (no. 294), and facilitating active participation by all the faithful (no. 294). A freestanding altar as the focal point of the space remains important, with the presider facing the people during the liturgy (no. 299). Additional instructions in the 2003 edition are fairly few in number. A few examples here will illustrate. New churches are admonished to erect a single altar in their church (no. 303), a revision of the earlier instruction which suggested that minor altars be few in number and be placed in chapels separated from the body of the church (no 267, 1975 edition). There are notations concerning seasonal expressions, such as the use of flowers (no. 305) and musical instruments (no. 313). Rather than simply mentioning the necessity of a cross on or near the altar (no. 270, 1975 edition), the new instruction adds, "with the figure of Christ crucified" (no. 308). And this edition grants more latitude in locating the tabernacle, with what appears to be slightly less emphasis on the necessity of a separate reservation chapel (no. 315; compare to no. 276 in the 1975 edition).

The National Conference of Catholic Bishops of the United States has recognized and responded to perceived limitations of the 1978 directive *Environment and Art in Catholic Worship* (EACW). In the year 2000 *Built of Living Stones: Art, Architecture, and Worship* (BLS) was released as a new document for guiding art and architecture in service to the church.[5] BLS was composed to help address some of the requests for further clarity in implementing the less directive approach of EACW. BLS is approximately eighty pages in length, with far more extensive footnoting of the material. In response to the perceived overemphasis on the role of the people in worship in EACW, BLS sometimes emphasizes the role of the clergy and the presence of God. It provides more direction for attention to the tabernacle and private

---

4. The full text of the 2003 English edition of the General Instruction of the Roman Missal is available on the web site of the United States Conference of Catholic Bishops at www.usccb.org. The text is also reprinted in *The Liturgy Documents*, 4th ed. (Chicago: Liturgy Training Publications, 2004), pp. 31-118.

5. National Conference of Catholic Bishops, *Built of Living Stones: Art, Architecture, and Worship* (Washington, D.C.: United States Catholic Conference, 2000). Reprinted in *The Liturgy Documents*, 4th ed., pp. 417-98.

devotional activities. It also contains a whole new chapter concerning some basic guidelines for building and renovating a church, including discussions of an appropriate process to follow and practical issues to consider. Like its predecessor, this document has received some criticism. Those who have been unhappy with the liturgical changes of Vatican II think BLS is too "open-ended" because it does not prescribe a return to pre–Vatican II norms. Those who appreciated the brevity and latitude of EACW sometimes find the document too prescriptive and more cumbersome. Certainly both EACW and BLS have helped to foster a living relationship between liturgical renewal and the arts in the life of the church. But tension will remain as our present pluralism takes concrete form in various communities.[6]

Additional contemporary guidance for church building and design continues to emerge for Catholic faith communities today.[7] Three examples are *God's House Is Our House, Our Place of Worship,* and *Meeting House Essays. God's House Is Our House: Re-imagining the Environment for Worship* by Richard S. Vosko is a practical guide for those considering church design.[8] Vosko is a priest in the diocese of Albany and has been a design consultant since 1970. He addresses all aspects of planning for the renovation or new design of a worship environment, from foundational liturgical concerns to implementation issues. Historical and theological insights root his guidance in the larger tradition of the church and provide inspiration for creative thought. *Our Place of Worship* is a recent eighty-page document produced by the Canadian Conference of Catholic Bishops to guide church building and renovation.[9]

---

6. Some dioceses have also chosen to articulate additional guidelines concerning normative practices for church design. An example would be from the Archdiocese of Chicago, Office for Divine Worship, *Guidelines for the Building and Renovation of Churches* (Chicago: Liturgy Training Publications, 2004).

7. Although only three particular resources are mentioned in this paragraph, four recent books from the Liturgical Press would also be of tremendous value to building committees. For thoughtful, critical reflection on tensions over church design today, see Michael E. DeSanctis, *Building from Belief: Advance, Retreat, and Compromise in the Remaking of Catholic Church Architecture* (Collegeville, Minn.: Liturgical Press, 2002). For their practical suggestions for considering church design in community, see Marchita B. Mauck, *Places for Worship: A Guide to Building and Renovating* (Collegeville, Minn.: Liturgical Press, 1995), and Joyce Ann Zimmerman, *The Ministry of Liturgical Environment* (Collegeville, Minn.: Liturgical Press, 2004). And for a thorough and accessible collection of official church statements concerning the physical environment for worship, see Mark G. Boyer, *The Liturgical Environment: What the Documents Say,* 2d ed. (Collegeville, Minn.: Liturgical Press, 2004).

8. Richard S. Vosko, *God's House Is Our House: Re-imagining the Environment for Worship* (Collegeville, Minn.: Liturgical Press, 2006).

9. Canadian Conference of Catholic Bishops, *Our Place of Worship* (Ottawa: Canadian Conference of Catholic Bishops, 1999).

First published in 1999, *Our Place of Worship* represents a synthesis of the priorities of the mid-century liturgical reforms with lessons learned from those early post–Vatican II years of experimentation with liturgical space. A sound approach for planning church building is combined with extended reflections on ritual space, the building process, and rites for dedicating church and altar. The bibliography blends enduring resources from the mid-twentieth century (e.g., works by Frédéric Debuyst, Peter Hammond, and Edward Sövik) with more recent publications from the 1990s. One series of booklets that has provided some significant focused guidance on particular aspects of church design is *Meeting House Essays*.[10] The very title of this series from Liturgy Training Publications indicates the extent to which concern over God's immanent presence remains a vital emphasis in relation to church design. Topics addressed include the importance of sacred space, acoustics, aesthetics, places for devotion, iconography, lighting, font design, and recent historical analysis of Catholic church design. Both scholars and practitioners are included as authors for these booklets,[11] which give evidence of continuing ecumenical respect and appreciation.

Protestant traditions need to be familiar with and learn from Catholic reflections concerning church design. Issues related to active communal worship, devotional opportunities for personal faith expression, beauty, and public witness, mentioned in the above materials, transcend all denominational boundaries. Protestant denominations have also continued to hone their suggestions for contemporary church design.[12] Examples of recent statements to guide congregational church design

10. The Meetinghouse Essays are ten booklets published by Liturgy Training Publications, Chicago, Illinois, between 1991 and 1999.

11. Titles and authors include "Sacred Places and the Pilgrimage of Life" by Lawrence A. Hoffman; "Acoustics for Liturgy: A Collection of Articles of The Hymn Society in the U.S. and Canada" by Dennis Fleisher, Edward Anders Sövik, Austin C. Lovelace, George Taylor, Walter R. Bouman, and Terry K. Boggs; "Cherubim of Gold" by Peter E. Smith; "Places for Devotion" by John Buscemi; "Renewing the City of God" by Michael E. DeSanctis; "Iconography and Liturgy" by Michael Jones-Frank; "Lighting the Liturgy" by Viggo Bech Rambusch; "Designing Future Worship Spaces" by Richard S. Vosko; "Ancient Fonts, Modern Lessons" by T. Jerome Overbeck; and "Path, Portal, Path: Architecture for the Rites" by Christopher Stroik.

12. Beyond the specific denominational resources mentioned in this paragraph, some useful titles that will be of particular value to those considering issues of contemporary church design include the following: James F. White and Susan J. White, *Church Architecture: Building and Renovating for Christian Worship* (Akron: Order of St. Luke Publications, 1998; originally published by Abingdon Press in 1988); William Seth Adams, *Moving the Furniture: Liturgical Theory, Practice, and Environment* (New York: Church Publishing Incorporated, 1999); Richard Giles, *Re-Pitching the Tent: Re-Ordering the Church Building for Worship and Mission,* revised and expanded edition (Norwich: Canterbury Press, 1999; Collegeville: Liturgical Press, 1999); *Searching for Sacred Space: Essays on Architecture and Liturgical Design in the Episcopal Church,* ed. John Ander Runkle (New York:

include *The Church for Common Prayer* and *A Congregational Planning Process* (from the Episcopal Church Building Fund),[13] *Church Building Space: An Architectural Planning Guide and Manual of Procedures, Manual of Procedures for Church Building Programs,* and *Architect Selection Process* (from the United Methodist Church),[14] "Worship Space and the Christian Assembly," principles found in the provisional series Renewing Worship (from the Evangelical Lutheran Church in America),[15] and the *Architectural Handbook* (from the Lutheran Church Extension Fund, Missouri Synod).[16] The Presbyterian Church (USA) has tended to communicate its suggestions for church design through its liturgical journals *Reformed Liturgy and Music*[17] and *Call to Worship.*[18] And

---

Church Publishing Incorporated, 2002); and D. Foy Christopherson, *A Place of Encounter: Renewing Worship Spaces* (Minneapolis: Augsburg/Fortress, 2004). Although these resources come from denominational publishing companies, all of them reference both Roman Catholic and Protestant materials and would be helpful across denominational lines.

13. Charles N. Fulton, Patrick J. Holtkamp, and Fritz Frurip, *The Church for Common Prayer: A Statement on Worship Space for the Episcopal Church* (New York: Episcopal Church Building Fund, 1994). A videotape by the same title was produced to accompany this 32-page booklet. A more detailed 48-page guide for the process of church building was also released in the 1990s: *A Congregational Planning Process* (New York: Episcopal Church Building Fund, n.d.). *The Church for Common Prayer* briefly outlines some theological and liturgical issues to consider in relation to church architecture. *A Congregational Planning Process* describes a specific strategy by which to actualize a tangible project.

14. Architect Douglas R. Hoffman wrote *Church Building Space: An Architectural Planning Guide* (New York: Evangelization and Church Growth, General Board of Global Ministries, The United Methodist Church, 1997), an 84-page booklet concerning many practical aspects of church design. Douglas R. Hoffman wrote *Manual of Procedures for Church Building Programs* (New York: Evangelization and Church Growth, General Board of Global Ministries, The United Methodist Church, 1997), a 74-page companion to *Church Building Space* that discusses a pragmatic approach to implementing a church building project. Roger L. Patterson wrote *Architect Selection Process* (New York: Evangelization and Church Growth, General Board of Global Ministries, The United Methodist Church, 1998), a 17-page booklet that specifically guides a church through selecting an architect appropriate for them. All of these booklets and other useful materials are available from The General Board of Global Ministries of The United Methodist Church in a single resource packet.

15. Evangelical Lutheran Church in America, "Worship Space and the Christian Assembly," in *Principles for Worship* (Minneapolis: Augsburg Fortress, 2002), pp. 67-96. This essay offers an excellent series of principles to guide the process of church design, with background and application notes to help explain the significance of the statements provided.

16. Lutheran Church Extension Fund, *Architectural Handbook* (St. Louis: Lutheran Church Extension Fund, 2005). This 48-page booklet is available as a downloadable file via www.lcef.org

17. See, for example, the issues entitled "Church Architecture," vol. 22, no. 2 (Spring 1988) and "The Art of Worship," vol. 31, no. 3 (1997).

18. See, for example, the issue entitled "Church Architecture," vol. 36, no. 3 (2003). *Reformed Liturgy and Music* was eventually replaced by *Call to Worship.*

the Christian Reformed Church occasionally produces articles and reflections connected to church design for the journal *Reformed Worship* and for the extensive web site of the Calvin Institute of Christian Worship.[19]

All of the above resources have similar emphases: a concern for fullness in relation to communal ritual celebrations, the significance of beauty (whether simple or complex), the importance of public witness, the importance of flexibility in relation to change of various kinds, and the significance of hospitality. Resources from a variety of traditions also continue to be affirmed in many of these sources, a testimony to the lasting effects of ecumenism in the twentieth century.

The Value of a Common Christian Witness and an Attention to Beauty

Conversations between Christian traditions about the design, theological meaning, and practical functioning of churches ought to continue in a climate of ecumenical respect and dialogue.[20] The mutual respect that has been established among the majority of Christian traditions can be expected to continue to foster the fairly easy movement of believers between churches. Committees charged with the responsibility of considering either renovation suggestions or plans for a new church design can benefit greatly from visiting recently renovated and built churches across traditions. Seeing how various theological emphases in worship (such as those pertaining to Christian initiation, proclamation of God's Word, and celebration of the Eucharist) visibly affect the organization and articulation of environments can spark new ideas and more intentional consideration of a host of options. Through such visits, committee members can preview the actual design work of architects and ask questions about how a particular architect worked with a community. And they can explore questions about common issues related to church renovation and design with others who have recently negotiated the many challenges associated with such a venture

19. See for example, the issue of *Reformed Worship* discussing worship and various arts (no. 64, June 2002). The web site address for the Calvin Institute of Christian Worship is www.calvin.edu/worship. An abundance of resources for considering church design, drawing on insights from multiple denominations, can be found in and through this web site.

20. A recent series of essays bears witness to the interest in and potential of continuing work oriented to ecumenical and liturgical renewal. See *Liturgical Renewal as a Way to Christian Unity,* ed. James F. Puglisi (Collegeville, Minn.: Liturgical Press, 2005).

(including fund-raising, selecting an architect, and maintaining good communication with a congregation during the project).

The migrating of parishioners (and sometimes clergy!) between various churches and their learning from one another will very likely continue to encourage similarities between built environments for worship and ministry. People appreciate recognizable features and artifacts for their ability to maintain a sense of continuity between Christian communities. Church design can facilitate this sense of unity in Christ. From the time of the Protestant Reformation there has often been an emphasis on visually marking denominational distinctiveness in church buildings (although this began to erode with the replication of revival designs in the nineteenth century). Perhaps as a consequence of the intense ecumenical activity of the twentieth century, concerns about denominational distinctiveness seem to be less important to people today. In a culture that even appears to be increasingly less predisposed to explicit denominational affirmations of the Christian faith (thinking here of the decline of many mainline traditions and the recent growth of so-called nondenominational churches), the similarities in design between Christian churches may provide a positive unified witness to the continuity between Roman Catholic and Protestant expressions of the church.

Roman Catholic and Protestant churches will probably continue to resemble one another to a significant degree in light of continuing liturgical renewal also. The liturgical activities of Christian churches are often quite similar. Eucharist, baptism, and preaching will remain central to Christian celebrations. We can anticipate interactive and celebratory manifestations of these rituals, which will require liturgical space that continues to enhance a sense of active, communal participation. Technological advances, a variety of postures in worship, and flexibility to accommodate a variety of patterns for ritual celebrations will need to remain a priority of design, at least among those who value such expressions and their artifacts in worship. While fully multipurpose worship spaces may always find a place in the life of some communities (if only as transitional spaces), it seems likely that they will remain a minority. Concern for having spaces dedicated to worship will probably gain momentum among many congregations in light of the recognized importance of accenting the transcendence of God and having places set apart for daily prayer and meditation. Many people are also rediscovering the value of attaching memory and maintaining traditions in relation to specific geographical locations associated with religious beliefs.

In an architectural world concerned with options and economics in design, beauty is an issue worth mentioning. Our churches become tangible public statements by virtue of their very existence in the landscape. Beauty is a notoriously difficult concept to define precisely, but in community a sense for what is attractive and enduring can be discerned over time.[21] Some Christian communities today are eschewing any concern for beauty. A common reason for ignoring a developed aesthetic concern is related to financial stewardship, a desire to dedicate the maximum amount of money for ministry to people rather than to a building fund. While it is certainly responsible to prioritize financial resources for public ministry, it is naive to believe that the visible presence of a church does not express a particular understanding of God and communicate the priorities of a community. Historically the church has affirmed that God is the author and source of all beauty, and a church building is inevitably connected to theological understandings of God. Accordingly, a church devoid of beauty misrepresents God as a God who is not concerned with beauty. In the wake of a century accused of producing banal architecture (and consequently of communicating a distorted view of God), Christians today need to be particularly careful about cultivating the theological connection between God and beauty.[22] Beauty enhances the world for all people, both those inside and those outside Christian communities.

21. In church design, beauty is not found only in great simplicity or great complexity, nor is it restricted to any particular architectural style. From the perspective outlined here, all architectural styles are *capable* of being articulated in beautiful forms. However, such an affirmation does not presuppose that every expression is necessarily beautiful. Beautiful church designs emerge from the collaborative work of excellent artists (architects are considered artists in their own right here) and people in the community, distilled through a thoughtful process of conviction, intention, and evaluation over an extended period of time. A final ruling on whether or not a church has truly fulfilled its goal of beauty will probably not reside with the generation that designed the structure. In truth, any lasting judgment and assignment of the label "beautiful" will fall to later generations that encounter and use a particular church building. For this reason alone, any notion of "disposable" church architecture ought to be banished from the lexicon of every faith community.

22. Resources such as Ray Bowman and Eddy Hall, *When Not to Build* (Grand Rapids: Baker Book House, 1992), encourage a pragmatic approach to church building that appeals to many congregations, an approach based primarily on square footage, multiple uses of interior space, and minimal expense. While such issues are important for church planning and building, references to the role of beauty and public witness are absent from Bowman and Hall's consideration. So-called design-and-build architectural firms frequently take a similar approach to church building. While economic benefits do emerge from such a "bottom-line" financial approach, unintended consequences can also emerge from this reductionistic thinking process. Christian communities today need to think long and hard about their testimony through church architecture and decide if considering economy alone is the best possible way to create a continuing visible witness to Jesus Christ.

The Importance of Sustainable Church Design

Sustainability is a concept of architectural design that will be important for future church building. Sustainable architectural design (sometimes called "green" architecture) recognizes the social, economic, and environmental ramifications of each new building project.[23] Ancient Israelite laws and the teachings of Jesus Christ provide a firm foundation for caring for all kinds of people in our communities. Care for others is expressed in part through choices that benefit the social and economic structures of a local community. Supporting local artisans and businesses (including using local building materials when possible) is an example of a strategy that contributes to sustainable architecture. Christian communities frequently use passages from the creation accounts in the book of Genesis to ground their affirmation of a need to be environmentally responsible (e.g., Gen. 1:28 and Gen. 2:15). Often we will speak of bearing the responsibility of being stewards of the gift of the earth and its resources. Christian communities of the future will have the opportunity to model good stewardship of the earth and be socially gracious by choosing to pursue designs that demonstrate a commitment to environmental responsibility. Churches could even become community leaders in showcasing sustainable design and thus demonstrating their commitment to be "good neighbors." The connection between sustainable design and social and environmental responsibility can be further illustrated in several ways.

First, architectural sustainability includes concern about the social and environmental impact that a new building has on a particular geographical location. Every site has a particular ecology with existing soil and water systems to consider. Churches need to be conscious of how a proposed new building or renovation might impact the ecology of the site in both the short term and the long term. Every site also has a relationship to other buildings and transportation systems. Decades of dependence on the car as a primary means of transportation have created a pattern of significant physical distance between many of our people and our church build-

---

23. Fiona Cousins and Michelle Murosky, "Sustainable Design," in Nicholas W. Roberts, *Building Type Basics for Places of Worship* (New York: John Wiley & Sons, Inc., 2004), p. 97. This chapter presents a useful overview of some of the basic understandings grounding sustainable design and provides practical ideas for implementing such designs. The United States Green Building Council (USGBC) has developed a rating system to help establish and standardize sustainable design. The rating system is called Leadership in Engineering and Environmental Design (LEED). Buildings can be measured against LEED standards, and their creators can seek recognition for meeting these objective criteria. Additional information about the LEED rating system can be found at the USGBC web site: www.usgbc.org.

ings. Churches of the twenty-first century have the opportunity to begin to reverse the trend toward what some critics now call urban or suburban sprawl.[24] Locating our churches in the midst of existing urban and suburban environments can help to resist sprawl. If churches pursued choices that encouraged people to walk or bike or use public transportation to reach the facilities, it would help to build more intimate connections with people in the community. There could also be economic advantages to such choices: individuals would spend less on transportation and do less damage to the environment (in terms of air quality and ground contamination).[25] For all these reasons, site selection and evaluation are important components of sustainability.

Second, a building can be planned in ways that demonstrate concern for the use of natural resources in relation to heating, cooling, and lighting. The insulation and sealing of a building will have a direct effect on the amount of energy needed to heat and cool the interior environment. Window sizing and location will have a bearing on both temperature control and lighting for the space. The type of lighting used in the church will impact the energy costs incurred over time. And the use of alternative technologies (such as solar or wind-related systems) and / or high-efficiency mechanical systems will help to reduce the amount of energy required to provide temperature control. Thoughtful choices in the early planning stages of a project can contribute to minimizing energy consumption throughout the life of the building.

Third, paying attention to the building materials used for a project can contribute to sustainability. Limiting the amount of scarce resources used in a church (such as particular woods or minerals) can help to preserve world supplies of rare materials and contribute to preserving the natural environments of those materials. In some cases, it may even be wiser to select alternative — more readily available or renewable — materials that might yield similar effects. Using materials from recycled sources is good for the earth and a tangible sign of responsible stewardship. Everything from incorporating previously used brick, stone, and glass to using innovative materials created from post-consumer waste can be considered. And using products that are environmentally friendly includes seeking out materials that required minimal energy resources to produce (saving initial energy costs) and that will not release toxins into the environment over time as they decay (whether while part of the church structure or when discarded).

24. For an accessible discussion of this topic, see Eric O. Jacobsen, *Sidewalks in the Kingdom: New Urbanism and the Christian Faith* (Grand Rapids: Brazos Press, 2003).

25. It is even possible to conceive of possible cost savings in relation to medical care: if people walked and biked to churches, they could improve their overall health and possibly strengthen their cardiovascular systems.

The Importance of Maintaining a
Unique Testimony and a Public Presence

For most Christian communities, it is not wise to imitate the approach of the structures used by megachurches, with their sprawling campuses, theater-like auditoriums for worship, and facilities for ministry that rival local restaurants, coffeehouses, bookstores, and recreational/exercise centers.[26] The financial resources required for constructing and maintaining such facilities are enormous. Auditorium spaces resembling fine-arts performance centers are noted for being particularly effective for introducing people to the faith by virtue of their size (allowing the self-conscious to feel anonymous in a vast space), for facilitating an entertaining format (retaining the attention of the uninitiated), and for providing comfortable, stationary seating that inhibits movement (conveying a certain notion of safety/distance).[27] But some have begun to question whether or not the church ought to create its own "Christian version" of community resources such as restaurants, theaters, and retail outlets.[28] Some ask whether it might not be a more powerful witness for Christians to be active in community establishments

---

26. Historically, churches have been known for providing their surrounding communities with various goods and services, such as food, clothing, and shelter for those in need and recreational facilities for younger people. These services have been provided without charge. Churches today that serve the community by developing and maintaining restaurants and retail outlets are redefining the traditional ways of caring for those in need. Such efforts do add a competitive component to local economies, a consequence that will continue to increase pressure to eliminate the tax-exempt status of churches and call into question their overall purpose in society.

27. Charles G. Finney (1792-1875) noted this phenomenon in the nineteenth century and adapted the Chatham Street Theatre in New York City for his evangelistic meetings. He renamed the theatre Chatham Street Chapel and led worship services there with an evangelistic focus. A number of twentieth-century congregations have gone on to reproduce this model of theatre/auditorium space for worship. For an excellent historical analysis of the use of auditorium spaces, see Jeanne Halgren Kilde, *When Church Became Theatre: The Transformation of Evangelical Architecture and Worship in Nineteenth-Century America* (New York: Oxford University Press, 2002). For a brief history and useful survey of churches using auditoriums in the twentieth century, see Anne C. Loveland and Otis B. Wheeler, *From Meetinghouse to Megachurch: A Material and Cultural History* (Columbia: University of Missouri Press, 2003).

28. Churches associated with the "emerging church" or "alternative worship" movement articulate such a concern. They are generally small communities of believers that often intentionally gather in local establishments for worship and ministry to witness to the presence of Christ in the world. For additional information on this movement, see Mike Riddell, Mark Pierson, and Cathy Kirkpatrick, *The Prodigal Project: Journey into the Emerging Church* (London: SPCK, 2001), and Dan Kimball, *The Emerging Church* (Grand Rapids: Zondervan, 2003).

in order to be "salt and light in the world" rather than setting aside resources to duplicate existing facilities.

That said, it is important to remember that megachurches do often function as wonderful centers of evangelism. They may come to establish a niche as locations that help those unfamiliar with or disenfranchised from the church to become connected to Christian community.[29] While these campuses and auditoriums will probably not dominate the church landscape in any significant way, it will be interesting to see if their architectural expressions exhibit any increasing use of Christian iconography. At present, they tend to exhibit either an absence or a minimal inclusion of traditional symbols. As this church movement matures, congregations may choose to become more visibly explicit about their Christian presence in the community through their architectural vocabulary.

A final thought on twenty-first-century church building concerns the increasing presence of worship structures for the world's religions in the United States and Europe. As the members of world religions such as Islam, Buddhism, Hinduism, and Jainism continue to increase in the West, their places for communal worship will eventually become more prevalent. Often these other faith traditions make ample use of traditional forms of religious architecture for mosques or temples, which function to call attention to their presence in the larger community. Many world religions value the use of architectural forms that associate them with historical roots, ethnic artistic expressions, and specific theological interpretations. They rely upon a recognizable, communal language of design that communicates clearly the God or gods that are referenced by their buildings.

In the decades to come, Christian communities may decide that "blending in" with the common architectural expressions of the day places them at a disadvantage in a landscape populated by unique religious architecture.[30] Distinctive symbols and architectural features may again become increasingly important for both exterior

---

29. Some who have shared in the ministries of the large megachurches have found that the opportunity to renew their faith in this environment (often including healing from past hurts) is of great value; they then return to denominational churches with a new energy for service.

30. So-called spiritual seekers are often curious about the unique traits of different religious belief systems. While "blending in" may give a church the advantage of establishing connections with familiar cultural expressions, it may have the unintended consequence of making a church appear to be no different from other cultural manifestations. Christian communities would do well to begin to think about what sets their testimony of faith apart from other religious messages that are becoming more prevalent (aurally and visually). Can our architectural manifestations be shaped in such a way that they work toward communicating the alternative vision of life and the world espoused by the whole Christian tradition?

and interior church design. Christian traditions may find the pluralism of the religious architectural landscape of their communities an increasing challenge in which to visually represent the Christian God.

RECENT RESOURCES FOR VISUALIZING NEW CHURCH DESIGNS

A number of valuable resources for church design have recently been published. One of them is *Building Type Basics for Places of Worship* by Nicholas W. Roberts, a technical guide to help people understand the ways in which site planning, structural, mechanical, electrical, and communication systems, materials, and acoustic and audiovisual concerns can be addressed.[31] This is a book written by an architect for architects to familiarize them with specific expectations and issues related to church design and building. While not written only for Christian communities, churches factor heavily into the text and photographs of this volume. (Liturgical consultant Richard Vosko also functioned as a significant resource person for this guidebook.) Those interested in comprehending many of the more technical aspects of church building will revel in the photographs, charts, graphs, drawings, and textual descriptions explaining the fundamentals of worship space design. By reading this work, they may be able to better understand some of the jargon peculiar to the world of architecture.

Picture books abound in the publishing world today, and a number of them feature recent churches from Europe, the United States, and around the world. Two of the more impressive oversize books are *Church Builders* by Edwin Heathcote and Iona Spens[32] and *New Spiritual Architecture* by Phyllis Richardson.[33] *Church Builders* begins with a wonderful summation of the theological and architectural movements that inspired church designs in the twentieth century. Following this essay is a host of pictures of Christian churches from Europe and the United States, and some from other nations as well. The photographs are excellent and provide a marvelous window into creative solutions for a wide range of Christian traditions. *New Spiritual Architecture* is not limited to Christian churches, although just over one half of the projects featured are churches located primarily in Europe and the United States.

---

31. Nicholas W. Roberts, *Building Type Basics for Places of Worship* (Hoboken, N.J.: John Wiley & Sons, Inc., 2004).

32. Edwin Heathcote and Iona Spens, *Church Builders* (New York: Academy Books, 1997).

33. Phyllis Richardson, *New Spiritual Architecture* (New York: Abbeville Press Publishers, 2003).

The spaces are grouped thematically, featuring those that are experimental in form, those that fit well into their context, those that are humble, and those that are grand in scale. The outstanding photographs are accompanied by minimal text describing the projects featured. Examples of excellent churches included are the Chapel of Ignatius (Seattle, Washington, 1997) designed by Steven Holl, the Jubilee Church (Rome, Italy, 2004) designed by Richard Meier, Christ Church (Donau City, Vienna, Austria, 2000) designed by Heinz Tesar, the Monastery of Novy Dvur (Plzen, Czech Republic, 2004) designed by John Pawson, Cathedral Church of Our Lady of the Angels (Los Angeles, California, 2002) designed by Rafael Moneo, Church of San Giovanni Rotondo (Foggia, Italy, 2004) designed by Renzo Piano, and Antioch Baptist Church (Perry County, Alabama, 2002) designed by Sam Mockbee and Rural Studio. Seeing and reading about these varied spaces for worship and ministry will fire the imagination and provoke thoughtful ways of cultivating interesting relationships between beauty and utility in meeting the needs of faith communities today.

Wolfgang Jean Stock has edited *European Church Architecture, 1950-2000* and written *Architectural Guide: Christian Sacred Buildings in Europe since 1950,* both of which feature a wide range of Roman Catholic and Protestant church designs exclusively from Europe.[34] Churches by Le Corbusier and Rudolf Schwarz are included in these collections, as well as a wide variety of offerings by many other architects. Although the buildings featured indicate a movement away from the rigid standards of the International Style, there is ample use of basic geometric forms, light, reinforced concrete, and steel, and the application of a minimalist aesthetic palette. As the new century begins, the churches seem to incorporate more complex forms of design. The plurality of design evident in postmodern architecture is abundant. Additional color is incorporated into some spaces. The churches seem to be fairly split between exhibiting longitudinal, processional spaces and centralized spaces that minimize the distance between the people and the liturgical appointments. There is a general absence of reliance on historical models of expression in the churches Stock has chosen to feature, but this should not be read as indicating that all churches in Europe are avoiding historical referents. A more thorough examination of all new churches would need to be conducted to make such a determination. Given the tremendous

34. The first book by Stock, *European Church Architecture, 1950-2000* (Munich: Prestel Publishing House, 2002), represents a basic overview of recent church architecture in Europe, documenting 60 buildings in some detail. The second book by Stock, *Architectural Guide: Christian Sacred Buildings in Europe since 1950* (Munich: Prestel Publishing House, 2004), adds a level of specific content to the first, featuring 130 sacred buildings from 20 European countries.

number of historic churches that exist throughout Europe, it seems likely that historical styles of design would be evident in at least a portion of new churches.

Michael J. Crosbie, architect and scholar, is the current editor in chief of *Faith and Form,* the journal of the Interfaith Forum on Religion, Art, and Architecture.[35] Crosbie has edited two volumes featuring recent religious architecture in the United States (from the 1990s to the millennium, a period of time that saw a marked resurgence of church building): *Architecture for the Gods* and *Architecture for the Gods, Book Two.*[36] Crosbie's collections feature new church buildings and renovations for Roman Catholic and Protestant traditions. One can discern both familiar and unfamiliar patterns in relation to historical designs for churches. Occasionally Gothic and colonial designs are referenced in creative ways. Many new designs are featured — again, a testimony to the impact of postmodern architecture. Contemporary materials and building techniques are evident. Vertical dimensions of space are used, employing a traditional way of referring to God's transcendence. Centralized planning of worship spaces is abundant, among both the Roman Catholic and the Protestant churches featured. This could be interpreted as evidence of a modern design feature that has moved from innovation to tradition.

A particular church reflective of the influences of ecumenism, liturgical renewal, and postmodern concerns for context is St. Theresa Church, Sherborn, Massachusetts (designed by Keefe Associates). Located in a town southwest of Boston that has many buildings designed in the tradition of wood-frame New England village architecture, this Catholic parish chose a facade resembling a Congregational meetinghouse church. The interior of the worship space features a semicircular seating arrangement around the liturgical appointments of ambo and altar. The appointments are centrally located along one long side of the space, not unlike the arrangement of the earliest meetinghouses. As this example shows, it has become possible at the end of the twentieth century for Roman Catholic communities to

---

35. The journal *Faith and Form* is another excellent source for viewing new building solutions for religious communities and for thoughtful reflections on church design today.

36. The first book by Crosbie, *Architecture for the Gods* (Mulgrave: Images Publishing Group, 1999), features 40 buildings — 34 Christian, 5 Jewish, and 1 Muslim. The second book by Crosbie, *Architecture for the Gods, Book Two* (Mulgrave: Images Publishing Group, 2002), features 54 buildings — 41 Christian, 10 Jewish, 1 Muslim, 1 Buddhist, and 1 Interfaith. Both Crosbie and Stock chose not to segregate the buildings featured in their books into specific tradition-related sections such as "Roman Catholic" and "Protestant." Perhaps this is a testimony to the similar needs of all denominational churches today and another by-product of continuing ecumenical activity.

adopt designs originally used exclusively by Protestant communities, surely evidence of the appreciation and respect fostered by ecumenical activities. And the centrally planned model of the worship space suggests the effectiveness of a design recovered under the influence of the liturgical movement.

Conclusions

There has perhaps never been a time that has held more potential than today for renovating and designing new churches with the intent of renewing Christian worship and ministry. Our twentieth century of church building has provided us with a large array of expressions. We have lived with them and come to see both the positive and the negative aspects of many of those buildings. The process we pursue in relation to the design of our churches needs to be evaluative, reflective, and communal. Exploring the architectural designs we have inherited and their impact on our current patterns of worship and ministry will be essential for shaping constructive new expressions. Appreciating the many expressions of churches in our communities will expand our horizons, helping us to recognize what can be accomplished through material manifestations of faith and enhancing relationships between Christian communities. And working together in community grants us the opportunity to share passionate impressions and ideas, envision what we believe in new ways, and grow in respect and understanding of one another.

Immanence will remain important to future church design. Many of the churches we occupy today demonstrate the positive qualities of spaces that accent the theological affirmation of a God who is present in us and active through us. But immanence alone is inadequate in conceiving of the fullness of God. Attention to God's transcendence needs to bring a healthy tension to the church buildings we occupy. Our challenge to creatively express both the immanence and the transcendence of God through material means is not new, but it remains critical to the spiritual formation of the faithful and public proclamation of the God we serve. We can learn much from the artifacts and testimonies of those who have gone before us. And we are granted the awkward privilege of constructing churches that will outlast us, the supporters of their creation.

Our world continues to change. As followers of Jesus Christ, the fundamental charge to honor God and serve humanity remains with us. A primary challenge for us as Christian communities will be to process the abundance of knowledge we have at our disposal and translate these insights into structures that will be cost effective, earth friendly, useful to both the initiated and the uninitiated, and reflective of the beauty of the very creation in which our buildings are located. Our hearts may always be made restless by the inevitable inadequacies of our church buildings. But our collective striving to inspire powerful encounters with God through our built environments for worship and ministry can also produce deep joy and great anticipation.

APPENDIX

THE FOLLOWING HISTORICAL documents have been reproduced in English to assist the reader in visualizing the development of theological reflection on church design from the 1940s to the 1970s. All of the documents below originated from within the Roman Catholic Church. The size and influence of the Catholic Church in Europe and the United States facilitated a wide distribution of these materials. Citations from these sources and references to these texts in bibliographies appeared in both Protestant and Catholic publications for many decades. The ecumenical spirit of the times encouraged consideration of this material across denominational lines.

Of particular note in the documents below is the gradual emphasis on the significance of the presence and role of the congregation in the liturgy. A corresponding concern for function and its implications for design is evident. Directives are provided for facilitating more communal, active participation in worship. A growing sympathy for embracing contemporary expressions of art and architecture is also present. Churches are admonished to "speak" in the visual language of their day. Initial concerns about avoiding secular building designs as a source for inspiring church architecture eventually dissipate. Ultimately, what is evident in this collection of writings is a movement toward conceiving of the church as a house for the people of God.

Directives for the Building of a Church
(German Liturgical Commission, 1947)

This document was composed by the Reverend Theodor Klauser, Rector Magnificus, of the University of Bonn, by order of and in cooperation with the Liturgical Commission established by the Catholic bishops of Germany. It appeared in Documents for Sacred Architecture *(Collegeville, Minn.: Liturgical Press, 1957) and is reproduced here by permission of Liturgical Press.*

The Christian church, a house of God, is a sacred place filled with the divine presence (even apart from the holy Eucharist), a place where the people of God assemble, and that for several purposes:

First and above all, to celebrate the re-presentation of the redeeming Sacrifice of our Lord.

Secondly, to partake of the fruits of Christ's redeeming Sacrifice in the holy sacraments.

Thirdly, to hear the preaching of the word of God.

Fourthly, to render homage and adoration to the presence of our Lord in the eucharistic Bread.

Fifthly, to engage in various non-liturgical devotions.

The Christian church building, however, serves not only as the assemblying place for the Christian community, whether for liturgical or non-liturgical worship; it is also a place for individual private devotion.

2. Such being the character and the purposes of the Christian church edifice, it bears a distinction of incomparable dignity.

It is, firstly, in a unique way "the tabernacle of God among men" (Apoc. 21:3), the place where by His mercy His people may surely find Him; it is our Father's house (Luke 15:17); it is the "basilica," the palace of the King.

Secondly, this house of God is the holy place in which the Church, the Mystical Body of Christ, is formed and upbuilded and hence the visible edifice is a symbol of this Mystical Body.

Thirdly, this house of God is the place in which the eternal union of God with His people in life everlasting is anticipated, and therefore the Christian church edifice is rightly regarded as the heavenly Sion descended upon earth.

3. These various purposes which the church building must serve present a peculiar problem in its construction. The eucharistic Sacrifice requires an arrangement

of space different from that required by the administration of the sacraments of baptism and penance; the requirements in the administration of these sacraments differ from those which preaching demands; and differences appear again as between preaching and eucharistic adoration, as between eucharistic adoration and community worship, as between community worship and private devotion. It is the task of the architect to find a solution of the problem which will best satisfy these several purposes of the church edifice.

4. The services of Christian worship, the eucharistic Sacrifice, the administration of the sacraments, the preaching of the word of God, adoration of the eucharistic Christ — these are not rendered in precisely the same way in all churches throughout the world. In the course of the centuries divers methods have developed, the so-called "liturgies" or "rites." By far the most important of these are the Roman and the Byzantine rites, the former in the bishoprics of the West and the latter in those of the East.

While agreeing in all essentials, the Roman and the Byzantine rites have features that are definitely distinct. Therefore the church edifice in which the Roman liturgy is to be celebrated cannot be exactly like one which serves the Byzantine liturgy.

5. The church edifice today is intended for the people of our times. Hence it must be fashioned in such way that the people of our times may recognize and feel that it is addressed to them. The most significant and the most worthy needs of modern mankind must here find their fulfillment: the urge toward community life, the desire for what is true and genuine, the wish to advance from what is peripheral to central and essential, the demand for clarity, lucidity, intelligibility, the longing for quiet and peace, for a sense of warmth and security.

Conclusions

1. The several parochial buildings, church, school, parish library and charity bureau and hospice, rectory and janitor's dwelling, should not, except in case of necessity, be erected apart from each other in separate localities.

The ideal which should be desired is a juxtaposition of these several units so as to form one *"domus ecclesiae,"* a parish center where the close interrelation of temple and priesthood, of Eucharist and charity, of sacraments and education would be visibly expressed.

2. It is not desirable that the church edifice, except in cases of necessity, be located directly on a street filled with the noise of business and traffic, even though the people of our times who are so immersed in earthly things do greatly need a distinct reorientation of their mind toward God on high. It would be a commendable thing if the people assembling for divine worship might traverse a zone of quiet, a bordered fore-court, a formal atrium, and so inwardly disposed and attuned to the divine atmosphere of the sacred interior.

3. It would be a mistake to plan the exterior structure in its outlines and spatial proportions, in its structural members and its decoration, according to the style of profane architecture of the time and of the surroundings, lest the attractiveness of the church building be merely that of this world. A mistake also to point out to the public the direction to the church by means of showy sign-boards along the way.

Our effort should be no doubt to express by exterior appearance of the building the supernatural, the divine character of the worship that transpires within — and yet to adapt the edifice in harmony with its surroundings.

4. In planning the entrances to the church building the chief considerations should not be simply protection from wind and weather and the orderly coming and going of the congregation.

The portals of the church, and especially the main portal, should by their impressive design suggest to the faithful the symbolism of church portals as representing the gates of heaven.

5. The plans for the interior of the church should be determined chiefly by the requirements for the eucharistic Sacrifice; not, as one sometimes finds, primarily for the sake of devotion to our Lord's eucharistic Presence so that spatial arrangements are made to serve chiefly for adoration and contemplation. This latter procedure is incorrect, because in the gradation of purposes that of eucharistic adoration is not the first in order.

The problem presented by this gradation of purposes can best be solved by a spatial arrangement which provides areas for eucharistic adoration and for the administration of the sacraments of baptism and penance distinct from that which is required for the eucharistic Sacrifice. These several areas could then be given their appropriate architectural treatment.

6. It is a mistaken although a widespread notion that the altar should be placed in the midst of the congregation, and that therefore the circular form of edifice is the only satisfactory one.

The Christian church building is intended primarily for the celebration of the eucharistic Sacrifice. This holy Sacrifice is, according to the mind of the Roman liturgy, an action: above all the action of Christ, our High-priest, and of His representative in the priestly office; but it is also the action of the entire Christian community. Climactic moments in the action of the congregation are the acclamations before the preface, the *Amen* at the end of the Canon, as well as the offertory and communion processions, of which the former now rarely appears in our day. The concurrence and concord of these actions suppose a spatial arrangement directed toward the altar, so that there is exchange of address and response between sanctuary and nave, between priest and people, and processional movement to and from the altar. The ideal therefore is a church building arranged with regard to these wishes of the Roman liturgy: direction toward the altar, opposite positions of priest and people, provision for orderly procession to and fro; while at the same time the altar must not be too far removed from the nave.

7. The altar has a meaning from earliest times as a station from which earth looks up to heaven. In the Christian religion the altar is, according to its purpose, the sacrificial and banquet table of the people of God, and at the same time the place of God's eucharistic advent among us. Since at the Consecration in the Mass our divine Lord becomes present upon the altar, it is, even without the tabernacle, Christ's throne on earth. And since the altar is His throne, the faithful from patristic times saw in the altar a symbol of Christ Himself, for the throne symbolizes the person of the Ruler. Therefore it is evidently incorrect to fashion the altar as a mural console as though its purpose were merely or chiefly to serve as a pedestal for tabernacle and crucifix, for candelabra and reliquaries, for painted altar-pieces or groups of statues.

In the well-planned church interior the altar should appear with greatest prominence as the most sacred object, the very center and heart of the entire environment. This will be made evident by its isolated placement, its relative elevation, accessible from all sides, well proportioned, excellent in the given material, monumental in the measure which the edifice demands, situated in right perspective, at the most lightsome point, and surmounted by a baldaquin or canopy.

8. Whenever it is possible the venerable tradition according to which the main axis of the building proceeds from west to east, with the altar at the eastern end, should be retained.

The significant and beautiful symbolism contained in this eastward direction would profitably be restored in the consciousness of the faithful, and thus the eastward placing of our churches revived. Various evidences seem to show that in days to come the ancient custom will be restored whereby the position of the priest is at the farther side of the altar, facing toward the people, as is still the case in the old Roman basilicas. This alteration of the present custom apparently corresponds to the widely felt desire for a more distinct expression of community oneness at the table of the Lord. The rule of eastward direction would not thereby be infringed; for the ideal goal in this orientation is God our Father and His only-begotten Son; and their divine light is regarded as rising and enthroned in the East, like the sun in the natural firmament. Now, this theophany, this appearance of God among us, takes place upon the altar, and hence the eastward direction in our churches is not to-ward the extreme eastern wall but toward the altar. Thus both priest and people are rightly turned toward the altar.

9. Yet it is not desirable in churches of great size to place the altar invariably near the extreme end of the building as was done in some churches here and there in ancient times (the one-area church).

More in accord with the general tradition would be, in larger churches, a rectan-gular, or semicircular, or polygonal sanctuary (choir) evidently distinct from the nave (the two-area church).

10. The terminal wall of the sanctuary should not be pierced by windows, lest the clear vision of the altar be obscured. Nor should the terminal wall be adorned with figured paintings that bear no direct relation to the eucharistic Sacrifice or to the theme of the liturgical year.

The architecture and the decoration of the sanctuary should be so designed that the eye will not be distracted but rather drawn to the altar and to the action or the eucharistic Sacrifice. Where figured paintings or mosaics adorn the sanctuary, these should represent ideas drawn from the Canon of the Mass, i.e., from the *Sursum corda* to the final doxology. In all cases the representation should not be of historical events but of static motives.

11. It would be unfortunate if the interior of the church were planned in such a way that the congregation would lack the feeling of oneness, of family union in the rendering of divine worship. On the other hand it would be a mistake to plan the entire space in such way that nowhere would there be left a quiet corner for private prayer.

Where possible, it would be ideal to provide a larger area for the large Sunday and feast-day congregations, and also another distinct and smaller one for the lesser number on workdays, so that in both cases there would be the feeling of a well-knit community, with still some provision of retired spaces for private devotion.

12. The highly desirable concentration of the whole interior upon the altar may be considerably disturbed by side altars, the stations of the Way of the Cross, confessionals, poorly placed lighting fixtures and benches and chairs, all of which may distract the gaze of the faithful from the sanctuary.

Everything really superfluous should be eliminated, and such details as are indispensable should be placed as inconspicuously as possible, perhaps in a lower chapel. Whatever must remain in the main area should be so designed and placed as not to interfere with the lines converging upon the altar.

13. The sacristy should be located quite near to the sanctuary and not, as in ancient times, alongside the facade of the building.

But there should be some way of passage from the sacristy to the entrance of the church so that on Sundays and feast-days there may be a festive approach of the clergy to the altar through the midst of the congregation, and furthermore so that the entrance chant, the introit, may again be rendered as of old.

14. The vast interiors of cathedral churches and of churches in pilgrimage places and in our great cities have made it necessary that preaching be done not from the sanctuary but from an elevated pulpit usually located almost about the center of the nave and to one side, or again, fixed to a side wall. This example set by large churches has been adopted rather generally and without equal reason, and with the pulpit so placed the preacher is turned away from part of the congregation.

Preaching, according to the liturgy, that is, preaching which is in organic relation to the eucharistic Sacrifice, should be primarily an extension and explanation of the two readings which announce the word of God. Therefore, like the epistle and the gospel, the sermon should, wherever possible, issue forth from the sanctuary, that is, from a lectern or an ambo located near the sanctuary rail.

15. The choir or *schola cantorum* has a well-defined liturgical task to fulfill, namely, to lead the congregation in prayers and hymns and acclamations, to alternate with the congregation in the responsorial chants, and to represent the congregation now and then. Therefore it is a mistake to locate the choir in a high gallery to the rear of and out of sight of the congregation.

In a church which adheres to the strict rules of the liturgy, the choir is placed at the forward end of the congregation and next to the sanctuary. If the high gallery is retained at all, it may serve as the location for the organ. The function of this instrument is not to furnish solo pieces during the mis-called "pauses" in the sacred action, but rather to support the chant of the choir and the congregation, and occasionally to accentuate the spirit of festivity before and after the divine service. (The gallery would also be the proper place for a polyphonic choir and for an orchestra, which latter of course is never permitted in a truly liturgical service.)

16. In the sacrament of baptism we are born anew as children of God and we are incorporated into the Church, the Mystical Body of Christ. It is a deplorable fact that this full significance of baptism, so fundamental a truth in the ensemble of our faith, does not receive sufficient emphasis in our modern parochial life, and accordingly the baptismal font is usually one of the most neglected objects in the furnishings of our churches.

The baptismal font, which should be of imposing design and proportions, should be located in its own distinct area near to the entrance of the church. This area should be, according to venerable ecclesiastical tradition, in circular or polygonal form. The text of the rite of baptism also suggests this architectural treatment. For at the decisive moment in this ritual ceremony the baptised person appears not as an active agent in the process, but as the passive recipient of the divine mysterious action. Such being the case, the appropriate architectural form here is not the rectangular space, which is symbolic of an active process, but rather a circular space, the axis of which is vertical and suggestive of a passive experience.

17. It would be a mistake to arrange and decorate the interior of the church in such a way as to create the atmosphere of a comfortable and cozy bourgeois residence; and a mistake also to wish to imitate the poverty of a proletarian dwelling.

The church interior should be neither bourgeois nor proletarian. It should bespeak forcibly the grandeur of God which surpasses all earthly measure, so that it may exalt the worshiper above the sphere and atmosphere of his daily private life; and yet, it must still leave one with the friendly feeling of "the goodness and kindness of our Savior" (Titus 3:4).

18. It would be a mistake, and it is one that is often made in our times, to entrust the decoration of the church, in painting and sculpture, in the designing of its furnishings, above all in the artistic treatment of the main portal, of the sanctuary, the altar, the baptismal font and the pulpit, to the arbitrary action of a transient pastor or of a donor, or to the risk of mere haphazard.

In our efforts to erect an exemplary church edifice it is necessary to work out not only a structural plan, but also a well thought out plan of artistic expression which will be theologically and pedagogically correct. Such a plan will recognize that the decorative scheme of the finished house of God should present to the view of the congregation an ensemble of the theme of our holy faith, not in a fragmentary way, but with a certain completeness and in significant proportions and with right placing of accent.

19. In the planning of new churches there is often a desire to fix the dimensions at the maximum that financial resources and the ground area permit. It is a mistake to imagine that a larger church is necessarily a finer one.

There is an optimum size which should be kept in mind. That optimum is attained in a church in which the priest at the altar may be seen and may be heard without mechanical aid from the farthest reaches of the congregation, and in which the distribution of holy Communion to all of the faithful may be accomplished without disrupting the holy Sacrifice of the Mass. This optimum size should never be exceeded except in extraordinary cases such as a cathedral church or a pilgrimage church, which must of course be of larger dimensions.

20. It would be a mistake to provide for a church of average size a sanctuary of large dimensions sufficient to accommodate all the clergy of a cathedral chapter; and a mistake also to reduce the size of the sanctuary to such degree that the altar steps reach nearly to the sanctuary rail.

The dimensions of the sanctuary should be in proper proportion to those of the entire building, the area between the altar steps and the sanctuary being of such width and depth that the ceremonies of solemn high Mass may proceed in good order and harmony.

21. It would be a mistake to fill the church unnecessarily with pews to such degree that they would extend forward almost to the altar rail and sideways to contact the outer walls.

There should be center and side aisles of sufficient width, and space enough about the church entrances and before the altar rail. Thus there will be no unseemly crowding at Communion time, and on certain occasions processions may take place with ease, such as the entrance procession on Sundays and feast days and processions of Candlemas day and Palm Sunday.

A serious responsibility rests upon those who are entrusted with the task of church building. The result of their work will determine whether or not succeeding generations of the faithful will love this house of God with a true familiar feeling, and whether they will come joyfully or reluctantly to the sacred action of community worship. Therefore the planning of a new church edifice needs to be thought out with earnest conscience and with great care.

Diocesan Church Building Directives (Diocesan Liturgical Commission, Superior, Wisconsin, 1957; revised text)

This document is reproduced by permission of the Chair of the Liturgical Commission, Father William Wenninger.

I. THE CHURCH AND ITS ELEMENTS

Statement of Principle

A church is a sacred building dedicated to divine worship primarily that it should be at the disposal of all the faithful for the public exercise of divine worship.

CANON LAW

O how awesome is this place; this is the house of God and the gateway to heaven; it shall be called the majestic court of God.

THE MASS OF DEDICATION

The Christian church, a house of God, is a sacred place filled with the divine presence, even apart from the holy Eucharist, a place where the people of God assemble:
    First, to celebrate the re-presentation of the redeeming sacrifice of our Lord.
    Secondly, to partake of the fruits of Christ's redeeming sacrifice in the holy sacraments.
    Thirdly, to hear the preaching of the word of God.
    Fourthly, to render homage and adoration to the presence of our Lord in the eucharistic bread.
    Fifthly, to engage in various non-liturgical devotions.

THE GERMAN LITURGICAL COMMISSION

The primary purpose of the church is to serve the sacred liturgy. The church is the home of the risen Christ, who under sacramental sign and sacred rite continues his redemptive work among us. In this sacred enclosure the glorified Christ offers expiation for sin, sanctifies, heals, announces the good news of salvation. The church is likewise the dwelling place of God's holy people: Christ's mystical body. In this sacred edifice the whole Christ, Head and members, offers perfect worship to the Father in heaven. Through sacred signs (the sacraments) Christ continues his divine operations in the living community. The baptized laity, the ordained ministers of the altar and the priest form this one body, of which the visible church is the unique symbol.

The church edifice must be inspired by these profound truths to be truly beautiful, meaningful, and functional on the supernatural level. Unless these truths are the guiding principle of sacred building, church architecture cannot escape becoming static and lifeless. The Christian church will convey a message to the men of our day only to the extent that the builders have understood the nature and spirit of Christian worship. No architect, therefore, ought to presume to build a church without first acquainting himself with the meaning and spirit of the sacred liturgy. Failure in this regard will lead inevitably to an architecture devoid of true Christian meaning.

Application of Principle

1. The architect of a church, the overseer of the entire plan, should be of outstanding competence in his field in creative skill. Conversant with the rich tradition of sacred building, he should be able to interpret that tradition in a living architectural form.

2. The architect, to execute a work of true aesthetic and religious value, must possess a true understanding of the meaning of sacred worship. He must be able to distinguish the essential from the peripheral and to subordinate lesser values to the higher.

3. The pastor or patron should make certain that the whole parochial complex is studied as a unit before embarking upon the planning of a new church. Rectory, school and church should be organized in a purposeful relationship.

4. The pastor or patron should work in close collaboration with the architect. He ought to make certain that the architect assimilates the theological and liturgical principles which he is to interpret in the church edifice.

5. The pastor and architect ought to work as a team in the planning and building of the church. Neither one ought to act independently of the other in matters which relate both to the science or art of architecture and the dictates of sound theology and liturgical practice. Each should respect the role of the other in his distinctive field.

6. Benefactors and donors of the church furnishings and sacred art should not be permitted to dictate their design and content, since the church's appointments must be related to the architecture and liturgical function of the church.

7. The church edifice is constructed to serve men of our age. Its architectural language should not be archaic or foreign but contemporary and genuine in expression. True Christian tradition accepts the true, good, and beautiful in each age and culture.

8. When possible, materials indigenous to the locale or territory should be used in the construction of the church, if they are of good quality and serviceable. Both the architecture and materials should be related to the nature and character of the immediate surroundings. A pretence of magnificence or luxury by the importation of costly materials from foreign lands does not significantly enrich the sacred edifice. (This is above all applicable to the altar.)

9. The employment of a sacred artist or competent art consultant to aid the architect is highly commendable since sacred art plays such a significant role in Christian worship. This will ensure a unity of beauty and purpose which cannot be achieved by furnishing the church with articles of an inferior prefabricated nature purchased from divergent sources.

10. Nothing false, profane, or bizarre should degrade this holy temple in architecture or art. Shoddy craftsmanship and weak, stereotyped "art-objects" of mass production should be excluded as unworthy of the house of God.

11. The sacred art of the church must possess a certain symbolic character due to the invisible realities of faith of which it is the expository sign. Excessive naturalism absorbs the worshippers' activity in the object itself rather than the mystery it represents. The extreme abstractionist treatment of sacred mysteries renders their content unintelligible to the unschooled viewer.

12. The decoration of the church should be simple, organic, and unpretentious. All deceit and false enrichment of the basic structure must be strictly avoided. The structural qualities of the architecture should carry the weight of beauty and purpose. Art works and the furnishings of the church must find their proper place in the higher order of the architectural structure. The architect and artist should work in unity of purpose.

13. Since the Church is a hierarchical or graded society, not all of her members have the same function, but each participates in her worship of the Father according to his God-given capacity. This hierarchical differentiation of function of priest, ordained ministers of the altar (e.g., deacons, altar assistants), and baptized laity ought to be expressed in elevation and articulation by the architecture.

The profound fact of the Church's unity, however, must not be forgotten in the attempt to achieve this visible gradation. Since the mystical body of Christ is a living, corporate society, the church architecture must possess an organic unity. Although many, we are one body. Functions differ, but the articulation of graded membership ought not to destroy the organic relationship of member to member.

Although distinct in treatment, the sanctuary which contains the altar and the nave which houses the community of the baptized ought to be visually and psychologically one. Visual or architectural separation should be avoided. The arrangement of space relations should lend itself to the active participation of the laity in the sacred action of the liturgy. Clear vision of the sanctuary and easy dialogue between priest and people should be readily possible. Long, narrow churches which remove the laity from close contact with the altar are undesirable.

The *schola cantorum,* or choir, should be no exception to this oneness of the community in worship. The choir ought not to be placed in a loft apart from the assembly but should form an integral part with it. The choir's proper place is in an intermediary position between the priest and people. A space at the left of the sanctuary ought to be provided for the *schola cantorum* so that the director of liturgical song is visibly accessible to both the choir and the entire assembly.

14. As Christ is head of the Church, the altar is the heart of the sacred building. Nothing should hinder the architectural initiation of the entire building toward the altar. Stations of the cross, lighting fixtures, ornaments, and statuary, rather than break the continuity of the converging line ought to maintain it.

15. Shrines and areas of particular non-liturgical devotions ought not to conflict with the church's higher purpose of serving the official worship of the church. More private areas ought to be provided for the individual devotional needs of the community. These can be located at any part of the nave providing they do not disturb visible or physical access to the altar.

16. Architects should strive to attain good acoustical qualities and proper lighting to avoid the audio-visual strain of the members of the community. Stained glass and diminutive windows which make electrical substitutes necessary even during the day hours are to be avoided.

17. Since full participation in the liturgy implies procession of the faithful on various occasions, (e.g., procession to receive the Eucharist), the facility of easy mobility by the entire assembly is to be preserved. The kneeling benches and aisles must not be an impediment to processional movement.

18. Since the word of God is proclaimed to the faithful in the liturgical assembly, the ambo or pulpit, rather than being a portable stand for notes, should possess dignity without being unduly massive. A step of elevation properly depicts the apostolic

office of announcing the good news of redemption. The pulpit should be located in the sanctuary on the gospel side near the communion rail.

19. Second in importance to the altar is the baptistery of the church. Each church is to have a baptistery of reasonable size to accommodate the minister and participants with ample space.

20. The baptistery is to be located near the entrance of the church. The holy font should make a strong statement to the community entering for divine worship since it is a continual sign of the Christian's rebirth in Christ and his membership in the mystical body. An open grill with locked gate is required by rubric, unless the font itself is locked. The baptistery should not be used for any purpose (e.g., crying room) other than the administration of this holy sacrament of Christian initiation.

21. The sacred font should be strong and dignified with a certain suggestion of massiveness to indicate its importance. A bath of regeneration and font of life-giving water, it should be stationary and permanent rather than provisional or portable.

22. A step of descent toward the font is commendable to portray the rich Pauline doctrine of baptism. By this means the inner meaning of baptism as a mystical descent into the death of Christ and the corresponding ascent with him into the Easter life of resurrection is visually symbolized.

23. The entrance to the church ought to be prominent and significant of the redemptive mysteries which are re-enacted within. A space of transition (fore-court, vestibule, or atrium), of peace and quiet between the outside world and the inner sacred space, has been traditionally observed. The vestibule is a physical aid to those who enter to dispose their souls for the sacred mysteries of the liturgy. It should be spacious and share the atmosphere of reverence of the church proper.

24. The sacristy should provide ample space for the many works of a practical nature in preparation for the sacred liturgy. A more solemn entrance to the altar should be provided for Sundays and feast-days so as to lend greater significance to the entrance procession (introit).

II. The Altar and Its Setting

Statement of Principle

The altar of holy Church is Christ himself.

The rite of ordination

Christ Jesus is the Priest, the Victim, and the Altar.

The Roman Breviary

The altar stands for Christ.

St Thomas Aquinas

The tremendous table.

St John Chrysostom

As Christ is the Head of the Church, the altar which represents his presence in the Christian assembly is the heart and center of the Christian church. This sacred stone of sacrifice and holy table of the eucharistic meal must possess absolute prominence over all else contained by the church. Above all the furnishings of the church, the altar stands as the symbol of Christ *par excellence*. It is the most expressive sign-image of Christ's mediatorship between God and man. Standing between heaven and earth, the altar sanctifies man's gift to God and brings God's gift to man. Thus the altar is the most sacred symbol of the priesthood of our Lord Jesus Christ and a permanent sign of his presence among the holy people of God.

The altar, rather than a supplement or ornament of the church, is the reason of its being. The church is constructed to house the holy table; the altar is not furnished to complete the church. The church edifice is the extension and complement of the altar of sacrifice.

Application of Principle

1. The design of the church begins with the altar; the altar must be the unchallenged focal point of the sacred building. The church must not only "contain" the altar but also complement the altar in its architectural organization.

2. The altar, the holy symbol of Christ's priesthood, ought not to be needlessly multiplied. Where auxiliary altars are necessary for the private celebration of the eucharistic sacrifice, they should be placed out of view of the congregation. A portable altar of reposition can be furnished when liturgically required.

3. The altar's autonomy is to be secured by preserving its centrality and independence. It should not be placed against the sanctuary wall as a mere object of furniture but ought to be freestanding as required by rubric. A minimum of three feet from the wall is to be observed. A greater distance is recommended.

4. The altar should be accessible from at least three sides. The predella should be constructed to allow free circuit around the altar on a single plane.

5. Retables, reredos, gradines, and other superstructures should be excluded from the altar since they tend to obscure the altar proper. The sanctity of the altar precludes the use of the holy table as a pedestal or stand for multiple accessories.

6. The structure of the altar should be notable for simplicity, integrity, and beauty as befits this holy symbol of Christ and his redemptive work. The *mensa* (table) and the *stipes* (supports for the table), the essential parts of the altar, should be expressed boldly and directly in the visible structure.

7. The material of the altar (the stone or the wood extension) should not be denatured by over-refinement or high-gloss polish treatment. The preservation of the natural surface texture of stone or wood, rather than weakening the solidity of the altar-image, strengthens it. Materials and finishes of "dainty" color ought to be rejected as incongruous with the altar's dignity and function.

8. An unnecessary overstatement of the altar's size ought to be avoided. The significance of the altar as the stone of sacrifice is achieved not so much by size as by the strength of the altar's architectural statement. Small churches ought not to emulate the size of altars in large churches. The relations and proportion of altar, sanctuary, and church having been duly considered, altars varying from six to eight feet in length will be adequate.

9. Since the altar itself is the symbol of Christ and his sacrifice, symbolic ornamentation of the altar is unnecessary. If symbolism is applied, it should be visually uncomplicated and legible to the worshipping laity. Simplicity and directness [are] the norm for the form and content of the symbol. The symbol should be immediately related to the meaning of the altar or the sacrament-sacrifice.

10. The use of natural light should play an important part in maintaining the altar's focal position in the church. The altar should be the center of light concentration. Since artificial light does not supplant the need or beauty of natural light, archi-

tects should strive to achieve light emphasis without the use of electrical substitutes. Recessed or shielded source-lighting, a precaution against sanctuary glare, is commendable. Windows should never be located on the terminal wall of the sanctuary.

11. The altar's appointments (tabernacle, altar cross, candleholders, and canopy) should not detract from the altar's primacy of position. *The altar dictates the scale of proportion.*

12. Unduly large crucifixes or wall crucifixion groups ought to be avoided since they tend to usurp the altar's primacy of position. (The altar's primacy as an object of veneration is derived from the inherent sacredness bestowed by the constitutive blessing or consecration.) The altar cross, formerly a portable processional banner, is an extension of the altar.

13. The altar crucifix secured for the setting of the eucharistic celebration should not express a naturalistic interpretation of the sacrifice of Christ. Rather than emphasize the dramatic and emotional aspects of the crucifixion, the ideal crucifix depicts the dogmatic realities of this act of redemption. The Savior's interior sacrificial will and external physical oblation, which suggest triumph through death, are important notes of true representation.

14. The canopy or baldaquin should form one visual unit with the altar. The baldaquin's purpose is to enhance and enrich the altar in dignity as "God's dwelling place among men." The canopy should not draw attention to itself; reserve and simplicity of execution [are] required.

15. Care must be exercised that the sanctuary be not reduced to an abbreviated appendage to the church, as often occurs when the roof or wall line is broken at the sanctuary — e.g., for the intrusion of the sacristies. The spatial unity of the sanctuary and nave must be preserved.

16. The sanctuary which serves the ministers of the altar ought to be spacious, lightsome, uncluttered, and furnished in good taste. A solemn serenity, sobriety, and purity achieved by the direct use of natural materials should characterize this sacrificial space as well as be the distinguishing mark of the church as a whole.

17. The communion rail (not required by rubric) should not serve as a visual barrier between altar and people. Rather than separation it should suggest the distinction of function between the ordained ministers of the altar and the baptized laity.

18. The sanctuary should not house shrines of particular devotion. The sacred art contained by this reserved space, more than simple portraiture, should recall the great mysteries re-enacted in the sacred liturgy of the Church. Rather than relating to the cult of the saints or a particular feast of the liturgical year, art themes of the

sanctuary should be universal in character, developing the rich signification of the eucharistic sign. Eschatological themes of which the Eucharist is the prefiguration are especially appropriate. The art of the sanctuary, however, must remain subordinate to the church's most important possession, the altar.

Constitution on the Sacred Liturgy (*Sacrosanctum Concilium,* issued by the II Vatican Council, 4 December 1963)

These excerpts from the English translation of the Constitution on the Sacred Liturgy are from Documents on the Liturgy, 1963-1979: Conciliar, Papal, and Curial Texts, *copyright © 1982, International Committee on English in the Liturgy, Inc. All rights reserved.*

Chapter VII: Sacred Art and Sacred Furnishings

122. The fine arts are deservedly ranked among the noblest activities of human genius, and this applies especially to religious art and to its highest achievement, sacred art. These arts, by their very nature, are oriented toward the infinite beauty of God, which they attempt in some way to portray by the work of human hands. They are dedicated to advancing God's praise and glory to the degree that they center on the single aim of turning the human spirit devoutly toward God.

The Church has therefore always been the friend of the fine arts, has ever sought their noble help, and has trained artists with the special aim that all things set apart for use in divine worship are truly worthy, becoming, and beautiful, signs and symbols of the supernatural world. The Church has always regarded itself as the rightful arbiter of the arts, deciding which of the works of artists are in accordance with faith, with reverence, and with honored traditional laws and are thereby suited for sacred use.

The Church has been particularly careful to see that sacred furnishings worthily and beautifully serve the dignity of worship and has admitted changes in materials, design, or ornamentation prompted by the progress of the technical arts with the passage of time.

Wherefore it has pleased the Fathers to issue the following decrees on these matters.

123. The Church has not adopted any particular style of art as its very own but has admitted styles from every period, according to the proper genius and circumstances of peoples and the requirements of the many different rites in the Church. Thus, in the course of the centuries, the Church has brought into being a treasury of art that must be very carefully preserved. The art of our own days, coming from every race and region, shall also be given free scope in the Church, on condition that it serves the places of worship and sacred rites with the reverence and honor due to

them. In this way contemporary art can add its own voice to that wonderful chorus of praise sung by the great masters of past ages of Catholic faith.

124. In encouraging and favoring art that is truly sacred, Ordinaries should strive after noble beauty rather than mere sumptuous display. This principle is to apply also in the matter of sacred vestments and appointments.

Let bishops carefully remove from the house of God and from other places of worship those works of artists that are repugnant to faith and morals and to Christian devotion and that offend true religious sense either by their grotesqueness or by the deficiency, mediocrity, or sham in their artistic quality.

When churches are to be built, let great care be taken that they are well suited to celebrating liturgical services and to bringing about the active participation of the faithful.

125. The practice of placing sacred images in churches so that they may be venerated by the faithful is to be maintained. Nevertheless there is to be restraint regarding their number and prominence so that they do not create confusion among the Christian people or foster religious practices of doubtful orthodoxy.

126. When deciding on works of art, local Ordinaries shall give hearing to the diocesan commission on sacred art, and if need be, to others who are especially expert, as well as to the commissions referred to in articles 44, 45, and 46. Ordinaries must be very careful to see that sacred furnishings and valuable works of art are not disposed of or damaged, for they are the adornment of the house of God.

127. Bishops should have a special concern for artists, so as to imbue them with the spirit of sacred art and liturgy. This they may do in person or through competent priests who are gifted with a knowledge and love of art.

It is also recommended that schools or academies of sacred art to train artists be founded in those parts of the world where they seem useful.

All artists who, prompted by their talents, desire to serve God's glory in holy Church should ever bear in mind that they are engaged in a kind of sacred imitation of God the Creator and are concerned with works intended to be used in Catholic worship, to uplift the faithful, and to foster their devotion and religious formation.

128. Along with the revision of the liturgical books, as laid down in article 25, there is to be an early revision of the canons and ecclesiastical statutes regulating the supplying of material things involved in sacred worship. This applies in particular to the worthy and well-planned construction of places of worship, the design and construction of altars, the nobility, placement, and security of the eucharistic tabernacle, the practicality and dignity of the baptistery, the appropriate arrangement of

sacred images and church decorations and appointments. Laws that seem less suited to the reformed liturgy are to be brought into harmony with it or else abolished; laws that are helpful are to be retained if already in use or introduced where they are lacking.

With article 22 of this Constitution as the norm, the territorial bodies of bishops are empowered to make adaptations to the needs and customs of their different regions; this applies especially to the material and design of sacred furnishings and vestments.

129. During their philosophical and theological studies, clerics are to be taught about the history and development of sacred art and about the sound principles on which the production of its works must be grounded. In consequence they will be able to appreciate and preserve the Church's treasured monuments and be in a position to offer good advice to artists who are engaged in producing works of art.

130. It is fitting that the use of pontifical insignia be reserved to those ecclesiastical persons who have either episcopal rank or some definite jurisdiction.

Instruction for the Proper Implementation of the Constitution on the Sacred Liturgy *(Inter Oecumenici)*

This document was produced by the Sacred Congregation of Rites and issued on 26 September 1964. This version can be found in R. Kevin Seasoltz, The New Liturgy: A Documentation, 1903-1965 *(New York: Herder & Herder, 1966). It is reproduced here with permission of the author.*

CHAPTER V: THE PROPER CONSTRUCTION OF CHURCHES AND ALTARS IN ORDER TO FACILITATE THE ACTIVE PARTICIPATION OF THE FAITHFUL

1. The Arrangement of Churches

90. In the new construction, repair, or adaptation of churches, great care shall be taken that they are suitable for the celebration of divine services according to the true nature of the services and for the active participation of the faithful (cf. *Constitution on the Sacred Liturgy,* article 124).

2. The Main Altar

91. It is proper that the main altar be constructed separately from the wall, so that one may go around it with ease and so that celebration may take place facing the people; it shall occupy a place in the sacred building which is truly central, so that the attention of the whole congregation of the faithful is spontaneously turned to it.

In choosing the material for the construction or ornamentation of the altar, the prescriptions of law shall be observed.

Moreover, the presbyterium or sanctuary area around the altar shall be of sufficient size that the sacred rites may be conveniently celebrated.

3. The Seat of the Celebrant and Ministers

92. The seat for the celebrant and ministers, according to the structure of individual churches, shall be so placed that it may be easily seen by the faithful and that the celebrant may truly appear to preside over the entire community of the faithful.

Nevertheless, if the seat is placed behind the altar, the form of a throne is to be avoided, as this belongs to the bishop alone.

4. Minor Altars

93. The minor altars shall be few in number. In fact, to the extent permitted by the structure of the building, it is highly suitable that they be placed in chapels in some way separated from the principal part of the church.

5. Ornamentation of Altars

94. The cross and candlesticks, which are required on the altar for the individual liturgical services, may also, in accordance with the judgment of the local ordinary, be placed next to it.

6. The Reservation of the Most Holy Eucharist

95. The most holy Eucharist shall be reserved in a solid and inviolable tabernacle placed in the middle of the main altar or of a minor, but truly outstanding, altar, or, according to lawful customs and in particular cases to be approved by the local ordinary, also in some other noble and properly adorned part of the church.

It is lawful to celebrate Mass facing the people even if there is a tabernacle, small but suitable, on the altar.

7. The Ambo

96. It is fitting that there be an ambo for the proclamation of the sacred readings, so arranged that the ministers can be easily seen and heard by the faithful.

8. The Place of the Schola and Organ

97. The place for the schola and the organ shall be so arranged that it will be clearly evident that the singers and the organist form a part of the united community of the faithful and so that they may fulfill their liturgical function more suitably.

9. The Places of the Faithful

98. The places for the faithful shall be arranged with particular care, so that they may participate in the sacred celebrations visually and with proper spirit. It is desirable that ordinarily benches or seats be provided for their use. Nevertheless, the custom of reserving seats for certain private persons is to be reprobated, in accordance with article 32 of the constitution.

Care shall also be taken that the faithful may not only see the celebrant and the other ministers but may also hear them easily, with the use of present-day technical means.

10. Baptistery

99. In the construction and ornamentation of the baptistery, care shall be taken that the dignity of the sacrament of baptism is clearly apparent and that the place is suitable for the community celebration of the sacrament (cf. *Constitution on the Sacred Liturgy*, article 27).

General Instruction of the Roman Missal (GIRM)

The fourth edition of this document, by the Sacred Congregation for Divine Worship, was issued 27 March 1975. The following excerpts are from the English translation of this document as found in Documents on the Liturgy, 1963-1979: Conciliar, Papal, and Curial Texts, *copyright © 1982, International Committee on English in the Liturgy, Inc. All rights reserved.*

Chapter V: Arrangement and Furnishing of Churches for the Eucharistic Celebration

I. General Principles

253. For the celebration of the Eucharist, the people of God normally assemble in a church or, if there is none, in some other fitting place worthy of so great a mystery. Churches and other places of worship should therefore be suited to celebrating the liturgy and to ensuring the active participation of the faithful. Further, the places and requisites for worship should be truly worthy and beautiful, signs and symbols of heavenly realities.[1]

254. At all times, therefore, the Church seeks out the service of the arts and welcomes the artistic expressions of all peoples and regions.[2] The Church is intent on keeping the works of art and the treasures handed down from the past[3] and, when necessary, on adapting them to new needs. It strives as well to promote new works of art that appeal to the contemporary mentality.[4]

In commissioning artists and choosing works of art that are to become part of a church, the highest artistic standard is therefore to be set, in order that art may aid faith and devotion and be true to the reality it is to symbolize and the purpose it is to serve.[5]

255. It is preferable that churches be solemnly consecrated. The faithful should give due honor to the cathedral of their diocese and to their own church as symbols

---

1. See SC [*Sacrosanctum Concilium*] art. 122-124; PO [*Presbyterorum ordinis*] no. 5. SCR [Sacred Congregation of Rites], Instr. InterOec [Instruction *Inter Oecumenici*], 26 Sept. 1964, No. 90; Instr. EuchMyst [Instruction *Eucharisticum mysterium*], 25 May 1967, no. 24.

2. See SC art. 123.

3. See SCR, Instr. EuchMyst no. 24.

4. See SC art. 123, 129. SCR, Instr. InterOec no. 13c.

5. See SC art. 123.

of the spiritual Church that their Christian vocation commits them to build up and extend.

256. All who are involved in the construction, restoration, and remodeling of churches are to consult the diocesan commission on liturgy and art. The local Ordinary is to use the counsel and help of this commission whenever it comes to laying down norms on this matter, approving plans for new buildings, and making decisions on the more important issues.[6]

II. Arrangement of a Church for the Liturgical Assembly

257. The people of God assembled at Mass possess an organic and hierarchical structure, expressed by the various ministries and actions for each part of the celebration. The general plan of the sacred edifice should be such that in some way it conveys the image of the gathered assembly. It should also allow the participants to take the place most appropriate to them and assist all to carry out their individual functions properly.

The congregation and the choir should have a place that facilitates their active participation.[7]

The priest and his ministers have their place in the sanctuary, that is, in the part of the church that brings out their distinctive role, namely, to preside over the prayers, to proclaim the word of God, or to minister at the altar.

Even though these elements must express a hierarchical arrangement and the diversity of offices, they should at the same time form a complete and organic unity, clearly expressive of the unity of the entire holy people. The character and beauty of the place and all its appointments should foster devotion and show the holiness of the mysteries celebrated there.

III. Sanctuary

258. The sanctuary should be clearly marked off from the body of the church either by being somewhat elevated or by its distinctive design and appointments. It should be large enough to accommodate all the rites.[8]

6. See SC art. 126.

7. See SCR, InterOec nos. 97-98.

8. See ibid. no. 91.

IV. Altar

259. At the altar the sacrifice of the cross is made present under sacramental signs. It is also the table of the Lord and the people of God are called together to share in it. The altar is, as well, the center of the thanksgiving that the Eucharist accomplishes.[9]

260. In a place of worship, the celebration of the Eucharist must be on an altar, either fixed or movable. Outside a place of worship, especially if the celebration is only for a single occasion, a suitable table may be used, but always with a cloth and corporal.

261. A fixed altar is one attached to the floor so that it cannot be moved; a movable altar is one that can be transferred from place to place.

262. The main altar should be freestanding to allow the ministers to walk around it easily and Mass to be celebrated facing the people. It should be so placed as to be a focal point on which the attention of the whole congregation centers naturally.[10] The main altar should ordinarily be a fixed, consecrated altar.

263. According to the Church's traditional practice and the altar's symbolism, the table of a fixed altar should be of stone and indeed of natural stone. But at the discretion of the conference of bishops some other solid, becoming, and well-crafted material may be used.

The pedestal or base of the table may be of any sort of material, as long as it is becoming and solid.

264. A movable altar may be constructed of any becoming, solid material suited to liturgical use, according to the traditions and customs of different regions.

265. Altars both fixed and movable are consecrated according to the rite described in the liturgical books; but movable altars may simply be blessed. There is no obligation to have a consecrated stone in a movable altar or on the table where the Eucharist is celebrated outside a place of worship (see no. 260).

266. It is fitting to maintain the practice of enclosing in the altar or of placing under the altar relics of saints, even of non-martyrs. Care must be taken to have solid evidence of the authenticity of such relics.

267. Minor altars should be fewer in number. In new churches they should be placed in chapels separated in some way from the body of the church.[11]

---

9. See SCR, Instr. EuchMyst no. 24.
10. See SCR, Instr. InterOec no. 91.
11. See ibid. no. 93.

V. Altar Furnishings

268. At least one cloth should be placed on the altar out of reverence for the celebration of the memorial of the Lord and the banquet that gives us his body and blood. The shape, size, and decoration of the altar cloth should be in keeping with the design of the altar.

269. Candles are to be used at every liturgical service as a sign of reverence and festiveness. The candlesticks are to be placed either on or around the altar in a way suited to the design of the altar and the sanctuary. Everything is to be well balanced and must not interfere with the faithful's clear view of what goes on at the altar or is placed on it.

270. There is also to be a cross, clearly visible to the congregation, either on the altar or near it.

VI. Chair for the Priest Celebrant and the Ministers, That Is, the Place Where the Priest Presides

271. The priest celebrant's chair ought to stand as a symbol of his office of presiding over the assembly and of directing prayer. Thus the best place for the chair is at the back of the sanctuary and turned toward the congregation, unless the structure or other circumstances are an obstacle (for example, if too great a distance would interfere with communication between the priest and people). Anything resembling a throne is to be avoided. The seats for the ministers should be so placed in the sanctuary that they can readily carry out their appointed functions.[12]

VII. Lectern (Ambo) or Place from Which the Word of God Is Proclaimed

272. The dignity of the word of God requires the church to have a place that is suitable for proclamation of the word and is a natural focal point for the people during the liturgy of the word.[13]

As a rule the lectern or ambo should be stationary, not simply a movable stand. In keeping with the structure of each church, it must be so placed that the ministers may be easily seen and heard by the faithful.

12. See ibid. no. 92.
13. See ibid. no. 96.

The readings, responsorial psalm, and the Easter Proclamation ("Exsultet") are proclaimed from the lectern; it may be used also for the homily and general intercessions (prayer of the faithful).

It is better for the commentator, cantor, or choir director not to use the lectern.

VIII. Places for the Faithful

273. The places for the faithful should be arranged with care so that the people are able to take their rightful part in the celebration visually and mentally. As a rule, there should be benches or chairs for their use. But the custom of reserving seats for private persons must be abolished.[14] Chairs or benches should be set up in such a way that the people can easily take the positions required during various celebrations and have unimpeded access to receive communion.

The congregation must be enabled not only to see the priest and the other ministers but also, with the aid of modern sound equipment, to hear them without difficulty.

IX. Choir, Organ, and Other Musical Instruments

274. In relation to the design of each church, the "schola cantorum" should be so placed that its character as a part of the assembly of the faithful that has a special function stands out clearly. The location should also assist the choir's liturgical ministry and readily allow each member complete, that is, sacramental participation in the Mass.[15]

275. The organ and other lawfully approved musical instruments are to be placed suitably in such a way that they can sustain the singing of the choir and congregation and be heard with ease when they are played alone.

X. Reservation of the Eucharist

276. Every encouragement should be given to the practice of Eucharistic reservation in a chapel suited to the faithful's private adoration and prayer.[16] If this is impossible

---

14. See SC art. 32. SCR, Instr. InterOec no. 98.

15. See SCR, Instr. MusSacr [Instruction *Musicum Sacrum*] no. 23.

16. See SCR, Instr. EuchMyst no. 53. RR, "Holy Communion and Worship of the Eucharist outside Mass, ed. typica," 1973, Introduction no. 9.

because of the structure of the church, the sacrament should be reserved at an altar or elsewhere, in keeping with local custom, and in a part of the church that is worthy and properly adorned.[17]

277. The Eucharist is to be reserved in a single, solid, unbreakable tabernacle. Thus as a rule there should be only one tabernacle in each church.[18]

XI. Images for Veneration by the Faithful

278. In keeping with the Church's very ancient tradition, it is lawful to set up in places of worship images of Christ, Mary, and the saints for veneration by the faithful. But there is need both to limit their number and to situate them in such a way that they do not distract the people's attention from the celebration.[19] There is to be only one image of any one saint. In general, the devotion of the entire community is to be the criterion regarding images in the adornment and arrangement of a church.

XII. General Plan of the Church

279. The style in which a church is decorated should be a means to achieve noble simplicity, not ostentation. The choice of materials for church appointments must be marked by concern for genuineness and by the intent to foster instruction of the faithful and the dignity of the place of worship.

280. Proper planning of a church and its surroundings that meets contemporary needs requires attention not only to the elements belonging directly to liturgical services but also to those facilities for the comfort of the people that are usual in places of public gatherings.

---

17. See SCR, Instr. EuchMyst no. 54; Instr. InterOec no. 95.

18. See SCR, Instr. EuchMyst no. 52; Instr. InterOec no. 95. SC Sacraments, Instr. "Nullo umquam tempore," 28 May 1938, no. 4: AAS 30 (1938) 199-200. RR, "Holy Communion and Worship of the Eucharist outside Mass," Introduction nos. 10-11.

19. See SC art. 125.

Environment and Art in Catholic Worship (Select Articles)

This document was produced by the Bishops' Committee on the Liturgy, National Conference of Catholic Bishops, 1978. The excerpts here are from Environment and Art in Catholic Worship, *copyright © 1978 by the United States Conference of Catholic Bishops, Washington, D.C. Used by permission. All rights reserved. In 2000, this document was replaced by* Built of Living Stones.

I. THE WORSHIP OF GOD AND ITS REQUIREMENTS

A Climate of Hospitality

11. As common prayer and ecclesial experience, liturgy flourishes in a climate of hospitality: a situation in which people are comfortable with one another, either knowing or being introduced to one another; a space in which people are seated together, with mobility, in view of one another as well as the focal points of the rite, involved as participants and *not* as spectators.[1]

12. The experience of mystery which liturgy offers is found in its God-consciousness and God-centeredness. This involves a certain beneficial tension with the demands of hospitality, requiring a manner and an environment which invite contemplation (seeing beyond the face of the person or the thing, a sense of the holy, the numinous, mystery). A simple and attractive beauty in everything that is used or done in liturgy is the most effective invitation to this kind of experience. One should be able to sense something special (and nothing trivial) in everything that is seen and heard, touched and smelled, and tasted in liturgy.

13. Incarnation, the paschal mystery, and the Holy Spirit in us are faith's access to the transcendence, holiness, otherness of God. An action like liturgy, therefore, has special significance as a means of relating to God, or responding to God's relating to us. This does not mean that we have "captured" God in our symbols. It means only that God has graciously loved us on our own terms, in ways corresponding to our condition. Our response must be one of depth and totality, of authenticity, genuineness, and care with respect to everything we use and do in liturgical celebration.

---

1. GI [*General Instruction of the Roman Missal*] 4, 5.

The Serving Environment

24. By environment we mean the larger space in which the action of the assembly takes place. At its broadest, it is the setting of the building in its neighborhood, including outdoor spaces. More specifically it means the character of a particular space and how it affects the action of the assembly. There are elements in the environment, therefore, which contribute to the overall experience, e.g., the seating arrangement, the placement of liturgical centers of action, temporary decoration, light, acoustics, spaciousness, etc. The environment is appropriate when it is beautiful, when it is hospitable, when it clearly invites and needs an assembly of people to complete it.

Furthermore, it is appropriate when it brings people close together so that they can see and hear the entire liturgical action, when it helps people feel involved and become involved. Such an environment works with the liturgy, not against it.

II. The Subject of Liturgical Action: The Church

The Action of the Assembly

29. The most powerful experience of the sacred is found in the celebration and the persons celebrating, that is, it is found in the action of the assembly: the living words, the living gestures, the living sacrifice, the living meal. This was at the heart of the earliest liturgies. Evidence of this is found in their architectural floor plans which were designed as general gathering spaces, spaces which allowed the whole assembly to be part of the action.

30. Because liturgical celebration is the worship action of the entire Church, it is desirable that persons representing the diversity of ages, sexes, ethnic and cultural groups in the congregation should be involved in planning and ministering in the liturgies of the community. Special competencies in music, public reading, and any other skills and arts related to public worship should be sought, respected and used in celebration. Not only the planners and ministers, however, are active in the liturgy. The entire congregation is an active component. There is no audience, no passive element in the liturgical celebration. This fact alone distinguishes it from most other public assemblies.

31. The assembly's celebration, that is, celebration in the midst of the faith community, by the whole community, is the normal and normative way of celebrating

any sacrament or other liturgy. Even when the communal dimension is not apparent, as sometimes in communion for the sick or for prisoners, the clergy or minister functions within the context of the entire community.

32. The action of the assembly is also unique since it is not merely a "celebration of life," reflecting all of the distinctions stemming from color, sex, class, etc. Quite the contrary, liturgy requires the faith community to set aside all those distinctions and divisions and classifications. By doing this the liturgy celebrates the reign of God, and as such maintains the tension between what is (the status quo of our daily lives) and what must be (God's will for human salvation — liberation and solidarity). This uniqueness gives liturgy its key and central place in Christian life as seen from the perspective of an actual community. Just as liturgy makes its own demands on the environment and the arts, so, too, does the assembly. When the assembly gathers with its own varied background, there is a commonness demanded which stems from our human condition. The commonality here seeks the best which people can bring together rather than what is compromised or less noble. For the assembly seeks its own expression in an atmosphere which is beautiful, amidst actions which probe the entire human experience. This is what is most basic and most noble. It is what the assembly seeks in order to express the heart of the Church's liturgy.

Contemporary

33. Contemporary art forms belong to the liturgical expressions of the assembly as surely as the art forms of the past. The latter are part of our common memory, our communion (which extends over time as well as over geographical boundaries). Contemporary art is our own, the work of artists of our time and place, and belongs in our celebrations as surely as we do. If liturgy were to incorporate only the acceptable art of the past, conversion, commitment and tradition would have ceased to live. The assembly should, therefore, be equally unhesitating in searching out, patronizing and using the arts and media of past and present. Because it is symbolic communication, liturgy is more dependent on past tradition than many human activities are. Because it is the action of a contemporary assembly, it has to clothe its basically traditional structures with the living flesh and blood of our times and our arts.

Beautiful

34. Because the assembly gathers in the presence of God to celebrate his saving deeds, liturgy's climate is one of awe, mystery, wonder, reverence, thanksgiving and praise. So it cannot be satisfied with anything less than the beautiful in its environment and all its artifacts, movements, and appeals to the senses.[2] [footnoted to *General Instruction of the Roman Missal,* no. 253] Admittedly difficult to define, the beautiful is related to the sense of the numinous, the holy. Where there is evidently no care for this, there is an environment basically unfriendly to mystery and awe, an environment too casual, if not careless, for the liturgical action. In a world dominated by science and technology, liturgy's quest for the beautiful is a particularly necessary contribution to full and balanced human life.

Servant

37. Different ministries in such an assembly do not imply "superiority" or "inferiority." Different functions are necessary in the liturgy as they are in any human, social activity. The recognition of different gifts and talents and the ordination, institution or delegation for the different services required (priest, reader, acolyte, musician, usher, etc.) is to facilitate worship. These are services to the assembly and those who perform them are servants of God who render services to the assembly. Those who perform such ministries are indeed servants of the assembly.

38. The liturgical assembly, as presented, is Church, and as Church is servant to the world. It has a commitment to be sign, witness, and instrument of the reign of God. That commitment must be reflected and implemented not only in the individual lives of its members but also in the community's choices and in its use of its money, property and other resources. Liturgical buildings and spaces should have the same witness value. Their planning should involve representatives of oppressed and disadvantaged parts of the communities in which they are located.

2. GI 253.

III. A House for the Church's Liturgical Celebrations

39. The congregation, its liturgical action, the furniture and the other objects it needs for its liturgical action — these indicate the necessity of a space, a place, a hall, or a building for the liturgy. It will be a place for praying and singing, for listening and speaking — a place for human interaction and active participation — where the mysteries of God are recalled and celebrated in human history. The servant nature of the Church in relation to the rest of the community in its area (and in the world) invites it to consider the broader needs of the community, especially in the community's deprived, handicapped and suffering members, and therefore to consider a breadth of possible uses of its buildings.

Primary Demand: The Assembly

40. In no case, however, should this mean a lack of attention to the requirements of the liturgical celebration or a yielding of the primary demands that liturgy must make upon the space: the gathering of the faith community in a participatory and hospitable atmosphere for word and Eucharist, for initiation and reconciliation, for prayer and praise and song.

41. Such a space acquires a sacredness from the sacred action of the faith community which uses it. As a place, then, it becomes quite naturally a reference and orientation point for believers. The historical problem of the church as a *place* attaining a dominance over the faith community need not be repeated as long as Christians respect the primacy of the living assembly.

42. The norm for designing liturgical space is the assembly and its liturgies. The building or cover enclosing the architectural space is a shelter or "skin" for a liturgical action. It does not have to "look like" anything else, past or present. Its integrity, simplicity and beauty, its physical location and landscaping should take into account the neighborhood, city and area in which it is built.

43. Many local Churches must use spaces designed and built in a former period, spaces which may now be unsuitable for the liturgy. In the renovation of these spaces for contemporary liturgical use, there is no substitute for an ecclesiology that is both ancient and modern in the fullest sense. Nor is there any substitute for a thorough understanding of ritual needs in human life and the varied liturgical tradition of the Church. With these competencies, a renovation can respect both the best qualities of the original structure and the requirements of contemporary worship.

Teamwork

44. Whether designing a new space for the liturgical action or renovating an old one, teamwork and preparation by the congregation (particularly its liturgy committee), clergy, architect and consultant (liturgy and art) are essential.[3] A competent architect should have the assistance of a consultant in liturgy and art both in the discussion stages of the project (dialogue with congregation and clergy as well as among themselves) and throughout the stages of design and building. Recent competitions in the design of buildings for liturgy have indicated the advantages of such consultation.

45. The congregation, or local Church, commonly acting through its delegates, is a basic and primary component in the team. The congregation's work is to acquaint the architect and consultant with its own self-image as Church and its sense of the larger community in which it exists. It is important for the congregation and clergy to recognize the area of their own competence. This will also define the limits beyond which they should not go. Respect for the competence of others in their respective fields is essential for good teamwork.

46. If a community has selected competent and skilled persons, they will receive from the architect and the consultant a design which will stimulate and inspire, as well as serve the assembly's needs as they have been described. When financial benefactors are involved, they have the same part in this process as the congregation and the clergy, subject to the same prior requirements of good liturgy.

47. A good architect will possess both the willingness to learn from the congregation and sufficient integrity not to allow the community's design taste or preference to limit the freedom necessary for a creative design. The architect will look to the congregation and clergy for an understanding of the character and purpose of the liturgical assembly. With that rapport, it is the architect's task to design the space, using contemporary materials and modes of construction, in dialogue with consultants who are expert in the areas of liturgical art, rites, acoustics and other specialized issues.

48. The liturgical-artistic consultant is an invaluable partner of the architect, for the purposes of space can be imagined and the place creatively designed only by a competent designer (architect) who is nourished with liturgy's tradition, its current shape, together with the appropriate furniture and other objects used. The feeling of liturgical action is as crucial as the craft of the designer in producing a worthy space and place.

3. CSL [*Constitution on the Sacred Liturgy*] 126; GI 258.

Visibility and Audibility

49. One of the primary requirements of the space is visibility of all in the assembly: others in the congregation as well as the principal focal point of the ritual action.

50. Visibility speaks more to the quality of view than merely the mechanics of seeing. A space must create a sense that what is seen is proximate, important and personal. The arrangement of the space should consider levels of priority in what is seen, allowing visual flow from one center of liturgical action to another. Furthermore, the sense and variety of light, artificial or natural, contribute greatly to what is seen.

51. Audibility of all (congregation and ministers) is another primary requirement. A space that does not require voice amplification is ideal. Where an amplifying system is necessary, provision for multiple microphone jacks should be made (e.g., at the altar, ambo, chair, font, space immediately in front of the congregation, and a few spots through the congregation). Since the liturgical space must accommodate both speech and song, there must be a serious acoustical consideration of the conflicting demands of the two. The services of an acoustical engineer can enable architect and builder to be aware of certain disadvantages in rooms that are exclusively "dry" or "live." A room designed to deaden all sounds is doomed to kill liturgical participation.

The Scale of a Space

52. The liturgical space should have a "good feeling" in terms of human scale, hospitality and graciousness. It does not seek to impress, or even less, to dominate, but its clear aim is to facilitate the public worship and common prayer of the faith community.

Unity of Space

53. Special attention must be given to the unity of the entire liturgical space. Before considering the distinction of roles within the liturgy, the space should communicate an integrity (a sense of oneness, of wholeness) and a sense of being the gathering place of the initiated community. Within that one space there are different areas corresponding to different roles and functions, but the wholeness of the total space should be strikingly evident.

54. Planning for a convergence of pathways to the liturgical space in a concourse or foyer or other place adequate for gathering before or after liturgies is recom-

mended. In some climates this might be outdoors. Such a gathering space can encourage introductions, conversations, the sharing of refreshments after a liturgy, the building of the kind of community sense and feeling recognized now to be a prerequisite of good celebration.

GLOSSARY

Altar or communion rail
A railing of wood or stone that stands in front of the altar/table and usually creates a distinct separation between the chancel and the nave. The rail is sometimes used for kneeling for prayer and receiving the elements during celebration of the Eucharist.

Altar or communion table
The primary liturgical appointment from which a celebration of the Eucharist is led in corporate worship. The altar is usually made of stone or wood.

Ambo or pulpit
The primary liturgical appointment from which the Word of God is read in public and/or proclaimed in a homily or sermon. Historically an ambo has been associated with reading God's Word and a pulpit with its proclamation. In practice today, the terms appear to be used interchangeably.

Ambry or Aumbry
A recess in a church wall used to store sacramental vessels for worship.

Apse
A semicircular, usually vaulted projection at the east end of a church.

Baldachino
A canopy or dome located over the altar/table or bishop's chair. This covering may be made of cloth, stone, wood, or metal.

Baptismal font and pool
A font is usually a vessel large enough to allow for the sprinkling or pouring of water onto a person during baptism. A deep font may accommodate the immersion of an infant. A pool is large enough to allow for substantially covering (or fully immersing) both children and adults in water during baptism.

Baptistery

The location of the primary liturgical appointment used for facilitating Christian initiation or baptism. The baptistery contains a font and/or pool for baptism and adequate space to accommodate those participating in the ritual, as well as oils (as required) and a Paschal candle (as required).

Baroque architecture

An expression of architectural design developed in Europe from the sixteenth to the seventeenth centuries. The design was usually elaborate (even exaggerated at times, seeking to create an illusionary effect), with many curves and swirls in the detailing. It is recognized through its incorporation of a style of visual art that uses a large scale and sweeping movement, and exhibits a tendency to break away from the picture plane (toward the viewer).

Basilican design

A type of church design rooted in the architecture of the basilica of the third and fourth centuries A.D. of the Roman Empire. Often the design used a rectangular gathering hall and had an apse at one or both ends from which a political leader could address the people.

Bauhaus, The

A school of art and design founded by architect Walter Gropius in 1919 in Weimar, Germany. Gropius sought to establish a form of art education that combined aesthetic theory with modern industrial production techniques. To encourage the integration of theory and production, he divided the school into workshops rather than fields of study or departments.

Bishop's chair or throne

A seat for the bishop, permanent in a cathedral, located near the altar/table.

Cambridge movement

A theological renewal movement begun in England, initiated by the Cambridge Camden Society in the early 1840s. The Cambridge movement was characterized by its promotion of Gothic revival or "neo-Gothic" church design.

Centrum

The name that Edward Sövik gave to the primary space used for corporate worship and other nonliturgical activities. At one point Sövik sought to develop new terms like this to help encourage a multipurpose approach to church space.

Chancel

The area within a worship space that frequently contains the altar/table and ambo/pulpit. Usually this area is raised above the level of the nave.

CIAM

The Congres Internationaux de l'Architecture Moderne or International Congress for Modern Architecture. CIAM was founded by architects such as Walter Gropius, Ludwig Mies van der Rohe, and Le Corbusier in Switzerland in 1928. The organization promoted a modern ideology of design, rejecting historical models as sources for contemporary building. CIAM supported a rational approach to architecture, encouraging the use of simplified geometric forms, volume over mass, a breaking away from classical symmetry and axiality, and an avoidance of ornamentation. Eventually the architectural design the organization promoted would come to be identified as the International Style.

Clerestory
An arcade of windows located in the upper portion of the walls of a church, usually in the nave and/or choir areas.

Communion rail
See "Altar or communion rail."

Communion table
See "Altar or communion table."

Credence
A shelf or table near the altar/table where sacramental vessels are set until needed in the Eucharistic celebration.

Cross
A primary symbol of the Christian faith, rendered in various ways by various faith traditions. The Greek style cross has arms of equal length; the Latin style cross has a shorter horizontal arm that intersects the longer vertical arm about two-thirds of the way up. The corpus (Latin for "body") is a representation of the body of Jesus Christ. When a corpus is attached to the Latin cross, it is generally referred to as a crucifix.

Crucifix
See "Cross."

Georgian architecture
An expression of architectural design that developed in England from the reign of King George I (ascended the throne in 1714) to King George IV (died in 1830). Georgian design is rooted in design principles related to ancient Greek and Roman architecture. It came to be popular in the United States, influencing the design of many types of buildings, including churches. Details characteristic of early Georgian design include finished stones at the corners of the building that often protruded (quoins), a gently pitched gable above a portico (an entrance that is open or partially roofed), and shallow vertical masonry supports or squared columns attached to a wall (pilasters).

Gothic architecture
An expression of architectural design developed in later medieval Europe (from the twelfth to the fifteenth centuries). The design was usually elaborate (including extraordinary glass work) and is recognized through its use of pointed arches, ribbed vaulting, and slender spires.

Gothic revival

An architectural movement that lasted from about 1730 to 1930 in which medieval European Gothic designs were studied and reproduced in contemporary buildings, producing neo-Gothic architecture.

International Style

An expression of modern architectural design (especially from 1925 to 1965) associated with particular architectural figures who sought to disconnect their work from historical patterns of design. The International Style is recognized for its use of simplified geometric forms, its emphasis on volume over mass and regularity over symmetry, and its lack of ornamentation.

Liturgical appointment

An object that functions as a focal point in relation to a particular expression of corporate worship. Three common liturgical appointments for Christian worship have been the altar/table for the Eucharist, the font/pool for baptism, and the ambo/pulpit for sharing God's Word.

Mass

See "Eucharist."

Modern architecture

An expression of architectural design developed in Europe and the United States from the mid-nineteenth to the twentieth centuries. Modern design was especially concerned with reflecting the industrial age of its day, and thus focused on emulating an aesthetic reflected in the design of machines. Proponents of modern architecture emphasized a disconnection from historical designs, functionality, simplified geometric forms, volume over mass, and a dramatic reduction of ornamentation.

Narthex

The area where people gather when they come into a church by its main entrance.

Nave

The area of a worship space that provides a place for the congregation during services. Seating is frequently found in this area.

Oils

Many Christian traditions use various consecrated oils for initiation, healing, and ordination. They are often located near the baptistery, sometimes near the altar/table.

Postmodern architecture

A form of architectural design that developed in the latter part of the twentieth century which seeks to challenge many presuppositions of modern architectural design. A key challenge is found in the reclaiming of historical styles of design as sources for architectural inspiration. Complexity in design (instead of mere simplicity) is also reclaimed, and ornamentation is once again valued.

Presider's chair
A seat for the one presiding at worship, usually located near the altar/table and/or ambo/pulpit.

Pulpit
See "Ambo or pulpit."

Raked floor
An inclined or slanted floor surface. A raked floor may be a smooth incline or consist of small terraces.

Reredos
An architectural framework located above and behind the altar/table. Elaboration of the reredos varies widely.

Reserved sacrament/reserved sacrament chapel
The reserved sacrament consists of the consecrated elements that are set aside for distribution to those who cannot share in the communal celebration. The reserved sacrament is usually stored in the tabernacle before it is distributed. The tabernacle is frequently located in a chapel set aside for private prayer and adoration of the reserved sacrament.

Romanesque architecture
An expression of architectural design based on Roman building techniques that developed in Europe from the fifth to the twelfth centuries. The design was usually rather unadorned, identifiable through its use of round arches and barrel vaults.

Sacristy
A room in a church used to store liturgical vessels and supplies and to prepare materials for worship celebrations. The cleaning of vessels and the appropriate disposal of the Eucharistic elements is accomplished here. Paraments (cloth coverings used for the ambo/pulpit and altar/table, usually in colors coordinated with the liturgical season) and clergy vestments may also be stored here.

Stations of the Cross
Markers established in a church, either in the primary corporate worship environment or in a devotional chapel, that remind the faithful of the final journey of Christ, from his condemnation to death before Pilate to his burial in the tomb.

Tabernacle
A small, usually decorated receptacle or cabinet that contains the consecrated elements from a Eucharistic celebration. The elements stored in the tabernacle are distributed to those who were unable to join in the initial corporate celebration.

Vernacular architecture
An expression of architectural design associated with structures used for commercial purposes such as barns, grain elevators, and warehouses. Often vernacular buildings are designed by non-architects and exhibit a keen sense for functional pragmatism.

BIBLIOGRAPHY

The following bibliography includes primarily sources of information used in this book. (It is not an exhaustive bibliography of materials addressing church architecture.) The titles are organized chronologically. I have sorted the material in this way to help give the reader an impression of the volume of titles that appeared during particular time periods. Materials reflecting the concerns of the liturgical movement and its impact on church design begin to surface in the 1930s. Surges in published materials tend to correspond with active periods of church building. The 1950s and 1960s exhibit a large number of documents, as does the period from 1990 to 2005. Foreign-language titles included in this bibliography represent materials often cited in English-language resources, illustrating the tremendous sharing of ideas between Western Europe and the United States. Short annotations accompany some of the titles.

Pre-1900

Kidder, F. E. *Churches and Chapels: Designs and Suggestions for Church-Building Committees, Architects, and Builders.* New York: William T. Comstock, 1895.

Architect and scholar Kidder created a guide for church building at the turn of the century. Kidder reminds the reader that a church is to be a temple to God and suggests that Gothic or Romanesque designs will more easily give a "religious impression."

Pugin, A. Welby. *True Principles and Revival of Christian Architecture.* 1895.

———. *The True Principles of Pointed or Christian Architecture.* London: John Weale, 1841.

Ruskin, John. *Seven Lamps of Architecture.* London: Elder Smith, 1849.

1900 to 1909

Cram, Ralph Adams. *Church Building: A Study of the Principles of Architecture in Their Relation to the Church*. Boston: Small, Maynard & Company, 1901.

———. *The Gothic Quest*. New York: Baker & Taylor, 1907.

Kidder, F. E. *Churches and Chapels: Designs and Suggestions for Church-Building Committees, Architects, and Builders*. Second edition. New York: William T. Comstock, 1900.

This is an expanded and revised edition of Kidder's earlier guide.

1910 to 1919

Baker, James McFarlan. *American Churches*. Volume two. New York: The American Architect, 1915.

Bond, Francis. *English Church Architecture*. London: H. Milford, 1913.

Cram, Ralph Adams. *Church Building: A Study of the Principles of Architecture in Their Relation to the Church*. Second edition. Boston: Small, Maynard & Company, 1910.

Cram's reflections have grown to approximately 270 pages in this edition.

———. *The Gothic Quest*. Second edition. New York: Baker & Taylor, 1907.

This is a revised and expanded work, now over 400 pages, promoting the use of Gothic design in church architecture.

———, ed. *American Churches*. Volume one. New York: The American Architect, 1915.

Kidder, F. E. *Churches and Chapels: Designs and Suggestions for Church-Building Committees, Architects, and Builders*. Fourth edition. New York: William T. Comstock, 1910.

This is a final revised edition of Kidder's guide.

Scott, Geoffrey. *The Architecture of Humanism: An Episode in Taste*. London: Constable & Company, 1914.

1920 to 1929

Conover, Elbert M. *Building the House of God*. New York: Methodist Book Concern, 1928.

Le Corbusier. *The City of Tomorrow and Its Planning*. Trans. Frederick Etchells. New York: Payson & Clarke Ltd., 1929.

———. *Urbanisme*. Paris: Éditions Crès, 1924.

———. *Vers une Architecture*. Paris: G. Crès et Cie, 1923.

Cram, Ralph Adams. *Church Building: A Study of the Principles of Architecture in Their Relation to the Church*. Third edition. Boston: Marshall Jones, 1924.

Cram's reflections have grown to approximately 350 pages in this edition.

———, ed. *American Church Building of Today*. New York: Architectural Book Publishing Company, Inc., 1929.

This volume contains a selection of church designs that coincide with Cram's approach to church architecture.

Short, Ernest. *A History of Religious Architecture*. London: Eyre & Spottiswoode, 1925.

This is a history of sacred architecture across time and geographical space, culminating in church architecture. The final chapter concludes with an appreciation of Gothic revival designs in England and the United States. Four editions of this volume would ultimately be produced.

1930 to 1939

Bartning, D. Otto. *Die Stahl Kirche*. New York: Copper & Brass Research Association, 1930.

Bonhoeffer, Dietrich. *Gemeinsames Leben*. München: Chr. Kaiser Verlag, 1938.

———. *Nachfolge*. München: Chr. Kaiser Verlag, 1937.

Brannach, Frank. *Church Architecture: Building for a Living Faith*. Milwaukee: The Bruce Publishing Company, 1932.

Dix, Gregory, ed. *The Treatise on the Apostolic Tradition of St. Hippolytus of Rome, Bishop and Martyr*. New York: Macmillan, 1937.

Herbert, A. G. *Liturgy and Society: The Function of the Church in the Modern World.* London: Faber & Faber, 1935.

————, ed. *The Parish Communion: A Book of Essays by W. S. Baker, D. R. Blackman, J. F. Briscoe, and Others.* London: SPCK, 1937.

Hitchcock, Henry-Russell, Jr., and Philip Johnson. *The International Style: Architecture Since 1922.* New York: W. W. Norton, 1932.

Parsch, Pius, and Robert Kramreiter. *Neue kirchenkunst im geist der liturgie.* Wien-Klosterneuburg: Volksliturgiescher Verlag, 1939.

This is a collaborative effort between Austrian liturgical movement leader Parsch and architect Kramreiter, seeking to promote liturgical renewal in concert with modern art and architectural designs in Catholic churches.

Reinhold, H. A. "The Architecture of Rudolf Schwarz." *Architectural Forum* 70, no. 1 (January 1939): 22-27.

————. "A Revolution in Church Architecture." *Liturgical Arts* 6 (1937-1938): 123-33.

Schwarz, Rudolf. *Vom bau der Kirche.* Heidelberg: Verlag Lambert Schneider, 1938.

This book represents Schwarz's exploration of a variety of models for church design. Centrally planned worship spaces receive positive attention in this work. An English version of the text was released in 1958. Schwarz's work was admired and widely read in the United States.

Short, Ernest. *A History of Religious Architecture.* Second edition. London: Eyre & Spottiswoode, 1936.

This is a revised and expanded edition of Short's work, which was cited in some bibliographies on church building in the first half of the twentieth century.

Watkin, William Ward. *The Church of Tomorrow.* New York: Harper & Brothers Publishers, 1936.

In this volume Watkin seeks primary inspiration from the cathedrals of the eleventh to the thirteenth centuries, attempting to fuse contemporary needs and materials with insights from medieval models.

1940 to 1949

Addleshaw, G. W. O., and Frederick Etchells. *The Architectural Setting of Anglican Worship.* London: Faber & Faber, 1948.

This book provides a thorough historical survey of Anglican church architecture to the twentieth century. The information contained in this volume was useful for those seeking to embody insights from the liturgical movement in contemporary churches, for it located particular architectural features of the past in their appropriate context. This book remained in bibliographies of church architecture design books for decades.

Anderson, Martin. *Planning and Financing the New Church.* Second revised edition. Minneapolis: Augsburg Publishing House, 1949.

Anson, Peter F. *Churches: Their Plan and Furnishing.* Revised and edited by Thomas F. Croft-Fraser and H. A. Reinhold. Milwaukee: The Bruce Publishing Company, 1948.

Conover, Elbert M. *The Church Builder.* New York: The International Bureau of Architecture, 1948.

Dix, Gregory. *The Shape of the Liturgy.* London: Dacre Press, 1945.

German Liturgical Commission. "Directives for the Building of a Church." *Orate Fratres* 24 (December 1949): 9-18.

This was originally published in 1947 under the title Richtlinien für die Gestaltung des Gotteshauses aus dem Geiste der römischen Liturgie. *This English translation represents an early statement intended to guide church builders in the Roman Catholic tradition according to the concerns of the liturgical movement. The document was primarily composed by the Rev. Dr. Theodore Klauser. It was reproduced in many places and was influential in guiding post-war church construction.*

Leach, William H. *Protestant Church Building: Planning, Financing, Designing.* New York: Abingdon-Cokesbury Press, 1948.

Le Corbusier. *Towards a New Architecture.* Trans. Frederick Etchells. London: Architectural Press, 1946.

McNally, R. J. *Fifty Modern Churches: Photographs, Ground Plans, and Information regarding Thirty-five Consecrated and Fifteen Dedicated Churches Erected during the Years 1930-1945.* London: Incorporated Church Building Society, 1947.

This book contains over 150 pages of photographs and plans of Anglican churches, with minimal information about each church. No essays or narratives are included in this volume. Some churches appear to exhibit the influence of modern design, but the influence of the priorities of the liturgical movement appears largely absent.

Maufe, Edward. *Modern Church Architecture*. London: Incorporated Church Building Society, 1948.

Pfammatter, Ferdinand. *Betonkirchen*. Zürich: Benziger Verlag Einsieldeln, 1948.
This is a thorough exploration of concrete churches in Europe (with a few from the United States) from the 1920s to the 1940s. Ample technical information, drawings, and photographs accompany the sites chosen.

Roulin, Dom E. *Modern Church Architecture*. St. Louis: B. Herder Book Company, 1947.

Schwarz, Rudolf. *Vom bau der Kirche*. Heidelberg: Verlag Lambert Schneider, 1947.
This is a reprint of Schwarz's 1938 text, which was now gaining a wider audience.

Scotford, John R. *The Church Beautiful: A Practical Discussion of Church Architecture*. Boston: Pilgrim Press, 1945.
Congregational minister Scotford seeks to help congregations consider simple ways in which they might enhance their present church environment in light of beauty and function.

Short, Ernest. *The House of God: A History of Religious Architecture*. Third edition. London: Eyre & Spottiswoode, 1951.
This is a third edition of his 1925 book with an expanded title.

―――. *The House of God: A History of Religious Architecture*. Fourth edition. London: Eyre & Spottiswoode, 1955.
This is the final revised edition of Short's book.

―――, ed. *Post-War Church Building: A Practical Handbook*. London: Hollis & Carter, 1947.

Wright, Frank Lloyd. *An Organic Architecture: The Architecture of Democracy*. Second edition. London: Lund Humphries & Co., Inc., 1941.

1950 to 1959

Betts, Darby Wood, ed. *Architecture for the Church*. Greenwich, Conn.: Seabury Press, 1952.

Biedrzynski, Richard. *Kirchen Unserer Zeit*. Munich: Hirmer Verlag, 1958.

This book provides an excellent survey of primarily German churches (with other notable exceptions), especially those built in the 1950s. Text and floor plans accompany the churches featured. Select churches are well-illustrated in the 148 full-page, black-and-white plates included.

Bonhoeffer, Dietrich. *The Cost of Discipleship*. New York: Macmillan, 1955.

————. *Letters and Papers from Prison*. Edited by Eberhard Bethge. Translated by Reginald H. Fuller. New York: Macmillan, 1953.

————. *Life Together*. Translated by John W. Doberstein. New York: Harper & Row, 1954.

Burchard, John Ely. "A Pilgrimage: Ronchamp, Raincy, Vézelay." *Architectural Record* 123, no. 3 (March 1958): 171-78.

"Church Building as an Expression of the Presence of the Church in the World." In *Report of the Conference for Architects and Theologians, May 6th-13th, 1959*. Bossey, Switzerland: The Ecumenical Institute, 1959.

This is a report of a conference of architects and theologians from Europe and the United States, initiated by the World Council of Churches, gathered to share ideas concerning contemporary church-building. Concerns for pursuing modern designs that could reflect servanthood, mission, and beauty were highlighted.

Collins, Peter. "The Doctrine of Auguste Perret." *Architectural Review* 114 (August 1953): 90-98.

Crichton, J. D. "The Church — The House of God's People." *Liturgy* 28 (1959): 43-47.

Davies, J. G. *The Origin and Development of Early Christian Church Architecture*. New York: Philosophical Library, 1953.

Diocesan Liturgical Commission, Superior, Wisconsin. "Diocesan Building Directives, Part One: The Church and Its Elements." *Liturgical Arts* 26, no. 1 (November 1957): 7-9.

Inspired, in part, by the guidelines produced by the 1947 German directives for church building, the principles outlined in this article accent active participation of the assembly in worship, service to those in our cities, and a contemporary, simplified expression of beauty in church building.

————. "Diocesan Building Directives, Part Two: The Altar and Its Setting." *Liturgical Arts* 26, no. 2 (February 1958): 43-44.

This is a companion article to the more general guidelines published in the previous issue of Liturgical Arts. The principles mentioned here discuss the significance of having a freestanding altar that is appropriately proportioned. The altar needs to utilize qualities of simplicity, integrity, and beauty in its design. The importance of natural light around the altar and in the immediate surrounding area is noted, as well as the optional use of communion rails.

Documents for Sacred Architecture: James Cardinal Lercaro: The Christian Church, and The Bishops of Germany Directives for the Building of a Church. Collegeville, Minn.: Liturgical Press, 1957.

This volume contains English translations of two important documents seeking to guide mid-century Roman Catholic church-building. The first document, "The Christian Church," was an address given by Cardinal Lercaro at the First National Congress of Sacred Architecture, Bologna, Italy, in 1955. The second document comprises the guidelines published in 1947 by bishops in Germany. Both accent the significance of the communities for which churches are built and remain open to contemporary expressions of design.

Feldtkeller, Andreas, and Rudolf Schwarz. *Kirchen von heute.* Stuttgart: Karl Krämer Verlag, 1959.

Issue number 27 in an architectural series of competitive designs, "Churches Today" is divided into two sections, Protestant and Catholic, with a lead article concerning contemporary Protestant churches by Feldtkeller and a lead article concerning contemporary Catholic churches by Schwarz. Following each article is a host of photographs, models, and plans that won various European church competitions.

Henze, Anton, and Theodore Filthaut. *Kirchliche Kunst der Gegenwart.* Recklinghausen: Paulus Verlag, 1954.

Text exploring the insights of the liturgical movement as they apply to the utilization of modern art and architecture in the church composes the first half of this book. The essays by Henze and Filthaut are clear and helpful for grasping mid-century priorities and thinking. More than one hundred pages of photographs of churches and artifacts of the church follow the text, illustrating the arguments of the authors quite well.

————. *Contemporary Church Art.* Translated by Cecily Hastings. Edited by Maurice Lavanoux. New York: Sheed & Ward, 1956.

This English translation of Kirchliche Kunst der Gegenwart was released just two years after the German publication. There is variation between the plates that accompany this translation and those that appear in the original.

Johe, Herbert W. *Architecture and the Church*, vol. 1: *A Bibliography on Architecture for the Church*. New York: Department of Worship and the Arts, National Council of Churches of Christ in the USA, 1959.

Kirchenbauten von Hermann Bauer und Fritz Metzger. Würzburg: Echter Verlag, 1956.
This volume is a survey of the work of two prolific and noteworthy modern church architects. Brief essays by Metzger, Bauer, P.-R. Régamey, R. Schwarz, and A.-M. Cocagnac are included. Many photographs and plans accompany the text.

McClinton, Katharine Morrison. *The Changing Church: Its Architecture, Art, and Decoration*. New York: Morehouse-Gorham Company, 1957.

Manual for Organizing and Managing the Building Program. New York: Department of Church Architecture, The United Lutheran Church in America, 1958.

Meinberg, Cloud. "The New Churches of Europe." *Worship* 31 (1957): 68-77.

Mills, Edward D. *The Modern Church*. London: Architectural Press, 1956; New York: Frederick A. Praeger, 1956.
Written from an English perspective, this is a practical guide addressing general issues connected to church building. Modern building sensibilities are found in the work. An appendix contains specific planning information for Roman Catholic and a variety of Protestant traditions.

O'Connell, J. B. *Church Building and Furnishing: The Church's Way*. Notre Dame: University of Notre Dame Press, 1955.

Organizing and Operating the Building Program. New York: Department of Church Architecture, The United Lutheran Church in America, 1954.

Powell, James Marvin, and M. Norvel Young. *The Church Is Building*. Nashville: Gospel Advocate Company, 1956.
This book of pragmatic advice from non-architects is intended to guide the process of building a church for congregations of a more "free church" Protestant tradition. Emphasis falls in these pages on the building as a tool that can enhance ministry. Ideal qualities for a church building include functionalism, sincerity, beauty, simplicity, and proportion.

Reinhold, H. A. *Speaking of Liturgical Architecture*. Notre Dame: University of Notre Dame Press, 1952.

Schwarz, Rudolf. *The Church Incarnate*. Translated by Cynthia Harris. Chicago: Henry Regnery Company, 1958.

Scotford, John R. *When You Build Your Church*. Doniger & Raughley, Inc., 1955.

Congregational minister Scotford outlines in very basic language a process by which a building committee or others can consider the building process for their church. Scotford raises many pragmatic questions that will need to be answered by congregations. His emphasis lies on simple, modern expressions of architecture for service. A second edition of this book appeared in 1958 and a third edition in 1968.

————. *When You Build Your Church*. Second edition. New York: Channel Press, 1958.

Shear, John Knox, ed. *Religious Buildings Today: An Architectural Record Book*. New York: F. W. Dodge Corporation, 1957.

Martin Halverson, executive director of the Department of Worship and the Arts, National Council of Churches, introduces this volume largely devoted to images of contemporary churches. Short articles discuss aspects of church design in general. The churches featured in the photographs (from a variety of denominations) are accompanied by brief remarks concerning each project.

Sherman, Jonathan G. *Church Buildings and Furnishings: A Survey of Requirements*. Greenwich, Conn.: Seabury Press, 1958.

Sixty Post-War Churches: Churches, Church Centers, and Dual-Purpose Churches. London: Incorporated Church Building Society, 1956.

Smith, George Cline. "Seventy Thousand Churches in Ten Years." In *Religious Buildings for Today*. New York: F. W. Dodge Corporation, 1957, p. 33.

Stoddard, Whitney S. *Adventure in Architecture: Building the New St. John's*. New York: Longmans, Green & Company, 1958.

Thiry, Paul; Richard M. Bennett; and Henry L. Kamphoefner. *Churches and Temples*. New York: Reinhold Publishing Company, 1953.

The authors divide their study into three sections: examinations of Roman Catholic, Jewish, and Protestant places of worship. Each section contains brief remarks concerning the ritual requirements of the group, historical development of their places of worship, and descriptions (with photographs and drawings) of contemporary structures for worship. Projects featured are generally drawn from North America.

Watkin, William Ward. *Planning and Building the Modern Church*. New York: F. W. Dodge Corporation, 1951.

This book is intended to be a basic guide for Roman Catholic and Protestant church-building. Watkins exhibits a clear preference for the designs of neo-Gothic churches (he speaks highly of the work of Magginis, Cram, and Goodhue, and features their churches). He generally dismisses pre-war and post-war European churches. Watkins' comments are general, with little reference to theological concerns. He embraces modern materials, and in the photographs he gives some examples of modern style.

Weyres, Willy. *Neue Kirchen im Erzbistum Köln, 1945-1956.* Dusseldorf: Verlag L. Schwann, 1957.

This is a well-written survey of post-war German churches in the archdiocese of Cologne. Dominikus and Gottfried Böhm, Rudolf Schwarz, and Emil Steffann are among the many architects featured in this work.

Weyres, Willy, Otto Bartning, et al. *Kirchen: Handbuch für den Kirchenbau.* Munich: Verlag Georg D. W. Callwey, 1959.

This is a more technical guide of nearly 450 pages, providing background and practical information on building Roman Catholic and Protestant churches. Historical and theological issues are discussed in specific sections. Following the descriptive chapters are examples of churches in Europe built after World War II (with photographs, drawings, and some text), and even a few examples from other countries (such as the United States). Many authors contributed to this work under the direction of Weyres and Bartning.

White, James F. "Church Architecture: Some Standards." *The Christian Century* 18, February 1959, p. 196.

Wright, Frank Lloyd. *The Natural House.* New York: Bramhall House, 1954.

1960 to 1969

Abbott, Walter M. *The Documents of Vatican II.* Translated and edited by Joseph Gallagher. New York: America Press, 1966.

The Architects' Journal, eds. *Church Buildings.* London: Architectural Press, 1967.

Arnold, Henry C. F. "Religious Buildings: Stability after the Boom." *Architectural Record* 134 (July 1963): 18.

Atkinson, Harry C. *How to Get Your Church Built.* Garden City, N.Y.: Doubleday, 1964.

Biéhler, André. *Architecture in Worship: The Christian Place of Worship.* Translated by Odette and Donald Elliott. Philadelphia: Westminster Press, 1965.

This is an English translation of Biehler's Liturgie et Architecture, *first published in 1961 by Labor et Fides in Geneva.*

Bonhoeffer, Dietrich. *Ethics.* Edited by Eberhard Bethge. New York: Macmillan, 1962.

Bouyer, Louis. *Liturgy and Architecture.* Notre Dame: University of Notre Dame Press, 1967.

Bruggink, Donald J., and Carl H. Droppers. *Christ and Architecture: Building Presbyterian/Reformed Churches*. Grand Rapids: Wm. B. Eerdmans Publishing Company, 1965.

Buildings and Breakthrough: Report of the Diocese of Chichester Buildings Study Group. Chichester: Diocese of Chichester Buildings Study Group/The Institute for the Study of Worship and Religious Architecture, University of Birmingham, n.d.

Callahan, Daniel, ed. *The Secular City Debate*. New York: Macmillan, 1966.

Canty, Donald. "Strength or Banality? A New Reformation Challenges Church Design." *Architectural Forum* 119, no. 6 (December 1963): 69-72.

Casel, Odo. *The Mystery of Christian Worship and Other Writings*. Translated by Burkhard Neunheuser. Westminster, Md.: Newman Press, 1962.

Christ-Janer, Albert, and Mary Mix Foley. *Modern Church Architecture: A Guide to the Form and Spirit of Twentieth-Century Religious Building*. New York: McGraw-Hill, 1962.

This book is divided into three primary sections, two featuring contemporary Roman Catholic and Protestant (eleven denominations) architecture, one featuring three Catholic monasteries and two Protestant seminaries. Introductory essays by theologians (E. Sutfin/M. Lavanoux and P. Tillich) accompany the first two sections. Individual projects contain substantial text, photographs, and drawings. Forty projects are featured in all.

Church Architecture: The Shape of Reform. Proceedings of a Meeting on Church Architecture Conducted by The Liturgical Conference in Cleveland, Ohio, February 23-25, 1965. Washington, D.C.: The Liturgical Conference, 1965.

Commission on Church Architecture of The Lutheran Church–Missouri Synod. *Architecture and the Church*. St. Louis: Concordia Publishing House, 1965.

Cope, Gilbert, ed. *Christianity and the Visual Arts: Studies in the Art and Architecture of the Church*. London, 1964.

————. *Making the Building Serve the Liturgy: Studies in the Re-ordering of Churches*. London: A. R. Mowbray & Company, 1962.

Le Corbusier. *The Radiant City: Elements of a Doctrine of Urbanism to Be Used as the Basis of Our Machine-Age Civilization.* Translated by Pamela Knight, Eleanor Levieux, and Derek Coltman. New York: Orion Press, 1967.

Cox, Harvey. *The Secular City: Secularization and Urbanization in Theological Perspective.* New York: Macmillan, 1965.

Dahinden, Justus. *New Trends in Church Architecture.* New York: Universe Books, 1967.

Davies, J. G. *The Architectural Setting of Baptism.* London: Barrie & Rockliff, 1962.
Director of the Institute for the Study of Worship and Religious Architecture, University of Birmingham, Davies wrote this book as a historical examination of fonts, pools, and spaces used for baptism. He provides insight for communities seeking to facilitate contemporary choices based on lessons learned from Christians of the past.

—————. *The Early Christian Church: A History of Its First Five Centuries.* New York: Holt, Rinehart & Winston, 1965.

—————. *The Secular Use of Church Buildings.* London: SCM Press, 1968; New York: Seabury Press, 1968.

Davies, Lawrence E. "Building of Lavish Churches Criticized at Coast Conference." *New York Times,* 27 April 1966, p. 47, cols. 1-2.

Debuyst, Frédéric. *Modern Architecture and Christian Celebration.* London: Lutterworth Press; Richmond, Va.: John Knox Press, 1968.
Debuyst was the editor of Art D'Eglise *for its last twenty years (to 1980). This book represents material presented in a lecture series in 1966 at the Institute for the Study of Worship and Religious Architecture, University of Birmingham (headed by J. G. Davies and G. Cope). Debuyst especially accents domesticity in design, seeking to promote "Paschal meeting rooms" for liturgical celebrations.*

Dix, Gregory, ed. *The Treatise on the Apostolic Tradition of St. Hippolytus of Rome, Bishop and Martyr.* Corrections by Henry Chadwick. London: SPCK, 1968.

"Down with the Cathedral!" *Newsweek,* 10 May 1965, p. 74.

Evers, Father Paul, and William Stolte. *An Incarnational Church: Saint Leo Catholic Church.* Pipestone, Minn.: Nicollet Press, 1969.

Fiddes, Victor. *The Architectural Requirements of Protestant Worship.* Toronto: Ryerson Press, 1961.

Filthaut, Theodor. *Kirchenbau und Liturgiereform*. Mainz: Matthias-Grunewald Verlag, 1965.

An early, thoughtful book reflecting on the implications of the new Roman Catholic reforms from Vatican II for church design. Filthaut continues to speak of the church as a "house of God," but brings a significant accent on the faithful as composing the temple and dwelling place of God. He remarks that the building is intended to serve the people. "Noble simplicity" is suggested as a guiding principle of design and organization of the space. There are ample suggestions in line with the emphases of the liturgical movement.

————. *Church Architecture and Liturgical Reform*. Translated by Gregory Roettger. Baltimore: Helicon, 1968.

Robert Hovda wrote the foreword to this English translation of Filthaut's book. The photographs included in the American edition exhibit a modern aesthetic.

Frey, Edward S. *This Before Architecture*. Jenkintown, Pa.: Foundation Books, 1963.

At the time of this writing, Frey was the Executive Director of the Commission on Church Architecture, Lutheran Church in America. The book is a compilation of six addresses delivered by Frey in various cities from 1957 to 1962. Frey's focus is on Christian communities articulating their theological and ministry needs clearly so that architects can provide appropriate buildings for their expressed needs. Familiar themes of active participation and service are present, with quotes from authors such as J. F. White, R. Schwarz, J. Jungmann, H. A. Reinhold, P. Hammond, and E. A. Sövik.

Giedion, Sigfried. *Space, Time, and Architecture: The Growth of a New Tradition*. Fifth edition. Cambridge, Mass.: Harvard University Press, 1967.

Gieselmann, Reinhard, and Werner Aebli. *Kirchenbau*. Zürich: Verlag Girsberger, 1960.

Gropius, Walter. *Apollo in the Democracy: The Cultural Obligation of the Architect*. New York: McGraw-Hill, 1968.

————. *The New Architecture and the Bauhaus*. Cambridge, Mass.: MIT Press, 1965.

Hammond, Peter. *Liturgy and Architecture*. London: Barrie & Rockliff, 1960.

————, ed. *Towards a Church Architecture*. London: Architectural Press, 1962.

Hovda, Robert W., and Gabe Huck. *There's No Place Like People: Liturgical Celebrations in Home and Small-Group Situations*. Washington, D.C.: The Liturgical Conference, 1969.

Hunt, Rolfe Lanier, ed. *Revolution, Place, and Symbol: Journal of the First International Congress on Religion, Architecture, and the Visual Arts, New York City and Montreal,*

August 26 through September 4, 1967. New York: The International Congress on Religion, Architecture, and the Visual Arts, 1969.

Irish Episcopal Commission for Liturgy. *The Place of Worship: Pastoral Directory on the Building and Reordering of Churches.* The Irish Institute of Pastoral Liturgy, 1966.

This is the first edition of a short book meant to educate and guide Roman Catholic communities in thoughtfully considering the design and use of their worship spaces in light of Vatican II reforms seeking "full and active participation." The suggestions are fairly brief, with emphases on an active assembly, simplicity, hospitality, and the role of the arts in worship.

Kidder-Smith, G. E. *The New Churches of Europe.* New York: Holt, Rinehart & Winston, 1964.

Lockett, W., ed. *The Modern Architectural Setting of the Liturgy.* London: SPCK, 1964.

McManus, Frederick. "Some Principles for Church Planning." *Worship* 35 (1961): 657-60.

Maguire, Robert, and Keith Murray. *Modern Churches of the World.* New York: E. P. Dutton, 1965.

Morse, John E. *To Build a Church.* New York: Holt, Rinehart & Winston, 1969.

Intended for both Protestant and Roman Catholic communities, this book focuses on practical issues related to planning and building churches. The introduction to the book is written by Edward A. Sövik, whom Morse thanks for his guidance and his many insights. Morse discusses concerns for meeting the needs of the congregation and the larger community, ecumenicity, contemporary forms, and hospitality.

"New Church Designs Reflect Changes in Liturgy." *New York Times,* 6 July 1968, pp. 23, 42, cols. 1-3, 2-5.

Pevsner, Nikolaus. *The Sources of Modern Architecture and Design.* New York: Oxford University Press, 1968.

Pichard, Joseph. *Les Églises nouvelles a travers le Monde.* Paris: Éditions des deux-mondes, 1960.

This is largely a picture book illustrating the diversity of modern churches being built in the first half of the twentieth century around the world (although the majority of churches featured are European). Attention is given to the role of modern art and its influence on church building. A limited amount of introductory text is present at the beginning of each chapter, highlighting some important architects and influences on modern design.

————. *Modern Church Architecture.* Translated by Ellen Callamann. New York: Orion Press, 1960.

This English version of Pichard's text Les Églises nouvelles a travers le Monde *was released in the same year that the French original was published.*

Rabinovich, Abraham. "The Old Church Steeple a Fading Symbol." *Suffolk Sun,* 24 December 1966, sec. 5-B, pg. 1, cols. 7-8.

Robinson, John A. T. *Honest to God.* Philadelphia: Westminster Press, 1963.

————. *Liturgy Coming to Life.* London: A. R. Mowbray, 1960.

Rubin, William S. *Modern Sacred Art and the Church at Assy.* New York: Columbia University Press, 1961.

Ruf, Sep. *German Church Architecture of the Twentieth Century.* Munich: Schnell & Steiner, 1964.

Schwarz, Rudolf. "The Eucharistic Building." *Faith and Form* 2 (April 1969): 20-23.

————. *Kirchenbau: Welt vor der Schwelle.* Heidelberg: F. H. Kerle Verlag, 1960.

Scotford, John R. *When You Build Your Church.* Third edition. New York: Meredith Press, 1968.

Seasoltz, R. Kevin. *The House of God: Sacred Art and Church Architecture.* New York: Herder and Herder, 1963.

Father Seasoltz discusses appropriate historical and theological contexts for church building here, applying insights from the liturgical movement to contemporary church design in light of early twentieth-century European churches by architects such as D. Böhm, R. Schwarz, and W. Moser. Frederick McManus provides a foreword, mentioning the significance of the church's function to "house the People of God at worship."

Smalley, Stephen. *Building for Worship: Biblical Principles in Church Design.* London: Hodder & Stoughton Limited, 1967.

Sövik, Edward A. "The Architecture of Kerygma." *Worship* 40, no. 4 (April 1966): 196-208.

————. "The Building and the Music." *The Diapason* 58, no. 4 (March 1967): 42-45.

————. "Church Design and the Communication of Religious Faith." *Architectural Record* 128 (December 1960): 137-40.

————. "Comment on Multi-Purpose Worship Spaces." *Faith and Form* 2 (April 1969): 20-21.

————. "The Faith Our Forms Express." *Dialog* 4 (Autumn 1965): 292-98.

————. "The Faith Our Forms Express." *Protestant Church Buildings and Equipment* 12, no. 1 (May 1964): 11, 30-31, 33, 48-50.

————. "Fundamentals for Church Builders." *Your Church* 7, no. 3 (July/August/September 1961): 18-19, 29-37.

————. "House of God to House of God's People." *The Priest* 25, no. 4 (April 1969): 214-20.

————. "Images of the Church." *Worship* 41, no. 3 (1967): 130-41.

————. "New Visions for Church Builders." *Church Management* 38 (October 1961): 10, 12, 14, 26-27, 39.

————. "Reformation Is Still Needed." *The Lutheran Standard*, 18 October 1966, pp. 12-13.

————. Review of *L'architecture religieuse contemporaine en France*, by Georges Mercier. *Faith and Form* 2 (April 1969): 4.

————. Review of *EuropÖische Kirchenkunst der Gegenwart*, by Erich Widder. *Faith and Form* 2 (April 1969): 4.

————. Review of *Modern Architecture and Christian Celebration*, by Frédéric Debuyst. *Faith and Form* 2 (January 1969): 30.

————. Review of *The Radiant City*, by Le Corbusier. *Liturgical Arts* 36, no. 4 (August 1968): 120.

————. "Revolution, Place, and Symbol: Reflections Two Years Later." *Worship* 43, no. 8 (October 1969): 496-500.

————. "Tea and Sincerity." *Liturgical Arts* 37, no. 1 (November 1968): 4-7.

————. "A Theology of Architecture." *Study Encounter* 2, no. 4 (1966): 170-83.

————. "The Valley of Decision." *Dodge Construction News* (Chicago edition), 25 August 1967, sec. 2, pp. 18 and 22.

———. "Westwood Lutheran Church, St. Louis Park, Minnesota." *Northwest Architect* 28, no. 3 (May/June 1964): 39, 41, 59-64.

———. "What Is an Altar? What Is a Pulpit? What Is a Baptismal Font? Why?" *World Encounter* 5, no. 4 (April 1968): 14-19.

———. "What Is a Church? A Place for Holding Family Reunions." *World Encounter* 5, no. 4 (April 1968): 8-13.

———. "What Is Religious Architecture?" *Discourse* 9 (Winter 1966): 67-82.

———. "What Is Religious Architecture?" *Faith and Form* 1 (special issue, 1967): 8-9, 22-26.

Stanton, Phoebe B. *The Gothic Revival and American Church Architecture: An Episode in Taste, 1840-1856.* Baltimore: Johns Hopkins Press, 1968.

Tegels, Aelfred. "The Church: House of God's People." *Worship* 35 (1961): 494-501.

Van Buren, Paul. *The Secular Meaning of the Gospel: Based on an Analysis of Its Language.* New York: Macmillan, 1963.

Venturi, Robert. *Complexity and Contradiction in Architecture.* New York: Museum of Modern Art, 1966.

Von Allmen, J. J. "A Short Theology of the Place of Worship." *Studia Liturgica* 3, no. 3 (1964): 155-71.

White, James F. *The Cambridge Movement: The Ecclesiologists and the Gothic Revival.* Cambridge: Cambridge University Press, 1962; reissued, 1979.

———. "Current Trends in American Church Building." *Studia Liturgica* 4, no. 1 (Spring 1965): 94-113.

———. *Protestant Worship and Church Architecture: Theological and Historical Considerations.* New York: Oxford University Press, 1964 (reprinted by Wipf & Stock, 2003).

———. "Some Contemporary Experiments in Liturgical Architecture." *Religion in Life* 30 (1961): 285-95.

Worship in the City of Man. Twenty-seventh North American Liturgical Week, Houston, Texas, August 22-25, 1966. Washington, D.C.: The Liturgical Conference, 1966.

Wunderlich, Robert E. *Worship and the Arts: A Study of the Life of the Church Expressed in Worship and the Arts.* St. Louis: Concordia Publishing House, 1966.
Chapter four of this volume concerns architecture and the church, highlighting themes of function, symbol, and service. A helpful balance between temple and meetinghouse is maintained. Suggested readings include books by A. Christ-Janer and Foley, E. Frey, P. Hammond, J. Jungmann, Pritchard, J. Shear, and P. Thiry.

1970 to 1979

The Architects' Journal, ed. *Church Buildings.* London: Architectural Press, 1970.

Bishops' Committee on the Liturgy. *Environment and Art in Catholic Worship.* Washington, D.C.: National Conference of Catholic Bishops, 1978.

Book of Common Prayer. New York: Seabury Press, 1979.

Bruggink, Donald J., and Carl H. Droppers. *When Faith Takes Form: Contemporary Churches of Architectural Integrity in America.* Grand Rapids: Wm. B. Eerdmans Publishing Company, 1971.

Centre National de Pastorale Liturgique. *L'eglise: Maison du people de Dieu: Liturgie et architecture.* Paris: Les Éditions du Cerf, 1971.
This is a primer for thinking through the design of new churches in light of the reforms of Vatican II. The emphasis falls on creating a "house for the people of God," both encouraging full and active participation in the liturgy and relating the ministries of the church to the needs of the world.

Davies, J. G. *Everyday God: Encountering the Holy in World and Worship.* London: SCM Press, 1973.

————, ed. *Looking to the Future: Papers Read at an International Symposium on Prospects for Worship, Religious Architecture, and Socio-Religious Studies, 1976.* Birmingham: Institute for the Study of Worship and Religious Architecture, 1976.

Gieselmann, Reinhard. *Contemporary Church Architecture.* London: Thames & Hudson, 1972.

Irish Episcopal Commission for Liturgy. *The Place of Worship: Pastoral Directory on the Building and Reordering of Churches*. Revised edition. The Irish Institute of Pastoral Liturgy, 1972.

Jencks, Charles. *The Language of Post-Modern Architecture*. New York: Rizzoli, 1977.

Johnson, Philip C. *Mies van der Rohe*. Third edition. New York: The Museum of Modern Art, 1978.

Lercaro, J., et al. *Espace sacré et architecture moderne*. Paris: Les Éditions du Cerf, 1971.
This is a series of eight essays concerning liturgical reform and church architecture by authors such as J. Lercaro, E. A. Sövik, J. G. Davies, and F. Debuyst. Four of the essays were first presented at the First International Congress on Religion, Architecture, and the Visual Arts. A strong theme of hospitable architecture, to provide for the assembly and meet the needs of the world, is present in this collection.

Lutheran Book of Worship. Minneapolis: Augsburg Publishing House, 1978.

Lynn, Edwin C. *Tired Dragons: Adapting Church Architecture to Changing Needs*. Boston: Beacon Press, 1972.

Randolph, David James, ed. *Sacred Space: Meaning and Form*. New York: The International Congress on Religion, Architecture, and the Arts, 1976.

The Sacramentary. New York: Catholic Book Publishing Company, 1973, 1985.

Schnell, Hugo. *Twentieth-Century Church Architecture in Germany: Documentation, Presentation, Interpretation*. Translated by Paul J. Dine. Munich: Verlag Schnell & Steiner, 1974.
This volume is a comprehensive examination of the development of church design — Roman Catholic and Protestant — in Germany from the 1870s to the 1970s. Attention is given to both theological and architectural issues. The book is broken into four time periods: before 1918, 1918 to 1945, 1945 to 1960, and after 1960. Each section is composed of a clearly written narrative with many ground plans, followed by extensive bibliographies and photographs.

Sövik, E. A. *Architecture for Worship*. Minneapolis: Augsburg Publishing House, 1973.

―――――. "Church Architecture — A Public Language." *Cutting Edge* 7, no. 4 (July-August 1978): 1-5.

―――――. "Ecumenics and High Art." *Liturgy* 23, no. 5 (September 1978): 19-20.

―――――. "House of God to House of God's People." *The Priest* 25, no. 4 (April 1969): 214-20.

———. "The Place of Worship: Environment for Action." In *Worship: Good News in Action,* edited by Mandus A. Egge, pp. 94-110. Minneapolis: Augsburg Publishing House, 1973.

———. "The Return to the Non-Church." *Faith and Form* 5 (Fall 1972): 12-15.

———. Review of *An Organic Architecture: The Architecture of Democracy,* by Frank Lloyd Wright. *Liturgical Arts* 39, no. 2 (February 1971): 53-54.

———. "The Second International Congress: The Architecture of Religion." *Faith and Form* 4 (Spring 1971): 20-21.

———. "Triumphalism, Sacred and Secular — A Christian Architect's Reflections." *Living Worship* 6, no. 1 (January 1970): 1-4.

Thompson, Elizabeth Kendall. "Building Types Study 450: Flexible Space in Religious Buildings." *Architectural Record* 145, no. 1 (July 1973): 117-32.

Van Loon, Ralph R. *Space for Worship: Some Thoughts on Liturgy, Art, and Architecture.* Philadelphia: Lutheran Church in America, 1975.

This twenty-page booklet was produced for the Lutheran Church in America by van Loon, the denominational coordinator for the Church Architecture Division for Parish Services. The emphasis here is on renewing worship with a focus on the people, flexible spaces (even to accommodate nonliturgical activities), and moveable furnishings. The brief bibliography includes writings by Bieler, Bruggink/ Droppers, Cope, Debuyst, Filthaut, Hammond, and Sövik.

Walker, Williston. *A History of the Christian Church.* Third edition. New York: Charles Scribner's Sons, 1970.

1980 to 1989

Blankenship, N. Vernon. "Planning the Worship Space." *Cutting Edge* 15, no. 2 (second quarter, 1986): 1-8.

Bradshaw, Paul. "The Liturgical Use and Abuse of Patristics." In *Liturgy Reshaped,* edited by Kenneth Stevenson, pp. 134-45. London: SPCK, 1982.

———. "The Search for the Origins of Christian Liturgy: Some Methodological Reflections." *Studia Liturgica* 17 (1987): 26-34.

"Church Architecture." Special issue. *Reformed Liturgy and Music* 22, no. 2 (Spring 1988).

Cunningham, Joseph L. "An Orderly Journey: A Diocesan Response." In *The Environment for Worship: A Reader,* edited by Secretariat, The Bishops' Committee on the Liturgy, National Conference of Catholic Bishops and The Center for Pastoral Liturgy, The Catholic University of America, pp. 71-75. Washington, D.C.: United States Catholic Conference, 1980.

Divita, James J. *Indianapolis Cathedral: A Construction History of Our Three Mother Churches.* Indianapolis: The Catholic Archdiocese of Indianapolis, 1986.

"Edward A. Sövik, FAIA." In *Liturgical Consultants for Worship Space,* pp. 60-63. Washington, D.C.: Federation of Diocesan Liturgical Commissions, 1989.

Faith and Order Commission. *Baptism, Eucharist, and Ministry.* Faith and Order Paper No. III. Geneva: World Council of Churches, 1982.

Guiton, Jacques. *The Ideas of Le Corbusier on Architecture and Urban Planning.* Translated by Margaret Guiton. New York: Braziller, 1981.

Hayes, Bartlett. *Tradition Becomes Innovation: Modern Religious Architecture in America.* New York: Pilgrim Press, 1983.

Huffman, Walter C., and S. Anita Stauffer. *Where We Worship.* Minneapolis: Augsburg Publishing House, 1987.

Huffman, Walter C., and Ralph R. Van Loon. *Where We Worship: Leader Guide and Process Guides.* Edited by S. Anita Stauffer. Minneapolis: Augsburg Publishing House, 1987.

Kennedy, Roger G. *American Churches.* New York: Crossroad Publishing Company, 1982.

Lane, George A. *Chicago Churches and Synagogues.* Chicago: Loyola University Press, 1981.

Lindstrom, Randall S. *Creativity and Contradiction: European Churches since 1970.* Washington, D.C.: The American Institute of Architects, 1988.

McGregory, Angus W. Review of *Architecture for Worship,* by Edward A. Sövik. *Reformed Liturgy and Music* 16, no. 2 (Spring 1982): 94.

Macmillan Encyclopedia of Architects. First edition (1982). S.v. "Böhm, Dominikus."

Macmillan Encyclopedia of Architects. First edition (1982). S.v. "Schwarz, Rudolf."

McNally, Dennis. *Sacred Space: An Aesthetic for the Liturgical Environment.* Wyndham Hall Press, 1985.

Using insights from comparative religion scholars, Father McNally seeks to argue for the creation of Christian worship spaces that exhibit qualities such as silence, darkness, emptiness, profusion, and monumentality. He seeks to restore a sense of mystery in modern worship spaces through the pursuit of these qualities of space.

Middleton, Arthur Pierce. *New Wine in Old Skins: Liturgical Change and the Setting of Worship.* Wilton, Conn.: Morehouse-Barlow, 1988.

This is a brief discussion of liturgical changes through the history of the church, with a focus on the Anglican tradition and its spaces for worship. Comments on a host of topics related to objects for worship are included too, all with an eye toward helping parishes make intelligent decisions when they seek to renew worship through altering the designs of their churches.

Pelikan, Jaroslav. *Jesus through the Centuries: His Place in the History of Culture.* New Haven: Yale University Press, 1985.

Riedel, Scott R. *Acoustics in the Worship Space.* Church Music Pamphlet Series. St. Louis: Concordia Publishing House, 1986.

Written by an acoustical and organ-design consultant, this 30-page pamphlet explains basic sound issues important for both spoken and musical expressions in worship.

Simon, Thomas G. *The Ministry of Liturgical Environment.* Collegeville, Minn.: Liturgical Press, 1984.

This 45-page guide is intended to instruct those who are to prepare environments for worship. It emphasizes achieving unity in the space, visibility, audibility, flexibility, and simplicity during worship events. The guide was prepared in relation to Environment and Art in Catholic Worship *and other contemporary documents.*

Sövik, Edward A. "Church Architecture — A Public Language." *Liturgy* 4, no. 4 (1985): 82-89.

———. "Elements of the Christian Tradition in Building." *Reformed Liturgy and Music* 16, no. 2 (Spring 1982): 81-83.

———. "The Environment for Sight, Sound, and Action." *Dialog* 25, no. 4 (Fall 1986): 272-76.

———. "The Mirror of the Church." *Faith and Form* 22 (Fall 1988): 16-18.

———. "Notes on Sacred Space." *Christian Century*, 31 March 1982, pp. 362-66.

Stauffer, S. Anita. "Fonts for Function and Meaning: Three Worthy Examples." *Catechumenate* (March 1988): 22-29.

———. "A Place for Burial, Birth, and Bath." *Liturgy* 5, no. 4 (1986): 51-57.

———. "Theology and Worship Space: Some Reflections." *Reformed Liturgy and Music* 22, no. 2 (Spring 1988): 61-65.

Tillich, Paul. *On Art and Architecture.* Edited by John and Jane Dillenberger. New York: Crossroad Publishing Company, 1987.

Van Loon, Ralph R. *Space for Worship: Some Thoughts on Liturgy, Art, and Architecture.* Revised edition. Philadelphia: Lutheran Church in America, 1982.

This is Van Loon's revised edition of his booklet, which exhibits more precision in the text (minor rewriting) and enhanced illustrations.

Vosko, Richard. *Through the Eye of a Rose Window: A Perspective on the Environment for Worship.* Saratoga, Calif.: Resource Publications, Inc., 1981.

The author of this 70-page book is a Roman Catholic priest, an architect, and a liturgical consultant. Vosko emphasizes the importance of the gathered community of the people of God at worship, community process in planning, stewardship, beauty, flexibility, and service to others in considering church designs. He also notes the significance of planning for the use of multimedia resources in worship.

White, James F., and Susan J. White. *Church Architecture: Building and Renovating for Christian Worship.* Nashville: Abingdon Press, 1988; reprinted by OSL Publications, 1998.

This practical handbook is intended to guide congregations through the building and renovation process. Focused primarily on assessing the various liturgical needs of both Roman Catholic and Protestant communities, the authors provide historical insights that assist communities in making wise architectural choices according to their theological beliefs.

Wuthnow, Robert. *The Restructuring of American Religion: Society and Faith Since World War II.* Princeton: Princeton University Press, 1988.

1990 to 1999

Adams, William Seth. *Moving the Furniture: Liturgical Theory, Practice, and Environment.* New York: Church Publishing Incorporated, 1999.

"The Art of Worship." Special issue. *Reformed Liturgy and Music* 31, no. 3 (1997).

Book of Common Worship. Louisville: Westminster/John Knox Press, 1993.

Bowman, Ray, and Eddy Hall. *When Not to Build: An Architect's Unconventional Wisdom for the Growing Church.* Grand Rapids: Baker Book House, 1992.

Boyer, Mark G. *The Liturgical Environment: What the Documents Say.* Collegeville, Minn.: Liturgical Press, 1990.

In this single volume Boyer has compiled references to and suggestions for the liturgical environment in official Catholic documents. Theological reflections and practical suggestions are also included.

Bradshaw, Paul. *The Search for the Origins of Christian Worship: Sources and Methods for the Study of Early Liturgy.* Oxford: Oxford University Press, 1992.

Buscemi, John. *Places for Devotion.* Meeting House Essay Series, Number Four. Chicago: Liturgy Training Publications, 1993.

Canadian Conference of Catholic Bishops. *Our Place of Worship.* Ottawa, Ontario: Publications Service, Canadian Conference of Catholic Bishops, 1999.

Chiat, Marilyn J. *America's Religious Architecture: Sacred Places for Every Community.* New York: John Wiley & Sons, 1997.

Clausen, Meredith L. *Spiritual Space: The Religious Architecture of Pietro Belluschi.* Seattle: University of Washington Press, 1992.

This is a thoughtful examination of the churches designed by one of the outstanding architects of the twentieth century.

Crosbie, Michael J. *Architecture for the Gods.* Mulgrave, Australia: Images Publishing Group, Ltd., 1999.

Crosbie, an architect, scholar, and editor of the journal Faith and Form, *compiled this oversized picture book featuring places of worship in the United States from the previous decade (thirty-four Christian, eight Jewish, and one Muslim). Excellent photographs are joined by drawings and minimal text concerning each project.*

Cunningham, Colin. *Stones of Witness: Church Architecture and Function.* Stroud, U.K.: Sutton Publishing Limited, 1999.

Debuyst, Frédéric. "The Church: A Dwelling Place of Faith." *Studia Liturgica* 24, no. 1 (1994): 29-44.

In this article, Debuyst reiterates his familiar themes (the familial nature of the Christian community, "living rooms" for worship, and hospitality) with a focus on models for church design provided by the work of Emil Steffann. Debuyst laments a "return" of monumental, neo-sacred spaces, urging a renewal of earlier reform emphases.

DeSanctis, Michael E. *Renewing the City of God.* Meeting House Essay Series, Number Five. Chicago: Liturgy Training Publications, 1993.

Episcopal Church Building Fund. *A Congregational Planning Process.* New York: Episcopal Church Building Fund, n.d.

"Evangelicals and Catholics Together: The Christian Mission in the Third Millennium." *First Things* 43 (May 1994): 15-22.

Fenwick, John, and Bryan Spinks. *Worship in Transition: The Liturgical Movement in the Twentieth Century.* New York: Continuum Publishing Company, 1995.

Fleisher, Dennis, et al. *Acoustics for Liturgy: A Collection of Articles of The Hymn Society in the U.S. and Canada.* Meeting House Essay Series, Number Two. Chicago: Liturgy Training Publications, 1991.

Fulton, Charles N., and Patrick J. Holtkamp. *Church Sites and Buildings.* New York: The Episcopal Church Building Fund, 1991.

Fulton, Charles N.; Patrick J. Holtkamp; and Fritz Frurip. *The Church for Common Prayer: A Statement on Worship Space for the Episcopal Church.* New York: The Episcopal Church Building Fund, 1994.

This 32-page booklet touches on theological and practical issues related to church designs for Episcopal communities. Authors such as P. Hammond, W. Huffman, E. A. Sövik, A. Stauffer, and R. Van Loon are included in the bibliography.

"The Gift of Salvation." *First Things* 79 (January 1998): 20-23.

Giles, Richard. *Re-Pitching the Tent: Re-Ordering the Church Building for Worship and Mission.* Norwich: Canterbury Press, 1996. A revised and expanded edition was published by the Liturgical Press in 1999.

Hammel, Bette. "A New Architecture in Post-War America: Ed Sövik." *Architecture Minnesota* 18, no. 6 (November/December 1992): 54-55.

Hardy, Daniel W. "God in the Ordinary: The Work of J. G. Davies (1919-1990)." *Theology* 99 (November-December 1996): 427-40.

Heathcote, Edwin, and Iona Spens. *Church Builders.* New York: Academy Editions, 1997.

Hitchcock, Henry-Russell, and Philip Johnson. *The International Style.* New York: W. W. Norton, 1995.

Hoffman, Douglas R. *Church Building Space: An Architectural Planning Guide.* New York: Evangelization and Church Growth, General Board of Global Ministries, the United Methodist Church, 1997.

————. *Manual of Procedures for Church Building Programs.* New York: Evangelization and Church Growth, General Board of Global Ministries, the United Methodist Church, 1997.

Hoffman, Lawrence A. *Sacred Places and the Pilgrimage of Life.* Meeting House Essay Series, Number One. Chicago: Liturgy Training Publications, 1991.

Holgate, Alan. *Aesthetics of Built Form.* Oxford: Oxford University Press, 1992.

Irish Episcopal Commission for Liturgy. *The Place of Worship: Pastoral Directory on the Building and Reordering of Churches.* Veritas Publications and the Irish Institute of Pastoral Liturgy, 1994.
This is an expanded and revised edition of a third edition that first appeared in 1991.

Jencks, Charles. *What Is Post-Modernism?* Fourth edition. London: Academy Books, 1996.

Jones-Frank, Michael. *Iconography and Liturgy.* Meeting House Essay Series, Number Six. Chicago: Liturgy Training Publications, 1994.

Krieg, Robert. *Romano Guardini: Proclaiming the Sacred in a Modern World.* Chicago: Liturgy Training Publications, 1995.

Kuehn, Regina. *A Place for Baptism.* Chicago: Liturgy Training Publications, 1992.

Matisse, Henri; M.-A. Couturier; and L.-B. Rayssiguier. *The Vence Chapel: The Archive of a Creation.* Translated by Michael Taylor. Milan: Menil Foundation/Skira Editore, 1999.

McCormick, Gwenn E. *Planning and Building Church Facilities.* Baptist Sunday School Board, 1993.

McNorgan, David. *Preparing the Environment for Worship.* Collegeville, Minn.: Liturgical Press, 1997.

Mauck, Marchita. *Places for Worship: A Guide to Building and Renovating.* American Essays in Liturgy. Collegeville, Minn.: Liturgical Press, 1995.

—————. *Shaping a House for the Church.* Chicago: Liturgy Training Publications, 1990.

"ML 20th Anniversary Bene, Most Influential Architect." *Modern Liturgy* 20, no. 9 (November 1993): 46.

Noll, Mark A. *A History of Christianity in the United States and Canada.* Grand Rapids: Wm. B. Eerdmans Publishing Company, 1992.

Norman, Edward R. *The House of God: Church Architecture, Style, and History.* New York: Thames & Hudson, 1990.
This study explores the origin and meaning of church design through the centuries. It focuses primarily on architecture before the modern period.

Olson, Roger E. *The Story of Christian Theology: Twenty Centuries of Tradition and Reform.* Downers Grove, Ill.: InterVarsity Press, 1999.

Overbeck, T. Jerome. *Ancient Fonts, Modern Lessons.* Meeting House Essay Series, Number Nine. Chicago: Liturgy Training Publications, 1998.

Patterson, Roger L. *Architect Selection Process.* New York: Evangelization and Church Growth, General Board of Global Ministries, the United Methodist Church, 1998.

Popecki, Joseph T. *The Parish of St. Mark in Burlington, Vermont, 1941-1991.* Burlington, Vt.: The Parish of St. Mark, 1991.

Purdy, Martin Terrence. *Churches and Chapels: A Design and Development Guide.* London: Butterworth Architecture, 1991.

Rambusch, Viggo Bech. *Lighting the Liturgy.* Meeting House Essay Series, Number Seven. Chicago: Liturgy Training Publications, 1994.

Schloeder, Steven J. *Architecture in Communion: Implementing the Second Vatican Council through Liturgy and Architecture.* Ignatius Press, 1998.

Schwebel, Horst. "Liturgical Space and Human Experience, Exemplified by the Issue of the 'Multi-Purpose' Church Building." *Studia Liturgica* 24, no. 1 (1994): 12-28.

In this study of post-war, German, "multi-purpose" worship spaces, Schwebel notes the gradual sacralization of the spaces. He also notes the disjunction between theological ideals and anthropological realities.

Senn, Frank C. *Christian Liturgy: Catholic and Evangelical.* Minneapolis: Fortress Press, 1997.

Smith, Peter E. *Cherubim of Gold.* Meeting House Essay Series, Number Three. Chicago: Liturgy Training Publications, 1993.

Sövik, Edward A. "Sitting Proper: Notes on Seating for the Assembly." *Environment and Art Newsletter* 3, no. 12 (February 1991): 90-93.

Stauffer, S. Anita. *Re-examining Baptismal Fonts: Baptismal Space for the Contemporary Church.* Collegeville, Minn.: Liturgical Press, 1991.

This is a videotape production discussing the features and the significance of locations and artifacts for Christian initiation.

Stroik, Christopher V. *Path, Portal, Path: Architecture for the Rites.* Meeting House Essay Series, Number Ten. Chicago: Liturgy Training Publications, 1999.

Stroik, Duncan. "Environment and Art in Catholic Worship: A Critique." *Sacred Architecture* 2, no. 1 (Summer 1999).

————. *Reconquering Sacred Space, 2000: Rediscovering Tradition in Twentieth-Century Liturgical Architecture.* Edited by Cristiano Rosponi and Giampaolo Rossi. Rome: Editrice il Bosco e la Nave, 1999.

————. "The Roots of Modernist Church Architecture." *Catholic Dossier* (May-June 1997).

————. "Ten Myths of Contemporary Church Architecture." *Sacred Architecture* 1, no. 1 (Fall 1998).

This Is the Night: A Parish Welcomes New Catholics. Chicago: Liturgy Training Publications, 1992.
This is a videotape (accompanied by a discussion guide) featuring Christian initiation at the Easter Vigil. The fullness of sign, symbol, and congregational participation is outstanding.

Torgerson, Mark Allen. "Edward Anders Sövik and His Return to the 'Non-church.'" Ph.D. diss., University of Notre Dame, 1995.

Trieb, Marc. *Sanctuaries of Spanish New Mexico.* Berkeley and Los Angeles: University of California Press, 1993.

Tuzik, Robert L., ed. *How Firm a Foundation: Leaders of the Liturgical Movement.* Chicago: Liturgy Training Publications, 1990.

The United Methodist Book of Worship. Nashville: The United Methodist Publishing House, 1992.

Upton, Dell. *Holy Things and Profane: Anglican Parish Churches in Colonial Virginia.* New Haven: Yale University Press, 1997.

Vander Molen, James. "A Self-Guided Tour." Grand Rapids: Church of the Servant, n.d.

Vosko, Richard S. *Designing Future Worship Spaces: The Mystery of a Common Vision.* Meeting House Essay Series, Number Eight. Chicago: Liturgy Training Publications, 1996.

Webber, Robert E. *Ancient-Future Faith: Rethinking Evangelicalism for a Postmodern World.* Grand Rapids: Baker Book House, 1999.

White, James F. "From Protestant to Catholic Plain Style." In *Seeing Beyond the Word: Visual Arts and the Calvinist Tradition,* edited by Paul Corby Finney, pp. 457-77. Grand Rapids: Wm. B. Eerdmans Publishing Company, 1999.

————. "Liturgical Architecture." In *Christian Worship in North America: A Retrospective, 1955-1995,* pp. 211-91. Collegeville, Minn.: Liturgical Press, 1997.
White was a significant liturgical historian who examined church architecture issues for some fifty years. The articles reprinted in this volume of collected writings are a good example of his insight into the relationship between worship and architecture.

————. *Roman Catholic Worship: Trent to Today.* New York: Paulist Press, 1995.

White, Susan J. *Art, Architecture, and Liturgical Reform: The Liturgical Arts Society (1928-1972)*. New York: Pueblo Publishing Company, 1990.

The Liturgical Arts Society and its quarterly journal, Liturgical Arts, were important in disseminating the ideas and modern aesthetic choices of those promoting liturgical renewal in North America. Conversations between European and American laity, clergy, and scholars are evident in the articles and exchanges in the journal. White documents and explains the significance of the Society's work.

—————. "Liturgical Architecture, 1960-1990: A Select Bibliography." *Studia Liturgica* 20, no. 2 (1990): 219-38.

Williams, Peter W. *Houses of God: Region, Religion, and Architecture in the United States.* Urbana: University of Illinois Press, 1997.

This is an insightful examination of church and other religious structures throughout the country, organized by geographical region. Williams includes references to theological, political, cultural, and economic factors that were formative in the establishment and proliferation of various church designs.

From 2000

Archdiocese of Chicago, Office for Divine Worship. *Guidelines for the Building and Renovation of Churches.* Chicago: Liturgy Training Publications, 2004.

This is an example of a brief document — 26 pages — produced by a particular diocese to assist their churches in adding more precision to documents such as Built of Living Stones.

Architecture for Worship. St. Paul: Luther Productions, 2002.

This videotape discusses various aspects of worship space design featuring the thought and work of Edward A. Sövik. The videotape is set up for group discussion and includes a discussion guide.

Berger, Robert, and Alfred Wills. *Sacred Spaces: Historic Houses of Worship in the City of Angels.* Glendale, Calif.: Balcony Press, 2003.

Best, Thomas F., and Dagmar Heller, eds. *Worship Today: Understanding, Practice, Ecumenical Influences.* Faith and Order Paper No. 194. Geneva: WCC Publications, 2004.

Boyer, Mark G. *The Liturgical Environment: What the Documents Say.* Second edition. Collegeville, Minn.: Liturgical Press, 2004.

This second edition was compiled by Boyer to incorporate the new statement Built of Living Stones *and other documents since the publication of the first edition in 1990. This edition is designed to be helpful for educating parishes on worship space and design also; it includes discussion questions at the end of each chapter.*

Bradshaw, Paul. *The Search for the Origins of Christian Worship: Sources and Methods for the Study of Early Liturgy.* Second edition. Oxford: Oxford University Press, 2002.

Christopherson, D. Foy. *A Place of Encounter: Renewing Worship Spaces.* Minneapolis: Augsburg Fortress Press, 2004.

This guide explores the 25 principles for worship space raised in the Renewing Worship initiative of the Evangelical Lutheran Church in America. The role and articulation of the worship environment are discussed in general terms, with discussions focused on sacrality, evangelism, and spiritual formation in relation to space.

"Church Architecture." Special issue. *Call to Worship* 36, no. 3 (2003).

Common Worship: Services and Prayers for the Church of England. London: Church House Publishing, 2000.

Crosbie, Michael J. *Architecture for the Gods. Book Two.* Mulgrave, Australia: Images Publishing Group, Ltd., 2002.

This is a second book by Crosbie of recent places of worship in the United States — forty-one Christian, ten Jewish, one Buddhist, one Muslim, and one interfaith. Primarily a picture book, it features excellent photographs accompanied by some drawings and minimal text pertaining to featured projects.

DeSanctis, Michael E. *Building from Belief: Advance, Retreat, and Compromise in the Remaking of Catholic Church Architecture.* Collegeville, Minn.: Liturgical Press, 2002.

Dix, Dom Gregory. *The Shape of the Liturgy.* New edition. New York: Continuum International Publishing Group, 2005.

Doordan, Dennis P. *Twentieth-Century Architecture.* New York: Harry N. Abrams, Inc., Publishers, 2002.

Dunlap, David W. *From Abyssinian to Zion: A Guide to Manhattan's Houses of Worship.* New York: Columbia University Press, 2004.

Earney, Mark, and Gilly Myers, eds. *Common Worship Today: An Illustrated Guide to Common Worship.* London: HarperCollins Publishers, 2001.

Evangelical Lutheran Church in America. *Principles for Worship.* Minneapolis: Augsburg Fortress Press, 2002.

The section in this book entitled "Worship Space and the Christian Assembly" (pp. 67-96) articulates a useful set of general principles to consider in relation to the design and use of worship spaces.

Farrelly, Elizabeth M. "How Great Thou Aren't." *Faith and Form* 38, no. 2 (2005): 20-21.

Fiorentinos, Panos. *Ecclesia: Greek Orthodox Churches of the Chicago Metropolis.* Chicago: Kantyli, Inc., 2004.

Greenagel, Frank L. *The New Jersey Churchscape.* New Brunswick, N.J.: Rutgers University Press, 2001.

Hawn, C. Michael. *Gather into One: Praying and Singing Globally.* Grand Rapids: Wm. B. Eerdmans Publishing Company, 2003.

Hoffman, Douglas R. "From Maybeck to Megachurches: The Evolution of Religious Architecture in Twentieth-Century America." *Faith and Form* 33, no. 2 (2000): 7-11.

Hoover, Stewart M. "The Cross at Willow Creek: Seeker Religion and the Contemporary Marketplace." In *Religion and Popular Culture in America,* edited by Bruce David Forbes and Jeffrey H. Mahan, pp. 145-59. Berkeley and Los Angeles: University of California Press, 2000.

Howe, Jeffrey. *Houses of Worship: An Identification Guide to the History and Styles of American Religious Architecture.* San Diego: Thunder Bay Press, 2003.

This is a helpful visual primer for becoming familiar with the range of church and other religious architecture throughout the United States.

Jacobsen, Eric O. *Sidewalks in the Kingdom: New Urbanism and the Christian Faith.* Grand Rapids: Brazos Press, 2003.

Jencks, Charles. *The New Paradigm in Architecture: The Language of Post-Modernism.* New Haven: Yale University Press, 2002.

Kieckheffer, Richard. *Theology in Stone: Church Architecture from Byzantium to Berkeley.* New York: Oxford University Press, 2004.

Kilde, Jeanne Halgren. *When Church Became Theatre: The Transformation of Evangelical Architecture and Worship in Nineteenth-Century America*. New York: Oxford University Press, 2002.

Kimball, Dan. *The Emerging Church*. Grand Rapids: Zondervan Publishing House, 2003.

Lathrop, Alan K. *Churches of Minnesota: An Illustrated Guide*. Minneapolis: University of Minnesota Press, 2003.

The Liturgy Documents: Volume One. Fourth edition. Chicago: Liturgy Training Publications, 2004.

Loveland, Anne C., and Otis B. Wheeler. *From Meetinghouse to Megachurch: A Material and Cultural History*. Columbia: University of Missouri Press, 2003.

Lutheran Church Extension Fund. *Architectural Handbook*. St. Louis: Lutheran Church Extension Fund, 2005.

McNamara, Denis R. *Heavenly City: The Architectural Tradition of Catholic Chicago*. Chicago: Liturgy Training Publications, 2005.

Morgan, William. *American Country Churches*. New York: Harry N. Abrams, 2004.

Moss, Roger W. *Historic Sacred Places of Philadelphia*. Philadelphia: University of Pennsylvania Press, 2005.

National Conference of Catholic Bishops. *Built of Living Stones: Art, Architecture, and Worship: Guidelines of the National Conference of Catholic Bishops*. Washington, D.C.: United States Catholic Conference, 2000.

Nelson, Louis P., ed. *American Sanctuary: Understanding Sacred Spaces*. Bloomington: Indiana University Press, 2006.

Ostdiek, Gilbert. "Introduction, Godfrey Diekmann, O.S.B., Award." *Proceedings of the North American Academy of Liturgy Annual Meeting* (2003): 29-31.

Puglisi, James F., ed. *Liturgical Renewal as a Way to Christian Unity*. Collegeville, Minn.: Liturgical Press, 2005.

Richardson, Phyllis. *New Spiritual Architecture*. New York: Abbeville Press, 2003.

Riddell, Mike; Mark Pierson; and Cathy Kirkpatrick. *The Prodigal Project: Journey into the Emerging Church*. London: SPCK, 2001.

Roberts, Nicholas W. *Building Type Basics for Places of Worship.* Hoboken, N.J.: John Wiley & Sons, Inc., 2004.

Rose, Michael S. *The Renovation Manipulation: The Church Counter-Renovation Handbook.* Cincinnati: Aquinas Publishing Ltd., 2000.

———. *Ugly as Sin: Why They Changed Our Churches from Sacred Places to Meeting Spaces — and How We Can Change Them Back Again.* Manchester, N.H.: Sophia Institute Press, 2001.

Runkle, John Ander, ed. *Searching for Sacred Space: Essays on Architecture and Liturgical Design in the Episcopal Church.* New York: Church Publishing, 2002.

This collection of essays discusses current issues related to Episcopal and Anglican church design. The theological notion of sacrality receives special attention, especially relevant in a cultural context where many are seeking a sense of divine mystery.

Rusch, William G. "Ecumenism, Ecumenical Movement." In *The Encyclopedia of Christianity,* vol. 2, edited by Erwin Fahlbusch et al. Grand Rapids: Wm. B. Eerdmans Publishing Company, 2001.

Seasoltz, R. Kevin. *A Sense of the Sacred: Theological Foundations of Christian Architecture and Art.* New York: Continuum Publishing Group, 2005.

This volume examines the use and development of art and architecture in the life of the Christian church, beginning with reflections in the Bible and continuing to the present day. Theological and liturgical issues are both addressed in the text. Chapters eight to ten are especially helpful for understanding the modern period.

———. "Transcendence and Immanence in Sacred Arts and Architecture." *Worship* 75, no. 5 (September 2001): 403-31.

Stock, Wolfgang Jean. *Architectural Guide: Christian Sacred Buildings in Europe Since 1950.* Munich: Prestel Verlag, 2004.

This is a field guide for exploring Roman Catholic and Protestant European churches of the last fifty years, featuring 130 buildings from twenty countries. Brief descriptions accompany the many photographs and plans of the churches and chapels, along with the specific building locations.

———. *European Church Architecture, 1950-2000.* Munich: Prestel Verlag, 2002.

This is an overview of Roman Catholic and Protestant churches of Western Europe from the last fifty years. Sixty churches are featured with some level of detail (including many photographs and floor plans). References (sometimes including photographs) are made to many other churches in the brief essays that precede the regional examinations.

Vosko, Richard S. *God's House Is Our House: Re-imagining the Environment for Worship.* Collegeville, Minn.: Liturgical Press, 2006.

———. "A House for the Church: Structures for Public Worship in a New Millennium." *Worship* 74, no. 3 (May 2000): 194-212.

"Your Word Is Truth." *First Things* 125 (August/September 2002): 38-42.

Zimmerman, Joyce Ann. *The Ministry of Liturgical Environment.* Collegeville, Minn.: Liturgical Press, 2004.

This 80-page guide is intended to instruct those who are to prepare environments for worship, taking the place of a guide by the same title issued in 1984. Attention is paid to aesthetics, symbols, and traditions. This guide was prepared in relation to Built of Living Stones *and other contemporary documents.*

INDEX

Aalto, Alvar, 64

Adams, T. W., 19

Adams, William Seth, 92, 214n.12

Alternative worship movement, 221n.28

Anson, Peter F., 80-81

Architecture for Worship by E. Sövik, 22, 93, 150-151, 154, 162n.35, 165n.48, 168n.57, 174n.67

Architectural Handbook (Lutheran Church, Missouri Synod), 215

Armour Institute (see Illinois Institute of Technology)

Art D'Eglise (journal), 71

Associated Parishes for Liturgy and Mission, 39

Bak, Bronislaw, 121

Baptism, Eucharist and Ministry (BEM), 183-184

Barth, Karl, 13

Bartning, Otto, 76n.18, 101-104, 112, 114, 165

Bauhaus, 54-56, 121

Baur, Hermann, 114

Beauduin, Dom Lambert, 33

Beauty in contemporary design, 83, 88-89, 151, 158-159, 162, 163, 168, 169, 179, 203, 214, 216, 218, 224, 227

Belluschi, Pietro, 64, 124-125, 131-132

Benedictine Abbey of St. John the Baptist, Collegeville, 34, 121-123

Betts, Darby Wood, 90

Birkerts, Gunnar, 140-142

Böhm, Dominikus, 37, 77n.18, 104-107, 109-110n.17, 112, 114, 153-155, 165, 191n.28

Bonhoeffer, Dietrich, 13-18, 19, 21-23, 152-155

Book of Common Prayer (1979), 40, 187

Book of Common Worship (1993), 40, 187

Bradshaw, Paul, 188-189

Brannach, Frank, 80

Breuer, Marcel, 54, 64, 121-123

British and Foreign Bible Society, 27

Bruggink, Donald J., 93n.69, 94-95

Built of Living Stones (2000), 212-213

Bultmann, Rudolf, 17

Burg Rothenfel, 33-34, 71, 111, 166

Burgee, John, 125

Caesar, Doris, 122

Call to Worship (journal), 215. *See also Reformed Liturgy and Worship*

Called to Common Mission document (2001), 185

Calvin Institute of Christian Worship, 216

Cambridge Camden Society, 44

Casel, Dom Odo, 33, 89n.52

Cathedral of St. Mary of the Assumption, San Francisco, 124-125

Charta Oecumenica (2001), 185

Chicago school of architecture, 49-50

Christopherson, D. Foy, 215n.12

Church for Common Prayer (Episcopal Church), 215

Church of the Blessed Sacrament, East Hartford, 135-137

Church of Corpus Christi, Aachen, 107-109, 113n.22, 131, 166

Church of England, 39, 72-73, 74-75, 187

Church of Notre Dame, Le Raincy, 98-101

Church of the Servant, Grand Rapids, 140-142

Church Service Society, 39

CIAM (International Congress for Modern Architecture), 61-64, 67, 108, 194-195

Commission on Architecture, Department of Worship and the Arts, National Council of Churches, 76n.18

Common Worship Project (Church of England), 187

Congres Internationaux de L'Architecture Moderne (see CIAM)

Conover, Elbert M., 29-30

Constitution on the Sacred Liturgy (1963), 31-32, 35-38, 78, 84-85, 87

Contemporary Christian music, 190

Cope, Gilbert, 74-75, 93n.69

Couturier, M. A., 76-77n.18

Cox, Harvey, 18-19, 23, 79, 159

Cram, Ralph Adams, 46-47

Critique of modern church design, 197-204

Crosbie, Michael J., 225-226

Crystal Cathedral (see Garden Grove Community Church)

Davies, John Gordon, 20-22, 74-76, 79, 91, 151-153, 204

Death of God theology, 16n.9

Decree on Ecumenism, 31

Debuyst, Frédéric, 71, 79-80, 93n.69, 160, 164n.42, 165-166, 188, 214

Department of Church Architecture of the United Lutheran Church in America, 92

Diekmann, Godfrey, 35, 78

Diocesan Church Building Directives, Superior, Wisconsin (1957), 73, 83-84

Directives for the Building of a Church (German Liturgical Commission, 1947), 73, 81-83

Directives of the Bishops of France regarding Sacred Art (1952), 82

Dix, Gregory, 38-39, 157

Dreyer, Otto, 114

Droppers, Carl H., 93n.69, 94-95

Ecumenical movement, 22, 26-33, 38-41, 64, 70-73, 76ff., 88, 91-94, 113, 145, 157ff., 182-186, 190, 216-217

Emerging church, 221n.28

Environment and Art in Catholic Worship (1978), 87-89, 161, 201-202, 212-213

Episcopal church, 90-92; resources for design, 214-215

Evangelical Lutheran Church in America, 148, 185, 187n.18; resources for design, 215

Evangelicals and Catholics Together, 185

Faith and Form (journal), 166, 225

Faith and Order Commission, World Council of Churches, 28

Federal Council of Churches in Christ in the United States (FCC), 27, 29

Ferguson, Frank W., 46

First Christian Church, Columbus, 128-131

Freeman, French and Freeman, architects, 37

Full communion accord, Evangelical Lutheran Church in America and the Episcopal Church (see *Called to Common Mission*)

Fulton, Charles, 91

Garden Grove Community Church, Garden Grove, 125-127

General Instruction of the Roman Missal, 86, 212

Giles, Richard, 91-92, 214n.12

Goodhue, Bertram G., 46

Gothic revival movement, 37, 44-47, 80n.28, 89, 113n.22, 144, 151, 197

Gropius, Walter, 54-55, 121, 195

Guardini, Romano, 33-34, 70-71, 108

Guiding Principles for the Design of Churches according to the Spirit of the Roman Liturgy (see *Directives for the Building of a Church* [German Liturgical Commission, 1947])

Hammond, Peter, 65n.49, 71-74, 76n.18, 82n.35, 83n.39, 91, 93n.69, 112, 114n.23, 214

Harnack, Adolf von, 12

Heathcote, Edwin, and Iona Spens, 223

Herbert, Arthur Gabriel, 38

Herkommer, Hans, 109n.16

Herwegen, Abbot Ildephons, 33

Hillenbrand, Reynold, 35

Hitchcock, Henry-Russell, 63-64, 125

Hoffman, Douglas R., 215n.14

Holtkamp, Patrick, 91

Holy Family Church, Oberhausen, 109-110

Honest to God by J. A. T. Robinson, 16-17

Hovda, Robert, 88, 159

Howe, Jeffrey, 211

Huffman, Walter C., 93-94

Illinois Institute of Technology, 56

Immanence: definition in relation to God, 2; meaning attached to church design, 3-10, 88-89, 151

Institute for the Study of Worship and Religious Architecture, 74

Instruction for the Proper Implementation of the Constitution on the Sacred Liturgy (1964), 85-86

Interdenominational Bureau of Architecture, 29

Interfaith Forum on Religion, Art, and Architecture, 148, 225

International Congresses on Religion, Architecture, and the Visual Arts, 19ff., 79-80, 159-160

International Missionary Council, 28

International style, 55, 63-64, 80, 108, 125n.8, 145, 161, 194-197, 202, 205, 208, 224

Jacobsen, Eric O., 220n.24

Japanese teahouse, 167-169

Jeanneret, Charles Edouard (see Le Corbusier)

Jencks, Charles, 194-196

Johnson, Philip, 63-64, 125-127

John XXIII, 30-31

Joint Commission on Architecture and the Allied Arts of the Protestant Episcopal Church, 90

Joint Declaration on the Doctrine of Justification (Roman Catholic and Lutheran churches, 1999), 184-185

Kacmarcik, Frank, 174, 202

Kahn, Louis, 63

Keefe Associates, architects, 225-226

Kepes, Gyorgy, 125

Kramer Chapel, Fort Wayne, 131n.10

Lavanoux, Maurice, 65n.49

Le Corbusier (Charles Edouard Jeanneret), 59-63, 77n.18, 112n.20, 161-163, 166, 195, 224

Leadership in Engineering and Environmental Design (LEED), 219n.23

Letters and Papers from Prison by D. Bonhoeffer, 14-16

Leuenberg Agreement (1973), 184

Liberal theology, 12-13, 16, 19, 23, 144, 207

Life and Work Commission, World Council of Churches, 28

Lippold, Richard, 125

Liturgical Arts Society, 80, 303

Liturgical Conference, 38, 78, 88, 148n.2, 158-160

Liturgical movement, 32-41, 70, 72-73, 75, 76n.18, 80-82, 89n.52, 90, 92, 101, 104-105, 107, 114, 120-121, 123, 144-145, 157, 165, 178, 186-193, 198, 207-208, 226

Liturgical Press, 34, 213n.7

Liturgical Week, 38

Liturgy and Architecture by P. Hammond, 21n.23, 65n.49, 72-74, 93n.69, 112, 114n.23, 164n.42

Lutheran Book of Worship (1978), 40

Lutheran Church, Missouri Synod, 40, 92-94, 131ff., 187; resources for design, 215

Lutheran Church in America, 40, 41n.37, 93-94, 167, 187

Lutheran World Federation, 184

Maginnis, Charles, 46n.7

Maguire, Robert, 73, 110n.16

Maria Laach Abbey, 33

Mary the Queen, Cologne-Riehl, 106-107

McSweeney, Ryan and Lee, architects, 124

Megachurch, 6, 143-144, 221-222

Meeting House Essays, 214

Metzger, Fritz, 114

Michel, Dom Virgil, 34

Middleton, Arthur Pierce, 91

Mies van der Rohe, Ludwig, 55-59, 63, 73, 91, 112, 121, 125, 161-163, 166, 195

Modern architecture, 22-23, 29, 37, 44n.1, 47ff., 72-75, 80, 87, 90-92, 95-96, 98, 104-105, 108, 114, 120, 144-146, 149, 156, 161ff., 178-179, 189, 194-198, 200, 203, 205, 208-210

Modern Architecture and Christian Celebration by F. Debuyst, 79-80, 166-167

Mont César Monastery, Louvain, 33
Moser, Karl, 114-115
Mott, John R., 27
Multipurpose church, 21-22, 88, 92, 137, 140-145, 153, 155, 204, 217
Murray, Keith, 73, 110n.16

National Conference of Catholic Bishops, 87ff., 212-213
National Council of Churches of Christ, 27, 32, 76, 92, 182-183
"Neo-gothic" architecture (see Gothic revival design)
Nervi, Pier Luigi, 124-125
Neutra, Richard, 63
New Church Research Group, 72-74
New Testament, locations for worship, 8-9
Nonchurch design, 16, 22, 149ff., 165-178
Nondenominational churches, 137-139, 143-144, 185-186
North American Academy of Liturgy, 39, 149
North Christian Church, Columbus, 133-134
Norwegian Lutheran Church of America, 150
Notre Dame du Haut, Ronchamp, 61-62, 98-101, 161n.35, 166

O'Connell, J. B., 81-82
O'Donnell, Wicklund, and Pigozzi, architects, 137-139
Oldham, Joseph H., 27
Orate Fratres (journal), 34
Order of St. Luke (United Methodist Church), 39
Ostreicher, Siegfried, 110n.16
Our Divine Saviour, Chico, 137n.11
Our Lady of Peace, Frankfurt, 105
Our Place of Worship, 213-214

Pasma, Douglas, 139n.12
Patterson, Roger L., 215n.14
Paul VI, 31-32
Pentecostal movement, 183n.5, 190
Perret, Auguste, 37, 77n.18, 98-101, 104, 112, 114, 165
Pfammatter, Ferdinand, 90, 112, 164, 165n.49
Pius XI, 30
Postmodern architecture, 196-197, 208-210, 224-225

Post World War II church building, 76, 118-121
Presbyterian and Reformed traditions, 32, 39, 40, 46, 47, 74n.10, 94-95, 125ff., 140ff., 160, 187; resources for design, 215-216
Pruitt-Igoe housing project, St. Louis, 195
Pugin, Augustus Welby Northmore, 44-45, 47

Quickborn movement, 33-34

Rambusch Company, 177
Reformed Liturgy and Worship (journal), 215
Reformed Worship (journal), 216
Reinhold, Hans Anscar, 35, 76n.18, 80-81, 164n.42, 191n.28
Religionless Christianity, 14-16
Renewing Worship Project (Lutheran, ELCA), 187, 215
Resurrection Church, Essen, 101-103
Richardson, Phyllis, 223-224
Ringenberg parish church, Germany, 105, 109n.16
Ritschl, Albrecht, 12
Robinson, John A. T., 16-19, 23, 39, 75
Roberts, Nicholas W., 223
Roman Catholic Church, resources for design, 212-214
Roman Missal (1969), 38, 40, 86, 187, 212
Rose, Michael, 202-203
Runkle, John Ander, 214n.12

Saarinen, Eero, 64, 131n.10, 133-134
Saarinen, Eliel, 64, 128-131
St. Anna Church, Düren, 108-109
St. Antony Church, Basel, 114
St. Christopher Church, Cologne-Niehl, 110-111, 166-167
St. Columba Church, Glenrothes, 110n.16
St. Engelbert Church, Cologne-Riehl, 105-106
St. Francis de Sales Church, Muskegon, 121n.5
St. John's Benedictine Abbey Church, Collegeville (see Benedictine Abbey of St. John the Baptist, Collegeville)
St. Laurentius Church, Munich, 110n.16
St. Leo's Roman Catholic Church, Pipestone, 148n.2, 172-175, 178
St. Mark's Roman Catholic Church, Burlington, 37

St. Paul Church, Bow Common, London, 110n.16

St. Saviour Chapel, IIT, Chicago, 57-59, 91, 162-163, 166

St. Theresa Church, Sherborn, 225-226

Schleiermacher, Friedrich, 12

Schloeder, Steven, 201

Schwarz, Rudolf, 34, 37, 70-71, 73, 76n.18, 105, 107-111, 112, 114, 131, 157, 163, 164n.42, 165, 166-167, 191n.28, 224

Schwippert, Hans, 107

Secretariat for Promoting Christian Unity, 30, 32

Secular Christianity, 16-18

Secular city debate, 18, 67, 87, 159

Secular Use of Church Buildings, The by J. G. Davies, 21-22, 151-153, 204

Sherman, Jonathan G., 90

Skidmore, Owings, and Merrill (SOM), 64, 131-132

Societas Liturgica, 39

Sövik, Edward Anders, 16, 22, 78, 79, 89n.51, 93-94, 147-179, 188, 202, 214

Star Church, 101-102

Stauffer, S. Anita, 93-94

Steel Church, Cologne-Essen, 102-103

Steffann, Emil, 73, 110n.16

Stewardship, 5, 92, 142, 159, 179, 218-221

Stock, Wolfgang Jean, 118n.1, 224-225

Stroik, Duncan, 49n.20, 201-202

Sullivan, Louis, 49

Sustainable church design, 219-220

Synagogue, 8

Tabernacle Church of Christ, Columbus (see First Christian Church)

Tabernacle of Moses, 6-7

Temple of Solomon, 7-8

Tillich, Paul, 17, 77n.18, 193

Towards a Church Architecture ed. by P. Hammond, 72n.5, 73, 82n.35

Transcendence, definition in relation to God, 2; meaning attached to church design, 3-10, 88-89, 151

Trinity Lutheran Church, Walnut Creek, 131-132

Trinity United Methodist Church, Charles City, 148n.2, 174, 176-178

Twenty-first Ecumenical Council (see Vatican II)

United Methodist Book of Worship (1992), 40, 187

United Methodist Church, 39, 95, 160, 176-178, 187; resources for design, 215

United Methodist Society for Worship, 39

Unity Temple, Oak Park, 52-54, 98, 162n.35

Universal Christian Council for Life and Work, 28

Van Loon, Ralph R., 93

Vatican II, 30-32, 34, 35, 37-38, 73-74, 80-82, 84, 88, 110n.16, 120, 157-158, 174, 189, 191n.27, 192, 193n.32, 201-202, 213-214

Venturi, Robert, 196

Von Dohlen, Russell Gibson, 135-137

Vosko, Richard S., 202, 213, 214n.11, 223

Webber, Robert E., 144n.19, 209n.1

Weber, Martin, 105

Wentworth, Charles Francis, 46

Wheeler and Sproson, architects, 110n.16

White, James F., 214n.12

White, Susan J., 214n.12

Williams, Peter W., 210-211

Willow Creek Community Church, South Barrington, 137-139, 143-144, 198

Witness potential, 221-223

World Council of Churches, 28, 32, 76-78, 182-184

World Missionary Conference, Edinburgh, 27-28

Wright, Frank Lloyd, 50-54, 56, 60, 61, 80, 98, 112n.20, 161-162

Yamasaki, Minoru, 195

Zion Lutheran Church, Portland, 131n.10